Exam Ref AZ-203
Developing Solutions for
Microsoft Azure

Santiago Fernández Muñoz

Exam Ref AZ-203 Developing Solutions for Microsoft Azure

Published with the authorization of Microsoft Corporation by:
Pearson Education, Inc.

ISBN-13: 978-0-13-564380-8
ISBN-10: 0-13-564380-5

Library of Congress Control Number: 2019948004

1 2019

TRADEMARKS

Microsoft and the trademarks listed at http://www.microsoft.com on the "Trademarks" webpage are trademarks of the Microsoft group of companies. All other marks are property of their respective owners.

WARNING AND DISCLAIMER

Every effort has been made to make this book as complete and as accurate as possible, but no warranty or fitness is implied. The information provided is on an "as is" basis. The author, the publisher, and Microsoft Corporation shall have neither liability nor responsibility to any person or entity with respect to any loss or damages arising from the information contained in this book or from the use of the programs accompanying it.

SPECIAL SALES

For information about buying this title in bulk quantities, or for special sales opportunities (which may include electronic versions; custom cover designs; and content particular to your business, training goals, marketing focus, or branding interests), please contact our corporate sales department at corpsales@pearsoned.com or (800) 382-3419.

For government sales inquiries, please contact governmentsales@pearsoned.com.

For questions about sales outside the U.S., please contact intlcs@pearson.com.

CREDITS

EDITOR-IN-CHIEF
Brett Bartow

EXECUTIVE EDITOR
Loretta Yates

DEVELOPMENT EDITOR
Songlin Qiu, Charvi Arora

MANAGING EDITOR
Sandra Schroeder

SENIOR PROJECT EDITOR
Tracey Croom

COPY EDITOR
Rick Kughen

INDEXER
Erika Millen

PROOFREADERS
Abigail Manheim and
Betty Pessagno

TECHNICAL EDITOR
Dave McCollough

ASSISTANT EDITOR
Charvi Arora

EDITORIAL ASSISTANT
Cindy Teeters

COVER DESIGNER
Twist Creative, Seattle

COMPOSITOR
codeMantra

*To my wonderful wife, because of her support and inspiration,
especially in the hard times.*

— SANTIAGO FERNÁNDEZ MUÑOZ

Contents at a glance

Contents

Acknowledgments

I want to say thank you to the people who gave me the opportunity to write this book and who also helped me during the entire process. Without their support, this book would not be a reality.

I also want to say thank you to my friend Rafa Hueso for his support and guidance during the last years of my professional career.

About the Author

I started my career as a Linux and Windows instructor. At the same time, I also started to learn scripting programming languages such as bash and VBS that were useful for my work. During that period of my career, I realized scripting languages were helpful, but they were not enough to meet all my needs, so I started learning other languages like Java, PHP, and finally C#.

I've been working as a Microsoft technologies consultant for the last 14 years, and over the last 6 years, I've consulted on Azure-related technologies. I've participated in different types of projects— From .NET developer to Solution Architect—and I've served in a variety of capacities. Now I'm focused on developing custom Industrial IoT solutions for my company and clients.

Introduction

Most books take a very low-level approach, teaching you how to use individual classes and accomplish fine-grained tasks. Through this book, we review the main technologies that Microsoft offers for deploying different kinds for solutions into Azure. From the most classical and conservative approaches using Azure Virtual Machines to the latest technologies, implementing event-based or message-based patterns with Azure Event Grid or Azure Service Bus, this book reviews the basics for developing most types of solutions using Azure services. The book also provides code examples for illustrating how to implement most of the concepts covered through the different sections. This should be used as the introduction to implementing more complex solutions. Although the book covers some basic concepts, you should have basic programming experience using ASP.NET, .NET Framework, or .NET Core, as well as using Git.

This book covers every major topic area found on the exam, but it does not cover every exam question. Only the Microsoft exam team has access to the exam questions, and Microsoft regularly adds new questions to the exam, making it impossible to cover specific questions. You should consider this book a supplement to your relevant real-world experience and other study materials. If you encounter a topic in this book that you do not feel completely comfortable with, use the "Need more review?" links you'll find in the text to find more information and take the time to research and study the topic. Great information is available on MSDN, TechNet, and in blogs and forums.

Organization of this book

This book is organized by the "Skills measured" list published for the exam. The "Skills measured" list is available for each exam on the Microsoft Learn website: *http://aka.ms/ examlist*. Each chapter in this book corresponds to a major topic area in the list, and the technical tasks in each topic area determine a chapter's organization. If an exam covers six major topic areas, for example, the book will contain six chapters.

Microsoft certifications

Microsoft certifications distinguish you by proving your command of a broad set of skills and experience with current Microsoft products and technologies. The exams and corresponding certifications are developed to validate your mastery of critical competencies as you design and develop, or implement and support, solutions with Microsoft products and technologies both on-premises and in the cloud. Certification brings a variety of benefits to the individual and to employers and organizations.

> **MORE INFO** **ALL MICROSOFT CERTIFICATIONS**
>
> For information about Microsoft certifications, including a full list of available certifications, go to http://www.microsoft.com/learn.

Check back often to see what is new!

Errata, updates, & book support

We've made every effort to ensure the accuracy of this book and its companion content. You can access updates to this book—in the form of a list of submitted errata and their related corrections—at:

MicrosoftPressStore.com/ExamRefAZ203/errata

If you discover an error that is not already listed, please submit it to us at the same page.

For additional book support and information, please visit *http://www.MicrosoftPressStore.com/Support.*

Please note that product support for Microsoft software and hardware is not offered through the previous addresses. For help with Microsoft software or hardware, go to *http://support.microsoft.com.*

Stay in touch

Let's keep the conversation going! We're on Twitter: *http://twitter.com/MicrosoftPress.*

Important: How to use this book to study for the exam

Certification exams validate your on-the-job experience and product knowledge. To gauge your readiness to take an exam, use this Exam Ref to help you check your understanding of the skills tested by the exam. Determine the topics you know well and the areas in which you need more experience. To help you refresh your skills in specific areas, we have also provided "Need more review?" pointers, which direct you to more in-depth information outside the book.

The Exam Ref is not a substitute for hands-on experience. This book is *not* designed to teach you new skills.

We recommend that you round out your exam preparation by using a combination of available study materials and courses. Learn more about available classroom training and find free online courses and live events at *http://microsoft.com/learn*. Microsoft Official Practice Tests are available for many exams at *http://aka.ms/practicetests*.

This book is organized by the "Skills measured" list published for the exam. The "Skills measured" list for each exam is available on the Microsoft Learn website: *http://aka.ms/examlist*.

Note that this Exam Ref is based on this publicly available information and the author's experience. To safeguard the integrity of the exam, authors do not have access to the exam questions.

CHAPTER 1

Develop Azure Infrastructure as a Service Compute Solution

Today, cloud computing is a consolidated reality that any company or professional should consider when developing or maintaining new or existing products. When you are planning for developing or deploying an application, you can choose between two main models of cloud services, Infrastructure as a Service (IaaS) or Platform as a Service (PaaS), and each model has its own pros and cons.

In this chapter, we will review how to work with the options that Azure makes available to you for developing your solutions based on the Infrastructure as a Service model.

Skills covered in this chapter:

- Skill 1.1: Implement solutions that use virtual machines (VM)
- Skill 1.2: Implement batch jobs by using Azure Batch Services
- Skill 1.3: Create containerized solutions

> **IMPORTANT**
> ## Have you read page xvii?
> It contains valuable information regarding the skills you need to pass the exam.

Skill 1.1: Implement solutions that use virtual machines (VM)

One of the main characteristics of the IaaS model is the greater level of control that it offers when deploying the infrastructure needed for your application. Typically, you need to work with this model because you need more control over the different elements of your application. Using IaaS, you deploy your own virtual machines where you will deploy all the needed components for solution.

Azure will provide you with all the underlying hardware and configuration needed for your virtual machine to run correctly, but you still need to manage all administrative tasks related to the VM's operating system, such as installing operating system upgrades or security patches. Even Microsoft manages the configuration needed for providing the fault tolerance for the physical hardware that supports your virtual machine. If you require that your application or software solution be highly available, you need to manage the configuration of the VMs that host your application.

Provision VMs

Deploying a VM in Azure is a straightforward process, but you still need to think about some key points if you want to achieve the best balance between the costs and your requirements. Perhaps the most obvious decision is which operating system you should use. The good news is that Azure fully supports Windows, Windows Server, and the main distributions of Linux.

> *NOTE* **SUPPORTED OPERATING SYSTEMS**
>
> You can review the full list of supported operating systems to be used in Azure VMs in the following URLs:
>
> - Windows: *https://support.microsoft.com/en-us/help/2721672/ microsoft-server-software-support-for-microsoft-azure-virtual-machines*
> - Linux: *https://docs.microsoft.com/en-us/azure/virtual-machines/linux/endorsed-distros*

All these Windows and Linux OSes are preinstalled and available to you in the Azure Marketplace as VM Images. Apart from these default VM images, you will also find other images in the marketplace from other vendors containing preconfigured solutions that may better match with your needs.

Once you have chosen your operating system, you need to decide other important aspects of the virtual machine:

- **Name** This will be the name of the virtual machine. Names may be up to 15 characters long.
- **Location** You need to select the geographical region where your virtual machine will be deployed. Azure has several datacenters deployed across the globe that are grouped in geographical regions. Choosing the wrong region or location may have negative effects.
- **Size** This is the amount of resources that you will assign to your virtual machines. These resources include amount of memory, processing power, number of virtual NICs that you can attach to your virtual machine, and total storage capacity that will be available for your virtual machine.

- **Limits**   Every subscription has default quota limits. These limits can affect you when deploying new virtual machines. By default, each subscription is limited to 20 VMs per region. However, this limit can be raised by contacting Azure's support service.
- **Extensions**   Extensions give you additional capabilities after the deployment of the virtual machine has finished correctly. Extensions allow you to automate some tasks or configuration once your VM has been deployed. Some of the most common extensions are
  - Run custom scripts
  - Deploy and manage configurations
  - Collect diagnostic data
- **Related resources**   When you deploy a virtual machine, you need to think about the amount and type of storage, such as whether this VM will be connected to the Internet and need a public IP or which type of traffic is allowed to go to or from the virtual machine. Some of these related resources, as shown below, are mandatory for deploying a VM.
  - **Resource group**   Every virtual machine needs to be contained in a resource group. You can create a new resource group or re-use an existing one.
  - **Storage account**   The virtual disks needed by the VM are .vhd files stored as page blobs in a storage account. Depending on the performance requirements of your VM, you can use standard or premium storage accounts. If you configure managed disks when deploying a VM, the storage account is automatically managed by Azure and won't appear in the VM configuration.
  - **Virtual network**   To be able to communicate with the rest of the world, your new VM needs to be connected to a virtual network.
  - **Network interface**   As in the physical world, your VM needs a network interface to connect to the virtual network for sending and receiving information.

Once you have gathered all the information that you need to deploy your VM, you are ready for deployment. You have several ways for doing this task:

- Using the Azure Portal
- Using PowerShell
- Using Azure CLI
- Programmatically using REST API or C#

In general, when you want to deploy a new virtual machine, you need to follow these steps:

1. Create a resource group for the virtual machine. You can also use an existing resource group for this VM.
2. Create a virtual network. If you are using the Azure Portal, you can do this while you are creating the VM. For PowerShell and Azure CLI, you need to specify the virtual network. However, if a virtual network doesn't already exist, one is created automatically.

3. Create a virtual NIC. If you are using Azure Portal, PowerShell, or Azure CLI, you don't need to do this because it is automatically done for you during the deployment.

4. Create the virtual machine.

The following piece of code shows how to create a virtual machine with managed disks in your Azure subscription.

LISTING 1-1 Creating a virtual machine

```
//dotnet core 2.2
/* You need to create an authentication file with the following structure:
    subscription=<subscription-id>
    client=<client-id>
    key=<client-secret>
    tenant=<tenant-id>
    managementURI=https://management.core.windows.net/
    baseURL=https://management.azure.com/
    authURL=https://login.windows.net/
    graphURL=https://graph.windows.net/
*/
//Create the management client. This will be used for all the operations that we will
//perform in Azure.
var credentials = SdkContext.AzureCredentialsFactory.FromFile("./azureauth.properties");

var azure = Azure.Configure().WithLogLevel(HttpLoggingDelegatingHandler.Level.Basic)
                        .Authenticate(credentials)
                        .WithDefaultSubscription();

//First of all, we need to create a resource group where we will add all the resources
//needed for the virtual machine.
var groupName = "az203-ResoureGroup";
var vmName = "az203VMTesting";
var location = Region.USWest2;
var vNetName = "az203VNET";
var vNetAddress = "172.16.0.0/16";
var subnetName = "az203Subnet";
var subnetAddress = "172.16.0.0/24";
var nicName = "az203NIC";
var adminUser = "azureadminuser";
var adminPassword = "Pa$$w0rd!2019";

//Create the management client. This will be used for all the operations that we will
perform in Azure.
var credentials = SdkContext.AzureCredentialsFactory.FromFile("./azureauth.properties");
var azure = Azure.Configure()
    .WithLogLevel(HttpLoggingDelegatingHandler.Level.Basic)
    .Authenticate(credentials)
    .WithDefaultSubscription();

//We need to create the resource group where we will add the virtual machine.
var resourceGroup = azure.ResourceGroups.Define(groupName)
    .WithRegion(location)
    .Create();
```

```
//Every virtual machine needs to be connected to a virtual network.
var network = azure.Networks.Define(vNetName)
    .WithRegion(location)
    .WithExistingResourceGroup(groupName)
    .WithAddressSpace(vNetAddress)
    .WithSubnet(subnetName, subnetAddress)
    .Create();
//Any virtual machine needs a network interface for connecting to the virtual network.
var nic = azure.NetworkInterfaces.Define(nicName)
    .WithRegion(location)
    .WithExistingResourceGroup(groupName)
    .WithExistingPrimaryNetwork(network)
    .WithSubnet(subnetName)
    .WithPrimaryPrivateIPAddressDynamic()
    .Create();
//Create the virtual machine.
azure.VirtualMachines.Define(vmName)
    .WithRegion(location)
    .WithExistingResourceGroup(groupName)
    .WithExistingPrimaryNetworkInterface(nic)
    .WithLatestWindowsImage("MicrosoftWindowsServer", "WindowsServer",
    "2012-R2-Datacenter")
    .WithAdminUsername(adminUser)
    .WithAdminPassword(adminPassword)
    .WithComputerName(vmName)
    .WithSize(VirtualMachineSizeTypes.StandardDS2V2)
    .Create();
```

> **NOTE** **APPLICATION REQUIREMENTS**
>
> To run all the examples through this book, you need to have an Azure subscription. If you
> don't have an Azure subscription, you can create a free subscription for testing the code in
> this book.
>
> Also, you will need to create an Azure AD application and a security principal in your Azure
> subscription. You need to configure these elements to grant create and modify privileges to
> your application. Follow the instructions in this procedure for creating the Azure AD applica-
> tion and the security principal. See *https://docs.microsoft.com/en-us/azure/active-directory/
> develop/howto-create-service-principal-portal*.

As you can see in Listing 1-1, we need to create each of the related and required resources
separately and then provide all the needed dependencies to the Azure management client that
will create the virtual machine.

Before you proceed to deploy a new VM, you also need to take into account other consider-
ations that would affect the deployment. For example, if your application or software solution
must be highly available, you would typically use a load balancer. If your virtual machines use a
load balancer, you need to put your VMs that host the application into an availability set. This
will ensure that any virtual machine in the same availability set will never be on the same hardware and won't be restarted at the same time because of software upgrades on the servers

running the VM. A virtual machine may only be added to an availability set during creation of the VM. If you forget to add the VM to an availability set, you need to delete the VM and start from the beginning.

Create ARM templates

One of the biggest advantages of using Azure IaaS is the level of automation that you can achieve when deploying new services, resources, or infrastructure. One of the main reasons you can do this is because Microsoft provides you the Azure Resource Manager (ARM), which is the deployment and management service in Azure. The ARM service is in charge of creating, updating, and deleting the different kind of services you can deploy in your subscription. All actions offered by the ARM service are exposed through the same API. This means that no matter which mechanism you use—portal, PowerShell, Azure CLI, Rest API, or client SDKs—you will get a consistent behavior and result when interacting with ARM.

When we work with the Azure Resource Manager, there are some concepts and terms that we need to clearly understand:

- **Resource**   These are the items you can manage in Azure.
- **Resource group**   This is a container that we use for holding resources. You can use any grouping criteria for your resources, but you need to remember that any single resource needs to be contained in a resource group. You can also use resource groups for managing different levels of management access to different groups of users.
- **Resource provider**   A resource provider is a service that offers the different kinds of Azure resources, and they manage the resource's lifecycle. For example, the service in charge of offering virtual machine resources is the *Microsoft.Compute* provider. You can also use the *Microsoft.Storage* provider for storage accounts or *Microsoft.Network* for all networking resources.
- **Resource Manager template**   This is the file that you need to provide to the ARM API when you want to deploy one or more resources to a resource group or subscription. This file is written in JavaScript Object Notation (JSON).

The main advantage of using ARM templates is that you have the definition of all the resources that you want to deploy in a consistent structure. This allows you to reuse the same template for deploying the same group of resources in different subscriptions, resource groups, or regions. Some common scenarios in which you can take advantage of the ARM templates are disaster recovery plan implementations, high availability configurations, or automatic provisioning scenarios (such as continuous deployment scenarios). In the following code snippet, you can see the most basic structure for an ARM template.

```
{
    "$schema": "https://schema.management.azure.com/schemas/2015-01-01/
    deploymentTemplate.json#",
    "contentVersion": "",
    "parameters": {  },
    "variables": {  },
    "functions": [  ],
    "resources": [  ],
    "outputs": {  }
}
```

Insofar as the ARM template structure is concerned, only the *$schema*, *contentVersion*, and resources sections are required to be present in a valid template. Following is a brief description of each section in a template:

- *$schema*   This required section sets the JSON schema that describes the version of the template you will use in the file. You can choose between two different schemas depending on the deployment type:

  - **Resource group deployments**   You should use *https://schema.management.azure. com/schemas/2015-01-01/deploymentTemplate.json#*.

  - **Subscription deployments**   You should use *https://schema.management.azure.com/ schemas/2018-05-01/subscriptionDeploymentTemplate.json#*.

- *contentVersion*   In this required section, you set a value you can use for providing your internal version number to the template, such as *1.0.0*. This version number is only meaningful for you; Azure does not use it. Typically, you change the version of the template when you make significant changes to the template.

- *parameters*   This is an optional section that you can use to set the values provided to the Resource Manager when you are performing a deployment. You can use customizable template parameters for different deployments without changing the content of the template.

- *variables*   This optional section contains the values that you will reuse across the entire template. You use variables for improving the usability and readability of the template.

- *functions*   You can use this optional section for defining your own functions to be used in the template.

- *resources*   This is a required section that contains all the resources that will be deployed or updated by the template.

- *outputs*   This optional section defines the values that the Resource Manager should return once the deployment has finished.

The ARM template that you need to use for deploying new VMs with the same configuration is shown in Listing 1-2. You may modify the values of the parameters according to your needs.

LISTING 1-2 ARM template for deploying a VM

```
{
    "$schema": "https://schema.management.azure.com/schemas/2015-01-01/
    deploymentTemplate.json#",
    "contentVersion": "1.0.0.0",
    "parameters": {
        "virtualNetworks_az203VNET_name": {
            "defaultValue": "az203demoVNET",
            "type": "string"
        },
        "networkInterfaces_az203NIC_name": {
            "defaultValue": "az203demoNIC",
            "type": "string"
        },
        "virtualMachines_az203VMTesting_name": {
            "defaultValue": "az203demoVM",
            "type": "string"
        },
        "subnets_az203Subnet_name": {
            "defaultValue": "az203demoSubnet",
            "type": "string"
        },
        "virtualMachines_az203VMTesting_id": {
            "defaultValue": "[concat(parameters('virtualMachines_
            az203VMTesting_name'),'_OSDisk1_1')]",
            "type": "string"
        },
        "virtualMachines_adminUser": {
            "defaultValue": "azureadminuser",
            "type": "string"
        },
        "virtualMachines_adminpassword": {
            "defaultValue": "Pa$$w0rd",
            "type": "securestring"
        }
    },
    "variables": {
        "osDiskName": "_OSDisk1_1_39c654d89d88405e968db84b722002d1"
    },
    "resources": [
        {
            "type": "Microsoft.Compute/virtualMachines",
            "name": "[parameters('virtualMachines_az203VMTesting_name')]",
            "apiVersion": "2018-06-01",
            "location": "westus2",
            "tags": {},
            "scale": null,
            "properties": {
                "hardwareProfile": {
                    "vmSize": "Standard_DS2_v2"
                },
                "storageProfile": {
                    "imageReference": {
                        "publisher": "MicrosoftWindowsServer",
```

```
                "offer": "WindowsServer",
                "sku": "2012-R2-Datacenter",
                "version": "latest"
            },
            "osDisk": {
                "osType": "Windows",
                "name": "[concat(parameters('virtualMachines_az203VMTesting_name'),
                variables('osDiskName'))]",
                "createOption": "FromImage",
                "caching": "ReadWrite"
            },
            "dataDisks": []
        },
        "osProfile": {
            "computerName": "[parameters('virtualMachines_az203VMTesting_name')]",
            "adminUsername": "azureadminuser",
            "adminPassword": "Pa$$w0rd",
            "windowsConfiguration": {
                "provisionVMAgent": true,
                "enableAutomaticUpdates": true
            },
            "secrets": [],
            "allowExtensionOperations": true
        },
        "networkProfile": {
            "networkInterfaces": [
                {
                    "id": "[resourceId('Microsoft.Network/networkInterfaces',
                    parameters('networkInterfaces_az203NIC_name'))]",
                    "properties": {
                        "primary": true
                    }
                }
            ]
        }
    },
    "dependsOn": [
        "[resourceId('Microsoft.Network/networkInterfaces',
        parameters('networkInterfaces_az203NIC_name'))]"
    ]
},
{

    "type": "Microsoft.Network/networkInterfaces",
    "name": "[parameters('networkInterfaces_az203NIC_name')]",
    "apiVersion": "2018-10-01",
    "location": "westus2",
    "tags": {},
    "scale": null,
    "properties": {
        "ipConfigurations": [
            {
                "name": "primary",
                "properties": {
                    "privateIPAllocationMethod": "Dynamic",
```

```
                "subnet": {
                    "id": "[resourceId('Microsoft.Network/virtualNetworks/
                    subnets', parameters('virtualNetworks_az203VNET_name'),
                    parameters('subnets_az203Subnet_name'))]"
                },
                "primary": true,
                "privateIPAddressVersion": "IPv4"
            }
        }
    ],
    "dnsSettings": {
        "dnsServers": [],
        "appliedDnsServers": []
    },
    "enableAcceleratedNetworking": false,
    "enableIPForwarding": false,
    "primary": true,
    "tapConfigurations": []
},
"dependsOn": [
    "[resourceId('Microsoft.Network/virtualNetworks/
    subnets', parameters('virtualNetworks_az203VNET_name'),
    parameters('subnets_az203Subnet_name'))]"
]
},
{
    "type": "Microsoft.Network/virtualNetworks",
    "name": "[parameters('virtualNetworks_az203VNET_name')]",
    "apiVersion": "2018-10-01",
    "location": "westus2",
    "tags": {},
    "scale": null,
    "properties": {
        "resourceGuid": "145e7bfc-8b00-48cf-8fa1-082448a30bae",
        "addressSpace": {
            "addressPrefixes": [
                "172.16.0.0/16"
            ]
        },
        "dhcpOptions": {
            "dnsServers": []
        },
        "subnets": [
            {
                "name": "[parameters('subnets_az203Subnet_name')]",
                "properties": {
                    "addressPrefix": "172.16.0.0/24"
                }
            }
        ],
        "virtualNetworkPeerings": [],
        "enableDdosProtection": false,
        "enableVmProtection": false
    },
    "dependsOn": []
},
```

```
    {
        "type": "Microsoft.Network/virtualNetworks/subnets",
        "name": "[concat(parameters('virtualNetworks_az203VNET_name'), '/',
        parameters('subnets_az203Subnet_name'))]",
        "apiVersion": "2018-10-01",
        "scale": null,
        "properties": {
            "addressPrefix": "172.16.0.0/24"
        },
        "dependsOn": [
            "[resourceId('Microsoft.Network/virtualNetworks',
            parameters('virtualNetworks_az203VNET_name'))]"
        ]
    }
  ]
}
```

This example has some interesting features to which we should pay attention. We have defined parameters and variables that we will use throughout the template. If you look at any parameter definition, you can see that it has three elements—*paramenterName*, *defaultValue,* and *type*. The *type* element is almost self-explanatory; it sets the kind of the value that this parameter will contain. The allowed types are string, securestring, int, bool, object, secureObject, and array. The *parameterName* is also quite straightforward and is any valid JavaScript that represents the name of the parameter. However, why use a *defaultValue* element instead of a *value* element? You use *defaultValue* because when you define a parameter in the template file, the only required elements are *parameterName* and type. The parameter's value is actually provided during the deployment process. If you don't provide a value for a parameter that you defined in the template, then the *defaultValue* will be used instead. You should bear in mind that this element is optional.

You can provide values to the parameters that you define for your template by using the command line or creating a file with the values that you want to provide to each parameter. The following example shows the content of a parameter file for the template shown previously in Listing 1-2:

```
{
    "$schema": "https://schema.management.azure.com/schemas/2015-01-01/
    deploymentParameters.json#",
    "contentVersion": "1.0.0.0",
    "parameters": {
        "virtualNetworks_az203VNET_name": {
            "value": "az203demoVNET"
        },
        "networkInterfaces_az203NIC_name": {
            "value": "az203demoNIC"
        },
        "virtualMachines_az203VMTesting_name": {
            "value": "az203demoVM"
        },
```

```
        "subnets_az203Subnet_name": {
            "value": "az203demoSubnet"
        },
        "virtualMachines_az203VMTesting_id": {
            "value": "[concat(parameters('virtualMachines_az203VMTesting_name'),
            '_OSDisk1_1_39c654d89d88405e968db84b722002d1')]"
        },
        "virtualMachines_adminUser": {
            "value": "azureadminuser"
        },
        "virtualMachines_adminpassword": {
            "value": "Pa$$w0rd"
        }
    }
}
```

When you are defining the value for a parameter, you can also use functions to construct dynamic values. If you take a look at the *virtualMachines_az203VMTesting_id* parameter, you can see that its value is set to a function. In this case, the function returns a string that is the result of adding the string *_OSDisk1_1_39c654d89d88405e968db84b722002d1* to the value of the parameter *virtualMachines_az203VMTesting_name*.

There are many predefined functions that you can use in your template. You can even define your own custom functions for those complicated pieces of code that repeats in your template. When working with custom functions, beware of some limitations:

- Custom functions cannot access template variables, although you can pass them as a parameter of your function.

- Your custom function cannot access the template's parameters; instead, they have access only to the parameters that you define in your function.

- Parameters on your custom function cannot have default values.

- Your custom function cannot call other custom functions; only predefined functions may be called.

- You cannot use the *reference()* predefined function.

> **NOTE   TEMPLATE REFERENCE**
>
> When you are working with ARM templates, is useful to consult the template reference for each type of resource you are configuring. You can review the complete template reference at *https://docs.microsoft.com/en-us/azure/templates/*. You can also review the complete reference of predefined functions at https://docs.microsoft.com/en-us/azure/azure-resource-manager/resource-group-template-functions.

When we initially talked about the resources that we need for deploying a VM, we saw that there are some resources that we need for the VM to run correctly. For example, we need at least one virtual disk for storing the operating system. We also need a virtual network for connecting the VM with the world, and we need a virtual network interface card for connecting the VM to the virtual network. All those dependencies are defined in an ARM template by using the element *dependsOn* on each resource type. This element accepts a list of resource names, separated by commas, that define the resources that need to be deployed before the resource can be deployed. As a best practice to avoid ambiguity, you should reference any resource that you put on the *dependsOn* element by using its provider namespace and type. You can do this by using the *resourceId()* predefined function.

If we review our example, the virtual network *virtualNetworks_az203VNET_name* needs to be deployed before *subnets_az203Subnet_name* can be deployed (see Figure 1-1). The *dependsOn* element is needed because the resources defined in the template are not deployed in the same order that appears in the template.

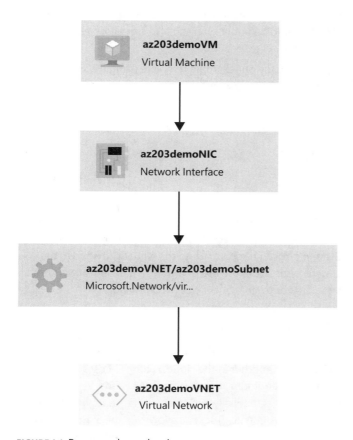

FIGURE 1-1 Resource dependencies

Once we are happy with our template, we can deploy it to our Azure subscription by using PowerShell, Azure CLI, Azure Cloud Shell, or REST API. Another interesting feature that we didn't mention before is that you can store your template JSON files in a remote location. This remote location needs to be publicly available. If your template contains information that shouldn't be public, you can provide that information as an inline parameter during the deployment. If you prefer your template not to be public, you can also store your template in a storage account and protect it by using an SAS token.

The following command shows how to deploy our example template using the template file *az203-template.json* and the properties file *az203-parameters.json*.

```
#!/bin/bash
#Azure CLI template deployment
az group create --name AZ203-ResourceGroup --location "West US"
az group deployment create \
  --name AZ203DemoDeployment \
  --resource-group AZ203-ResourceGroup \
  --template-file az203-template.json \
  --parameters @az203-parameters.json
```

The previous command creates the resource group called *AZ203-ResoureGroup* in the West US region. Then it creates a new deployment called *AZ203DemoDeployment* that will create the resources defined in the *az203-template.json* template using the values provided in the parameters file named *az203-parameters.json*. Note the use of the @ symbol in front of the parameters file. This is required by the *az group deployment create* command.

Configure Azure Disk Encryption for VMs

One of the main concerns of any organization is how to protect their data. Azure has the security of all data that is stored in one way or another in the cloud. Azure VM uses virtual disks for storing the operating system or any additional data that the VM needs. Virtual disks—managed or unmanaged disks—are automatically and transparently encrypted and decrypted by the Azure Storage Service Encryption (SSE) service. However, the SSE service only ensures the data protection at rest. This means the virtual disk file is encrypted, but the information inside the virtual disk is not encrypted.

The good news is that you can also encrypt the content of the virtual disk by using the Azure Disk Encryption service. This service is supported by the Azure Key Vault service for storing the encryption keys that you need for encrypting your disks. The Azure Disk Encryption service also depends on the BitLocker feature for Windows VMs and the *DM-Crypt* feature existing in Linux VMs.

> **NOTE** **AZURE KEY VAULT**
>
> Azure provides the Azure Key Vault service for securely storing your passwords, connection strings, and any other sensitive information that your application may need. You can get more detailed information about Azure Key Vault by reviewing the article at *https://docs.microsoft. com/en-us/azure/key-vault/.*

Before you enable disk encryption on one of your IaaS VMs, you should review the supported scenarios:

- **Enabling encryption on new Windows IaaS VMs.** You can enable the encryption for VMs created from a supported Azure Gallery image or from a pre-encrypted VHD with your own encryption keys.
- **Enabling encryption of existing IaaS VMs in Azure.** You can enable disk encryption for Windows or Linux VMs for the OS or data disks. Bear in mind that if you want to enable encryption on a Linux VM, you need to ensure the VM has a minimum of 7GB of memory.
- **Enabling encryption on virtual machine scale sets.** For Windows VMs in a scale set, you can enable the encryption for OS and data disks. For Linux VMs in a scale set, you can only enable the disk encryption for data disks.
- **Enabling encryption on managed disks.** You can also enable the encryption on IaaS VMs configured with managed disks.
- **Disabling encryption on IaaS VMs.** Depending on your operating system, you have different scenarios:
  - **Windows** You can disable disk encryption on the OS or data disk regardless of whether the VM is a member of a scale set or is a standalone VM.
  - **Linux** For standalone or members of scale-set VMs, you can disable disk encryption only on data disks.
- **Backup and restore encrypted VMs.** You can also protect your encrypted IaaS VMs by configuring their backups using the Azure Backup service.

You should also carefully review these non-supported scenarios:

- You cannot enable disk encryption on basic-tier IaaS VMs.
- You should disable encryption on OS drives for Linux IaaS VMs.
- You should disable encryption on data drives for Linux IaaS VMs when the OS drive is already encrypted.

- Classic IaaS VMs are not supported.
- You should enable encryption on Linux custom images.

You cannot use the disk encryption feature for encrypting

- Azure Files (shared folders)
- Network File Systems (NFS)
- Dynamic volumes
- Windows IaaS VMs configured with a software-based RAID

Once you have evaluated the supported scenarios, you should follow the next high-level workflow (see Figure 1-2) for encrypting a Windows or Linux VM:

1. If you plan to deploy a VM from an existing encrypted VHD from your on-premises infra-structure, you need to upload the VHD to an Azure storage account and the encryption key to your key vault.

2. If you want to create a new IaaS from your custom VHD or from a Marketplace image, you need to provide the encryption configuration.

3. Grant access to Azure platform to your key vault. Azure needs to be able to read needed encryption keys to be able to encrypt your IaaS VM.

4. Azure configures your encrypted VM with the needed encryption key and key vault settings.

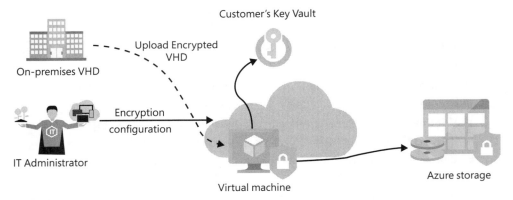

FIGURE 1-2 New VM encryption workflow

You can use following procedure for deploying the prerequisites and encrypt an existing Windows IaaS VM. In this procedure we will use Azure Cloud Shell and PowerShell:

1. If needed, create a new resource group:
   ```
   New-AzureRmResourceGroup -Name 'az203-EncryptionDemo' -Location 'West US'
   ```

2. Create a new key vault. Remember that your vault name needs to be universally unique.
   ```
   $keyVault = New-AzureRmKeyVault -VaultName 'az203DemoEncryptionVault'
   -ResourceGroupName 'az203-EncryptionDemo' -Location 'West US'
   ```

3. Grant Azure access to your key vault. Azure needs to access your key vault to make the encryption keys available to the VM during the boot and decryption processes:

```
Set-AzureRmKeyVaultAccessPolicy -VaultName 'az203DemoEncryptionVault'
-ResourceGroupName 'az203-EncryptionDemo' -EnabledForDiskEncryption
```

4. Grant Azure yourself access to your key vault. When you create a new key vault, all access is denied by default. You need to create an access policy for your Azure Active Directory user to be able to create a new key for encrypting disks:

```
Set-AzureRmKeyVaultAccessPolicy -VaultName 'az203DemoEncryptionVault'
-UserPrincipalName '<your_AAD_username>' -PermissionsToKeys Get,List,Update,Create,
Import,Delete -PermissionsToSecrets Get,List,Set,Delete,Recover,Backup,Restore
```

5. Create a new key for encrypting the disk:

```
$keyEncryptionKeyName = 'az203VMEncryptionKey';
Add-AzureKeyVaultKey -VaultName 'az203DemoEncryptionVault'
-Name $keyEncryptionKeyName -Destination 'Software';
$keyEncryptionKeyUrl = (Get-AzureKeyVaultKey -VaultName 'az203DemoEncryptionVault'
-Name $keyEncryptionKeyName).Key.kid;
```

6. Encrypt the disks of the Windows IaaS VM. You need to ensure that you set the *Resource-GroupName* parameter to the resource group where the VM exists. The VM also needs to be running to enable the disk encryption extension.

```
Set-AzureRmVMDiskEncryptionExtension -ResourceGroupName
'az203-EncryptionDemo' -VMName 'az203demoVM' -DiskEncryptionKeyVaultUrl
$keyVault.VaultUri -DiskEncryptionKeyVaultId $keyVault.ResourceId
-KeyEncryptionKeyUrl $keyEncryptionKeyUrl -KeyEncryptionKeyVaultId
$keyVault.ResourceId;
```

Skill 1.2: Implement batch jobs by using Azure Batch Services

When you start a new project, you need to evaluate how you are going to implement the requirements of the application or solution that you need to implement. Sometimes, one of those requirements is that the application needs to make a lot of calculations to prepare some amount of data that needs to be presented to the user; calculations also might be processed before other components of the solution so it can work with the data. These types of tasks are usually time consuming and heavy in terms of resource needs that can negatively affect the performance of an application.

Examples include running risk simulations for a financial service application, image process-ing for a geographic information system (GIS), or VFX or 3D image–rendering for a movie. In all these cases, a good option for your application is to have a specialized and separate system from your main application that can run all these heavy tasks.

You can implement this specialized and separate system by deploying your own VMs or scale sets in Azure. However, in this case, you need to take care of the overhead of managing those VMs or scale sets. Another downside is that you will be charged for all the time those

VMs are running, regardless of whether you are running your specialized workload (risk simulation, image analysis, 3D image–rendering, and the like).

Fortunately, Azure provides you with a service that is aimed to solve this need. Azure Batch allows you to run parallel workloads that can execute the application that makes the specialized calculations and provides you with the results. The advantages of this service are that you don't need to take care of configuring virtual machines, clusters, and the like, and you only will be charged for the resources that your application needs while it is running.

This skill covers how to:

- Manage batch jobs by using Batch Service API
- Run a batch job by using Azure CLI, Azure Portal, and other tools
- Write code to run an Azure Batch Services batch job

Manage batch jobs by using Batch Service API

When you plan to work with Azure Batch, there are some resources that are common to any workload that you may integrate into your application. These common resources are:

- **Batch account** Every single processing resource dedicated to run your workloads needs to be managed by a batch account. You can run more than one workload inside a single batch account. You can also associate a storage account to a batch account for storing all the files, programs, and resources that your workloads may need during their execution.

- **Compute node** A compute node is each of the computing resources that will actually run the application that performs the task you need to accomplish, such as image processing or data manipulation. Compute nodes are organized into pools.

- **Pool** A pool is a collection of compute nodes. A pool is the resource that manages the type, size, scaling policy communication, task scheduling, network configuration, and other settings that your workload needs for running correctly. A single pool can run multiple jobs and tasks. You should bear in mind that you configure the target or desired size of your pool, but the actual size could be limited by the quota of the number of cores in the batch account.

- **Job** Manages how the execution of the tasks is performed on each compute node in a pool. When you create a job, you can specify whether you want to create a new pool for this job or use an existing pool. It also manages other attributes, such as job priority, constraints, or the behavior of the job when all tasks are completed.

- **Task** This type of resource performs the actual execution of your command, script, or application in a single compute node. A task is always associated to a job, and it is scheduled, queued, and prioritized by its job.

All these elements are related to each other in the high-level workflow that you see in Figure 1-3.

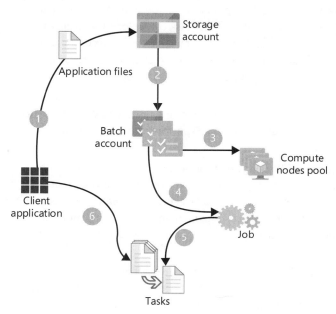

FIGURE 1-3 Creating a Batch service job

Following is a description of the workflow shown in Figure 1-3:

1. **Upload data files to a Storage Account.** Every Batch account can have an associated storage account where you will store the data files that you will need for your jobs. You will also use this storage account for storing the results of your tasks.

2. **Upload application files needed for your tasks.** You will use the storage account associated to the batch account to store the scripts or applications and their dependencies that need to be deployed on the compute nodes for the task to be able to run. Also, you can package all your application files and their dependencies into a zip file, called an application package, that will automatically be deployed to the compute nodes. Even if you decide to use an application package, you still need to have a storage account linked to the Batch account.

3. **Create a compute nodes pool.** At this point, you set the number, the size, and the operating system of the compute nodes that will be part of this pool.

4. **Create a job.** This job will be in charge of managing the tasks that will actually run the application on each compute node. You need to ensure that all needed files for the tasks are present on the compute node to be able to run the task. This is done by the job

preparation task, which is executed on each compute node that is scheduled to run a task and is the first task to run in the compute node. The Batch service waits for the job preparation task to finish before starting the actual task. On the other hand, when the job is marked as completed, you can also perform some cleanup operations by using a job-release task.

5. **Add tasks to the job.** A task is the actual script or application that you program for performing the desired action in the compute node. A task can upload the result of its operation to the storage account. Bear in mind that if you save the results of the task in the compute node itself, this data will be lost when the compute node is recycled or destroyed. As soon as you add the tasks to the job, the compute node starts scheduling their execution.

6. **Monitor tasks.** Once you have started the execution of the tasks, you should monitor the status of the tasks. This optional step allows you to perform additional actions based on the status of the execution.

When you need to implement this workflow in your application, you need to work with two main APIs—Azure Batch Services and Azure Storage. You will use Azure Storage API for uploading and downloading files from blob containers. You will use Azure Batch for creating and deleting the pool of compute nodes; you'll also use Azure Batch for creating, monitoring, deleting, starting, and stopping the job as well as managing, monitoring, and adding the tasks to the job.

During the configuration of a Batch job, you may have some additional requirements that are not covered with the default configuration. You can control the amount of time that a job is executing by configuring the *MaxWallClockTimeExpiry* setting. If the job didn't finish all the tasks in the max wall clock time, then the Batch Account terminates the job and any pending tasks with *MaxWallClockTimeExpiry*. You can also control the number of times that a failing task can be relaunched by setting the *MaxTaskRetryCount* parameter. A task is considered to have failed if it returns an exit code different from zero. If an error occurs while downloading the assets needed for the task to perform its actions, the task can fail. In this situation, a *failureInfo* object is created and attached to the task. The Azure Batch account uses this object for determining whether it should finish the job after the failure of one task in the job. This action is controlled by the *OnTaskFailure* property (you can see this property as the *When a task fails* setting in the Azure Portal), and its default value is to take no action.

As we already saw, a job is in charge of managing the execution of tasks on the compute node. Azure Batch provides you with a default task manager that performs this task management. However, you can also create a job manager task for implementing your own logic when deploying and running your tasks in the compute nodes. The job manager task is executed in one of the compute nodes, and it has all the information required for creating the tasks in the job. The job manager task is managed by the batch account and is created as one of the first steps when the job is created. Because of the importance of this task, it is monitored and automatically created if the task fails. This job manager task is also a requirement if you decide to use job schedules, which allow you to create recurring tasks when you need to control the duration, frequency, and schedule of jobs created during the scheduled period.

Microsoft offers a client Batch API for .NET, Python, Node.js, and Java. If your application doesn't use any of the previous languages, you can still work with Azure Batch from your application by using the provided REST API.

Whatever API you decide to use, you need to get the following information from your batch and storage account before you can make any API call:

- **Batch account name**   This is the name you gave to your batch account when you created it.

- **Batch account URL**   This URL has the form of *https://<batch_account_name>.<region>.batch.azure.com.*

- **Batch account key**   This key is used for authenticating the request to the batch account. Any batch account has two separate keys. You can use either of them for authenticating, although you should only use the same key on your application.

- **Storage account name**   This is the name of the storage account associated with the batch account.

- **Storage account key**   You need to provide one of the two available keys for accessing the storage account.

In the section "Write code to run an Azure Batch Services batch job," we will review an example of code that you can use for running jobs in Azure using C#.

Run a batch job by using Azure CLI, Azure Portal, and other tools

In the previous section, we looked at a high-level review of the Batch Service API for managing jobs. You can also use Batch Management API for managing batch accounts. However, you can also perform these actions by using other tools like PowerShell, Azure CLI, Azure Portal, Azure Batch Explorer, Azure Batch Shipyard, or Azure Storage Explorer. With the exception of Azure Storage Explorer, the main advantage of using any of these tools is that they unify the Batch Service and Batch Management APIs' capabilities into the same tool. Although Azure Storage Explorer cannot directly manage batch jobs or tasks, this tool makes developing and debugging your Batch solutions easier.

Azure Batch Explorer is a rich desktop client that you can download for Windows, Linux, or OSX. You can manage different batch accounts to view high level statistics and manage pools, jobs, job schedules, packages, or digital certificates. You can also troubleshoot the task execution by accessing to the content of each compute node in the pool.

Another interesting feature is that Azure Batch supports the execution of tasks using Docker or Singularity containers. For easing the provision, monitoring, and execution of batch workloads based on containers, you can use Batch Shipyard. The best part is that you don't need to download or install any tool in your local environment; simply open a Cloud Shell and type **shipyard** in your favorite shell to run this tool.

In the next few examples, we will review the procedure for running a batch job by using these tools. The job consists of discovering the type of data that your files contain. To do so, we will use the Linux *file* command. For this example, we will assume that all needed resources are already created:

- An Azure Batch account.
- A compute nodes pool.
- A storage account linked with the Azure Batch account.
- A container in the storage account. This container will store the files that will be analyzed in the tasks.
- A resource group that will contain all the resources needed for the Azure Batch account.

In this first example, we will review how to create a job and tasks using the Azure Portal. To start, we need to create the compute nodes pool that will execute the job:

1. Sign in to the management portal *(http://portal.azure.com)*.
2. In the search box at the top of the Azure Portal, type the name of your Batch account.
3. Click the search result that matches your Batch account.
4. On the Batch Account blade, in the left column, under Features, click the Pools entry. This will open the Batch's blade.
5. On the Batch Pools blade, click the Add button to add a new pool. This will open the Add Pool blade.
6. On the Add Pool blade, on the Pool Detail section, enter the Pool ID and optionally, the Display Name.
7. On the Operating System section, select Canonical in the publisher drop-down menu, ensure that *UbuntuServer* is selected in the Offer drop-down menu, and select *18.04-LTS* in the Sku drop-down menu. We won't need data disks for these compute nodes.
8. On the Node Size section, ensure that Standard A1 VM size is selected.
9. On the Scale section, set the number of Target Dedicated Nodes to *4*. Remember that the actual number of nodes depends on the quota limit of your subscription.
10. Click the OK button to create the pool.

> *NOTE* **ADVANCED SETTINGS CREATING POOLS**
>
> When you are creating a compute node pool, you have more advanced options that allow you to control how to dynamically scale the number of nodes associated to the pool or create nodes from custom images. For more detail about the pool's advanced settings, you can review Microsoft Docs at *https://docs.microsoft.com/en-us/azure/batch/batch-automatic-scaling.*

Once we have created the pool, we can create the job and tasks. Creating a task for a job is a separate procedure that you need to perform once you have created a job:

1. Sign in to the management Portal (*http://portal.azure.com*).

2. In the search box at the top of the Azure Portal, type the name of your Batch account.

3. Click the search result that matches your Batch account.

4. On the Batch Account blade and on left side column under the Features section, click on the Jobs entry. This will open the Jobs blade.

5. On the Jobs blade, click on the Add button to add a new job. This will open the Add Job blade shown in Figure 1-4.

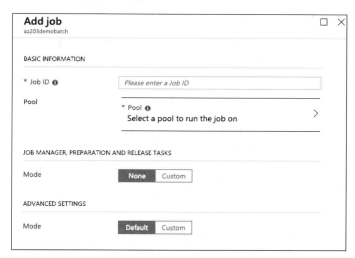

FIGURE 1-4 Creating a new Batch Service job dialog

6. In the Job ID field, enter the value. You will need this value later if you want to manage this job from PowerShell, Azure CLI, or programmatically.

7. On the Select A Pool To Run The Job On control, select the pool that you created in the previous procedure.

8. Leave the remaining options as is and click OK.

Once you have created the job, you need to create the tasks that will be run by this job:

1. On the Azure Batch Job blade, click on the job that you configured in the previous procedure. This will open a blade with the specific details of your job.

2. In the General section, click the Tasks option, which will open the Tasks blade. You will use this blade for adding tasks to the job.

3. On the Tasks blade, click the Add button located in the upper-right corner of the blade, which will open the Add Task blade.

4. On the Add Task blade, in the General section, provide a Task ID and the Command Line that will be executed by this task.

5. Complete the Advanced Settings according to your requirements. At the least, you will need to add resource files to your task. These Advanced Settings are explained below in more detail.

6. Click Submit to create the task and add it to the job.

While you have been adding the task, you can also adjust some Advanced Settings:

- **Max Wall Clock Time**   This controls the maximum time that the task is allowed to run. If the task is not completed before this time is exhausted, the Batch account terminates the job and all its tasks.

- **Max Task Retry Count**   If a task completes with a non-zero return code, the task is considered to have failed. This setting controls the maximum times that a failed task can be retried.

- **Retention Time**   This is the time that the Batch account will maintain the data in the working directory of the task. By default, this time is 7 days, but you can customize it with this setting.

- **User Identity**   Controls the user privileges that will be used for running this task. You can select between auto-user accounts with or without admin privileges. Auto-user accounts are built-in user accounts used for running the task. You can also define your own named user accounts, but you can only programmatically attach a named user account to a task.

- **Multi-Instance Settings**   By default, tasks cannot communicate with other tasks. This setting allows your tasks to be able to communicate between them, using MPI (Message Passing Interface).

- **Resource Files**   This is a list of files that will be downloaded to the task before it runs. These files are needed for the task to do the job.

- **Environment Settings**   Defines any environment variable that your task may require to run.

- **Task Dependencies**   You can define a hierarchy of tasks by defining dependencies between them. The child task won't run until the parent task has successfully executed. You can define the following Task Dependency types:

  - **One-To-One**   A child task won't run until its parent task has finished successfully.

  - **One-To-Main**   A child task has two or more parents. Child tasks won't run until all parent tasks have finished successfully. The parent task ID can be any string that best fits your needs.

  - **Task ID Range**   This is similar to the One-To-Many dependency type, but parent task IDs need to be resolved to an integer. For example, this means that *5*, *7*, *008*, and *256* are valid task IDs, but *3monkeys* is not a valid task ID.

- **Application Packages**   An application package contains all the needed dependencies and binaries for the task to run. This setting controls the application package that will be uploaded to the task before starting its execution.

Just as we have configured a pool, a job, and its tasks using the Azure Portal, we can use PowerShell or Azure CLI to do the same. In the following procedure, we will configure a pool, a job, and its tasks using PowerShell:

1. Open a PowerShell in an elevated session.

2. Install the Azure PowerShell module by using the *Install-Module -Name Az -AllowClover* cmdlet in the PowerShell window. Alternately, you can use Azure Cloud Shell. If you decide to use Azure Cloud Shell, skip ahead to step 5.

3. Connect to your subscription:

```
Connect-AzAccount
```

4. Register the Azure Batch provider namespace. You need to perform this step only once per subscription:

```
Register-AzResourceProvider -ProviderName Microsoft.Batch
```

5. Get the access keys for your Batch Account. In this procedure, we will use the primary account key. This is also known as the Batch context for the cmdlets. You will need to use this context on the next steps:

```
$context = Get-AzBatchAccountKeys -AccountName <Batch_account_name>
```

6. Create a Batch pool. This will create a pool with four dedicated nodes. Each node is a Ubuntu 18.04.0-LTS virtual machine.

```
$vmImage = New-Object -TypeName "Microsoft.Azure.Commands.Batch.Models.
PSImageReference" -ArgumentList @("UbuntuServer","Canonical","18.04.0-LTS")
$vmConfig = New-Object -TypeName "Microsoft.Azure.Commands.Batch.Models.
PSVirtualMachineConfiguration" -ArgumentList @($vmImage, "batch.node.ubuntu
18.04")
New-AzBatchPool -Id <your_pool_id> -VirtualMachineSize "Standard_a1"
-VirtualMachineConfiguration $vmConfig -AutoScaleFormula '$TargetDedicated=4;'
-BatchContext $context
```

7. Create a Job. When you create a job, you cannot use directly the pool object that you created in the previous step. You need to construct an *PSPoolInformation* object that contains the information about the pool where you will create the job:

```
$poolInformation = New-Object -TypeName "Microsoft.Azure.Commands.Batch.Models.
PSPoolInformation"
$poolInformation.PoolID = <your_pool_id>
New-AzBatchJob -Id <your_job_id> -PoolInformation $poolInformation -BatchContext
$context
```

8. Create as many Batch tasks as you need:

```
$tasks = @()
1..4 | foreach {
    $task = New-Object Microsoft.Azure.Commands.Batch.Models.
PSCloudTask("SampleTask$_", "uname -a")
    $tasks += $task
    }
New-AzBatchTask -JobId "jobPStesting" -Tasks $tasks -BatchContext $Context
```

Write code to run an Azure Batch Services batch job

Although Azure Portal, PowerShell, Azure CLI, and Azure Batch Explorer are powerful tools for
managing or even defining Batch pools, jobs, and tasks, the most flexible approach for integrating your solution with Azure Batch is using one of the available client SDKs in your code.

In this section, we will review how to perform the same tasks that you already performed
in the previous section using Azure Portal or PowerShell, but we'll use the .Net client library.
Also, we will add a little bit of complexity by including some interaction with the Azure Storage
account linked to the Batch account. The tasks in the job will get information about the file
type of the files that we will provide to the tasks. You will upload to the storage account all the
files that the tasks will need to run. Microsoft provides separate SDKs for working with pools,
jobs, and tasks, and for managing a Batch account. Azure Batch Client library is the SDK used
for creating your pools, jobs, and tasks. If you need to manage a Batch account, you need to
use the Azure Batch Management library.

When you are writing code for Batch jobs, you are not limited to write your code for Windows Operating System if you want to use the .NET client library. The example that we will
review in this section is written in .NET Core, and you can execute it on Windows, Linux, or
MacOS X.

Before you can proceed to compile this example, you need to meet some requirements:

- Create an Azure Batch account.
- Create an Azure Storage account and link it to the Azure Batch account.
- You need .NET Core 2.1 or newer.
- You need the *Microsoft.Azure.Batch* nuget package.
- You need the *WindowsAzure.Storage* nuget package.

Before you can start programming the batch pools, jobs, and tasks, you need to upload the
files to the storage account. You need to do this as one of the first steps because you need the
references to the files in the storage account to pass them as the resource files for the tasks.
You need to create a *CloudBlobClient* object. This object will be used for managing the access
to your storage account.

```
//.Net Core 2.2
//Create a blob client. We will use this client for accessing the images that we need to
//process
string storageConnectionString = $"DefaultEndpointsProtocol=https;AccountName={ STORAGE_
ACCOUNT_NAME };AccountKey={ STORAGE_ACCOUNT_KEY }";
CloudStorageAccount storageAccount = CloudStorageAccount.Parse(storageConnectionString);
CloudBlobClient blobClient = storageAccount.CreateCloudBlobClient();
```

Once you have the *CloudBlobClient* object, you need to ensure that the container that you
will use for storing the images already exists. You need to get a *CloudBlobContainer* object for
working with blob containers. Then you call the method *CreateIfNotExistsAsync()*, which ensures
that the container is created even if it didn't exist on your storage account. Then you need to
upload the files to the blob storage by using the *UploadFromFileAsync()* method. This method
requires the *CloudBlobClient* that you created for uploading the images (see Listing 1-3).

LISTING 1-3 Uploading files to a Storage account

```
//Get a reference to the blob container. We will create if it not exist.
const string STORAGE_ACCOUNT_IMAGES_CONTAINER_NAME = "images";
CloudBlobContainer imagesContainer = blobClient.
GetContainerReference(STORAGE_ACCOUNT_IMAGES_CONTAINER_NAME);
imagesContainer.CreateIfNotExistsAsync().Wait();

//List of images your local computer that will be uploaded
List<string> inputFilePaths = new List<string>(Directory.GetFiles("images/"));

//Create a list of references of files once they have been uploaded to the blob
container
List<ResourceFile> inputImages = new List<ResourceFile>();
foreach (string imagePath in inputFilePaths)
{
    Console.WriteLine("Uploading file {0} to container [{1}]...", filePath,
    STORAGE_ACCOUNT_IMAGES_CONTAINER_NAME);
    string blobName = Path.GetFileName(imagePath);
    imagePath = Path.Combine(Environment.CurrentDirectory, imagePath);
    CloudBlobContainer container = blobClient.
    GetContainerReference(STORAGE_ACCOUNT_IMAGES_CONTAINER_NAME);
    CloudBlockBlob blobData = container.GetBlockBlobReference(blobName);
    blobData.UploadFromFileAsync(imagePath).Wait();
    //We access the storage account by using a Shared Access Signature (SAS) token.
    //You need to start the upload operation as soon as possible, so we set no start
    //time for making the token immediately available.
     SharedAccessBlobPolicy sasConstraints = new SharedAccessBlobPolicy
    {
        SharedAccessExpiryTime = DateTime.UtcNow.AddHours(2),
        Permissions = SharedAccessBlobPermissions.Read
    };
    // Construct the SAS URL for blob
    string sasBlobToken = blobData.GetSharedAccessSignature(sasConstraints);
    string blobSasUri = String.Format("{0}{1}", blobData.Uri, sasBlobToken);
    ResourceFile resourceFile = new ResourceFile(blobSasUri, blobName);
    inputImages.Add(resourceFile);
}
```

Once you have all the files needed for the tasks to run, you need to create the Batch pool, job, and tasks. When you work with Batch Client Library for .NET, the first thing you need to do is create a batch client that will be in charge of authenticating and performing all the communication tasks with the Azure Batch account. To create a *BatchClient*, you need to provide the credentials that your application will use for connecting to your Batch account. These credentials are managed by a *BatchSharedKeyCredentials*. You need to provide the Batch account name, URL, and key for creating the *BatchSharedKeyCredentials* object. You can get the value for the name and URL from the Overview page in your Batch Account blade. The value for the key parameter can be obtained from the Keys sections in your Batch Account blade. You will find two different keys. You can use either of them. As a best practice, you should always use the same key for all your applications that need to access to your Batch account.

```
//We start by getting a Batch Account client.
BatchSharedKeyCredentials batchCredentials = new BatchSharedKeyCredentials(BATCH_
ACCOUNT_URL, BATCH_ACCOUNT_NAME, BATCH_ACCOUNT_KEY);
using (BatchClient batchClient = BatchClient.Open(batchCredentials))
{
...
```

Now you can create the pool, job, and tasks that will run in your Batch account. First, you need to create the compute nodes pool. To do this, you need to create an image reference for the VMs that will be included in the pool. Then, using the image reference, you can create the VM configuration. The last step will be to create the pool itself. When creating the Batch pool, you need to create a *BatchPool* object, fill all the required properties—such as pool ID, number of target nodes, size of the nodes, and VM configuration—and then commit the changes to the Batch account for creating the pool. See Listing 1-4.

LISTING 1-4 Create a compute node pool

```
//Create the compute nodes pool
Console.WriteLine($"Creating pool {POOL_ID} ...");
//We will use Linux VMs for this pool.
//We need to create a Linux Server image reference, VM configuration and Batch pool
ImageReference imageReference = new ImageReference(
                                publisher: "Canonical",
                                offer: "UbuntuServer",
                                sku: "18.04-LTS",
                                version: "latest");
VirtualMachineConfiguration vmConfiguration = new VirtualMachineConfiguration(
                                        imageReference: imageReference,
                                        nodeAgentSkuId: "batch.node.ubuntu 18.04");
//Create the Batch pool
try
{
    CloudPool pool = batchClient.PoolOperations.CreatePool(
                        poolId: POOL_ID,
                        targetDedicatedComputeNodes: POOL_NODE_COUNT,
                        virtualMachineSize: POOL_VM_SIZE,
                        virtualMachineConfiguration: vmConfiguration);
```

```
        pool.Commit();
}
catch (BatchException be)
{
    // Accept the specific error code PoolExists as that is expected if the pool already
    // exists
    if (be.RequestInformation?.BatchError?.Code == BatchErrorCodeStrings.PoolExists)
    {
        Console.WriteLine("The pool {0} already existed when we tried to create it",
        POOL_ID);
    }
    else
    {
        throw; // Any other exception is unexpected
    }
}
```

Now that you have the Batch pool, you can create the job and the tasks for getting the information from the uploaded files. You need to create a *CloudJob* object for working with any job in the Batch pool. The way you create a job is similar to creating a pool. You need to create the *CloudJob* object, fill the required properties ID and *PoolInformation*, and then commit the changes to the Batch account for actually creating the job (see Listing 1-5).

LISTING 1-5 Creating a CloudJob object

```
//Create the actual Batch Job
Console.WriteLine($"Creating job [{JOB_ID}]...");

try
{
    CloudJob job = batchClient.JobOperations.CreateJob();
    job.Id = JOB_ID;
    job.PoolInformation = new PoolInformation { PoolId = POOL_ID };

    job.Commit();
}
catch (BatchException be)
{
    //If the job already exists, we just accept it and register in the log.
    if (be.RequestInformation?.BatchError?.Code == BatchErrorCodeStrings.JobExists)
    {
        Console.WriteLine($"The Job {JOB_ID} already exists...");
    }
    else
    {
        throw;
    }
}
```

Now that you have your pool ready, you can create the tasks that will get the information from the files that you uploaded previously. In this case, you are going to create a task for every file that you uploaded to the storage account. You need to create a *CloudTask* object and use the *ResourceFiles* property for indicating which file will be analyzed by the task. When creating the task, you need to set the command line that will be run by the task. In this example, your task will run the file command to get the information about the file uploaded in the *Resource-Files* property. Place all the tasks that you need to create in a *List* object that you use for storing *CloudTask* objects. Then you will use this list to pass the tasks to the job for so they can be executed (see Listing 1-6).

LISTING 1-6 Creating the tasks to add to a job

```
//Now, we need to create the tasks that we will add to the job.
System.Console.WriteLine($"Adding {inputImages.Count} tasks to the job [{JOB_ID}]...");
List<CloudTask> tasks = new List<CloudTask>();
//We put each file to be processed in a separate task. We created the inputImages List
//when you uploaded the files to the storage account
for (int i = 0; i < inputImages.Count; i++)
{
    string taskId = $"Task{i}";
    string imageFilename = inputImages[i].FilePath;
    string taskCommandLine = $"file {imageFilename}";

    CloudTask task = new CloudTask(taskId, taskCommandLine);
    task.ResourceFiles = new List<ResourceFile> { inputImages[i]};
    tasks.Add(task);
}
```

Now you can attach the list of your tasks to your job. As soon as you add the tasks to the job, the job manager will try to deploy to an available node and execute the task.

```
//Add all tasks to the job.
batchClient.JobOperations.AddTask(JOB_ID, tasks);
```

Once you have your tasks running inside your job in your compute nodes tool, you need to monitor them to ensure all the tasks have completed successfully. You can monitor the status of the added task by creating a *TaskStateMonitor*. Before you can create this monitor, you need to get the list of added tasks to the job by using the method *ListTasks()* in the *JobOperations* property of your Batch client.

```
//At this point, we need to monitor if tasks are failing or not. We need to set the
//maximum amount of time to wait for the tasks to complete.
TimeSpan timeout = TimeSpan.FromMinutes(30);
System.Console.WriteLine($"Monitoring all tasks to be completed, timeout in
{timeout}...");
IEnumerable<CloudTask> addedTasks = batchClient.JobOperations.ListTasks(JOB_ID);
batchClient.Utilities.CreateTaskStateMonitor().WaitAll(addedTasks, TaskState.Completed,
timeout);
```

To get the result of the execution of each task, you need to read the content of the stdout.txt file from the node where the task was executed.

```
//Print tasks results
System.Console.WriteLine();
System.Console.WriteLine("Printing tasks results...");
System.Console.WriteLine("Printing tasks results...");

IEnumerable<CloudTask> completedTasks = batchClient.JobOperations.ListTasks(JOB_ID);

foreach (CloudTask task in completedTasks)
{
    System.Console.WriteLine($"Task: {task.Id}");
    System.Console.WriteLine($"Node: {task.ComputeNodeInformation.ComputeNodeId}");
    System.Console.WriteLine("Standard output:");
    System.Console.WriteLine(task.GetNodeFile(Constants.StandardOutFileName).
    ReadAsString());
}
```

Finally, you can perform some clean up by deleting the job and the pool, directly from your code.

```
//Clean up Batch resources
batchClient.JobOperations.DeleteJob(JOB_ID);
batchClient.PoolOperations.DeletePool(POOL_ID);
```

Skill 1.3: Create containerized solutions

With the evolution of technology and the emergence of the cloud, we need to meet other challenges presented by this technical evolution. One of these requirements is the ability to deploy pieces of software in a reliable and quick manner. Virtualization technologies were one of the keys for making this kind of reliable and quick deployment possible.

However, when we talk about operating system virtualization using virtual machines, one of the main drawbacks is the fact that we have a complete set of binaries, libraries, and resources that are duplicated between virtual machines. This is where containerization provides a different approach to deploying pieces of software across multiple servers in a reliable and quick manner.

A container is piece of software that packages your code and all its dependencies in a single package that can be run directly by the computer environment. When a container is executed, it uses a read-only copy of the common libraries of the operating system that your code needs to run. This reduces the required amount of resources that a container needs to run your code when compared to running the same code on a virtual machine. Container technology was originally born in Linux environments, but it also has been ported to the Microsoft Windows environment. There are several implementations of container technology in the Linux ecosystem, but Docker Containers are the most widely used.

When you move the container technology to an enterprise environment, scaling dynamically and automatically is a problem, just as it is with virtual machines. There are several available solutions, such as Docker Swarm, DC/OS, or Kubernetes. All these solutions are orchestration solutions that automatically scale and deploy your containers in the available resources.

Microsoft offers the ability to work with containers using two different services:

- **Azure Container Service (ACS)**   This is a service that allows you to deploy a production-ready cluster of Docker Swarm, DC/OS, or Kubernetes. With this service, you still need to manage and fine-tune the cluster.
- **Azure Managed Kubernetes Service (AKS)**   This is a managed Kubernetes cluster in which you only need to worry about deploying your containers and images.

This skill covers how to:

- Create an Azure Managed Kubernetes Service (AKS) cluster
- Create container images for solutions
- Publish an image to the Azure Container Registry
- Run containers by using Azure Container Instance or AKS

Create an Azure Managed Kubernetes Service (AKS) cluster

Kubernetes is an open-source system for orchestrating the deployment, management, and scaling of application running in containers. This means that the containers that you upload to a Kubernetes cluster are automatically balanced and distributed across the different nodes of the cluster.

Azure allows you to deploy a managed Kubernetes cluster, which means you only need to worry about the cluster nodes that run the containers. You don't need to manage the other components that comprise the cluster and are needed to run correctly. Before we can continue with creating a managed Kubernetes service in Azure, we should review the components that are part of any Kubernetes cluster and the advantage of using a managed service like AKS.

Any AKS cluster is divided in two main components:

- **Cluster master nodes**   These are the nodes that manage the cluster and provide the core orchestration services.
- **Nodes**   A node contains the VMs where your container will be executed.

When you create an AKS cluster, all the elements are automatically created and configured for you, including the cluster master nodes. Because this is a managed service, the cluster master nodes are included in the managed part of the service. That is, they are managed by Azure. You are not charged for any of these cluster master nodes. Even these cluster master nodes are managed by Azure, and they are single tenant. This means that all master nodes are dedicated to the same tenant. Every master node has deployed the following components:

- **API Server**   The *kube-apiserver* is the component that exposes the needed APIs that Kubernetes needs to run. These APIs are managed by tools like kubectl or the Kubernetes Dashboard.

- **Scheduler**   This component determines what nodes can run the workloads that are part of your application. Once a node is selected as valid for running a workload, the scheduler is also in charge of starting the workload.

- **Etcd**   This component is a key-value store that maintains the configuration and the state of the Kubernetes cluster.

- **Controller Manager**   The kube-controller-manager is in charge of managing other controllers. A controller is control loop that watches for the shared state of the cluster. The controller works with the API server for querying the current state and making the needed changes to achieve the desired state. You can have controllers for deployments, cron jobs, garbage collecting, namespaces, and most of the operations in the cluster.

Because the master nodes are managed by Azure, you cannot directly connect to these nodes to perform any configuration or troubleshooting. If you need to troubleshoot your AKS cluster, you can do so by reviewing the AKS cluster logs in the Azure Monitor logs. Other administrative operations, like the version upgrade, can be performed using the Azure Portal or Azure CLI.

Cluster master nodes are only one part of any AKS cluster. Other important parts are the nodes or node pools. In Kubernetes, a node is each of the VMs that run the workloads of your application. A node pool is a group of nodes that share the same configuration. When you create your AKS cluster, Azure creates a default node pool with the number of nodes that you set during the initial deployment.

Each node in the AKS cluster has deployed some default components needed for the AKS cluster to run correctly.

- **The Kubernetes agent**   The Kubernetes agent (also known as a kubelet) receives the orders from the orchestrator and executes them in the node. One of these orders could be launching the container that holds your application.

- **Proxy**   The proxy or kube-proxy manages the virtual network on each node. This process routes the network traffic and manages the IP addressing for the services and pods running in the node.

- **Container runtime**   This is the component that allows your containers to run and interact with the resources, such as the network or the storage that is available in the node.

When you create the AKS node, you set the size of the VM that will be used for the AKS nodes. This setting defines the amount of resources available to your containers. Bear in mind that the Kubernetes agent reserves some resources to ensure that it has enough resources to manage the requests from the master nodes. These reservations are 60ms of CPU and 20 percent of memory, up to 4GiB. This means that if you use a DS2 v2 node size with 2vCPU and 7GiB, the amount of memory reserved for the agent will be 1.4 GiB (20% * 7 GiB = 1.4 GiB). If you use an E4s V3 node with 4 vCPI and 32 GiB of memory, then 4 GiB of memory will be reserved, even if the 20 percent of 32GiB is equal to 6.4GiB.

> **NOTE** **RUNNING WINDOWS CONTAINERS IN AKS**
>
> At the time of this writing, you can only use Ubuntu VMs as nodes of an AKS cluster. If you need to use a different host OS for the containers, you need to deploy your own Kubernetes cluster using aks-engine. You can review the official aks-engine GitHub page for more details. See *https://github.com/Azure/aks-engine*.

Before explaining how to delay an AKS cluster, we need to discuss how to deploy the containers to the AKS cluster. From the most basic to the most complex, these concepts are:

- **Pod** This is a logical resource that Kubernetes uses for running an instance of your container. The container is where the code actually runs. A pod is a structure needed by Kubernetes to define resource limits, plan the schedule, and deploy the container. A Pod usually has a 1:1 relationship with a container, although there can be advanced scenarios in which a single pod can contain multiple containers.

- **Deployments** One or more identical pods can be grouped in a deployment. When deploying a pod using a deployment structure, if you deploy a single pod without using a deployment and a problem occurs, it could be finished and wouldn't be restarted or migrated to another healthy node. Every deployment is managed by the Deployment Controller. You can also update the deployment definition. When you apply that updated definition to an existing deployment, the Deployment Controller manages the termination or creation of new pods according to the new definition. When a pod in a deployment is drained from a node, any resource attached to the pod is also removed.

- **YAML manifests** Any deployment is defined using a YAML file that contains the definition of the resource that will be deployed. Depending on the type of the resource, you will set the key *kind* to the correct value: *Deployment*, *StatefulSet*, or *DaemonSet*. The manifest contains the entire definition of the resource that needs to be deployed to the AKS cluster.

- **StatefulSets** These work similarly to deployment managing pods. The big difference is that any pod managed by a *StatefulSet* is assigned a static network identifier, the storage assigned to the pod is persistent, the deployment and scaling of the pod is ordered and graceful across the nodes, as well as updates on the nodes are also managed in an ordered way. The storage assigned to a pod in a *StatefulSet* is persisted even if the pod is deleted. *StatefulSets* are managed by the StatefulSet Controller.

- **DaemonSets** Pods in a *DaemonSets* are guaranteed to be deployed in every node specified in the manifest. The sets are usually used for log collection in the monitoring workloads.

Once you have reviewed the main concepts needed to work with an AKS cluster, you should be able to better understand the requirements when creating a cluster in Azure. The following procedure shows how to create an AKS cluster using the Azure Portal:

1. Sign in to the management portal (*http://portal.azure.com*).

2. Click on the Create A Resource Link at the upper-left corner, and then select Containers | Kubernetes Service.

3. On the Create Kubernetes cluster blade, on the Basics tab, create a new resource group using the Create New link below the resource group drop-down menu for the Resource group option. You can also use an existing resource group.

4. In the Cluster Details section, shown in Figure 1-5, type a name for your cluster in Kubernetes Cluster Name box.

CLUSTER DETAILS

* Kubernetes cluster name ❶	
* Region ❶	West US ⌄
* Kubernetes version ❶	1.12.6 ⌄
* DNS name prefix ❶	

FIGURE 1-5 Creating a new managed Kubernetes cluster

5. Select the Region where this cluster will be deployed.

6. Select the Kubernetes Version. The last available version is selected by default.

7. Provide a value for the DNS Name Prefix. This value will be appended to the FQDN of the managed API server. You need to connect to the API Server when you need to manage containers once they have been deployed into the cluster.

8. In the Scale section, select the size of each node that will be added to the cluster. Bear in mind that you won't be able to change the size of the nodes after you have created the cluster. You can change the number of nodes associated to the cluster.

9. In the Scale section, select the number of nodes that you want to connect to your cluster. For production environments, you should deploy at least three nodes for achieving a good level of resiliency.

10. Click the Next: Authentication button at the bottom of the tab to move to the Authentication tab.

11. On the Authentication tab, in the Cluster Infrastructure section, ensure that Service Principal is configured to create a new default service principal. This service principal is used by the Kubernetes service cluster for accessing other resources in Azure, such as the Azure Container Registry or Azure Load Balancers.

12. In the Kubernetes Authentication And Authorization section, ensure Enable RBAC is configured to No. The Role-Based Access Control (RBAC) provides fine-grained granularity for managing the access to the cluster resources.

13. Click the Next: Networking button at the bottom of the tab to move to the Networking tab.

14. On the Networking tab, ensure that the option HTTP Application Routing is not enabled. This option will create an HTTP ingress controller that routes HTTP traffic to your application. This configuration is not recommended for production environments; it's recommended only for testing or developing environments.

15. On the Networking tab, ensure that the Network Configuration option is configured to Basic. This will create a new VNet for your cluster. If you prefer to connect your new cluster to an existing VNet, select the Advanced option.

16. Click the Next: Monitoring button at the bottom of the tab to move to the Monitoring tab.

17. On the Monitoring tab, ensure that the option Enable Container Monitoring is enabled. This will connect your Kubernetes cluster with Azure Monitor. You can then monitor the performance of your cluster, monitor the resources consumed by your containers, identify which containers are running in which nodes, and so on.

18. Click the Review + Create button at the bottom of the tab.

19. On the Review + Create tab, ensure that all settings looks right for you. When you open this tab, Azure performs a validation of your settings, and if everything is okay, the Create button will be enabled.

20. On the Review + Create tab, make sure the Create button is enabled; click Create to create the cluster.

Create container images for solutions

Azure provides several services that allow you to deploy your application in a container. It doesn't matter if you decide to use Azure Kubernetes Services, Service Fabric, Azure Web Apps for Containers, Azure Container Registry, or Azure Container Instances; all these services use the same container technology implementation, Docker.

Before you can deploy your application to any of these services, you need to put your application into a container by creating an image of your container. A container image is a package that contains everything you need—code, libraries, environment variables, and configuration files—to run your application. Once you have your container images, you can create instances of the image for running the code, each of which is a container.

When you create your container image, you must define your application's requirements, which are placed in a file called Dockerfile. This Dockerfile contains the definition and requirements needed for creating your container image. Use the following high-level procedure for creating an image:

1. **Create a directory for the new image.** This directory will contain your Docker file, your code, and any other dependencies that need to be added to the image and that are not already published as an image.

2. **Create the Dockerfile.** This file contains the definition of your image. Listing 1-7 shows an example of a functional Dockerfile.

3. **Open a command line.** You use this command line to run the Docker commands.

4. **Create the container image.** Use the command *docker build* for creating the image. When you create an image, you should add a tag to clearly identify the image and the image version. If you don't set a version number, it will be automatically assigned the default value *latest*. You need to provide the path of the folder that contains the Dockerfile. This command has following structure:

   ```
   docker build --tag=<tag_name>[:<version>] <dockerfile_dir>
   ```

5. **List the new created image.** Once Docker finishes downloading all the dependencies for your image, you can ensure that your image has been created by executing this command:

   ```
   docker image ls
   ```

LISTING 1-7 Dockerfile example

```
# Use an official Python runtime as a parent image
FROM python:2.7-slim

# Set the working directory to /app
WORKDIR /app

# Copy the current directory contents into the container at /app
COPY . /app

# Install any needed packages specified in requirements.txt
RUN pip install --trusted-host pypi.python.org -r requirements.txt

# Make port 80 available to the world outside this container
EXPOSE 80

# Define environment variable
ENV NAME World

# Run app.py when the container launches
CMD ["python", "app.py"]
```

NEED MORE REVIEW? **BEST PRACTICES FOR WRITING DOCKERFILES**

When you are writing your own Dockerfile, you should bear in mind some best practices detailed at *https://docs.docker.com/develop/develop-images/dockerfile_best-practices/*.

For complex applications, creating an image for each component of the application can become a complex task. For scenarios in which you need to define and run multiple containers, you can use Docker Compose. You can also think of Docker Compose as the definition of your images for a production environment. If your application is comprised of several images, you can define the relationship between those images and how they are exposed to the external world. Also, you can set the limits of resources that will be assigned to each container and what happens if one container associated to a service fails.

A service in the Docker world is each of the pieces of that are part of your application. A service has a one-to-one relationship with an image. It's important to remember that a service can have multiple instances of the same image; this means you can have multiple containers. The definitions of these relationships and requirements are stored in the *docker-composer.yaml* file.

> **NEED MORE REVIEW?** **FULLY FUNCTIONAL EXAMPLE**
>
> You can run a fully functional example in your local environment by reviewing the instructions published by Microsoft at *https://docs.microsoft.com/en-us/azure/aks/ tutorial-kubernetes-prepare-app*.

Publish an image to the Azure Container Registry

The main purpose for creating an image is to make your code highly portable and independent from the server that executes your code. To achieve this objective, your image needs to be accessible by all the servers that can execute your image. Therefore, you need to store your image in a centralized storage service.

Azure Container Registry (ACR) is the Microsoft's implementation of a Docker registry service, based on the Docker Registry 2.0 definition. Using this managed Docker registry service, you can privately store your images for later distribution to container services, such as Azure Managed Kubernetes Service. You can also use ACR for building your images on the fly and automating the building of the image based on the commits of your source code.

Before you can upload an image to your private container registry, you need to tag the image. To do this, you need to include the name of your private container registry in the tag. You will use the name structure *<acr_name>.azurecr.io/[repository_name][:version]*. The following list breaks down each part of the tag:

- **acr_name**   This is the name that you gave to your registry.
- **repository_name**   This is an optional name for a repository in your registry. ACR allows you to create multi-level repositories inside the registry. If you want to use a custom repository, just put its name in the tag.
- **version**   This is the version that you use for the image.

Use following procedure for pushing your image to your ACR registry. We assume that you already created an Azure Container Registry and you have installed the latest Azure CLI:

1. Log in to your registry using this command:

   ```
   az acr login -name <acr_name>
   ```

2. Tag the image that you want to upload to the registry using this command:

   ```
   docker tag foobar <acr_name>.azurecr.io/<repository_name>/<image_name>
   ```

3. Push the image to the registry using this command:

   ```
   docker push <acr_name>.azurecr.io/<repository_name>/<image_name>
   ```

When docker finishes pushing your image to the registry, you can browse the repositories in your registry, as shown in Figure 1-6, to verify that has been successfully uploaded.

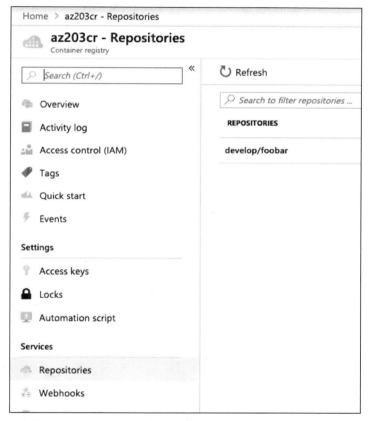

FIGURE 1-6 Browse container repository

In the next section, we will review how to run the container from the image you have already pushed to the registry.

Run containers by using Azure Container Instance or AKS

Once you have created your image and made it available to Azure services by pushing it to your container registry, it is time to run the container in any of the services that Azure offers to you. Follow this high-level procedure:

1. Create as many images as your application needs to run correctly.

2. Upload or push your application images to a container registry.

3. Deploy the application.

When you want to create an image in the Azure Container Instance (ACI) service from your Azure Container Registry (ACR), you need to authenticate before you can pull the image from your ACR. For the purpose of demonstration, we will use Admin account authentication in the following procedure showing how to create and run a container in ACI:

1. Sign in to the Azure cloud shell (*https://shell.azure.com*).

2. In the Shell Selector, select Bash.

3. Open the online editor by clicking on the curly brace icon to the right of the Shell Selector.

4. Use the script in Listing 1-8 to create a service principal password and to create a container from your images in the registry.

LISTING 1-8 Creating a service principal password

```
#!/bin/bash

#Some variable definition useful for the script
ACR_NAME=az203cr
SP_NAME=az203cr_sp
IMAGE_TAG=az203cr.azurecr.io/develop/foobar:latest
RESOURCE_GROUP=AKSdemo-RG
APP_NAME=foobar
APP_DNS_NAME=prueba


#Get the registry ID. You will need this ID for creating the authorization to the
//service principal
ACR_ID=$(az acr show --name $ACR_NAME --query id --output tsv)

#Get the ACR login server
ACR_SERVER=$(az acr show --name $ACR_NAME --query loginServer --output tsv)

#Get the service principal password. We will grant pull only privileges to the service
//principal
echo "Generating Service Principal password"
SP_PASS=$(az ad sp create-for-rbac --name http://$SP_NAME --scopes $ACR_ID --role
acrpull --query password --output tsv)

#Get the App ID associated to the service principal
SP_ID=$(az ad sp show --id http://$SP_NAME --query appId --output tsv)
```

```
echo "Service principal ID: $SP_ID"
echo "Service principal password: $SP_PASS"

#Create the container in the Container Instance service
az container create --resource-group $RESOURCE_GROUP --name $APP_NAME --image
$IMAGE_TAG --cpu 1 --memory 1 --registry-login-server $ACR_SERVER --registry-username
$SP_ID --registry-password $SP_PASS --dns-name-label $APP_DNS_NAME --ports 80
```

5. In the top right corner, below the user information, click the ellipsis icon, and then click Save. Provide a name for the script.

6. In the Azure Cloud Shell, execute the script by typing following command in the bash shell:

```
sh <your_script_name>
```

Once you have executed this procedure, you can access your container by looking for your container's name in the Azure Portal. You can also access the application that you put in this container by entering the URL of the container into a browser. The URL for this container will be in the form of *<APP_DNS_NAME>.<region>.azurecontainer.io*, based on the value of the variable *APP_DNS_NAME* that you provided in the previous script.

EXAM TIP

You can use several authentication mechanisms, such as an individual login with Azure AD, an Admin account, or a Service Principal. Authentication with Azure AD is a good approach for your development and testing environment. Using the Admin account is disabled by default and is discourage for production environments because you need to put the Admin account password in your code. For production environments, the recommended way to pull images is using service principals for authentication with the ACR.

Chapter summary

- Azure provides computing services for deploying your own virtualized infrastructure directly in the cloud. You can also deploy hybrid architectures to connect your on-premises infrastructure with your IaaS resources.

- Azure Resource Manager is the service in Azure that manages the different resources that you can deploy in the cloud. You can define the resources and their dependencies by using a JSON-based file called an ARM template.

- You can secure the data stored in your VMs by encrypting the virtual disks of the VM. This encryption is performed by the operating system of the VM. By default, Managed and Unmanaged virtual disks are also encrypted at rest by the cloud storage system.

- Azure Batch offers the capability to unload your application of heavy or repetitive tasks by executing these tasks on a separate group of compute nodes.

- You typically use Azure Batch for executing an image analysis, prediction or simulation model calculations, and 3D- or FX-image rendering.
- Azure Managed Kubernetes Service (AKS) service is a managed version of the Kubernetes open-source solution. This solution provides you high-availability and load balancing for your application containers.
- A container image is a package of software in which you store your code and any library or dependencies for running your application in a highly portable environment.
- When you create a new instance of a container image, each of these instances is named a "container."
- You can store your container images in a centralized store called a registry.
- Azure Container Registry is a managed registry, which is based on the open-source specification of Docker Registry 2.0.
- You can run your containers in several Azure services, such as Azure Managed Kubernetes Service, Azure Container Instance, Azure Batch, Azure App Service, or Azure Container Service.

Thought experiment

In this Thought Experiment, you can demonstrate your skills and knowledge about the topics covered in this chapter. You can find the answers to this Thought Experiment in the next section.

You are developing an application for making the analysis of images from a Geographic Information System. You decide to use containers for packaging the code that will make the image analysis. You use an Azure Container Registry for storing all the images of your application. The result of the image analysis will be in another image file and additional data will be stored in a database. The resulting images won't be stored in the database. The users of your application need to access a web portal for reviewing the results of the analysis.

With this information in mind, answer the following questions:

1. Which technology should you use for providing the needed compute resources that will run the containers that will execute the image analysis code?
2. What is the most secure way of accessing the Azure Container Registry?

Thought experiment answers

This section contains the solutions to the Thought Experiment.

1. The most effective way of running the containers that create the image analysis would be to use an Azure Batch account. You can run your containers in the nodes of the compute pool of the Batch account. This ensures that the load of processing the GIS images won't affect the performance of your applications and the user's experience.

2. You should access your registry by using an Azure AD security principal. When you need to access an Azure Container Registry, you have three ways of accessing the images:

- Using Azure AD login
- Using Admin account
- Using Azure AD service principals

Azure AD login is an interactive authentication mechanism and won't work well on production workloads in which authentication needs to happen automatically. By using an Admin account, you will also need to interactively provide the username and password. Using service principles, you can also apply fine-grained authorization based on RBAC. You can even secure these credentials by using Azure Key Vault.

## CHAPTER 2

Develop Azure Platform as a Service compute solution

Traditionally, the deployment of any software has required not only the planning of the architecture from the development point of view but also the planning of the infrastructure that would support that software. Networking, load balancing, fault-tolerance, and highly available configurations are some of the things that any new enterprise-level software deployment must manage.

However, once the deployment in the production environment has finished, you need to maintain it. This maintenance means that you also need to allocate the budget for the infrastructure's maintenance, and you must have trained staff for conducting this maintenance.

Thanks to cloud technologies, you can drastically reduce these infrastructure planning and deployment requirements by deploying your software on a managed service known as Platform as a Service (PaaS). Doing so means you only need to worry about your code and how it interacts with other services in Azure. Platform as a Service products such as Azure App Service or Azure Functions release you from worrying about highly-available or fault-tolerant configurations because these things are already managed by the service provided by Azure.

In this chapter, we review the PaaS solutions that Azure provides, which allow you to focus on your code and forget about the underlying infrastructure.

Skills covered in this chapter:

- Skill 2.1: Create Azure App Service web apps
- Skill 2.2: Create Azure App Service mobile apps
- Skill 2.3: Create Azure App Service API apps
- Skill 2.4: Implement Azure functions

Skill 2.1: Create Azure App Service web apps

Azure App Service is a Platform as a Service (PaaS) solution that Microsoft offers to assist with developing your applications, mobile app back-end, or REST APIs without worrying about the underlying infrastructure.

You use most of the more popular programming languages—.NET, .NET Core, Java, Ruby, Node.js, PHP, or Python—on top of your preferred platform (Linux or Windows). Azure App Service provides you with enterprise-level infrastructure capabilities, such as load balancing, security, autoscaling, and automated management. You can also include Azure App Service in your continuous deployment life cycle thanks to the integration with GitHub, Docker Hub, and Azure DevOps.

This skill covers how to:

- Create an Azure App Service web app
- Create an Azure App Service background task by using WebJobs
- Enable diagnostics logging

Create an Azure App Service web app

When you plan to create an Azure App Service, there are some concepts about how your application performs that you need to understand. Every App Service needs resources to execute your code. Virtual machines are the base of these resources. Although the low-level configuration for running these virtual machines is automatically provided by Azure, you still need to provide some high-level information. The group of virtual machines that host your web application is managed by an App Service plan.

You can think of an App Service plan like a server farm being run in a cloud environment. This also means that you are not limited to running a single App Service in an App Service plan and sharing the same computing resources.

When you create a new App Service plan, you need to provide the following information:

- **Region**   This is the region where your App Service plan is deployed. Any App Service in this App Service plan is placed in the same region as the App Service plan.
- **Number Of Instances**   This is the number of VMs that are added to your App Service plan. Bear in mind that the maximum number of instances that you can configure for your App Service plan depends on the pricing tier that you select. You can scale the number of instances manually or automatically.
- **Size Of The Instances**   You configure the size of the VM that is used in the App Service plan.
- **Operating System Platform**   This controls whether your web application runs on Linux or Windows VMs. Depending on the operating system, you have access to different pricing tiers. Beware that once you have selected the operating system platform, you cannot change the OS for the App Service without recreating the App Service.
- **Pricing Tier**   This sets the features and capabilities available for your App Service plan and how much you pay for the plan. For Windows VMs, there are two basic pricing tiers

that use shared VMs—F1 and D1. When you use the basic pricing tiers, your code runs alongside other Azure customers' code.

When you run an App Service in an App Service plan, all instances configured in the plan execute the app. This means that if you have five virtual machines, any app you run will run on each of the five VMs. Other operations related to the App Service, such as additional deployment slots, diagnostic logs, backups, or WebJobs, also are executed using the resources of each virtual machine in the App Service plan.

The following procedure shows how to create an App Service plan and upload an elementary web application based on .NET Core using Visual Studio 2017. Ensure that you have installed the ASP.NET and web development workload and you have installed the latest updates.

1. Open Visual Studio 2017 on your computer.

2. Click the Tools menu and choose Get Tools And Features. Verify that the ASP.NET And Web Development In The Web & Cloud section is checked.

3. In the Visual Studio 2017 window, click File > New > Project to open the New Project window.

4. In the New Project window, on the tree structure on the left side, expand the Installed node, expand the Visual C# node, and click the Web node.

5. In the list of templates in the center of the window, select ASP.NET Core Web Application.

6. In the Properties of the project at the bottom of the page, complete the following steps:

   ■ Select a Name for the project.

   ■ Enter a path for the Location of the solution.

   ■ In the Solution drop-down menu, select Create A New Solution.

   ■ Enter a Name for the solution.

7. Click the OK button in the bottom-right corner of the New Project window. This opens the New ASP.NET Core Web Application window.

8. In the New ASP.NET Core Web Application window, ensure that the following values are selected in the two drop-down menus on the top-left side of the window:

   ■ .NET Core

   ■ ASP.NET Core 2.1

9. Select Web Application from the Project Templates area in the center of the window.

10. Uncheck the option Configure For HTTPS on the bottom-left side of the window.

11. Click the OK button in the bottom-right corner of the New ASP.NET Core Web Application window.

At this point, you have created an elementary ASP.NET Core web application. You can run this application in your local environment to ensure that the application is running correctly before you publish the application to Azure.

Now we need to create the Resource Group and App Service plan that hosts the App Service in Azure:

1. In your Visual Studio 2017 window, ensure that you have opened the solution of the web application that you want to publish to Azure.

2. On the right side of the Visual Studio window, on the Solution Explorer window, right-click the project's name.

3. In the contextual menu, click Publish. This opens the Pick A Publish Target window.

4. In the Pick A Publish Target window, make sure that App Service is selected from the list of Available Targets on the left side of the window.

5. In the Azure App Service section, on the right side of the window, ensure that the Create New Option is selected.

6. In the bottom-right corner of the window, click Publish button, which opens the Create App Service window.

7. In the Create App Service window, add a new Azure account. This account needs to have enough privileges in the subscription for creating new resource groups, app services, and an App Service plan.

8. Once you have added a valid account, you can configure the settings for publishing your web application, as shown in Figure 2-1.

FIGURE 2-1 Creating an App Service

9. In the App Name text box, enter a name for the App Service. By default, this name matches the name that you gave to your project.

10. In the Subscription drop-down menu, select the subscription in which you want to create the App Service.

11. In the Resource Group drop-down menu, select the resource group in which you want to create the App Service and the App Service plan. If you need to create a new resource group, you can do so by clicking the New link on the right side of the drop-down menu.

12. To the right of the Hosting Plan drop-down menu, click the New link to open the Configure Hosting Plan window.

13. In the Configure Hosting Plan window, type a name for the App Service plan in the App Service Plan text box.

14. Select a region from the Location drop-down menu.

15. Select a virtual machine size from the Size drop-down menu.

16. Click the OK button in the bottom-right corner of the window. This closes the Configure Hosting Plan window.

17. On the bottom-right corner of the Create App Service window, click the Create button. This starts the creation of the needed resources and the upload of the code to the App Service.

18. Once the publishing process has finished, Visual Studio opens your default web browser with the URL of the newly deployed App Service. This URL will have the structure *https://<your_app_service_name>.azurewebsites.net*.

Depending on the pricing tier that you selected, some features are enabled, such as configuring custom domains or configuring SSL connections for your web applications. For production deployment, you should use Standard or, Premium pricing tiers. As your feature needs change, you can choose different pricing tiers. You can start by using the free tier, F1, in the early stages of your deployment and then increase to an S1 or P1 tier if you need to make backups of your web application or need to use deployment slots.

Even if the premium pricing tiers do not fit your computer requirements needs, you can still deploy a dedicated and isolated environment, called Isolated pricing tier. This tier provides you with dedicated VMs running on top of dedicated Virtual Networks where you can achieve the maximum level of scale-out capabilities. Bear in mind that Linux cannot be used with tiers F1 and D1.

When you are developing your web application, you need to test your code on both your local environment and in development or testing environments that are similar to the production environment. Starting with the Standard pricing tier, Azure App Service provides you with the deployment slots. These slots are deployments of your web application that reside in the same App Service of your web application. A deployment slot has its own configuration and hostname. You can use these additional deployment slots for testing your code before moving to the production slot. The main benefit of using these deployment slots is that you can swap these slots without any down time. You can even configure an automated swap of the slots by using Auto Swap.

When you plan for deploying your web application into an App Service, Azure offers you several options:

- **ZIP or WAR files**   When you want to deploy your application, you can package all your files into a ZIP or WAR package. Using the Kudu service, you can deploy your code to the App Service.

- **FTP**   You can copy your application files directly to the App Service using the FTP/S endpoint configured by default in the App Service.

- **Cloud synchronization**   Powered by the Kudu deployment engine, this method allows you to have your code in a OneDrive or Dropbox folder, and it syncs that folder with the App Service.

- **Continuous deployment**   Azure can integrate with GitHub, BitBucket, or Azure DevOps Services for deploying the most recent updates of your application to the App Service. Depending on the service, you can use the Kudu build server, Azure Pipelines, or Azure DevOps Service for implementing a continuous delivery process. You can also configure the integration manually with other cloud repositories like GitLab.

- **Your local Git repository**   You can configure your App Service as a remote repository for your local Git repository and push your code to Azure. Then the Kudu build server automatically compiles your code for you and deploys to the App Service.

- **ARM Template**   You can use Visual Studio and an ARM template for deploying your code into an App Service.

> *NOTE* **KUDU**
>
> Kudu is the platform that is in charge of the Git deployments in Azure App Service. You can find more detailed information on its GitHub site at *https://github.com/projectkudu/kudu/wiki*.

Azure App Service also provides you with the ability to integrate the authentication and authorization of your web application, REST API, a mobile app back-end, or even Azure Functions. You can use different well-known authentication providers, like Azure, Microsoft, Google, Facebook, and Twitter for authenticating users in your application. You can also use other authentication and authorization mechanisms on your applications. However, by using this security module, you can provide a reasonable level of security to your application with minimal or even no required code changes.

There are situations when your application may require access to resources on your on-premises infrastructure, and App Service provides you with two different approaches:

- **VNet Integration**   This option is available only for Standard, Premium, or PremiumV2 pricing tiers. This integration allows your web app to access resources in your virtual network. If you create a site-to-site VPN with your on-premises infrastructure, you can access your private resources from your web app.

- **Hybrid connections** This option depends on the Azure Service Bus Relay and creates a network connection between the App Service and an application endpoint. This means that hybrid connections enable the traffic between specific TCP host and port combinations.

Once you have created your App Service application, you can manage the different settings that may affect your application. You can access these settings in the Configuration menu on the Settings section in the App Service blade:

- **General Settings** These settings are related to the environment and platform in which your app runs. You can control the following items:
  - **Framework Versions** This setting controls which languages and versions are available to your application. You can enable or disable languages that will or won't be used by the App Service.
  - **Platform** This setting controls whether your application runs on a 32- or 64-bit platform.
  - **Web Sockets** If your application uses SignalR or socket.io, you need to enable web sockets.
  - **Always On** Enabling this setting means your app is always loaded. By default, the application is unloaded if it is idle for some amount of time. You can configure this idle timeout in the host.json project file. The default value for App Service is 30 minutes.
  - **Managed Pipeline Version** Only for IIS, this setting controls the pipeline mode.
  - **HTTP Version** This enables the HTTPS/2 protocol.
  - **ARR Affinity** Enabling this setting ensures that client requests are routed to the same instance for the life of the session. This setting is useful for stateful applications but can negatively affect stateless applications.
  - **Auto Swap** Used in conjunction with deployment slots, if you enable this option at the deployment slot level, it will be automatically swapped into the production deployment slot when the stage slot is updated.
  - **Debugging** Enable remote debugging options for Visual Studio so that it can connect directly to your app.
- **App Settings** You can load your custom settings in your application during startup. You use a key/value pair for each of your custom settings. These settings are always encrypted at rest, that is when they are stored.
- **Connection Strings** This will store the needed configurations that allow your application to connect to databases.
- **Default Documents** This setting configures which web page is displayed at the root URL of your app.
- **Handler Mappings** You can configure custom script processors for different file extensions.
- **Virtual Applications And Directories** This setting allows you to add additional virtual directories or applications to your App Service.

Create an Azure App Service background task by using WebJobs

Your web application may require you to run specific type of tasks that do not require interaction with the user. These types of tasks can usually be executed on background threads without affecting the user interface.

Azure App Service provides you with the capability to execute these background jobs by using WebJobs. WebJobs are executed in the same context as the web application, using the resources available in the App Service Plan where your app is executing. WebJobs can be either executables or scripts that you upload to the App Service using the Azure portal, or you can program your own custom WebJob using WebJobs SDK and include it with your web app project. Bear in mind that you cannot run WebJobs in an App Service running Linux.

> **NOTE** **RUNNING BACKGROUND TASKS**
>
> Azure provides you with different services—Microsoft Flow, Azure Logic Apps, Azure Functions, and WebJobs—that can be used for automating business processes and solving integration problems. This overlapping between these different services can lead to some confusion. You can review the differences between these services at *https://docs.microsoft.com/en-us/azure/azure-functions/functions-compare-logic-apps-ms-flow-webjobs*.

When you are working with WebJobs, you need to think about how many times your job should be executed and the circumstances under which it should be executed. Depending on your requirements, you should configure one of the two available WebJobs types:

- **Continuous** This type of job starts as soon as you create the WebJob. This job type runs inside every instance in which the web app is running. The job runs in an endless loop. Continuous jobs can be remotely debugged.

- **Triggered** This type of job is executed based on a schedule that you define. These jobs can also run when you manually fire a trigger. The job will be executed in a single instance, selected by Azure, between all instances of a web app running in the App Service Plan. You cannot remotely debug this kind of job.

When you work with WebJobs, you should enable the Always On setting so that the web app does not stop when it becomes idle. This setting is found in the App Service application's General Settings. Use the following procedure for creating a scheduled WebJob using the Azure Portal:

1. Sign in to the management portal at *http://portal.azure.com*.
2. In the Search box at the top of the Azure Portal, type the name of your App Service.
3. On the left side of the App Service blade, click the WebJobs item under the Settings section, as shown in Figure 2-2. This will open the WebJobs area on the center and right sections of the App Service blade.

Settings

- Application settings
- Configuration (Preview)
- Authentication / Authorization
- Application Insights
- Identity
- Backups
- Custom domains
- SSL settings
- Networking
- Scale up (App Service plan)
- Scale out (App Service plan)
- WebJobs

FIGURE 2-2 App Service settings

4. In the WebJobs area in the top-left corner, click the Add button to open the Add WebJob dialog box on the right side of the screen.

5. Type a name for the WebJob in the Name text box.

6. Click the folder icon for the File Upload control to open a file browser dialog box for uploading the executable or script that you want to use with this WebJob. Supported files are .cmd, .bat, .exe, .ps1, .sh, .php, .py, .js, .jar, and zip files. If you use a zip file, you can only add supported file types to it.

7. From the Type drop-down menu, select Triggered.

8. From the Triggers drop-down, select Scheduled.

9. In the CRON Expression text box, write the expression that represents the schedule for the execution of your job.

10. Click OK at the bottom of the Add WebJob dialog to create the WebJob and add it to the list in the WebJobs area.

NEED MORE REVIEW? **USING CRON EXPRESSIONS**

A CRON Expression is a single-line string that represents the schedule for the execution of your job. Each line is comprised of five fields that represent time attributes, in this order, from left to right: seconds, minutes, hours, days, months, and days-of-week. All time fields need to be present in a CRON line. If you don't need to provide a value for a field, use the asterisk character. A CRON Expression uses the following format:

```
<seconds> <minutes> <hours> <days of month> <months> <days of week>
```

For example, the CRON Expression 0 15 10 * * 6 runs at 10:15 AM on Fridays of every month.

For a detailed description of each field, as well as syntax and examples, see *https:// docs.microsoft.com/en-us/azure/azure-functions/functions-bindings-timer#cron-expressions*.

Using executables or external scripts is the simplest way to work with WebJobs, but you can also program your own WebJob using the WebJobs .NET SDK. This SDK allows you to create your own console application that you can include in your solution and upload directly to your Azure App Service. Using the WebJobs .NET SDK, you can create background tasks that can integrate with other Azure services, such as Storage Queue, Event Hub, Blob Storage, and so on. When you program your console application using WebJobs .NET SDK, you are not limited to using it with WebJobs. Although the association between WebJobs and WebJobs SDK is the best way to use both features, you are not constrained to this configuration.

Depending on the SDK version you use, WebJobs .NET SDK allows you to create .NET Core or .NET Framework console application. You should use version 3.0 for creating .NET Core console apps and use version 2.0 for .NET Framework apps. There are significant differences when working with each version that you should bear in mind when planning your WebJob. Some of the keys differences between versions are

- In version 3.0, you need to add a storage binding extension by installing the NuGet package *Microsoft.Azure.WebJobs.Extensions.Storage*. By default, this extension is available in WebJobs .NET SDK version 2.0.

- Only Version 3.0 does supports .NET Core.

- Visual Studio tools are different between version 2.0 and version 3.0. You cannot automatically deploy a WebJob .NET Core project with a web application project. You can only add existing or new WebJob .NET Framework projects.

When you are programming your own WebJob, you need to know about some concepts that you will use in your code:

- **host** This is the runtime container in which functions are executed. This object will listen for the configured triggers and will call the appropriate function. When using SDK version 3.0 , you need to build an *iHost* object; when using version 2.0, you need to create a new instance of the class *JobHost*.

- **trigger** This represents the different event types that fire the execution of the function that you program to perform a task. You can program two types of triggers:

  - **Automatic** This type of trigger calls a function in response to an event of a particular type. For example, you could add a trigger that calls a function every time you put a message in an Azure Queue.

  - **Manual** Using this type of trigger, you need to manually call the WebJob from your host or from the Azure Portal.

- **binding** This is how your job application can interact with the external world. Bindings provide input and output connectivity with Azure and other third-parties services. You can use input bindings to get information and data from external services and output bindings to update data in external services. How you install and configure the different binding types in your code depends on the version that you are using.

The following steps show how to program a console application using WebJob SDK 3.0. In this example, you will use .NET Core to program the application:

1. Open Visual Studio and create a new project by clicking File > New > Project. This will open the New Project window.

2. In the New Project window, on the tree structure on the left side of the window, select Installed > Visual C# > .NET Core.

3. Select the Console App (.NET Core) template project.

4. At the bottom of the Project Properties window, provide values for the Name, Location, Solution, and Solution Name. Then click the OK button.

5. You need to add some NuGet packages by clicking Tools > NuGet Package Manager > Manage NuGet Packages For Solution.

6. On the Manage NuGet Packages for Solution tab, click the Browse tab.

7. Install the following NuGet packages:

   - *Microsoft.Azure.WebJobs*
   - *Microsoft.Azure.WebJobs.Extensions*
   - *Microsoft.Azure.WebJobs.Extensions.Storage*
   - *Microsoft.Extensions.Logging.Console*

8. In the Solution Explorer window, click the Program.cs file.

9. From the Main method, remove all the code and add the code shown in Listing 2-1.

LISTING 2-1 Configuring a .NET Core Generic Host

```
//C# .NET Core. WebJobs SDK v3.0

//you need to add Microsoft.Extensions.Hosting and Microsoft.Extensions.Logging
//namespaces to your code
//var builder = new HostBuilder();
builder.UseEnvironment("development");
builder.ConfigureWebJobs(wj =>
{
    wj.AddAzureStorageCoreServices();
    wj.AddAzureStorage();
});
builder.ConfigureLogging((context,b) =>
{
    b.AddConsole();
});
var host = builder.Build();
using (host)
{
    host.Run();
}
```

The first thing you need to do to create a .NET Core Generic Host container is to create a *HostBuilder* object. This object will perform all the configuration needed before creating the actual host. This process is typical for any other .NET Core application that doesn't need to deal with HTTP. The generic host deals with the lifetime of the application.

You make the configuration that you want to apply to the new host by using the *ConfigureWebJobs()* method. This method will automatically add the appsettings.json file and environment variables as configuration sources. Inside this method, you configure the bindings that you will use for listening for the events that you want to monitor. In this example, you want to take some actions when a new message arrives at the Azure Queue. This means that you need to configure the Storage binding extension. You do so by calling the extension method *AddAzureStorage()* in your *HostBuilder* instance. The *AddAzureStorageCoreServices()* method is used by Azure WebJobs for saving log data that will be shown on the WebJobs dashboard.

When you are happy with your configuration, you can create the actual host by calling the *Build()* method on your *HostBuilder* instance. Then you only need to start the host's lifecycle by calling the *Run()* method for the *Host* instance.

1. In the Solution Explorer window, add a new *C#* class. Right-click the name of your project. On the contextual menu, click Add > New Item.

2. In the New Item window, select Class. Type a name for your new class and click the Add button. The new class will contain the triggers that will be listening to the events on the Azure Queue.

3. In the new class, add the method shown in Listing 2-2.

LISTING 2-2 New message queue trigger

```
//C# .NET Core. WebJobs SDK v3.0

//you need to add Microsoft.Azure.Webjobs and Microsoft.Extensions.Logging namespaces to
//your code
public static void NewMessageQueueTrigger(
    [QueueTrigger("<put_your_queue_name_here>")] string message,
    ILogger logger)
{
    logger.LogInformation($"New message from queue (<put_your_queue_name_here>):
    {message}");
}
```

You can create an automatic trigger associated with a binding by creating a public static function with the appropriate parameter attributes. In this case, the *QueueTrigger* parameter attribute configures the Azure Queue that will be listening for the new message. When a new message arrives, it will be passed to the function using the *message string* parameter. The parameter attributes and types depend on the triggers and bindings that you want to use in your code.

> **NEED MORE REVIEW?** **QUEUE STORAGE BINDING**
>
> You can review the full details about the available triggers and outputs associated with the storage binding by reviewing the online Microsoft Doc at *https://docs.microsoft.com/en-us/azure/azure-functions/functions-bindings-storage-queue*.

Now that you are done with your code, you need to configure the connection string that you will use for connecting with your storage account:

1. In the Azure Portal, create a storage account. You can also use an existing storage account for this example.

2. On the Storage Account blade, click the Access Key item in the Settings section. Copy the Connection string under the Key 1 section. You will need this value in an upcoming step.

3. In the Solution Explorer window, right-click the name of your project. On the contextual menu, click Add > New Item.

4. In the New Item window, select JavaScript JSON Configuration File. Type **appsettings.json** as the name for the new file and click the Add button.

5. In the Solution Explorer window, right-click the *appsettings.json* file and choose Properties.

6. In the Properties for the *appsettings.json file*, change the Copy To Output Directory option from Do Not Copy to Copy If Newer.

7. Replace the content of the *appsettings.json* file with the following string:

```
{
    "AzureWebJobsStorage": "<Put your storage account connection string here>"
}
```

At this point, you can start testing your application locally:

1. In the Visual Studio window, click Debug > Start Without Debugging.

2. In Visual Studio, open the Cloud Explorer window by clicking View > Cloud Explorer.

3. In the Cloud Explorer window, connect to your Azure Subscription.

4. Click the user icon at the top center of the Cloud Explorer window, which will open the Account Management section.

5. Click the Manage Accounts link, which will open the Account Settings window.

6. In the Account Settings window, click the Sign In button.

7. Once you have logged into your account, ensure that your Azure subscription appears on the Cloud Explorer window and click the Apply button to close the Account Management section.

8. In the Cloud Explorer, navigate to your storage account.

9. Expand your storage account node, right-click Queues and click Create Queue. You need to use the same queue name as the one you used for your code in the *QueueTrigger* parameter attribute.

10. Click the queue that you created in the previous step to open a new tab in Visual Studio with your queue's name.

11. On your queue's tab, create a new message by clicking the Add Message button (see Figure 2-3). This will open the Add Message window.

FIGURE 2-3 Creating a new message

12. In the Add Message window shown in Figure 2-4, write a message and configure an expiration value using the Expires In setting.

13. On the console application window, ensure that the new message that you published on your Azure Queue has appeared. If you refresh your Azure Queue, you will see that your message has disappeared. This happens because messages from the queue are removed once they are processed.

FIGURE 2-4 Adding a new message to the queue

At this point, you have tested your console application to confirm that it can connect to Azure and monitor an Azure Queue for a new message. Also, you have ensured that new messages come to the configured Azure Queue, and that your console application writes the message to the console. You used the WebJobs .NET SDK 3.0 to conduct the test by using the QueueTrigger from the Queue storage extension.

The last part of this example is to publish your console application as a WebJob in an App Service. You have two options:

- Publish your .NET Core application as a console application, package all binaries in a zip file, and create a run.cmd file that runs the application by using the command *dotnet run*. Then you can upload this zip file by using the procedure explained at the beginning of this section.

- Publish your .NET Core application directly from Visual Studio.

The following procedure shows how to publish your .NET Core application from Visual Studio:

1. In Visual Studio, right-click the name of your project.

2. Click Publish. This will open the Pick A Publish Target window.

3. On the Pick A Publish Target window, ensure that the Microsoft Azure App Service option on the left side of the window is selected.

4. Ensure that the Create New option is selected. If you need to publish your WebJob to an existing App Service, click the Select Existing option.

5. Click the Publish button at the right-bottom corner of the window to open the Create App Service window.

6. In the Create App Service window, provide the following information: App Name, Subscription, Resource Group, and Hosting Plan. This is the same procedure that you use for creating a new App Service from Visual Studio.

7. Once the publishing process has finished, your WebJob is ready to perform the tasks you have programmed.

In this example, you won't be able to see any results because you cannot access the console of the instance in which the WebJob is running. When you run your application in your local environment, any new messages that you receive from the queue are written to the console. When you publish your WebJob to Azure, you need to use an alternate method for viewing these results. You can use output bindings and write the message to a blob file or an alternate queue. The preferred way of visualizing these log messages is to integrate your WebJob with Application Insights.

> **NEED MORE REVIEW?** **USING WEBJOBS SDK**
>
> You can learn more about how to use WebJobs SDK by reviewing Microsoft Docs at *https://docs.microsoft.com/en-us/azure/app-service/webjobs-sdk-how-to.*
>
> You can also review how to add Application Insight logging support to your WebJob SDK application by reviewing the Microsoft Docs example at *https://docs.microsoft.com/en-us/azure/app-service/webjobs-sdk-get-started.*

Enable diagnostics logging

Troubleshooting and diagnosing the behavior of an application is a fundamental operation in the lifecycle of every application. This is especially true if you are developing your own application. Azure App Service provides you with some mechanisms for enabling diagnostics logging at different levels that can affect your application:

- **Web Server Diagnostics** These are message logs generated from the web server itself. You can enable three different types of logs:

  - **Detailed Error Logging** This log contains detailed information for any request that results in an HTTP status code 400 or greater. When an error 400 happens, a new HTML file is generated, containing all the information about the error. A separate HTML file is generated for each error. These files are stored in the file system of the instance in which the web app is running. A maximum of 50 error files can be stored. When this limit is reached, the oldest 26 files are automatically deleted from the file system.

- **Failed Request Tracing** This log contains detailed information about failed requests to the server. This information contains a trace of the IIS components that were involved in processing the request. It also contains the time taken by each IIS component. These logs are stored in the file system. The system creates a new folder for each new error, applying the same retention policies as for detailed error logging.

- **Web Server Logging** This log registers the HTTP transactions information for the requests made to the web server. The information is stored using the W3C extended log file format. You can configure custom retention policies to these log files. By default, these diagnostic logs are never deleted, but they are restricted by the space they can use in the file system. The default space quota is 35 MB.

- **Application diagnostics** You can send a log message directly from your code to the log system. You use the *System.Diagnostics.Trace* class for writing information in the application diagnostics logs. This is different from Application Insights because Application diagnostics are just logged information that you register from your application. If you want your application to send logs to Application Insights, you need to add the Application Insights SDK to your application.

- **Deployment diagnostics** This log is automatically enabled for you, and it gathers all information related to the deployment of your application. Typically, you use this log for troubleshooting failures during the deployment process, especially if you are using custom deployment scripts.

You can enable the different diagnostics logs, shown in Figure 2-5, using the Azure Portal. When you enable Application Logging, you can select the level of error log that will be registered on the files. These error levels are:

- **Disabled** No errors are registered.
- **Error** Critical and Error categories are registered.
- **Warning** Registers Warning, Error, and Critical categories.
- **Information** Registers Info, Warning, Error, and Critical log categories.
- **Verbose** Registers all log categories (Trace, Debug, Info, Warning, Error, and Critical).

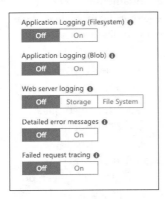

FIGURE 2-5 Enabling diagnostics logging

When you configure application logging, you can configure where the log files will be saved. You can choose between saving the logs in the file system or using blob storage. Storing application logs in the file system is intended for debugging purposes. If you enable this option, it will be automatically disabled after 12 hours. If you need to enable the application logging for a more extended period, you need to save the log files in blob storage. When you configure application logging for storing the log files in blob storage, you can also provide a retention period in days. When log files become older than the value that you configure for the retention period, the files are automatically deleted. By default, there is no retention period configured. You can configure the web server logging in the same way that you configure the storage for your application logging.

If you configure application or web server logging for storing the log files in the file system, the system creates the following structure for the log files:

- **/LogFiles/Application/** This folder contains the logs files from the application logging.

- **/LogFiles/W3SVC#########/** This folder contains the files from the Failed Request Traces. The folder contains an XSL file and several XML files. The XML files contain the actual tracing information, while the XSL file provides the formatting and filtering functionality for the content stored in the XML files.

- **/LogFiles/DetailedErrors/** This folder contains the *.htm files related to the Detailed Error Logs.

- **/LogFiles/http/RawLogs/** This folder contains the Web Server logs in W3C extended log format.

- **/LogFiles/Git** This folder contains the log generated during the deployment of the application. You can also find deployment files in the folder *D:\home\site\deployments*.

You will need this folder structure when you want to download the log files. You can use two different mechanisms for downloading the log files: FTP/S or Azure CLI. The following command shows how to download log files to the current working directory:

```
az webapp log download --resource-group <Resouce group name> --name <App name>
```

The logs for the application *<App name>* will be automatically compressed into a file named *webapp_logs.zip*. Then, this file will be downloaded in the same directory where you executed the command. You can use the optional parameter *--log-file* for downloading the log files to a different path in a different zip file.

There are situations in which you may need to view the logs for your application in near-real time. For these situations, App Service provides you with Log Streams. Using streaming, you can see the log messages as they are being saved to the log files. Any text file stored in the *D:\home\LogFiles* folder will be also displayed on the log stream. You can view log streams by using the embedded viewer in the Azure Portal, on the Log Stream item under the monitoring section in your App Service. You can also use the following Azure CLI command for viewing your application or web server logs in streaming:

```
az webapp log tail --resource-group <Resouce group name> --name <App name>
```

Skill 2.2: Create Azure App Service mobile apps

From the most basic to the more complex, most of the mobile applications are an excellent vehicle for exchanging information with the user. Mobile apps are usually the interface that the user uses for purchasing products, playing music, sending and receiving messages, playing games, and many other activities. All these mobile apps need to communicate with the services that provide the actual service to the user. The mobile apps receive the requests or the information from users and they return responses with information such as confirmation of a purchase, a stream with the song that the user wants to hear, a message from a friend, or the position of other players in the game.

Azure App Service provides you with the capabilities of programming these back-end services that will make your mobile app work correctly. It also provides you with the ability to remotely monitor your mobile apps to ensure that they are running correctly, and it gathers all the information that you may need when troubleshooting.

> **This skill covers how to:**
> - Add push notifications for mobile apps
> - Enable offline sync for mobile apps
> - Implement a remote instrumentation strategy for mobile devices

Add push notifications for mobile apps

When you develop a mobile app, there is a high probability that you will need to send information to your users when they are not using the app. For doing so, you will use push notifications. This asynchronous communication mechanism allows you to interact with your users when they are offline. For making this interaction happen, there are some key players that are part of this asynchronous communication:

- **The mobile app client**   This is your actual mobile app, which runs on your user's device. The user must register with the Platform Notification System (PNS) to receive notifications. This will generate a PNS handler that will be stored in the mobile app back end for sending notifications.
- **The mobile app back end**   This is the back end for your app client, and it stores the PNS handler that the client received from the PNS. Using this handler, your back end service can send push notifications to all registered users.
- **A Platform Notification System (PNS)**   These platforms deliver the actual notification to the user's device. Platform Notification Systems are platform dependent, and each vendor has its own PNS. Apple has the Apple Push Notification Service, Google uses the Firebase Cloud Messaging, and Microsoft uses the Windows Notification Service.

Even if your mobile app will be targeted to a single platform, implementing push notifications requires a good amount of effort. This is because some Platform Notification Systems only focus on delivering the notification to the user's device but doesn't deal with requirements like targeted notifications or broadcasting notifications. Another requirement for most Platform Notification Systems is that device tokens need to be refreshed every time you release a new version of your app. This operation requires that your back end deals with a large amount of traffic and databases updates simply to keep device tokes updated. If you need to support different mobile platforms, these tasks become even more complicated.

Microsoft provides you with the Azure Notification Hub. This service provides cross-platform push notification to your mobile app back end, allowing you to create an abstraction for managing each Platform Notification System and providing a consistent API for interacting with the Notification Hub. When you need to add push notifications to your mobile app, you will integrate the Notification Hub service with your back-end service hosted on the Mobile App Service. Figure 2-6 shows the workflow for sending push notifications to users using the Notification Hub.

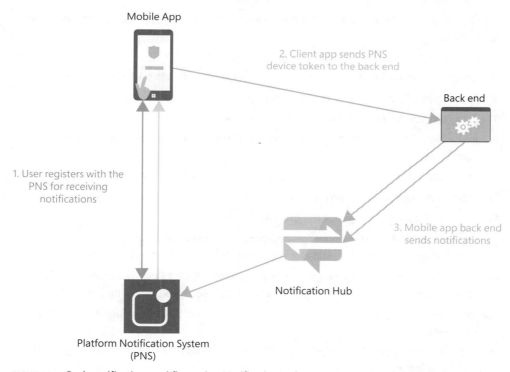

FIGURE 2-6 Push notification workflow using Notification Hub

The interaction between your back-end Mobile App and Notification Hub is performed using the Mobile App SDK for ASP.NET or Node.js web applications. Before your back-end application can send push notifications, you need to connect your App Service with your Notification Hub. Use following procedure to make this connection:

1. Sign in to the management portal (*http://portal.azure.com*).
2. On the left side of the portal, click Create A Resource.
3. On the New blade, in the Search the Marketplace text box, type **Mobile App** and press return.
4. On the Mobile App blade, click the Create button.
5. On the Create Mobile App blade, type a name for your mobile back-end application.
6. Type a name for the New Resource Group.
7. Click App Service Plan, and then click Create New.
8. In the New App Service Plan panel, in the App Service Plan text box, type a name for the App Service Plan.
9. Select the Location and Pricing Tier for the App Service Plan.
10. In the New App Service Plan panel, click OK.
11. In the Mobile App panel, click the Create button.
12. Once the Mobile App has been created, type the name of your new Mobile App in the Search Resources, Services, And Docs text box at the top of the Azure Portal.
13. On the App Service blade, on the left side of the blade, click Push in the Settings section. This will open the Push area on the center and right sections of the App Service blade.
14. In the top-left corner of the Push area, click the Connect button to open the Notification Hub panel.
15. In the Notification Hub panel, click the Notification Hub plus sign, which will open the New Notification Hub panel.
16. In the New Notification Hub panel, type a name for the Notification Hub.
17. In the Namespace section, click the Or Create New link to create a new namespace. A Notification Hub namespace is a group of hubs in the same region.
18. Leave the Pricing Tier set to Free.

19. Click the OK button to close the New Notification Hub panel.

20. The newly created Notification Hub should now be connected to your App Service. At this point, you can configure the integration of the Notification Hub with each Platform Notification System that you want to use for sending notifications.

The next step is to modify your back end code for integrating with the Notification Hub. Listing 2-3 shows a piece of code for sending notifications from your back end to the Notification Hub.

LISTING 2-3 Sending notifications from the ASP.NET back end

```
// C# ASP.NET Framework. Mobile App SDK

// Add following using statements to your code:
// using System.Collections.Generic;
// using Microsoft.Azure.NotificationHubs;
// using Microsoft.Azure.Mobile.Server.Config;

// We need to get the configuration for sending the logs to the correct tracer.
HttpConfiguration config = this.Configuration;
// We get the mobile settings for getting the Notification Hub credentials.
MobileAppSettingsDictionary mobileSettings = this.Configuration.
GetMobileAppSettingsProvider().GetMobileAppSettings();

// Get the Notification Hubs name and connection string. We will use these for creating
// a Notification Hub client.
string notificationHubName = mobileSettings.NotificationHubName;
string notificationHubConnection = mobileSettings
    .Connections[MobileAppSettingsKeys.NotificationHubConnectionString].ConnectionString;

// Create a new Notification Hub client that will perform all the interactions with the
// Notification Hub
NotificationHubClient hubClient = NotificationHubClient
.CreateClientFromConnectionString(notificationHubConnection, notificationHubName);

// We want to send notifications to all registered templates that contains the
"messageParam" parameter
// This includes templates for Apple, Google, Windows and Windows Phone PNS platforms
Dictionary<string,string> templateParams = new Dictionary<string,string>();
templateParams["messageParam"] = item.Text + " was processed.";

try
{
    // Send the actual push notification.
    var result = await hubClient.SendTemplateNotificationAsync(templateParams);

    // We register the notification was sent succesfully.
    config.Services.GetTraceWriter().Info(result.State.ToString());
}
catch (System.Exception ex)
{
    // There were some issues that we need to register in the logs.
    config.Services.GetTraceWriter()
        .Error(ex.Message, null, "Push.SendAsync Error");
}
```

The last step is to make the needed modifications on your mobile app client to register the device with its correspondent Platform Notification System and register with your Notification Hub through your back end. The details for how to make this implementation depend on the platform that you are using for your mobile app client.

> **MORE INFO**   **NOTIFICATION HUB EXAMPLES**
>
> You can review the details for implementing Notification Hub integration for your mobile app in Microsoft Docs:
>
> - **iOS:**   *https://docs.microsoft.com/en-us/azure/notification-hubs/notification-hubs-ios-apple-push-notification-apns-get-started*
>
> - **Android:**   *https://docs.microsoft.com/en-us/azure/notification-hubs/notification-hubs-android-push-notification-google-fcm-get-started*
>
> - **Windows Universal:**   *https://docs.microsoft.com/en-us/azure/notification-hubs/notification-hubs-windows-store-dotnet-get-started-wns-push-notification*

Enable offline sync for mobile app

When you plan and design any mobile app, you need to consider situations in which the user won't have access to a data network. Perhaps the user is in a zone with no coverage, or is on a plane and has enabled the plane mode; whatever the reason, users sometimes cannot access a data network.

For dealing with these offline scenarios, Azure Mobile Apps client and server SDKs allow your application to be functional even when the user has no access to a network. While your app is in offline mode, Mobile Apps SDKs allow your application to create, delete, or modify data. This modified data is saved to a local store, and when the user has access to a network and the app is online again, the SDK synchronizes the changes with your back end. Also, the SDK also deals with situations in which there are conflicts between the data on the server and the data in the application's local storage. This allows you to handle the conflicts on either the client or the server side.

When you work with the Azure Mobile App SDK, your client uses the /tables endpoint for performing CRUD (Create, Read, Update, Delete) operations on the data models used by your back end. The calls to this endpoint fail if the client application doesn't have a network connection. These online requests are managed by the IMobileServiceTable (.NET client SDK) or MSTable (iOS) interfaces. To implement offline sync in your application, you should use the "sync" version of these interfaces: *IMobileServiceSyncTable* and *MSSyncTable*. When you use these interfaces, you can still make any CRUD operation that you made before with the online interface version, but the data will be automatically read or written to local storage.

The local storage is a data-persistence layer provided by the Azure Mobile App client SDK. This persistence layer is provided by SQLite on Windows, Xamarin, and Android platforms.

For iOS, the persistence layer is provided by Core Data. This local store needs to be initialized before your client application can use it with the sync tables. This initialization consists on calling the method *IMobileServicesSyncContext.InitializeAsync(localstore)*.

The Mobile App client SDK tracks the changes made to the local store by using a sync context. This sync context consists of an ordered list or operation queue that contains all CUD (Create, Update, Delete) operations made with sync tables. These CUD operations will be sent later to the server when the client makes a push operation on the local changes. When you work with the sync context, you can perform the following operations:

- **Push** All the CUD changes will be sent to the server. This is an incremental action, which means only changes from the last push operation will be sent to the server. To ensure that the operations are sent in the correct order, you cannot send changes for individual tables.

- **Pull** This operation downloads the data in a table to the local storage. Pull operations are made on a per-table basis. By default, all records in the table are downloaded, although you can use customized queries for getting only a subset of the data. If you perform a pull operation on a table that has pending changes to be sent to the server, then the pull operation performs an implicit push to synchronize the data with the server. This allows the SDK to minimize the possibility of conflicts.

- **Incremental Sync** When you perform a pull operation, you can add a query name to the call. This query name is used only on the client side. You need to ensure that the query name is unique for each logical operation; otherwise, a different pull operation could return incorrect results. When you use a query name, Azure performs an incremental sync, retrieving only the most recent record in the table. This action depends on the *updateAt* field in the table.

- **Purge** This operation clears the contents of your local storage. If there is a CUD operation in the sync context pending to be uploaded to the server, the purge operation will fail and throw an exception. In this situation, you can still purge the data from your local store by setting the force purge parameter to *false* in the *PurgeAsync()* method.

Implement a remote instrumentation strategy for mobile devices

Once you have deployed your mobile app to any of the different distribution marketplaces such as Apple Store, Google Play, or Microsoft Store, it becomes difficult to get information about how your app is performing on the user's device.

Visual Studio App Center is a cloud tool that provides remote instrumentation for your mobile apps. Using App Center, you can get information about your mobile app's problems while running on users' devices. Also, you can also monitor the usage statistics for your apps.

You can integrate App Center with your mobile app using the App Center SDK. This SDK is available for most popular mobile platforms and programming languages, such as Android, iOS, React Native, Universal Windows Platform, Xamarin, and Apache Cordoba.

The App Center SDK is a modularized SDK in which each module corresponds with the different services offered by App Center:

- **Analytics**   This service allows you to analyze users' behavior and customer engagement. It offers information about the operating system version, session count, device model properties, application updates, and the number of times the user comes back to your application. Also, you can create your own custom events for measuring meaningful things for your business, such as whether a user played a video or started a purchase transaction and then decided to cancel it.

- **Diagnostics (Crashes)**   When your application crashes, App Center automatically generates a crash report including a stack trace of the execution at the moment of the crash, which module threw the exception that caused the crash, and other useful information for troubleshooting the crash. You can also integrate App Center with your favorite bug tracker, like Jira, VSTS, Azure DevOps, or GitHub, and it can automatically create a ticket or incident report on your bug-tracking platform.

- **Distribute**   During the testing phase, you can distribute your application to a group of users before publishing your app to Apple Store, Google Play, or Microsoft Store. Also, you can also use this distribution mechanism if you plan to use your mobile app as an internal corporate app that won't be publicly available.

- **Push**   App Center allows you to send push notifications to your users directly from the App Center portal.

The following procedure shows how to integrate an iOS Xamarin App with App Center:

1. Sign in to the App Center Management Portal (*https://appcenter.ms*).

2. In the top-right corner of the App Center Management Portal, click the Add New dropdown, and then click Add New App.

3. On the Add New App panel, type the name of your application in the App Name text box.

4. In the OS section, select iOS.

5. In the Platform section, select Xamarin.

6. Click the Add New App button in the bottom-right corner of the Add New App panel.

7. Open Visual Studio for Mac.

8. Click File > New Solution.

9. On the Choose Template For Your New Project window, click Multiplatform > App on the left side of the window.

10. Select the project template's Native App (iOS, Android).

11. Click the Next button in the bottom-right corner of the window.

12. Type a name for your application.

13. Click the Next button at the bottom-right corner of the window.

14. Select the location in which your project will be created.

15. Click the Create button at the bottom-right corner of the window.

16. In the Solution Explorer, right-click your iOS project, and then click Add > Add NuGet Packages.

17. On the NuGet packages manager window, type **App Center** in the search box in the top-right corner of the window.

18. Select the following packages:
    - *Microsoft.AppCenter*
    - *Microsoft.AppCenter.Crashes*
    - *Microsoft.AppCenter.Analytics*

19. Click the Add Packages button.

20. Accept the license terms.

21. Open the *AppDelegate.cs* file and add following using statements:

```
using Microsoft.AppCenter;
using Microsoft.AppCenter.Analytics;
using Microsoft.AppCenter.Crashes;
```

22. Add the following statement to the *FinishedLaunching()* method in the file *AppDelegate.cs*:

```
AppCenter.start("<your_app_center_key>", typeof(Analytics), typeof(Crashes));
```

23. You can get your App Center key from the Overview page of your app in the App Center Management Portal.

24. Now you see your active users, events, and diagnostics information in the App Center Management Portal using the Diagnostics and Analytics modules, as shown in Figure 2-7.

FIGURE 2-7 App Center modules

Skill 2.3: Create Azure App Service API apps

When you are designing the architecture of a web application, one of the layers that you will need is an API that allows the different layers of your architecture to communicate with each other. Regardless of the architecture of your application, there is a good chance that you will use a RESTful API to make that intercommunication happen.

In the same way that you can use Azure App Service for hosting your web application, you can use it for hosting your RESTful API. This allows you to take advantage of all the security, scalability, and serverless capabilities that we reviewed in previous skills.

> **This skill covers how to:**
> - Create an Azure App Service API app
> - Create documentation for the API by using open-source and other tools

Create an Azure App Service API app

Creating an Azure App Service API app is quite similar to creating a regular web application deployed in an App Service. You will have the same options available for your API app that you have for a web app. This means that you need to create or assign your API to App Service Plan. The following procedure shows how to create a new App Service API app, and it includes an ASP.NET API demo using the Azure Portal:

1. Sign in to the management portal (*http://portal.azure.com*).
2. Click the Create A Resource Link in the upper-left corner, and then select Web > API App. This will open the Create API App panel.
3. On the Create API App panel, type a name for your API.
4. In the subscription drop-down menu, select the subscription for which you want to create this API app.
5. In the Resource Group section, type a name for a new resource group. You can also use an existing resource group.
6. Click the App Service Plan/Location setting, which will open the App Service Plan pane.
7. On the App Service Plan pane, click Create New.
8. On the New App Service Plan pane, shown in Figure 2-8, type a name for the App Service Plan.

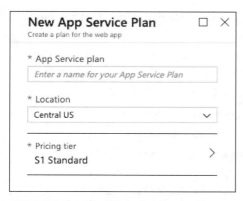

FIGURE 2-8 Creating a New App Service Plan

9. In the location drop-down menu, select the region in which you want to create the App Service Plan.

10. In the Pricing Tier control, select the F1 pricing tier under the Dev / Test tab.

Once you have created your App Service API app, you can create your demo API app:

1. In the newly created API app, click Quickstart from the Deployment section.

2. On the Quickstart pane, click ASP.NET from the General section.

3. On the ASP.Net Get Started pane, check the option I Acknowledge That This Will Overwrite All Site Contents.

4. Click the blank icon below the check box. This will deploy the example project to your App Service.

5. Click the Download button to download the code to your local environment. If desired, you can redeploy it to the App Service later.

At this point, you should be able to make requests to your API published in Azure. Your API is exposed using HTTP and HTTPS protocols. HTTP is not suitable for production environments, so you should secure your API access by enabling the HTTPS Only option on the SSL Settings pane in the Settings section. In this section, you can also configure SSL bindings for any additional fully qualified domain name (FQDN) added to your API app.

Another important security-related topic to consider is that other applications do not require authentication to interact with your API. Depending on your security requirements, you might want to authenticate all or some of the requests made to your API. Azure App Service allows you to secure the access to your API by providing authentication before users or applications make requests to your API. You can add this security layer to your API without making any modifications to your code. This security layer is provided by different authentication providers:

- **Azure Active Directory**   You can authenticate any user within your organization or any other organization with Office 365 deployed.
- **Facebook**   A user with a valid Facebook account could access your API.
- **Google**   A user with a valid Google account could access your API.
- **Twitter**   A user with a valid Twitter account could access your API.
- **Microsoft**   For Microsoft accounts, such as outlook.com, Xbox Live, MSN, OneDrive, and Bing.

Use the following procedure to enable Authentication for your API app using Azure Active Directory:

1. Sign in to the management portal (*http://portal.azure.com*).
2. In the search box at the top of the Azure portal, type the name of your App Service API app.
3. In the Settings section, click Authentication / Authorization.
4. In the Authentication / Authorization pane, choose On for the Switch Control App Service Authentication.
5. In the Action To Take When Request Is Not Authenticated drop-down menu, select Log In With Azure Active Directory.
6. In the Authentication Providers section, shown in Figure 2-9, click Azure Active Directory to configure this authentication provider.

FIGURE 2-9 Authentication providers

7. On the Azure Active Directory Settings pane, choose Express for the Management Mode.

8. Click Create New AD App for the Management Mode from the Current Active Directory section.

9. Type a name in the Create App text box. This will be the name of the application that will be created and registered on your Azure Active Directory domain. By default, only the users from your domain will be able to authenticate to your API.

> **NEED FOR REVIEW?   AUTHENTICATE ON BEHALF OF YOUR USERS**
>
> The API is not a service that will be typically used by users. It will be consumed by front-end web desktop, or mobile applications. If you require your users to authenticate to your front-end or mobile application, it will be quite usual to pass these credentials to your back-end API. The following article shows how to enable and configure authentication between a front-end web application and an API app. See *https://docs.microsoft.com/en-us/azure/app-service/app-service-web-tutorial-auth-aad#configure-auth*.

One additional security layer that you might like to add to your application is Cross-Origin Resource Sharing (CORS) protection. Using this protection, you are telling your web browser that your web application is allowed to use resources from another authorized domain. This scenario usually happens when your web application needs to make a request to your API back end using JavaScript. By default, web browsers don't allow requests from sources that don't match your web application domain, port, and protocol. This means that if you published your web application at *https://app.contoso.com/* and some JavaScript code in your application makes a request to *https://images.contoso.com*, the request will fail because of the CORS protection. In this example, the domain name doesn't match. You need to configure the Access-Control-Allow-Origin header for allowing the web application, *app.contoso.com*, to access resources from other trusted sources, such as *images.contoso.com*.

You can configure this CORS protection on your own code, but Azure App Service also provides you with this protection without making any changes to your code. Use the following procedure to enable CORS protection for your API app:

1. Sign in to the management portal (*http://portal.azure.com*).

2. In the search box at the top of the Azure portal, type the name of your App Service API app.

3. Click the CORS item in the API section.

4. On the CORS pane, on the Allowed Origins section, type the URL for your web application or any other URL that you want to allow to access to your API programmatically. For example, if your API is published at *https://api.contoso.com*, and your web application is published at *https://webapp.contoso.com*, you should add *https://webapp.contoso.com* to the list of allowed origins in the API App CORS configuration.

Bear in mind that you should not mix your own CORS configuration with Azure's built-in CORS configuration. You can use either of them—built-in or your own configuration—but you cannot mix them. Built-in configuration takes precedence over your own configuration, so if you mix both types of configurations, your own configuration won't be effective.

Create documentation for the API by using open-source and other tools

One crucial part of the lifecycle of every project is the documentation of the project. This is especially important for API software projects in which the functionality and details of each API endpoint need to be clearly identified for other developers to be able to use the API without accessing your code.

Swagger is an open-source tool that helps you document REST APIs. Swagger is language-agnostic, which means that you can use it with any language that you use for programming your REST API. The Swagger project has been donated to the OpenAPI Initiative, which was donated to the Linux Foundation in 2015. This means that you can also refer to Swagger as OpenAPI, which is the preferred way to name this specification.

OpenAPI not only helps you document your REST API, but it also helps with generating client SDKs or API discovery. Another advantage of using OpenAPI is that the tools that come with OpenAPI allows you to generate interactive documentation.

When you work with OpenAPI, you need to create a JSON or YAML file. Fortunately, you don't need to manually create this *swagger.json* or *swagger.yaml* file. There are tools that help you create these files. The appropriate tool depends on whether you need to document an existing REST API or you want to create your API from scratch. Regardless of whether you create the API documentation from scratch or you use the documentation from an existing API, you can use Swagger UI to view the API documentation interactively.

Swagger UI is a web-based UI, as shown in Figure 2-10, which provides interactive access to the information contained in the Swagger file. You can also embed this web-based UI in your web project, which allows you to have your project and documentation accessible from the same place. Using Swagger UI, you can even test the endpoint or function directly from the web UI without using external tools, such as Postman.

You can create your API documentation from scratch using Swagger Editor, which is an online and free tool that allows you to create your own API definition. Once you are done with the definition of your API, you can generate server and client code for that definition.

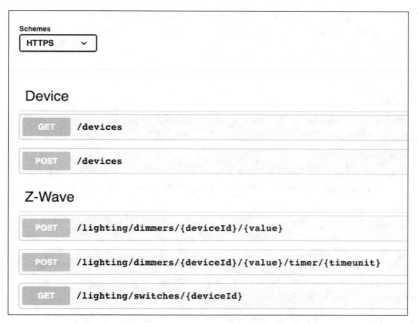

FIGURE 2-10 Swagger UI provides interactive access to the Swagger file

If you need to document an existing REST API, you can use tools like these:

- **Swashbuckle** This tool integrates with your ASP.NET project. It consists of three components that generate, store, and display the information obtained dynamically from your routes, controllers, and models. The tool publishes an endpoint that provides the *swagger.json* used by Swagger UI or other external tools.

- **NSwag** This tool also integrates with your ASP.NET project. It dynamically generates the documentation from your API, based on the routes, controllers, and models. It also provides an embedded version of Swagger UI. The main advantage of this tool is that it can also generate new code based on the definition of the API made in the *swagger.json* file.

> **NOTE   OPENAPI TOOLS**
>
> Swashbuckle and NSwag are not the only tools for documenting your API. You can review a more complete list at *https://swagger.io/tools/open-source/open-source-integrations/ ?_ga=2.264932431.1729815966.1553285867-1363801429.1553285867.*

Use the following NSwag procedure for adding OpenAPI documentation to your API project. In this procedure, we will assume that you are using ASP.NET Core for your REST API.

1. Open your API project.

2. Install the NuGet package *NSwag.AspNetCore* using the following code:

```
dotnet add <Your_project_name_here>.csproj package NSwag.AspNetCore.
```

3. In the *Startup* class, import the following namespaces:

- *NJsonSchema*
- *Nswag.AspNetCore*

4. In the *ConfigureServices* method, add following code for registering the required OpenAPI services:

```
services.AddOpenApiDocument();
```

5. In the *Configure* method of your *Startup* class, enable the middleware to serve the *swagger.json* file as an endpoint. This is useful for integration with third parties and API discovery:

```
app.UseSwagger();
app.UseSwaggerUi3();
```

6. Run your project to ensure that you have enabled OpenAPI correctly. From your web browser, navigate to the URL of your local project and append the */swagger* URI. You should have something like *http://localhost:5000/swagger.*

Listing 2-4 shows the code before making the modifications for adding OpenAPI documentation.

Listing 2-5 shows how your code should look after you make the modifications explained in the preceding set of steps.

LISTING 2-4 Adding NSwag for OpenAPI documentation

```csharp
// C# ASP.NET Core. Startup.cs file
using Microsoft.AspNetCore.Builder;
using Microsoft.EntityFrameworkCore;
using Microsoft.Extensions.DependencyInjection;
using TodoApi.Models;

namespace TodoApi
{
    public class Startup
    {
        public void ConfigureServices(IServiceCollection services)
        {
            services.AddDbContext<TodoContext>(opt => opt.UseInMemoryDatabase("TodoList"));
            services.AddMvc();
        }

        public void Configure(IApplicationBuilder app)
        {
            app.UseDefaultFiles();
            app.UseStaticFiles();

            app.UseMvc();
```

LISTING 2-5 Adding NSwag for OpenAPI documentation

```
// C# ASP.NET Core. Startup.cs file

using Microsoft.AspNetCore.Builder;
using Microsoft.EntityFrameworkCore;
using Microsoft.Extensions.DependencyInjection;
using TodoApi.Models;
using NJsonSchema;
using NSwag.AspNetCore;

namespace TodoApi
{
    public class Startup
    {
        public void ConfigureServices(IServiceCollection services)
        {
            services.AddDbContext<TodoContext>(opt => opt.UseInMemoryDatabase("TodoList"));
            services.AddMvc();

            // Register the Swagger generator, defining one or more Swagger documents
            services.AddOpenApiDocument();
        }

        public void Configure(IApplicationBuilder app)
        {
            app.UseDefaultFiles();
            app.UseStaticFiles();

            // Enable middleware to serve generated Swagger as a JSON endpoint.
            app.UseSwagger();
            app.UseSwaggerUi3();

            app.UseMvc();
        }
    }
}
```

Skill 2.4: Implement Azure Functions

Based on Azure App Service, Azure Functions allow you to run pieces of codes that solve particular problems inside the whole application. You use these functions in the same way that you may use a class or a function inside your code. That is, your function gets some input, executes the piece of code, and provides an output.

The big difference between Azure Functions and other app services models is that with Azure Functions (using the Consumption pricing tier), you will be charged per second only when your code is running. If you use App Service, you are charged hourly when the App Service Plan is running—even if there is no code executing. Because Azure Functions is based on App Service, you can also decide to run your Azure Function in your App Service Plan if you already have other app services executing.

Implement input and output bindings for a function

When you are writing a function in your code, that function may require data as input information for doing the job that you are writing. The function can also produce some output information as the result of the operations performed inside the function. When you work with Azure Function, you may also need these input and output flows of data.

Binding uses Azure Functions for connecting your function with the external world without hard-coding the connection to the external resources. An Azure Function can have a mix of input and output bindings, or it can have no binding at all. Bindings pass data to the function as parameters.

Although triggers and bindings are closely related, you should not confuse them. Triggers are the events that cause the function to start its execution; bindings are like the connection to the data needed for the function. You can see the difference in this example:

One publisher service sends an event—one that reads a new image that has been uploaded to blob storage—to an Event Grid. Your function needs to read this image, process it, and place some information in a CosmosDB document. When the image has been processed, your function also sends a notification to the user interface using SignalR.

In this example, you can find one trigger, one input binding, and two output bindings:

- **Trigger**   The Event Grid should be configured as the trigger for the Azure Function.
- **Input binding**   Your function needs to read the image that has been uploaded to the blob storage. In this case, you need to use blob storage as an input binding.
- **Output bindings**   Your function needs to write a CosmosDB document with the results of processing the image. You need to use the CosmosDB output binding. Your function also needs to send a notification to the user interface using the SignalR output binding.

Depending on the language that you use for programming your Azure Function, the way you declare a binding changes:

- **C#**   You declare bindings and triggers by decorating methods and parameters.
- **Other**   Updates the function.json configuration file.

When defining a binding for non-C# language functions, you need to define your binding using the following minimal required attributes:

- **type**   This string represents the binding type. For example, you would use *eventHub* when using an output binding for Event Hub.

- **direction**   The only allowed values are in for input bindings and out for output bindings. Some bindings also support the special direction *inout*.

- **name**   This attribute is used by the function for binding the data in the function. For example, in JavaScript, the key in a key/value list is an attribute.

Depending on the specific binding that you are configuring, there could be some additional attributes that should be defined.

> **NOTE**   **SUPPORTED BINDINGS**
>
> **For a complete list of supported bindings, please refer to this article at *https://docs.microsoft.com/en-us/azure/azure-functions/functions-triggers-bindings#supported-bindings*.**

Before you can use a binding in your code, you need to register it. If you are using C# for your functions, you can do this by installing the appropriate NuGet package. For other languages, you need to install the package with the extension code using the *func* command-line utility. The following example will install the Service Bus extension in your local environment for non-C# projects:

```
func extensions install –package Microsoft.Azure.WebJobs.ServiceBus
```

If you are developing your Azure Function using the Azure Portal, you can add the bindings in the Integrate section of your function. When you add a binding that is not installed in your environment, you will see the warning message shown in Figure 2-11. You can install the extension by clicking the Install link.

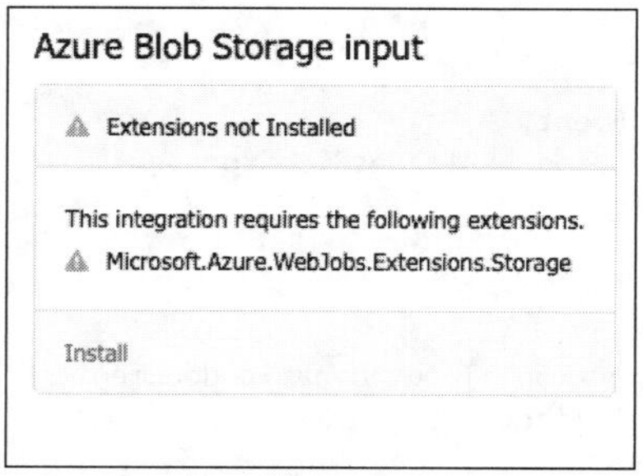

FIGURE 2-11 Missing extension warning message

If you decide to program your Azure Function using C#, the configuration of the bindings is made using decorators for function and parameters. The *function.json* file is automatically constructed based on the information that you provide in your code. Listing 2-6 shows how to configure input and output bindings using parameter decorators.

LISTING 2-6 Configuring input and output bindings

```csharp
// C# ASP.NET Core

using System;
using System.IO;
using Microsoft.Azure.WebJobs;
using Microsoft.Extensions.Logging;
using Microsoft.Azure.WebJobs.Extensions.SignalRService;
using Microsoft.Azure.WebJobs.Extensions.EventGrid;
using Microsoft.Azure.EventGrid.Models;
using System.Threading.Tasks;

namespace  Company.Functions
{
    public static class BlobTriggerCSharp
    {
        [FunctionName("BlobTriggerCSharp")]
        public static Task Run(
            [EventGridTrigger]EventGridEvent eventGridEvent,
            [Blob("{data.url}", FileAccess.Read, Connection = "ImagesBlobStorage")]
            Stream imageBlob,
            [CosmosDB(
                databaseName: "GIS",
                collectionName: "Processed_images",
                ConnectionStringSetting = "CosmosDBConnection")] out dynamic document,
            [SignalR(HubName = "notifications")]IAsyncCollector<SignalRMessage>
             signalRMessages,
            ILogger log)
        {
            document = new { Description = eventGridEvent.Topic, id = Guid.NewGuid() };
            log.LogInformation($"C# Blob trigger function Processed event\n Topic:
            {eventGridEvent.Topic} \n Subject: {eventGridEvent.Subject} ");
            return signalRMessages.AddAsync(
            new SignalRMessage
```

```
        {
            Target = "newMessage",
            Arguments = new [] { eventGridEvent.Subject }
        });
    }
}
}
```

Let's review the portions of Listing 2-6 that are related to the binding configuration. In this example, we configured one input binding and two output bindings. The parameter *imageBlob* is configured as an input binding. We have decorated the parameter with the attribute Blob, which takes following parameters:

- **Path** The value *{data.url}* configures the path of the blobs that will be passed to the function. In this case, we are using a binding expression that resolves to the full path of the blob in the blob storage.

- **Blob access mode** In this example, you will access the blob in read-only mode.

- **Connection** This sets the connection string to the storage account where the blobs are stored. This parameter sets the app setting name that contains the actual connection string.

We have also configured two output bindings, though we have configured them differently. The first output binding is configured using the keyword *out* in the parameter definition. Just as we did with the input parameter, we configured the output parameter document by using a parameter attribute. In this case, we used the *CosmosDB* attribute. We use following parameters for configuring this output binding:

- **databaseName** Sets the database in which we will save the document that we will create during the execution of the function.

- **collectionName** Sets the collection in which we will save the generated document.

- **ConnectionStringSetting** Sets the name of the app setting variable that contains the actual connection string for the database. You should not put the actual connection string here.

Setting a value for this output binding is as simple as assigning a value to the parameter document. We can also configure output bindings by using the *return* statement of the function. In our example, we configure the second output binding this way.

The function parameter *signalRMessages* is our second output binding. As you can see in Listing 2-6, we didn't add the *out* keyword to this parameter because we can return multiple output values. When you need to return multiple output values, you need to use *ICollector* or *IAsyncCollector* types with the output binding parameter, as we did with *signalRMessages*. Inside our function, we add needed values to the *signalRMessages* collection and use this collection as the return value of the function. We used the *SignalR* parameter attribute for configuring this output binding. In this case, we only used one parameter for configuring the output binding.

- **HubName**   This is the name of the SignalR hub where you will send your messages.
- **ConnectionStringSetting**   In this case, we didn't use this parameter, so it will use its default value *AzureSignalRConnectionString*. As we saw in the other bindings, this parameter sets the name of the app setting variable that contains the actual connection string *SignalR*.

When you are configuring bindings or triggers, there will be situations when you need to map the trigger or binding to a dynamically generated path or element. In these situations, you can use binding expressions. You define a binding expression by wrapping your expression in curly braces. You can see an example of a binding expression shown previously in Listing 2-6. The path that we configure for the input binding contains the binding expression *{data.url}*, which resolves to the full path of the blob in the blob storage. In this case, *EventGridTrigger* sends a JSON payload to the input binding that contains the *data.url* attribute.

> **NEED MORE REVIEW?   BINDING EXPRESSION PATTERNS**
>
> You can learn about more binding expression patterns by reviewing this article about Azure Functions binding expression patterns in Microsoft Docs at *https://docs.microsoft.com/en-us/azure/azure-functions/functions-bindings-expressions-patterns*.

The way you configure the bindings for your code depends on the language that you used for your Azure Function. In the previous example, we review how to configure input and output bindings using C# and parameters decorations. If you use any of the other supported languages in your Azure Function, the way you configure input and output bindings changes.

The first step when configuring bindings in non-C# languages is to modify the *function.json* configuration file. Listing 2-7 shows the equivalent *function.json* for the binding configuration made in Listing 2-6. Once you have configured your bindings, you can write your code to access the bindings that you configured. Listing 2-8 shows an example written in JavaScript for using bindings in your code.

LISTING 2-7 Configuring input and output bindings in *function.json*

```
{
  "disabled": false,
  "bindings": [
    {
      "name": "eventGridEvent",
      "type": "eventGridTrigger",
      "direction": "in"
    },
    {
      "name": "imageBlob",
      "type": "blob",
      "connection": "ImagesBlobStorage",
      "direction": "in",
      "path": "{data.url}"
    },
```

```
  {
    "name": "document",
    "type": "cosmosDB",
    "direction": "out",
    "databaseName": "GIS",
    "collectionName": "Processed_images",
    "connectionStringSetting": "CosmosDBConnection",
    "createIfNotExists": true
  },
  {
    "name": "signalRMessages",
    "type": "signalR",
    "direction": "out",
    "hubName": "notifications"
  }
  ]
}
```

LISTING 2-8 Using bindings in JavaScript

```
// NodeJS. Index.js

const uuid = require('uuid/v4');
module.exports = async function (context, eventGridEvent) {
    context.log('JavaScript Event Grid trigger function processed a request.');
    context.log("Subject: " + eventGridEvent.subject);
    context.log("Time: " + eventGridEvent.eventTime);
    context.log("Data: " + JSON.stringify(eventGridEvent.data));

    context.bindings.document = JSON.stringify({
        id: uuid(),
        Description: eventGridEvent.topic
      });

    context.bindings.signalRMessages = [{
        "target": "newMessage",
        "arguments": [ eventGridEvent.subject ]
    }];

    context.done();
};
```

Listings 2-7 and 2-8 represent the equivalent code in JavaScript to the code in the C# code shown in Listing 2-6. Most important is that *name* attributes in the binding definitions shown in Listing 2-7 correspond to the properties of the context object shown in Listing 2-8. For example, we created a *cosmosDB* output binding and assigned the value *document* to the *name* attribute in the *binding* definition in Listing 2-7. In your JavaScript code, you access this output binding by using *context.bindings.document*.

Remember that you need to install the extensions on your local environment before you can use bindings or triggers. You can use the *func* command-line command from the Azure Function CLI tools.

Implement function triggers by using data operations, timers, and webhooks

When you create an Azure Function, that function will be executed based on events that happen in the external world. Some examples include

- Executing a function periodically
- Executing a function when some other process uploads a file to blob storage or sends a message to a queue storage
- Executing a function when an email arrives in Outlook

All these events are programmatically managed by triggers.

You can configure function triggers in the same way that you configure input or output bindings, but you need to pay attention to some additional details when dealing with triggers. You configure a trigger for listening to specific events. When an event happens, the trigger object can send data and information to the function.

You can configure three different types of triggers:

- **data operation** The trigger is started based on new data that is created, updated, or added to system. Supported systems are CosmosDB, Event Grid, Event Hub, Blob Storage, Queue Storage, and Service Bus.
- **timers** You use this kind of trigger when you need to run your function based on a schedule.
- **webhooks** You use HTTP or webhooks triggers when you need to run your function based on an HTTP Request.

Triggers send data to the function with information about the event that caused the trigger to start. This information depends on the type of trigger. Listing 2-9 shows how to configure a data operation trigger for CosmosDB.

LISTING 2-9 Configuring a CosmosDB trigger

```
// C# ASP.NET Core
using System.Collections.Generic;
using Microsoft.Azure.Documents;
using Microsoft.Azure.WebJobs;
using Microsoft.Azure.WebJobs.Host;
using Microsoft.Extensions.Logging;
namespace Company.Function
{
    public static class CosmosDBTriggerCSharp
    {
        [FunctionName("CosmosDBTriggerCSharp")]
        public static void Run([CosmosDBTrigger(
            databaseName: "databaseName",
            collectionName: "collectionName",
            ConnectionStringSetting = "AzureWebJobsStorage",
```

```
        LeaseCollectionName = "leases",
        CreateLeaseCollectionIfNotExists = true)]IReadOnlyList<Document> input,
        ILogger log)
    {
        if (input != null && input.Count > 0)
        {
            log.LogInformation("Documents modified " + input.Count);
            log.LogInformation("First document Id " + input[0].Id);
            log.LogInformation("Modified document: " + input[0]);
        }
    }
  }
}
```

> **IMPORTANT** **WORKING WITH LEASES COLLECTION**
>
> At the time of this writing, Cosmos DB trigger does not support working with a partitioned lease collection. Microsoft is removing the ability to create a non-partitioned collection using Azure Portal. You can still create your non-partitioned collections using SDKs. CosmosDB trigger requires a second collection to store leases over partitions. Both collections—leases and the collection that you want to monitor—need to exist before your code runs. To ensure that the lease collection is correctly created as a non-partitioned collection, don't create the collection using the Azure Portal, and set the trigger parameter *CreateLeaseCollectionIfNotExists to true*.

Just as with bindings, you need to install the corresponding NuGet package with the appropriate extension for working with triggers. In this case, you need to install the package *Microsoft.Azure.WebJobs.Extensions.CosmosDB*. We used the *CosmosDBTrigger* parameter attribute for configuring our trigger with the following parameters:

- **databaseName**   This is the name of the database that contains the collection this trigger should monitor.

- **collectionName**   This is the name of the collection that this trigger should monitor. This collection needs to exist before your function runs.

- **ConnectionStringSetting**   This is the name of the app setting variable that contains the connection string to the CosmosDB database. If you want to debug your function in your local environment, you should configure this variable in the file *local.settings.json* file and assign the value of the connection string to your development CosmosDB database. This *local.settings.json* file is used by Azure Functions Core Tools to locally store app settings, connection strings, and settings and won't be automatically uploaded to Azure when you publish your Azure Function.

- **LeaseCollectionName**   This is the name of the collection that will be used for storing leases over partitions. By default, this collection will be stored in the same database as the *collectionName*. If you need to store this collection in a separate database, use the parameter *leaseDatabaseName* or *leaseConnectionStringSetting* if you need to store the database in a separate CosmosDB account.

- **CreateLeaseCollectionIfNotExists**   This creates the lease collection set by the *LeaseCollectionName* parameter if it does not exist in the database. Lease collection should be a non-partitioned collection and needs to exist before your function runs.

This trigger monitors for new or updated documents in the database that you configure in the parameters of the trigger. Once the trigger detects a change, it passes detected changes to the function using an *IReadOnlyList<Document>*. Once we have the information provided by the trigger in the input list, we can process the information inside our function. If you have enabled Application Insight integration, you will be able to see the log messages from your function, as show in Figure 2-12.

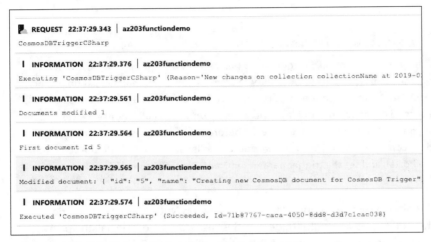

FIGURE 2-12 View Azure Function logs in Application Insight

> **NOTE**   **VERSION 1.0 VERSUS VERSION 2.0**
>
> When you work with Azure Functions, you can choose between versions 1.0 and 2.0. The main difference between the two versions is that you can only develop and host Azure Functions 1.0 on Azure Portal or Windows computers. Functions 2.0 can be developed and hosted on all platforms supported by .NET Core. The Azure Function you use affects the extension packages that you need to install when configuring triggers and bindings. Review the following overview of Azure Functions runtime versions. See *https://docs.microsoft.com/en-us/azure/ azure-functions/functions-versions*.

When you work with timer and webhooks triggers, the main difference between them and a data operations trigger is that you not need to explicitly install the extension package that supports the trigger.

Timer triggers execute your function based on a schedule. This schedule is configured using a CRON expression that is interpreted by the NCronTab library. A CRON expression is a string compound of six different fields with this structure:

```
{second} {minute} {hour} {day} {month} {day-of-week}
```

Each field can have numeric values that are meaningful for the field:

- **second** Represents the seconds in a minute. You can assign values from *0* to *59*.
- **minute** Represents the minutes in an hour. You can assign values from *0* to *59*.
- **hour** Represents the hours in a day. You can assign values from *0* to *23*.
- **day** Represents the days in a month. You can assign values from *1* to *31*.
- **month** Represents the months in a year. You can assign values from *1* to *12*. You can also use names in English, such as *January*, or you can abbreviations of the name in English, such as *Jan*. Names are case-insensitive.
- **day-of-week** Represents the days of the week. You can assign values from *0* to *6* where *0* is Sunday. You can also use names in English, such as *Monday*, or you can use abbreviations of the name in English, such as *Mon*. Names are case-insensitive.

All fields need to be present in an CRON expression. If you don't want to provide a value to a field, you can use the asterisk character *. This means that the expression will use all available values for that field. For example, the CRON expression * * * * * * means that the trigger will be executed every second, in every minute, in every hour, in every day, and in every month of the year. You can also use some operators with the allowed values in fields:

- **Range of values** Use the dash operator— – —for representing all the values available between two limits. For example, the expression *0 10-12 * * * ** means that the function will be executed at *hh:10:00*, *hh:11:00*, and *hh:12:00* where hh means every hour. That is, it will be executed three times every hour.
- **Set of values** Use the comma operator— , —for representing a set of values. For example, the expression *0 0 11,12,13 * * ** means that the function will be executed three times a day, every day, once at *11:00:00*, a second time at *12:00:00*, and finally at *13:00:00*.
- **Interval of values** Use the forward slash operator— / —for representing an interval of values. The function is executed when the value of the field is divisible by the value that you put on the right side of the operator. For example, the expression **/5 * * * * ** will execute the function every five seconds.

Listings 2-10 and 2-11 show how to configure a timer trigger and how to use the trigger with JavaScript code.

LISTING 2-10 Configuring a timer trigger in *function.json*

```
{
  "disabled": false,
  "bindings": [
    {
      "name": "myTimer",
      "type": "timerTrigger",
      "direction": "in",
      "schedule": "0 */5 * * * *",
      "useMonitor": true,
      "runOnStartup": true
    }
  ]
}
```

LISTING 2-11 Using a timer trigger with JavaScript

```
//NodeJS. Index.js file
module.exports = async function (context, myTimer) {
    var timeStamp = new Date().toISOString();

    if(myTimer.isPastDue)
    {
        context.log('JavaScript is running late!');
    }
    context.log('JavaScript timer trigger Last execution: ', myTimer.ScheduleStatus.Last);
    context.log('JavaScript timer trigger Next execution: ', myTimer.ScheduleStatus.Next);
};
```

Just as we did when we configured bindings in the previous section, when you configure a trigger for non-C# languages, you need to add them to the *function.json* configuration file. You configure your triggers in the bindings section. Listing 2-10 shows the appropriate properties for configuring a timer trigger:

- **name** This is the name of the variable that you will use on your JavaScript code for accessing the information from the trigger.

- **type** This is the type of trigger that we are configuring. In this example, the value for the timer trigger is *timerTrigger*.

- **direction** This is always included in a trigger.

- **schedule** This is the CRON expression used for configuring the execution scheduling of your function. You can also use a *TimeSpan* expression.

- **useMonitor** This property monitors the schedule even if the function app instance is restarted. The default value for this property is *true* for every schedule with a recurrence greater than one minute. Monitoring the schedule occurrences will ensure that the schedule is maintained correctly.

- **runOnStartup** This indicates that the function should be invoked as soon as the runtime starts. The function will be executed after the function app wakes up after going idle because of inactivity or if the function app restarts because of changes in the function. Setting this parameter to true is not recommended on production environments because it can lead to unpredictable execution times of your function.

> *NOTE* **TROUBLESHOOTING FUNCTIONS ON YOUR LOCAL ENVIRONMENT**
>
> While you are developing your Azure Functions, you need to troubleshoot your code in your local environment. If you are using non-HTML triggers, you need to provide a valid value for the AzureWebJobsStorage attribute in the *local.settings.json* file.

TimeSpan expressions are used to specify the time interval between the invocations of the function. If the function execution takes longer than the specified interval, then the function is invoked immediately after the previous invocation finishes. *TimeSpan* expressions are strings with the format *hh:mm:ss* where hh represents hours, *mm* represents minutes, and *ss* represents seconds. Hours in a *TimeSpan* expression need to be less than *24*. The *TimeSpan* expression *24:00:00* means the function will be executed every day. *02:00:00* means the function will be invoked every two hours. You can use *TimeSpan* expressions only on Azure Functions that are executed on App Service Plans. That is, you cannot use TimeSpan expressions when you are using the Consumption pricing tier.

You use HTTP triggers for running your Azure Function when an external process makes an HTTP request. This HTTP request can be a regular request using any of the available HTTP methods or a webhook. A web callback or webhook is an HTTP request made by third-party systems, or external web applications, or as a result of an event generated in the external system. For example, if you are using GitHub as your code repository, GitHub can send a webhook to your Azure Function each time a new pull request is opened. Webhooks are available only for version 1.x of the Azure Function runtime.

When you create an Azure Function using HTTP triggers, the runtime automatically publishes an endpoint with the following structure:

```
http://<your_function_app>.azurewebsites.net/api/<your_function_name>
```

This is the URL or endpoint that you need to use when calling to your function using a regular HTTP request or when you configure an external webhook for invoking your function. You can customize the route of this endpoint by using the appropriate configuration properties. This means that you can also implement serverless APIs using HTTP triggers. You can even protect the access to your function's endpoints by requesting authorization for any request made to your API using the App Service Authentication / Authorization. Listing 2-12 shows how to configure an HTTP trigger with a custom endpoint.

LISTING 2-12 Configuring an HTTP trigger

```csharp
// C# ASP.NET Core

using System.Security.Claims;
using System;
using System.IO;
using System.Threading.Tasks;
using Microsoft.AspNetCore.Mvc;
using Microsoft.Azure.WebJobs;
using Microsoft.Azure.WebJobs.Extensions.Http;
using Microsoft.AspNetCore.Http;
using Microsoft.Extensions.Logging;
using Newtonsoft.Json;

namespace Company.Function
{
    public static class HttpTriggerCSharp
    {
        [FunctionName("HttpTriggerCSharp")]
        public static async Task<IActionResult> Run(
            [HttpTrigger(AuthorizationLevel.Anonymous, "get", "post", Route = "devices/
            {id:int?}")] HttpRequest req,
            int? id,
            ILogger log)
```

```
{
        log.LogInformation("C# HTTP trigger function processed a request.");
        //We access to the parameter in the address by adding a function parameter
        //with the same name
        log.LogInformation($"Requesting information for device {id}");

        //If you enable Authentication / Authorization at Function App level,
        //information
        //about the authenticated user is automatically provided in the HttpContext
        ClaimsPrincipal identities = req.HttpContext.User;
        string username = identities.Identity?.Name;

        log.LogInformation($"Request made by user {username}");

        string name = req.Query["name"];

        string requestBody = await new StreamReader(req.Body).ReadToEndAsync();
        dynamic data = JsonConvert.DeserializeObject(requestBody);
        name = name ?? data?.name;

        //We customize the output binding
        return name != null
            ? (ActionResult)new JsonResult(new { message = $"Hello, {name}",
            username = username, device = id})
            : new BadRequestObjectResult("Please pass a name on the query string or
            in the request body");
    }
  }
}
```

The example in Listing 2-12 shows the following points when working with HTTP triggers:

- How to work with authentication.
- How to work with the authorization level.
- How to customize the function endpoint, using route parameters.
- How to customize the output binding.

HTTP triggers are automatically provided to you out-of-the-box with the function *runtime*. There is no need to install a specific NuGet package for working with this extension. You use the *HTTPTrigger* parameter attribute for configuring the HTTP trigger. This trigger accepts the following parameters:

- **AuthLevel**   This parameter configures the authorization key that you should use for accessing the function. Allowed values are
  - **anonymous**   No key is required.
  - **function**   This is the default value. You need to provide a function-specific key.
  - **admin**   You need to provide the master key.
- **Methods**   You can configure the HTTP methods that your function will accept. By default, the function runtime accepts all HTTP methods. Listing 2-12 reduces these accepted HTTP methods to *get* and *post*. Don't use this parameter if you set the *WebHookType* parameter.

- **Route** You can customize the route of the endpoint used for the function to listen to a new request. The default route is http://<your_function_app>.azurewebsites.net/api/<your_function_name>.

- **WebHookType** This parameter is available only for version 1.x runtime functions. You should not use the *Methods* and *WebHookType* parameter togethers. This parameter sets the *WebHook* type for a specific provider. Allowed values are

  - **Generic** This parameter is used for non-specific providers.
  - **Github** This parameter is used for interacting with GitHub webhooks.
  - **slack** This parameter for interacting with Slack webhooks.

When you declare the variable type that your function uses as the input from the trigger, you can use *HttpRequest* or a custom type. If you use a custom type, the runtime tries to parse the request body as a *JSON* object for getting needed information for setting your custom type properties. If you decide to use *HttpRequest* for the type of the trigger input parameter, you will get full access to the request object.

Every Azure Function App that you deploy automatically exposes a group of admin endpoints that you can use for accessing programmatically some aspects of your app, such as the status of the host. These endpoints look like

```
http://<your_function_app_name>.azurewebsites.net/admin/host/status.
```

By default, these endpoints are protected by an access code or authentication key that you can manage from your Function App in the Azure Portal, as shown in Figure 2-13.

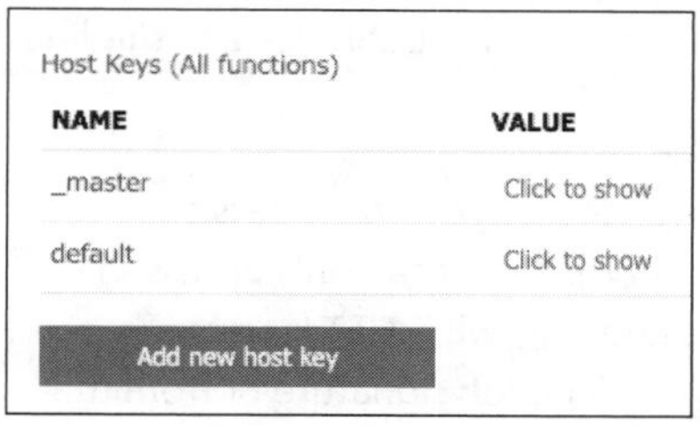

Host Keys (All functions)

NAME	VALUE
_master	Click to show
default	Click to show

Add new host key

FIGURE 2-13 Managing host keys for a Function App

When you use the HTTP trigger, any endpoint that you publish will also be protected by the same mechanism, although the keys that you will use for protecting those endpoints will be different. You can configure two types of authorization keys:

- **host** These keys are shared by all functions deployed in the Function App. This type of keys allows access to any function in the host.
- **function** These keys only protect the function where they are defined.

When you define a new key, you assign a name to the key. If you have two keys of a different type—*host* and *function*—with the same name, the *function* key takes precedence. There are also two default keys—one per type of key—that you can also use for accessing your endpoints. These default keys take precedence over any other key that you created. If you need access to the admin endpoints that we mentioned before, you need to use a particular host key called *_master*. You can also need to use this administrative key when you set the admin value to the *AuthLevel* trigger configuration parameter. You can provide the appropriate key when you make a request to your API by using the code parameter or using the *x-function-key* HTTP header.

Protecting your endpoints using the authorization keys is not a recommended practice for production environments. You should only use authorization keys on testing or development environments for controlling the access to your API. For a production environment, you should use one of the following approaches:

- **Enable Function App Authorization / Authentication**   This will integrate your API with Azure Active Directory or other third-party identity providers to authenticate clients.
- **Use Azure API Management (APIM)**   This will secure the incoming request to your API, such as filtering by IP address or using authentication based on certificates.
- **Deploy your function in an App Service Environment (ASE)**   ASEs provides dedicated hosting environments that allow you to configure a single front-end gateway that can authenticate all incoming requests.

If you decide to use any of the previous security methods, you need to ensure that you configure the *AuthLevel as anonymous*. You can see this configuration in Listing 2-12 in this line:

```
HttpTrigger(AuthorizationLevel.Anonymous…
```

When you enable the App Service Authentication / Authorization, you can access the information about the authentication users by using *ClaimPrincipal*. You can only access this information if you are running Azure Functions 2.x runtime and only with .NET languages. You can use *ClaimPrincipal* as an additional parameter of your function signature or from the code—using the request context—as shown previously in Listing 2-12.

```
ClaimsPrincipal identities = req.HttpContext.User;
string username = identities.Identity?.Name;
```

As we saw earlier in this section, Azure Functions runtime exposes your function by default using the following URL schema:

```
http://<your_function_app_name>.azurewebsites.net/api/<your_function_name>.
```

You can customize the endpoint by using the route *HTTPTrigger* parameter. In Listing 2-12, we set the route parameter to *devices/{id:int?}*. This means that your endpoint will look like this:

```
http://<your_function_app_name>.azurewebsites.net/api/devices/{id:int?}
```

When you customize the route for your function, you can also add parameters to the route, which will be accessible to your code by adding them as parameters of your function's signature. You can use any Web API Route Constraint (see *https://www.asp.net/web-api/overview/web-api-routing-and-actions/attribute-routing-in-web-api-2#constraints*) that you may use when defining a route using Web API 2.

By default, when you make a request to a function that uses an HTTP trigger, the response will be an empty body with these status codes:

```
HTTP 200 OK in case of Function 1.x runtime
HTTP 204 No Content in case of Function 2.x runtime.
```

If you need to customize the response of your function, you need to configure an output binding. You can use any of the two types of output bindings, using the return statement or a function parameter. Listing 2-12 shows how to configure the output binding for returning a JSON object with some information.

It is important to remember the limits associated with the function when you plan to deploy your function in a production environment. These limits are

- **Maximum request length**   The HTTP request should not be larger than 100MB.
- **Maximum URL length**   Your custom URL is limited to 4096 bytes.
- **Execution timeout**   Your function should return a value in less than 2.5 minutes. Your function can take more time to execute, but if it doesn't return anything before that time, the gateway will time out with an HTTP 502 error. If your function needs to take more time to execute, you should use an async pattern and return a ping endpoint to allow the caller to ask for the status of the execution of your function.

> **NEED MORE REVIEW?   HOST PROPERTIES**
>
> You can also make some adjustments to the host where your function is running by using the *host.json* file. Visit the following article for reviewing all the properties available in the *host.json* file at *https://docs.microsoft.com/en-us/azure/azure-functions/functions-bindings-http-webhook#trigger---hostjson-properties*.

Implement Azure Durable Functions

One crucial characteristic of Azure functions is that they are stateless. This characteristic means that function runtime does not maintain the state of the objects that you create during the execution of the function if the host process or the virtual machine where the function is running is recycled or rebooted.

Azure Durable Functions are an extension of the Azure Functions that provide stateful workflow capabilities in a serverless environment. These stateful workflow capabilities allow you to

- **Chain function calls together** This chaining means that a function can call other functions, which maintains the status between calls. These calls can be synchronous or asynchronous.

- **Define workflow by code** You don't need to create JSON workflow definitions or use external tools.

- **Ensure that the status of the workflow is always consistent** When a function or activity on a workflow needs to wait for other functions or activities, the workflow engine automatically creates checkpoints for saving the status of the activity.

The main advantage of using Azure Durable Functions is that it eases the implementation of complex stateful coordination requirements in serverless scenarios. Although Durable Azure Functions is an extension of Azure Functions, at the time of this writing, it doesn't support all languages supported by Azure Functions. The following languages are supported:

- **C#** Both precompiled class libraries and C# script are supported.

- **F#** Precompiled class libraries and F# script are supported. F# script is available only for Azure Functions runtime 1.x.

- **JavaScript** Supported only for Azure Functions runtime version 2.x runtime. Version 1.7.0 or later or Azure Durable Functions is required.

Durable Functions are billed using the same rules that apply to Azure Functions. That is, you are charged only for the time that your functions are running.

Working with Durable Functions means that you need to deal with different kinds of functions. Each type of function plays a different role in the execution of the workflow. These roles are:

- **Activity** These are the functions that do the real work. An activity is a job that you need your workflow to do. For example, you may need your code to send a document to a content reviewer before other activity can publish the document, or you need to create a shipment order to send products to a client.

- **Orchestrator** Any workflow executes activity functions in a particular order. *Orchestrator* functions define the actions that a workflow executes. These actions can be activity functions, timers, or waiting for external events or sub-orchestrations. Each instance of an *orchestrator* function has an instance identifier. You can generate this identifier manually or leave the Durable Function framework to generate it dynamically.

- **Client** This is the entry point of a workflow. Instances of a client function are created by a trigger from any source, such as HTTP, queue, or event triggers. Client functions create instances of *orchestrator* functions by sending an *orchestrator* trigger.

In the same way that Azure Function uses triggers and bindings for sending and receiving information from functions, you need to use triggers and bindings for setting the communication between the different types of *durable* functions. Durable functions add two new triggers to control the execution of *orchestration* and *activity* functions:

- **Orchestration triggers** These allow you to work with *orchestration* functions by creating new instances of the function or resuming instances that are waiting for a task. The most important characteristic of these triggers is that they are single-threaded. When you use orchestration triggers, you need to ensure that your code does not perform async calls—other than waiting for *durable* function tasks—or I/O operations. This ensures that the *orchestration* function is focused on calling *activity* functions in the correct order and waiting for the correct events or functions.

- **Activity trigger** This is the type of trigger that you need to use when writing your *activity* functions. These triggers allow communications between *orchestration* functions and *activity* functions. They are multi-threaded and don't have any restriction related to threading or I/O operations.

The following example shows how the different types of functions and triggers work together for processing and saving a hypothetical order generated from an external application and saved to a CosmosDB database. Although the example is quite simple, it shows how the different functions interact. Figure 2-14 shows a diagram of the workflow implemented on the functions shown in Listings 2-13 to 2-20. For running this example, you need to meet the following requirements:

- An Azure subscription.

- An Azure Storage Account. The *orchestration* function needs an Azure Storage Account for saving the status of each *durable* function instance during the execution of the workflow.

- An Azure CosmosDB database.

- Install following dependencies using this command:
  ```
  func extensions install -p <package_name> -v <package_version>
  ```

- CosmosDB:
  - Package name: *Microsoft.Azure.WebJobs.Extensions.CosmosDB*
  - Version: 3.0.3

- Durable Functions extension:
  - Package name: *Microsoft.Azure.WebJobs.Extensions.DurableTask*
  - Version: 1.8.0

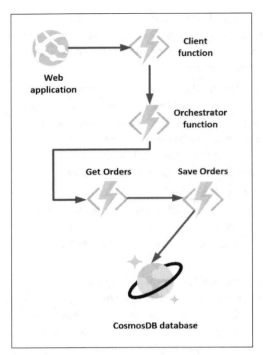

FIGURE 2-14 Durable function workflow

You can run this example using your favorite Integrated Development Environment (IDE). Visual Studio and Visual Studio Code offers several tools that make working with Azure projects more comfortable. Use the following steps for configuring your Visual Studio Code and creating the durable functions:

1. Open your Visual Studio Code.

2. Click the Extensions icon on the left side of the window.

3. On the Extensions panel, on the Search Extensions In Marketplace text box, type **Azure Functions**.

4. In the result list, on the Azure Function extension, click the Install button. Depending on your Visual Studio Code version, you may need to restart Visual Studio Code.

5. Click the Azure icon on the left side of the Visual Studio Code window.

6. In the Functions section, click Sign In To Azure For Log Into Azure.

7. In the Functions section, click the lightning bolt icon, which creates a new Azure Function.

8. In the Create New Project dialog, select JavaScript.

9. In the Select A Template For Your Project's First Function dialog box, select HTTP Trigger.

10. For the Provide A Function Name option, type **HTTPTriggerDurable**. This creates the first function that you need for this example.

11. Select Anonymous for the Authorization Level.

12. Select Open In Current Window to open the project that you just created.

Repeat steps 5 to 12 for all the durable functions that you need for this example. It is important to save all the functions you need in the same folder.

Listings 2-13 and 2-14 show the JavaScript code and the JSON configuration file that you need to create the client function that will call the *orchestration* function.

LISTING 2-13 Azure Durable Functions client function code

```
// NodeJS. HTTPTriggerDurable/index.js
const df = require("durable-functions");

module.exports = async function (context, req) {
    context.log('JavaScript Durable Functions example');
    const client = df.getClient(context);
    const instanceId = await client.startNew(req.params.functionName, undefined, req.body);

    context.log(`Started orchestration with ID = '${instanceId}'.`);

    return client.createCheckStatusResponse(context.bindingData.req, instanceId);
};
```

LISTING 2-14 Durable functions. Client function JSON configuration file

```
{
  "disabled": false,
  "bindings": [
    {
      "authLevel": "anonymous",
      "type": "httpTrigger",
      "direction": "in",
      "name": "req",
      "route": "orchestrators/{functionName}",
      "methods": [
        "get",
        "post"
      ]
    },
    {
      "type": "http",
      "direction": "out",
      "name": "$return"
    },
    {
      "name": "context",
      "type": "orchestrationClient",
      "direction": "in"
    }
  ]
}
```

Listings 2-15 and 2-16 show the JavaScript code and the JSON configuration file that you need to create the *Orchestration* function that invokes, in the correct order, all the other activity functions. This function also returns to the client the results of the execution of the different activity functions.

LISTING 2-15 Azure Durable Functions *Orchestrator* function code

```
// NodeJS. OrchestratorFunction/index.js
const df = require("durable-functions");

module.exports = df.orchestrator(function*(context) {
    context.log("Starting workflow: chain example");

    const order = yield context.df.callActivity("GetOrder");
    const savedOrder = yield context.df.callActivity("SaveOrder", order);

    return savedOrder;
});
```

LISTING 2-16 Durable functions. *Orchestrator* function JSON configuration file

```
{
  "disabled": false,
  "bindings": [
    {
      "type": "orchestrationTrigger",
      "direction": "in",
      "name": "context"
    }
  ]
}
```

Listings 2-17 and 2-18 show the JavaScript code and the JSON configuration file that you need to create the activity function *Get Order*. In this example, this function is in charge of constructing the information that will be used in the *Save Order* function. In a more complex scenario, this function could get information from the user's shopping cart from an e-commerce system or any other potential source.

LISTING 2-17 Azure Durable Functions *activity* function code

```
// NodeJS. GetOrder/index.js
module.exports = async function (context) {
    //Create a mock order for testing
    var order = {
        "id" : Math.floor(Math.random() * 1000),
        "name" : "Customer",
        "date" : new Date().toJSON()
    }
    context.log(order);
    return order;

};
```

LISTING 2-18 Azure Durable Functions *activity* function JSON configuration file

```
{
  "disabled": false,
  "bindings": [
    {
      "type": "activityTrigger",
      "direction": "in",
```

```
        "name": "name"
      }
    ]
}
```

Listings 2-19 and 2-20 show the JavaScript code and the JSON configuration file that you need to create the activity function that will save the order in a CosmosDB database. In a much more complex scenario, you could use this function to insert the order into your ERP system or send it to another activity function that could do further analysis or processing.

LISTING 2-19 Azure Durable Functions activity function code

```javascript
// NodeJS. SaveOrder/index.js
module.exports = async function (context) {

    //Saves the order object received from other activities to a CosmosDB document
    context.bindings.orderDocument = JSON.stringify({
        "id": `${context.bindings.order.id}`,
        "customerName": context.bindings.order.name,
        "orderDate": context.bindings.order.date,
        "cosmosDate": new Date().toJSON()
    });
    context.done();
};
```

LISTING 2-20 Azure Durable Functions activity function JSON configuration file

```json
{
  "disabled": false,
  "bindings": [
    {
      "type": "activityTrigger",
      "direction": "in",
      "name": "order"
    }
    ,
    {
      "name": "orderDocument",
      "type": "cosmosDB",
      "databaseName": "ERP_Database",
      "collectionName": "Orders",
      "createIfNotExists": true,
      "connectionStringSetting": "CosmosDBStorage",
      "direction": "out"
    }
  ]
}
```

The entry point in any workflow implemented using Durable Functions is always a client function. This function uses the orchestration client for calling the orchestrator function. Listing 2-14 shows how to configure the output binding.

```json
    {
      "name": "context",
      "type": "orchestrationClient",
      "direction": "in"
    }
```

When you are using JavaScript for programming your client function, the orchestrator client output binding is not directly exposed using the value of the *name* attribute set in the function.json configuration file. In this case, you need to extract the actual client from the context variable using the `getClient()` function declared in the durable-functions package, as shown in Listing 2-13.

```
const client = df.getClient(context);
```

Once you have the correct reference to the orchestrator client output binding, you can use the method *startNew()* for creating a new instance of the orchestrator function. The parameters for this method are:

- **Name of the orchestrator function**   In our example, we get this name from the HTTP request, using the *URL* parameter functionName, as previously shown in Listings 2-13 and 2-14.

- **InstanceId**   Sets the *Id* assigned to the new instance of the *orchestration* function. If you don't provide a value to this parameter, then the method creates a random *Id*. In general, you should use the autogenerated random *Id*.

- **Input**   This is where you place any data that your *orchestration* function may need. You need to use JSON-serializable data for this paramenter.

Once you have created the instance of the *orchestration* function and saved the *Id* associated to the instance, the client functions return a data structure with several useful HTTP endpoints. You can use these endpoints to review the status of the execution of the workflow, or terminate the workflow, or send external events to the workflow during the execution. Following is an example of the workflow management endpoints for the execution of our example in a local computer environment:

```
{
    "id": "789e7eb945a04ab78e74e9216870af28",
    "statusQueryGetUri":
"http://localhost:7071/runtime/webhooks/durabletask/
instances/789e7eb945a04ab78e74e9216870af28?taskHub=DurableFunctionsHub&connection=
Storage&code=AZNSvCSecL4w0RIRzPxLqbey1uJlThcwRE42UNuJavVIozMJhrNOzw==",
    "sendEventPostUri":
"http://localhost:7071/runtime/webhooks/durabletask/instances/789e7eb945a04ab78e74e92168
70af28/raiseEvent/{eventName}?taskHub=DurableFunctionsHub&connection=Storage&code=AZNSvC
SecL4w0RIRzPxLqbey1uJlThcwRE42UNuJavVIozMJhrNOzw==",
    "terminatePostUri":
"http://localhost:7071/runtime/webhooks/durabletask/instances/789e7eb945a04ab78e74e92168
70af28/terminate?reason={text}&taskHub=DurableFunctionsHub&connection=Storage&code=
AZNSvCSecL4w0RIRzPxLqbey1uJlThcwRE42UNuJavVIozMJhrNOzw==",
     "rewindPostUri":
"http://localhost:7071/runtime/webhooks/durabletask/instances/789e7eb945a04ab78e74e92168
70af28/rewind?reason={text}&taskHub=DurableFunctionsHub&connection=Storage&code=AZNSvCSe
cL4w0RIRzPxLqbey1uJlThcwRE42UNuJavVIozMJhrNOzw==",
"purgeHistoryDeleteUri":
"http://localhost:7071/runtime/webhooks/durabletask/instances/789e7eb945a04ab78e74e92168
70af28?taskHub=DurableFunctionsHub&connection=
Storage&code=AZNSvCSecL4w0RIRzPxLqbey1uJlThcwRE42UNuJavVIozMJhrNOzw=="
}
```

In this example, we used an Azure Function based on an HTTP trigger, but your client function is not limited to use this trigger. You can use any of the triggers available in the Azure Function framework.

Once you have created the instance of the orchestrator function, this function calls the activity functions by the order defined in the code, as previously shown in Listing 2-15.

```
const order = yield context.df.callActivity("GetOrder");
const savedOrder = yield context.df.callActivity("SaveOrder", order);
```

The orchestrator function uses an orchestration trigger for getting the information that the client function sends when it creates the instance. The *orchestration* trigger creates the instances of the different activity functions by using the *callActivity()* method of the durable-functions package. This method takes two parameters:

- **Name of the activity function**
- **Input** You put here any JSON-serializable data that you want to send to the activity function.

In our example, we execute the activity function *GetOrder*, previously shown in Listing 2-17, for getting the *order* object that we use as the input parameter for the next activity function *SaveOrder*, previously shown in Listing 2-19, for saving the information in the CosmosDB database configured in Listing 2-20.

You can test this example on your local computer by running the functions that we have reviewed in this section, in the same way that you test any other Azure function. Once you have your function running, you can test it by using curl or postman. You should make a *GET* or POST HTTP request to this URL: *http://localhost:7071/api/orchestrators/OrchestratorFunction*.

Notice that the parameter functionName of the URL matches with the name of our orchestrator function. Our *client* function allows us to call different *orchestration* functions, just by providing the correct *orchestration* function name.

You can use different patterns when you are programming the *orchestration* function, and the way it calls the activity functions:

- **Chaining** The activity functions are executed in a specific order, where the output of one activity function is the input of the next one. This is the pattern that we used in our example.
- **Fan out/fan in** Your *orchestratration* function executes multiple activity functions in parallel. The result of these parallel activity functions is processed and aggregated by a final aggregation activity function.
- **Async HTTP APIs** This pattern coordinates the state of long-running operations with external clients.
- **Monitor** This pattern allows you to create recurrent tasks using flexible time intervals.
- **Human Interaction** Use this pattern when you need to run activity functions based on events that a person can trigger. An example of this type of pattern is the document approval workflow, where publishing a document depends on the approval of a person.

Create Azure Function apps by using Visual Studio

When you are developing Azure Functions, if you decide to use C# for creating your function, your natural choice for the Integrated Development Environment (IDE) would be Visual Studio. Any function that you create needs to run in Azure Function App.

You can create Function Apps either using the Azure Portal or Visual Studio. The following procedure shows how to create an Azure Function project and an Azure Function App in Azure using Visual Studio 2017:

1. On your local computer, open Visual Studio 2017.
2. Click Tools > Get Tools And Features. Check the Azure Development Workload option in the Web & Cloud section.
3. Click the Modify button on the bottom-right corner of the window.
4. Click Tools > Extensions And Updates.
5. In the navigation tree on the left side of the window, click Installed > Tools.
6. In the installed tools, look for Azure Functions And Web Jobs Tools. Ensure that you have installed the latest version as listed in the release notes at *https://docs.microsoft.com/en-us/azure/azure-functions/durable/durable-functions-concepts*.
7. Create a new Azure Function project. Click File > New > Project.
8. On the left side of the New Project window, click Installed > Visual C# > Cloud.
9. On the New Project window, in the template area, click Azure Functions, as shown in Figure 2-15.

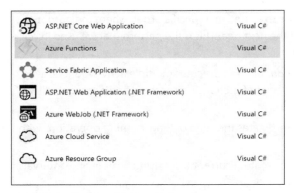

FIGURE 2-15 Cloud project templates

10. On the bottom of the New Project window, provide a Name, Location, and Solution Name for your project.

11. Click OK.

12. On the New Project *<your_project_name>* window, select Azure Functions v2 Preview (.NET Standard) from the Azure Function templates drop-down menu.

13. In the Azure Function Templates area, select HTTP Trigger.

14. Click OK.

15. Make the modifications that you need on the new project.

16. In the Solution Explorer, right-click the Azure Function project name.

17. Click Publish, which opens the Pick A Publish Target window

18. On the Pick A Publish Target window, click Publish. This opens the Create App Service window.

19. In the top-right corner of the Create App Service window, click the Add An Account Button For Connecting To Your Azure Subscription.

20. On the Create App Service window that is connected to you Azure Subscription, type the name of your function app in the App Name field, as shown in Figure 2-16.

FIGURE 2-16 Creating a Function App

21. On the Resource Group drop-down menu, click on the New link next to the drop-down menu.

22. Type a name for the new Resource Group and click OK.

23. Click the New link next to the Hosting Plan drop-down menu.

24. On the Configure Hosting Plan window, provide a name for the App Service Plan.

25. From the drop-down menu Location, select the location where your app service plan will be created.

26. Ensure the size consumption option is selected in the last drop-down menu.

27. Click OK to close the Configure Hosting Plan window.

28. In the Create App Service window, click on the New link next to the Storage Account drop-down menu.

29. Type a name for the new Storage Account and click OK.

30. In the bottom-right corner of the Create App Service window, click OK. This will create the Function app in Azure and deploy your code in the new function app.

Chapter summary

- Azure provides you with the needed services for deploying serverless solutions, allowing you to center on the code and forget about the infrastructure.

- Azure App Service is the base of the serverless offering. On top of App Service, you can deploy Web Apps, Mobile backend Apps, REST APIs or Azure Functions, and Azure Durable Functions.

- When you work with App Service, you are charged only for the time your code is running.

- App Service runs on top of an App Service Plan.

- An App Service Plan provides the resources and virtual machines needed for running your App Service code.

- You can run more than one App Service on top of a single App Service Plan.

- You can run non-interactive tasks in the background by using WebJobs tasks.

- WebJobs can be executed based on a schedule or triggers.

- When troubleshooting your App Service application, you can use several methods of diagnostics logging: web server logging and diagnostics, detailed error, failed requests, application diagnostics, and deployment diagnostics.

- Diagnostics logs are stored locally on the VM where the instance of your application is running.

- You can add push notifications to your mobile back-end app by connecting it with Azure Notification Hub.

- Azure Notification Hub offers a platform-independent way of managing and sending notifications to all mobile platforms to which you have deployed your mobile app.

- Offline sync for mobile apps allows your mobile app to create, update, and delete data while the user doesn't have access to a mobile network. Once the user is online again, the Azure Mobile Apps client SDK syncs the changes with your mobile app back end.

- You can track the activity of your mobile users and get automatically generated crash reports from your users' mobile apps by using Visual Studio App Center.

- You can configure CORS in your own code or at App Service level.

- If you configure CORS in your code and at App Service–level, the configuration on your code won't take effect because App Service level takes precedence.

- You can secure the access to your REST APIs deployed in App Service by enabling built-in Authentication / Authorization without modifying your code.

- Swagger / OpenAPI is an open-source tool for documenting your APIs.

- Swagger UI is the tool for visualizing the interactive API documentation generated by Swagger.

- You can use tools like Swashbuckle or NSwag to dynamically generate OpenAPI documentation based on the definition of the routes on your code.

- Azure Functions is the evolution of WebJobs.

- Azure Functions uses triggers and bindings for creating instances of Azure functions and sending or receiving data to or from external services, such as Queue Storage or Event Hub.

- There are two versions of Azure Functions. Version 1.0 only supports .NET Framework and Windows environments. Version 2.0 supports .NET Core and Windows and Linux environments.

- When you work with triggers and bindings, you need to install the appropriate NuGet package for function extensions that contain that triggers or bindings.

- Azure Function runtime already includes extensions for Timers and HTTP Triggers. You don't need to install specific packages for using these trigger bindings.

- Triggers that creates function instances can be based on data operations, timers, or webhooks.

- Azure Durable Functions is the evolution of Azure Functions that allows you to create workflows in which the state of the instances is preserved in the event of VM restart or function host process respawn.

- Orchestration functions define the activity and the order of execution of the functions that do the job.

- Activity functions contain the code that makes the action that you need for a step in the workflow, such as sending an email, saving a document, or inserting information in a database.

- Client functions create the instance of the orchestration function using an orchestration client.

- Azure Function Apps provides the resources needed for running Azure Functions and Durable Functions.

Thought experiment

In this Thought Experiment, you can demonstrate your skills and knowledge about the topics covered in this chapter. You can find the answers to this Thought Experiment in the next section.

You are developing a web application that is comprised of several pieces that communicate with each other. The web application has a REST API and a front-end application. This web application also needs to start a document publication workflow every time a document is saved in a Blob Storage Account.

With this information in mind, answer the following questions:

1. Which serverless technology should you use for implementing the REST API?
2. Which trigger should you use for starting the document publication workflow?
3. Which is the appropriate function type for using the trigger in the previous question?

Thought experiment answers

This section contains the solutions to the Thought Experiment.

1. You can use App Service API or Azure Function for implementing the REST API of your web application. If you use App Service API, you can use ASP.NET Web API 2 for implementing your API with C#. You can also use other languages like JavaScript or Python for this task. You can also use Azure Functions for your REST API. You can use HTTP Triggers with Azure Functions, customizing the route of each function for listening to the appropriate endpoint.

2. Because you need to start the workflow when a new document is saved to a Blob Storage account, you should use a Blob Trigger in your Azure Durable Function. You should use Durable functions because your workflow depends on humans for triggering some events, such as approving or declining the document. You should implement the Human Interaction pattern.

3. The appropriate function for using the Blob trigger is the Client function. This function waits for the *new document saved* event and then creates a new instance of the *orchestration* function that manages the document publication workflow. You need to implement the Human Interaction pattern on the *orchestration* function.

## CHAPTER 3

Develop for Azure storage

All applications work with information or data. Applications create, transform, model, or operate with that information. Regardless of the type or volume of the data that your application uses, sooner or later, you will need to save it persistently so that it can be used later.

Storing data is not a simple task and designing storage systems for that purpose is even more complicated. Perhaps your application needs to deal with terabytes of information, or you may work with an application that needs to be accessed from different countries, and you need to minimize the time required to access it. Also, cost efficiency is a requirement in any project. In general, there are many requirements that make designing and maintaining storage systems difficult.

Microsoft Azure offers different storage solutions in the cloud for satisfying your application storage requirements. Azure offers solutions for making your storage cost-effective and minimizing latency.

Skills covered in this chapter:

- Skill 3.1: Develop solutions that use storage tables
- Skill 3.2: Develop solutions that use Cosmos DB storage
- Skill 3.3: Develop solutions that use a relational database
- Skill 3.4: Develop solutions that use blob storage

Skill 3.1: Develop solutions that use storage tables

Storage tables allow you to store NoSQL data in the cloud. It's a schemaless storage design in which your data is stored using key/attribute pairs. A schemaless storage design means that you can change the structure of your data as your application requirements evolve. Another advantage of using storage tables is that they are more cost effective than using the same amount of storage on traditional SQL systems.

Azure offers two types of storage tables services: Azure Table Storage and Azure Cosmos DB Table. Azure Cosmos DB is a premium service that offers low latency, higher throughput, global distribution, and other improved capabilities. In this section, we review how to work with Azure Table storage using the Azure Cosmos DB Table API.

Azure Table storage can manage a large amount of structured, non-relational data. You can authenticate the calls that you make to the Storage Account. You can use OData and

LINQ queries with the WCF Data Service .NET libraries for accessing your data store in Azure Table Storage.

> **This skill covers how to:**
> - Design and implement policies for tables
> - Query Table Storage by using code
> - Implement partitioning schemes

Design and implement policies for tables

Before we can start designing and implementing policies for tables, we need to review some essential concepts for working with Table Storage. Azure Table storage is included and managed by the Azure Account Storage service. All scalability and performance features that apply to an Azure Account Storage account also apply to Azure Table Storage. (For simplicity, we refer to "Azure Account Storage" as a "Storage Account" and "Azure Table storage" as "Table Storage.")

You can think of a Storage Account as the parent namespace of Table Storage. The Storage account also provides the authentication mechanism to the Table Storage for protecting access to the data. You can create as many tables as you need inside a Storage account as long as the table names are unique inside the Storage Account.

Once you have created the Storage Account, you need to deal with following elements that are part of the table model:

- **Tables**   Tables are the storage containers for entities. You can create as many entities as you need inside a table. When you create a table, you need to bear in mind the following restrictions when naming your new table:
    - The table name must be unique inside the Storage Account.
    - The table name may only contain alphanumeric characters.
    - The table name cannot start with a number.
    - Table names are case-insensitive when you create the table. The name of the table preserves the case, but they are case-insensitive when you are using the table.
    - Table names must be between 3 and 64 characters long.
    - You cannot use reserved table names, such as "tables."
- **Entities**   You can think in an entity as a row in a table of a relational database. It has a primary key and a group of properties. Each entity in Azure Table Storage can be as big as 1MB and can have up to 252 properties to store data. When you create a new entity, the Table storage service automatically adds three system properties:
    - **Partition key**   The partition key defines a group of entities that can be queried more quickly.

- **Row key**   The row key is a unique identifier inside the partition.
- **Timestamp**   The timestamp properties set the time and date when you created the entity.
- **Properties**   These are pairs of key/values related to an entity. You can think of properties as each of the columns or fields that define the structure of a table in a relational database and are part of each row. When you create a property, remember that they are case-sensitive, and the name can be up to 255 characters long. When you are naming a property, you should follow the naming rules for C# identifiers. You can review these naming rules at *https://docs.microsoft.com/en-us/dotnet/standard/design-guidelines/naming-guidelines*.

NEED MORE REVIEW? **TABLE SERVICE DATA MODEL**

When you are working with tables, entities, and properties, you should review all types and details that apply to these elements. You can review a detailed description of each element in the Microsoft Docs article "Understanding the Table Service Data Model" at *https://docs.microsoft.com/en-us/rest/api/storageservices/understanding-the-table-service-data-model*.

When you are working with storage, you need to control who and how much time a process, person, or application can access your data. Azure Table storage allows you to control this access based on several levels of protection. Because Table storage is a child of Azure Storage, these authorization mechanisms are provided by Azure Storage:

- **Shared Key Authorization**   You use one of the two access keys configured at the Storage Account level to construct the correct request for accessing the Storage Account resources. You need to use the Authorization Header for using the access key in your request. The access key provides access to the entire Storage Account and all its containers, such as blobs, files, queues, and tables. You can consider Storage Account keys to be like the root password of the Storage Account.
- **Shared Access Signatures**   You use Shared Access Signatures (SAS) for narrowing the access to specific containers inside the Storage Account. The advantage of using SAS is that you don't need to share the Storage account's access keys. You can also configure a higher level of granularity when setting access to your data.

The drawback of using shared access keys is that if either of the two access keys are exposed, the Storage Account and all the containers and data in the Storage Account are also exposed. The access keys also allow you to create or delete elements in the Storage Account.

Shared Access Signatures provide you with a mechanism for sharing access with clients or applications to your Storage Account without exposing the entire Storage account. You can configure each SAS with different levels of access to each of the following:

- **Services**   You can configure SAS for granting access only to the services that you require, such as blob, file, queue, or table.

- **Resource types** You can configure the access to a service, container, or object. For the Table service, this means that you can configure the access to API calls at the service level, such as list tables. If you configure the SAS token at the container level, you can make API calls like create or delete tables. If you decide to configure the access at the object level, you can make API calls like create or updating entities in the table.

- **Permissions** Configure the action or actions that the user is allowed to perform in the configured resources and services.

- **Date expiration** You can configure the period for which the configured SAS is valid for accessing the data.

- **IP addresses** You can configure a single IP address or range of IP addresses that are allowed to access your storage.

- **Protocols** You can configure whether the access to your storage is performed using HTTPS-only or HTTP and HTTPS protocols. You cannot grant access to the HTTP-only protocol.

Azure Storage uses the values of previous parameters for constructing the signature that grants access to your storage. You can configure two different types of SAS:

- **Account SAS** Account SAS controls access to the entire Storage Account.

- **Service SAS** Service SAS delegates access to only specific services inside the Storage Account.

Regardless of the SAS type you need to configure, you need to construct an SAS token for access. You append this SAS token to the URL that you use for accessing your storage resource. You need to configure a policy for constructing the SAS. You configure this policy by providing the needed values to the SAS URI—or SAS token—that you attach to your URL request.

For constructing the SAS URI for an Account SAS, you need to use the parameters shown in Table 3-1.

TABLE 3-1 Account SAS URI parameters

PARAMETER NAME	URI PARAMETER	REQUIRED	DESCRIPTION
api-version	api-version	NO	You can set the version of the storage service API that processes your request.
SignedVersion	sv	YES	Sets the version of the signed storage service used to authenticate your request. This version should be 2015-04-05 or later.
SignedServices	ss	YES	Sets the services to which you grant access. You can grant access to more than one service by combining the allowed values: ■ **Blob** You need to use the value (b) in the SAS URI. ■ **Queue** You need to use the value (q) in the SAS URI. ■ **Table** You need to use the value (t) in the SAS URI. ■ **File** You need to use the value (f) in the SAS URI.

PARAMETER NAME	URI PARAMETER	REQUIRED	DESCRIPTION
Signed-ResourceTypes	srt	YES	Sets the resource type to which you grant access. You can configure more than one resource type simultaneously by combining more than one of the allowed values: ■ **Service** You need to use the value (s) in the SAS URI. ■ **Container** You need to use the value (c) in the SAS URI. ■ **Object** You need to use the value (o) in the SAS URI.
SignedPermission	sp	YES	Configures the permissions that you grant to the resource types and services configured on previous parameters. Not all permissions apply to all resource types and services. The following list only shows the permissions that apply to the table service: ■ **Read** You need to use the value (r) in the SAS URI. ■ **Write** You need to use the value (w) in the SAS URI. ■ **Delete** You need to use the value (d) in the SAS URI. ■ **List** You need to use the value (l) in the SAS URI. ■ **Add** You need to use the value (a) in the SAS URI. ■ **Update** You need to use the value (u) in the SAS URI. If you set a permission that is meaningful only for a service or resource type that you didn't set on the previous parameters, the permission is silently ignored.
SignedStart	st	NO	Sets the time and date at which the SAS token is valid. It must be expressed in UTC using ISO 8601 format: ■ YYYY-MM-DD ■ YYYY-MM-DDThh:mmTZD ■ YYYY-MM-DDThh:mm:ssTZD
SignedExpiry	se	YES	Sets the time and date in which the SAS token becomes invalid. It must be expressed in UTC using ISO 8601 format.
SignedIP	sip	NO	Sets the IP or range of IP addresses from which the storage service accepts requests. When using ranges of IPs, the limits are included in the range.
SignedProtocol	spr	NO	Sets the protocol allowed to request the API. Correct values are: ■ HTTPS only (https) ■ HTTP and HTTPS (https, http)
Signature	sig	YES	This is an HMAC-SHA256–computed string encoded using Base64 that the API uses for authenticating your request. You calculate the signature based on the parameters that you provided in the SAS URI. This signature must be valid to process your request.

Use the following procedure for constructing and testing your own account SAS token:

1. Sign in to the management portal (*http://portal.azure.com*).

2. In the search box at the top of the Azure portal, type the name of your Storage Account.

3. On the Storage Account blade, click Shared Access Signature in the Settings section.

4. On the Shared Access Signature panel, deselect the Blob, File, and Queue checkboxes under Allowed Services, as shown in Figure 3-1. Leave the Table checkbox selected.

5. Ensure that all options in Allowed Resource Types and Allowed Permissions are checked, as shown in Figure 3-1.

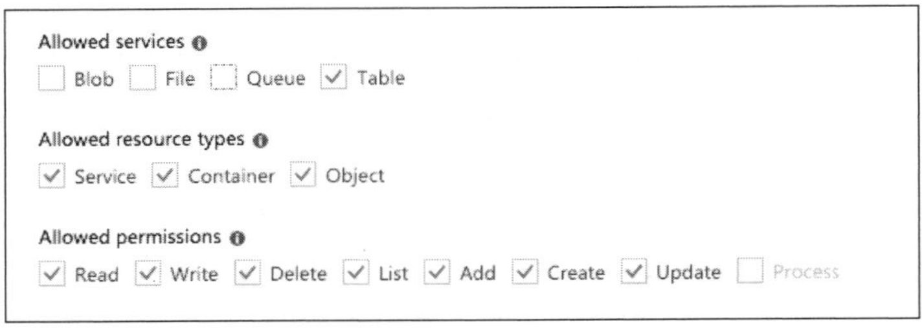

FIGURE 3-1 Configuring the Account SAS policy

6. Ensure that Allowed IP addresses have no value in the text box and HTTPS Only is selected in the Allowed Protocols section.

7. In the Signing Key drop-down menu, make sure that you have selected the Key1 value.

8. Click the Generate SAS And Connection String button at the bottom of the panel.

9. Copy the Table Service SAS URL. Now you can test your SAS token using a tool such as Postman, curl, or a web browser.

10. Open a web browser.

11. Paste the Table Service SAS URL in the address bar. Don't press Enter at this point.

12. In the Table Service SAS URL—after your Storage Account domain and before your SAS Token—add the bold text below. Your URL should look like this:

```
https://az203storagedemo.table.core.windows.net/tables?sv=2018-03-28&ss=bfqt&srt=s
co&sp=rwdlacup&se=2019-04-02T22:32:20Z&st=2019-04-02T14:32:20Z&spr=https&sig=ZnMBI
FxnmdOEyu%2FQJLQyYs1npP65o0No2u1KbrsGfd4%3D
```

13. Press Enter to navigate to the URL.

14. Confirm that you get an XML document with the list of existing tables in your Storage Account.

If you need to narrow the access to your resources and limit it only to tables or entities, you can create a Service SAS. This type of SAS token is quite similar to an Account SAS; you need to create a URI that you append to the URL that you use to request your Table storage service. Account and Service SAS share most of the URI parameters, although some parameters are specific to the service, and you need to take them into consideration when creating your Service SAS token. Table 3-2 shows the parameters that you need to set for creating a Table Service SAS. Other storage services require different parameters.

TABLE 3-2 Table Service SAS URI parameters

PARAMETER NAME	URI PARAMETER	REQUIRED	DESCRIPTION
SignedVersion	sv	YES	Sets the version of the signed storage service used to authenticate your request. This version should be 2015-04-05 or later.
TableName	tn	YES	Sets the name of the table to which you want to grant access.
SignedPermission	sp	YES	Configures the permissions that you grant to the table configured in the *TableName* parameter. You can set the following permissions on your SAS token: ■ **Query** You need to use the value (r) in the SAS URI. ■ **Add** You need to use the value (a) in the SAS URI. ■ **Update** You need to use the value (u) in the SAS URI. ■ **Delete** You need to use the value (d) in the SAS URI. You need to omit this parameter if you decide to use a Stored Access Policy.
SignedStart	st	NO	Sets the time and date at which the SAS token is valid. It must be expressed in UTC using ISO 8601 format: ■ YYYY-MM-DD ■ YYYY-MM-DDThh:mmTZD ■ YYYY-MM-DDThh:mm:ssTZD If you use an API version 2012-02-12 or later, the difference between *signedstart* and *signedexpiry* cannot be greater than one hour, unless you are using a container policy.
SignedExpiry	se	YES	Sets the time and date in which the SAS token becomes invalid. It must be expressed in UTC using ISO 8601 format. You need to omit this parameter if you decide to use a Stored Access Policy.
StartPK *StartRK*	spk srk	NO	Using these parameters, you can control access to a portion of the entities stored in the table, based on the partition and row keys of the table. If you use the *StartPK* parameter, you must also use the *StartRK* parameter. If you omit these parameters, there is no lower bound to the range of entities to which you grant access.

PARAMETER NAME	URI PARAMETER	REQUIRED	DESCRIPTION
EndPK *EndRK*	epk erk	NO	Using these parameters, you can control access to a portion of the entities stored in the table, based on the partition and row keys of the table. If you use the *EndPK* parameter, you must also use the *EndRK* parameter. If you omit these parameters, there is no upper bound to the range of entities to which you grant access.
SignedIP	sip	NO	Sets the IP or range of IP addresses from which the storage service accepts requests. When using ranges of IPs, the limits are included in the range. You need to omit this parameter if you decide to use a Stored Access Policy.
SignedProtocol	spr	NO	Sets the protocol allowed to request the API. Valid values are: ■ HTTPS only (https) ■ HTTP and HTTPS (https, http)
SignedIdentifier	si	NO	Relates the SAS URI that you are constructing with a Stored Access Policy on your Storage Account. Using Stored Access Policies provides a greater level of security.
Signature	sig	YES	This is an HMAC-SHA256 computed string encoded using Base64 that the API uses for authenticating your request. You calculate the signature based on the parameters that you provided in the SAS URI. This signature must be valid to process your request.

You can generate a Service SAS token by using the code shown in Listing 3-1. If you need to generate an SAS token and you don't want to write your own code for creating the token, you can create new Shared Access Signatures from the Azure Portal, using the Storage Explorer in the Storage account. On the Storage Explorer, navigate to the table for which you need to create the new SAS, right-click the name of the table, and click Get Shared Access Signature.

LISTING 3-1 Generate a Service SAS token

```
//C# .NET Core.

//you need to install WindowsAzure.Storage NuGet Package
using System;
using Microsoft.WindowsAzure.Storage;
using Microsoft.WindowsAzure.Storage.Auth;
using Microsoft.WindowsAzure.Storage.Table;

namespace ch3_1_1
{
    class Program
    {
        static void Main(string[] args)
        {
            string tablename = "az203tabledemo";
            string accountname = "az203storagedemo";
```

```
                string key = "<your_primary_or_secondary_access_key>";

                string connectionString = $"DefaultEndpointsProtocol=https;
                AccountName={accountname};AccountKey={key}";
                CloudStorageAccount storageAccount = CloudStorageAccount.Parse(connectionString);

                CloudTableClient tableClient = storageAccount.CreateCloudTableClient();
                CloudTable table = tableClient.GetTableReference(tablename);

                SharedAccessTablePolicy tablePolicyDefinition = new SharedAccessTablePolicy();
                tablePolicyDefinition.SharedAccessStartTime = DateTimeOffset.UtcNow;
                tablePolicyDefinition.SharedAccessExpiryTime = DateTimeOffset.UtcNow.
                AddHours(24);
                tablePolicyDefinition.Permissions = SharedAccessTablePermissions.
Query | SharedAccessTablePermissions.Add | SharedAccessTablePermissions.Delete |
SharedAccessTablePermissions.Update;

                string SASToken = table.GetSharedAccessSignature(tablePolicyDefinition);
                Console.WriteLine("Generated SAS token:");
                Console.WriteLine(SASToken);

        }
    }
}
```

One drawback of using Service SAS tokens is that if the URL is exposed, an unauthorized user could use the same URL to access your data as long as the access policy is valid. Stored Access Policies allows you to define access policies that are associated and stored with the table that you want to protect. When you define a Stored Access Policy, you provide an identifier to the policy. Then you use this identifier when you construct the Service SAS token. You need to include this identifier when you construct the signature that authenticates the token and is part of the SAS itself.

The advantage of using a Stored Access Policy is that you define and control the validity and expiration of the policy without needing to modify the Service SAS token. You can associate up to five different stored access policies. Listing 3-2 shows the piece of code for creating a Stored Access Policy. Because this code is quite similar to Listing 3-1, we have highlighted the lines that create the Stored Access Policy.

LISTING 3-2 Generate a Stored Access Policy

```
//C# .NET Core.
static void Main(string[] args)
        {
                string tablename = "az203tabledemo";
                string accountname = "az203storagedemo";
                string key = "<your_primary_or_secondary_access_key>";

                string connectionString = $"DefaultEndpointsProtocol=https;
                AccountName={accountname};AccountKey={key}";
```

```
CloudStorageAccount storageAccount = CloudStorageAccount.Parse(connectionString);

CloudTableClient tableClient = storageAccount.CreateCloudTableClient();
CloudTable table = tableClient.GetTableReference(tablename);

SharedAccessTablePolicy tablePolicyDefinition = new SharedAccessTablePolicy();
tablePolicyDefinition.SharedAccessStartTime = DateTimeOffset.UtcNow;
tablePolicyDefinition.SharedAccessExpiryTime = DateTimeOffset.UtcNow.
AddHours(24);
tablePolicyDefinition.Permissions = SharedAccessTablePermissions.
Query | SharedAccessTablePermissions.Add | SharedAccessTablePermissions.Delete |
SharedAccessTablePermissions.Update;

TablePermissions tablePermissions = Task.Run(async () => await table.
GetPermissionsAsync()).ConfigureAwait(false).GetAwaiter().GetResult();
SharedAccessTablePolicies policies = tablePermissions.SharedAccessPolicies;

policies.Add(new KeyValuePair<string, SharedAccessTablePolicy>(tablename +
"_all", tablePolicyDefinition));

Task.Run(async () => await table.SetPermissionsAsync(tablePermissions)).Wait();
}
```

Query table storage by using code

When you need to work with tables in Azure, you can choose between Azure Table Storage
and Table API for Azure Cosmos DB storage. Although Microsoft offers two different services
for working with tables, depending on the language that you use for your code, you can access
both services using the same library. You can work with tables by using .NET Framework and
Standard, Java, NodeJS, PHP, Python, PowerShell, C++, or REST API.

If you decide to use .NET Standard for your code, you need to use Azure Cosmos DB .NET
SDK. This SDK allows you to work with Azure Table Storage and Table API for Azure Cosmos DB.
You need to use the NuGet package *Microsoft.Azure.Cosmos.Table*. This package provides you
with the needed classes for working with tables, entities, keys, and values:

- **CloudStorageAccount** You use this class for working with the Storage Account where
  you want to create or access your tables. You need to provide the appropriate connection string to your instance of this class for connecting with your Storage Account. You
  can use SAS tokens when creating the instance of this class for authenticating to your
  Storage Account.

- **CloudTableClient** Use an instance of this class for interacting with the Table service.
  You need to use this object for getting references for existing tables or creating new
  references. Once you get the table reference, you need to create an instance of the
  CloudTable class for working with the table.

- **CloudTable**   This class represents a table in the Table service. You use an instance of this class for performing operations on the table, such as inserting or deleting entities. You need to use a *TableOperation* object for performing any action on the table's entities.

- **TableOperation**   Define an operation that you want to perform in your table's entities. You construct a *TableOperation* object for defining the insert, merge, replace, delete, or retrieve operations. Then you pass this *TableOperation* object to the *CloudTable* object for executing the operation.

- **TableResult**   This object contains the result of executing a *TableOperation* by a *CloudTable* object.

- **TableEntity**   Any document that you add to your table needs to be represented by a child of the *TableEntity* class. You define your model with the fields that match the keys of your document in your table.

***IMPORTANT*   NUGET PACKAGES**

Depending on the .NET version that you are using, you need to install different packages:

- **.NET Framework**   Use the NuGet package Microsoft.Azure.Cosmos DB.Tables.

- **.NET Standard**   Use the NuGet package Microsoft.Azure.Cosmos.Tables. If you use .NET Core, you also need to install the NuGet package Microsoft.Azure.Storage. Common.

You can use the following steps and Listings 3-3 to 3-8 to review a working example written in C# Core on how to work with Table Storage using Azure Cosmos DB Table Library for .NET. In this example, we use Visual Studio Code with the C# for Visual Studio Code extension installed, but you can use your preferred editor for this:

1. Open Visual Studio Code and open a folder on your computer where you want to store the files associated with this project.

2. Open a new Terminal by clicking Terminal > New Terminal.

3. Create a new folder named **az203TablesCodeDemo**. Change the location to this new folder.

4. Create a new project from the predefined Console Application template. Use the following command:

```
dotnet new console
```

5. Install the required NuGet packages by using the following commands:

```
dotnet add az203TablesCodeDemo.csproj package Microsoft.Azure.Cosmos.Table
dotnet add az203TablesCodeDemo.csproj package Microsoft.Azure.Storage.Common
dotnet add az203TablesCodeDemo.csproj package Microsoft.Extensions.Configuration
dotnet add az203TablesCodeDemo.csproj package Microsoft.Extensions.Configuration.Json
dotnet add az203TablesCodeDemo.csproj package Microsoft.Extensions.Configuration.Binder
```

6. In the Visual Studio Code window, create a new C# class file named **AppSettings.cs**. This helper class stores all needed information for your application.

7. Replace the content of the *AppSettings.cs* file with content in Listing 3-3.

LISTING 3-3 The AppSettings.cs file

```
//C# .NET Core.
using Microsoft.Extensions.Configuration;

namespace az203TablesCodeDemo
{
    public class AppSettings
    {
        public string SASToken { get; set; }
        public string StorageAccountName { get; set; }
        public static AppSettings LoadAppSettings()
        {
            IConfigurationRoot configRoot = new ConfigurationBuilder()
                .AddJsonFile("AppSettings.json")
                .Build();
            AppSettings appSettings = configRoot.Get<AppSettings>();
            return appSettings;
        }
    }
}
```

8. In the Visual Studio Code window, create a new file named **AppSetings.json**. Add the following content to the file:

```
{
    "SASToken": "<Your_SAS_Token>",
    "StorageAccountName": "<Your_Azure_Storage_Account_Name>"
}
```

9. Create a new C# class file and give it the name **Common.cs**. This class contains basic joint operations that you need for the rest of the examples, like creating the example table or the Storage Account object.

10. Replace the contents of the *Common.cs* file with the contents of Listing 3-4.

LISTING 3-4 The Common.cs file

```
//C# .NET Core.

using System;
using System.Threading.Tasks;
using Microsoft.Azure.Cosmos.Table;

namespace az203TablesCodeDemo
{
    public class Common
    {
```

```
public static CloudStorageAccount CreateStorageAccountFromSASToken(string SASToken,
string accountName)
{
    CloudStorageAccount storageAccount;
    try
    {
        //We required that the communication with the storage service uses HTTPS.
        bool useHttps = true;
        StorageCredentials storageCredentials = new StorageCredentials(SASToken);
        storageAccount = new CloudStorageAccount(storageCredentials,
        accountName, null, useHttps);
    }
    catch (FormatException)
    {
        Console.WriteLine("Invalid Storage Account information provided. Please
        confirm the SAS Token is valid and did not expire");
        throw;
    }
    catch (ArgumentException)
    {
        Console.WriteLine("Invalid Storage Account information provided. Please
        confirm the SAS Token is valid and did not expire");
        Console.ReadLine();
        throw;
    }

    return storageAccount;
}

public static async Task<CloudTable> CreateTableAsync(string tableName)
{
    AppSettings appSettings = AppSettings.LoadAppSettings();
    string storageConnectionString = appSettings.SASToken;
    string accountName = appSettings.StorageAccountName;

    CloudStorageAccount storageAccount = CreateStorageAccountFromSASToken
    (storageConnectionString, accountName);

    // Create a table client for interacting with the table service
    CloudTableClient tableClient = storageAccount.CreateCloudTableClient(new
    TableClientConfiguration());

    Console.WriteLine($"Creating the table {tableName}");

    // Create a table client for interacting with the table service
    CloudTable table = tableClient.GetTableReference(tableName);
    if (await table.CreateIfNotExistsAsync())
    {
    Console.WriteLine($"Created Table named: {tableName}");
    }
    else
```

```
            {
            Console.WriteLine($"Table {tableName} already exists");
            }

            Console.WriteLine();
            return table;
        }
    }
}
```

In this example, you are using an SAS token that you previously generated on your Azure Storage account. When you use an SAS token for authenticating the operations to your Table storage service, you also need to provide the account name.

11. In your project's folder, create a new folder named **Model**.

12. Create a new C# class file named **PersonEntity.cs** inside the folder Model.

13. Replace the contents of the **PersonEntity.cs** file with the contents of Listing 3-5.

LISTING 3-5 PersonEntity.cs file

```
//C# .NET Core.
using Microsoft.Azure.Cosmos.Table;

namespace az203TablesCodeDemo.Model
{
    public class PersonEntity: TableEntity
    {
        public PersonEntity() {}

        public PersonEntity(string lastName, string firstName)
        {
            PartitionKey = lastName;
            RowKey = firstName;
        }

        public string Email { get; set; }
        public string PhoneNumber { get; set; }
    }
}
```

The *PersonEntity* class that inherits from *TableEntity* is the C# representation of a document in your table. Pay particular attention to the *PartitionKey* and *RowKey* properties. These are the only two required properties that any entity needs to provide to the table. We will review these two properties in more detail in the next section.

14. Create a new C# Class file named **TableUtils.cs** in your project folder. This class contains some basic operations that you need to work with entities in a table.

15. Replace the *TableUtils.cs* contents with the contents of Listing 3-6.

LISTING 3-6 TableUtils.cs file

```csharp
//C# .NET Core.

using System;
using System.Collections.Generic;
using System.Threading.Tasks;
using az203TablesCodeDemo.Model;
using Microsoft.Azure.Cosmos.Table;

namespace az203TablesCodeDemo
{
    public class TableUtils
    {
        public static async Task<PersonEntity> InsertOrMergeEntityAsync(CloudTable table,
        PersonEntity entity)
        {
            if (entity == null)
            {
                throw new ArgumentNullException("entity");
            }
            try
            {
                // Create the InsertOrReplace table operation
                TableOperation insertOrMergeOperation = TableOperation.
                InsertOrMerge(entity);

                // Execute the operation.
                TableResult result = await table.ExecuteAsync(insertOrMergeOperation);
                PersonEntity insertedCustomer = result.Result as PersonEntity;

                return insertedCustomer;
            }
            catch (StorageException e)
            {
                Console.WriteLine(e.Message);
                Console.ReadLine();
                throw;
            }
        }

        public static async Task<TableBatchResult> BatchInsertOrMergeEntityAsync
        (CloudTable table, IList<PersonEntity> people)
        {
            if (people == null)
            {
                throw new ArgumentNullException("people");
            }
            try
            {
                TableBatchOperation tableBatchOperation = new TableBatchOperation();

                foreach (PersonEntity person in people)
                {
                    tableBatchOperation.InsertOrMerge(person);
                }
```

```
            TableBatchResult tableBatchResult = await table.ExecuteBatchAsync
            (tableBatchOperation);

            return tableBatchResult;
        }
        catch (StorageException e)
        {
            Console.WriteLine(e.Message);
            Console.WriteLine();
            throw;
        }
    }
    public static async Task<PersonEntity> RetrieveEntityUsingPointQueryAsync
    (CloudTable table, string partitionKey, string rowKey)
    {
        try
        {
            TableOperation retrieveOperation = TableOperation.Retrieve<PersonEntity>
            (partitionKey, rowKey);
            TableResult result = await table.ExecuteAsync(retrieveOperation);
            PersonEntity person = result.Result as PersonEntity;
            if (person != null)
            {
                Console.WriteLine($"Last Name: \t{person.PartitionKey}\n" +
                $"First Name:\t{person.RowKey}\n" +
                $"Email:\t{person.Email}\n" +
                $"Phone Number:\t{person.PhoneNumber}");
            }

            return person;
        }
        catch (StorageException e)
        {
            Console.WriteLine(e.Message);
            Console.ReadLine();
            throw;
        }
    }

    public static async Task DeleteEntityAsync(CloudTable table,
    PersonEntity deleteEntity)
    {
        try
        {
            if (deleteEntity == null)
            {
                throw new ArgumentNullException("deleteEntity");
            }

            TableOperation deleteOperation = TableOperation.Delete(deleteEntity);
            TableResult result = await table.ExecuteAsync(deleteOperation);

        }
```

```
        catch (StorageException e)
        {
            Console.WriteLine(e.Message);
            Console.ReadLine();
            throw;
        }
    }
}
}
```

16. Now that you have all the code that you need for interacting with the Azure Table Storage service, you can add some code to your *Program.cs* file to test it. Content in Listing 3-7 shows how to create a new testing table, then create three entities on the new table. You create the last two entities by using a batch operation, which allows you to create several entities at the same time. You need to ensure that the entities in the same batch operation share the same partition key. You also modify one of the entities, and then you retrieve an entity from your table.

LISTING 3-7 The Program.cs file

```
//C# .NET Core.

using System;
using System.Collections.Generic;
using System.Threading.Tasks;
using az203TablesCodeDemo.Model;
using Microsoft.Azure.Cosmos.Table;

namespace az203TablesCodeDemo
{
    class Program
    {
        static void Main(string[] args)
        {

            string tableName = "az203TableDemo" + Guid.NewGuid().ToString().Substring(0, 5);

            // Create or reference an existing table
            CloudTable table = Task.Run(async () => await Common.CreateTableAsync
            (tableName)).GetAwaiter().GetResult();

            try
            {
                // Demonstrate basic CRUD functionality
                Task.Run(async () => await CreateDemoDataAsync(table)).Wait();
            }
            finally
            {
                // Delete the table
                // await table.DeleteIfExistsAsync();
            }
        }
```

```
private static async Task CreateDemoDataAsync(CloudTable table)
{
    // Create an instance of a person entity. See the Model\personEntity.cs for
    //a description of the entity.
    PersonEntity person = new PersonEntity("Fernández", "Santiago")
    {
        Email = "santiago.fernandez@contoso.com",
        PhoneNumber = "123-555-0101"
    };

    // Demonstrate how to insert the entity
    Console.WriteLine($"Inserting person: {person.PartitionKey}, {person.RowKey}");
    person = await TableUtils.InsertOrMergeEntityAsync(table, person);

    // Demonstrate how to Update the entity by changing the phone number
    Console.WriteLine("Update an existing Entity using the InsertOrMerge Upsert
    Operation.");
    person.PhoneNumber = "123-555-0105";
    await TableUtils.InsertOrMergeEntityAsync(table, person);
    Console.WriteLine();

    //Insert new people with same partition keys.
    //If you try to use a batch operation for inserting entities with different
    //partition keys you get an exception.
    var people = new List<PersonEntity>();

    person = new PersonEntity("Smith", "John")
    {
        Email = "john.smith@contoso.com",
        PhoneNumber = "123-555-1111"
    };
    people.Add(person);

    person = new PersonEntity("Smith", "Sammuel")
    {
        Email = "sammuel.smith@contoso.com",
        PhoneNumber = "123-555-2222"
    };
    people.Add(person);

    TableBatchResult insertedPeopleResult = new TableBatchResult();
    insertedPeopleResult = await TableUtils.BatchInsertOrMergeEntityAsync(table,
    people);

    foreach (var res in insertedPeopleResult)
    {
        PersonEntity batchPerson = res.Result as PersonEntity;
        Console.WriteLine($"Inserted person in a batch operation:
        {batchPerson.PartitionKey}, {batchPerson.RowKey}");
    }
    // Demonstrate how to Read the updated entity using a point query
    Console.WriteLine("Reading the updated Entity.");
```

```
        person = await TableUtils.RetrieveEntityUsingPointQueryAsync(table,
        "Fernández", "Santiago");
        Console.WriteLine();

        // Demonstrate how to Delete an entity
        //Console.WriteLine("Delete the entity. ");
        //await SamplesUtils.DeleteEntityAsync(table, person);
        //Console.WriteLine();
        }
    }
}
```

17. Before you can run your code, you need to ensure that compilation includes the *AppSettings.json* file. Edit your *az203TablesCodeDemo.csproj* file and add the following code inside the *ItemGroup* section:

```
<None Update="AppSettings.json">
    <CopyToOutputDirectory>PreserveNewest</CopyToOutputDirectory>
</None>
```

18. In the Visual Studio Code window, start debugging your code by pressing F5.

19. Review the output of your code in the terminal window and ensure that all operations completed successfully. You can also check to ensure that the table and entities have been created successfully using Azure Portal Storage Explorer or Microsoft Azure Storage Explorer desktop app.

In the previous example, you retrieved a single entity by using the *Retrieve<>()* method from the *TableOperation* class. It is also quite common to need to retrieve a batch of entities stored in your tables. You can get a batch of different entities from your table by using OData or LINQ queries. If you need to use LINQ queries, you can use a *TableQuery* object for constructing your query. You can add code in Listing 3-8 to the previous example to review how *TableQuery* works.

LISTING 3-8 TableQuery example

```
//C# .NET Core.
//Add this code to the CreateDemoDataAsync method in Listing 3-6
TableQuery<PersonEntity> query = new TableQuery<PersonEntity>()
    .Where(TableQuery.GenerateFilterCondition("PartitionKey", QueryComparisons.Equal,
    "Smith"));

TableContinuationToken token = null;
do
{
    TableQuerySegment<PersonEntity> resultSegment = await table.ExecuteQuerySegmentedAsync
    <PersonEntity>(query, token);
    token = resultSegment.ContinuationToken;

    foreach (PersonEntity personSegment in resultSegment.Results)
    {
```

```
        Console.WriteLine($"Last Name: \t{personSegment.PartitionKey}\n" +
        $"First Name:\t{personSegment.RowKey}\n" +
        $"Email:\t{personSegment.Email}\n" +
        $"Phone Number:\t{personSegment.PhoneNumber}");
        Console.WriteLine();
    }
} while (token != null);
```

Implement partitioning schemes

When you create an entity in your table, you need to provide three system properties:

- **PartitionKey**   *PartitionKey* defines which partition belongs to the entity. A partition stores entities with the same *PartitionKey*.
- **RowKey**   The *RowKey* parameter uniquely identifies the entity inside the partition.
- **Timestamp**   The *Timestamp* property is the date and time when you create or modify the entity and is automatically provided for you by the system.

Because *PartitionKey* and *RowKey* are parameters of *string* type, the order applied to the entities uses lexical comparison. Using this type of comparison means that an entity with a *RowKey* value of *232* appears before an entity with a *RowKey* value of *4*.

Understanding how partitions store your data is essential because depending on the *PartitionKey* and *RowKey* that you define for your data, you can affect the performance when inserting, modifying, or retrieving data from your table. *PartitionKey* and *RowKey* define a clustered index that speeds up the entity searches on the table. You need to bear in mind that is the only index that exists in your table. You cannot define any new indexes. If you need to define a new index, you need to move to the Cosmos DB premium storage service using the Table API.

Each Table Storage service node services one or more partitions. The service can scale up and down dynamically by load balancing partitions across different nodes. When a node is under a heavy load, the storage service splits the range of partitions served by a particular node between several other nodes that have a lower load, as shown in Figure 3-2. When the pressure on the primary node lowers, the storage service merges the different parts of the partition into the original node.

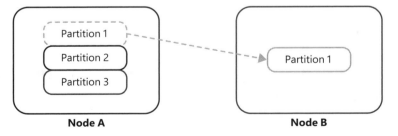

FIGURE 3-2 Configuring Account SAS policy

Another essential aspect that you need to consider when implementing your partitioning scheme is the Entity Group Transactions (EGT) built-in transaction mechanism. When you need to perform atomic operations across a batch of entities, the EGT built-in transaction mechanism ensures that all modifications happen consistently. The Entity Group Transaction can only operate on entities that share the same *PartitionKey*; that is, the entities need to be stored on the same partition. You need to carefully evaluate this feature because using fewer partitions means that you can use EGT more frequently, but it also means that you are decreasing the scalability of your application.

As we mentioned before in this section, the *PartitionKey* selection you make dramatically impacts the scalability and the performance of your solution. You can go from creating all your entities on a single partition to creating a partition for every single entity. Saving all entities in a single partition allows you to use entity group transactions on all your entities. If you put a significant number of entities in this single partition, you can prevent the Table Storage service from being able to scale and balance the partition efficiently. This happens because the node is reaching the scalability target of 500 entities per second too quickly. When the node reaches this limit, the Table service tries to load balance the partition to another node that has a lower load. Each time the Table service relocates your partition, it is disconnected and reconnected on the new node. Although this reconnection operation is quite fast, your application still can suffer timeouts and server busy errors.

When you choose your *PartitionKey*, you need to find the best balance between being able to use batch transactions or EGT and ensuring that your Table Storage solution is scalable. Other important aspects that you should take into consideration when designing and implementing your partition scheme is the type of operation that your application needs to do. Depending on how you update, insert, or delete entities in your table, you should select the correct *PartitionKey*. Independently of the modification operation that your application uses more frequently, and the impact that it can have on the performance when retrieving the results, you should carefully consider the different query types that you can use for locating your entities. You can use the following query types for working with your entities:

- **Point Query**   You set the *PartitionKey* and *RowKey* of your query. You should use these types of queries as often as possible because they provide better performance when looking up entities. In this case, you take advantage of the indexed values of *PartitionKey* and *RowKey* for getting a single entity. For example, you can use *$filter=(PartitionKey eq 'Volvo') and (RowKey eq '1234BCD').*

- **Range Query**   In this type of query, you set the *PartitionKey* to select a partition, and you filter a range of values using the *RawKey*. This type of query returns more than one entity. For example, you construct the filter as *$filter=PartitionKey eq 'Volvo' and RowKey ge '1111BCD' and RowKey lt '9999BCD'*. This filter will return all entities representing Volvo cars in which the plate number is greater than or equal to '1111BCD' and less than '9999BCD'. This type of query performs better than partition and table scans but worse than point queries.

- **Partition Scan**   In this case, you set the *PartitionKey* but use properties other than *RowKeys* for filtering the entities in the partition and returning more than one entity. For example, you can use this type of filter: *$filter=PartitionKey eq 'Volvo' and color eq 'blue'*. In this case, you look for entities representing blue Volvo cars. This type of query performs worse than range and point queries but better than Table Scans.

- **Table Scan**   You don't set the *PartitionKey*. This means that you don't take advantage of the indexed values in these system properties. Because you don't set the *Partition-Key*, it doesn't matter if you use *RowKey*; the Table Storage service performs a table scan lookup. This kind of query returns more than one entity. This type of query has the worst performance compared with partition scans and range and point queries. For example, you use the filter *$filter=Color eq 'Blue'* for getting all entities that represent blue cars.

Bearing in mind the types of queries and the characteristics and features of partition definition and management, you can use different Table design patterns. These patterns allow you to address some of the limitations, such as having only a single clustered index or working with transactions between partition boundaries:

- **Intra-partition secondary index pattern**   You can enable efficient lookups on different *RowKeys* with different sorting orders by creating multiple copies of the same entity in the same partition and using different values for the *RowKey* on each copy of the entity.

- **Inter-partition secondary index pattern**   You create multiple copies of the same entity in different partitions or even different tables using different *RowKey* values for setting different sort orders.

- **Eventually consistent transactions pattern**   Using Azure queues, you can bypass the limitation of using entity group transactions only inside the same partition.

- **Index entities pattern**   You use external storage, such as blob storage, for creating lists of indexed entities by using non-unique properties. For example, you have entities that represent employees in a company, and you used the department name as the *PartitionKey* and the Employee ID as the *RowKey*. You can create virtual indexes by creating a list for each value of the non-unique attribute that you want to index. This means you can have a list called *Smith* that contains all employee IDs for employees that have the Smith surname. You can also use the intra-partition and inter-partition secondary index pattern in conjunction with this pattern.

- **Denormalization pattern**   Because Table Storage is a schemaless NoSQL database, you are not restricted to normalization rules. This means you can store detailed information in the same entity that you should store in separate entities if you were using an SQL database.

- **Data series pattern**   You can minimize the number of requests that you need to make for getting a data series related to an entity. For example, consider an entity that stores the temperature of an industrial oven every hour. If you need to make a graph for showing the evolution of the temperature, you need to make 24 requests, one each hour.

Using this pattern, you create a copy of the entity that stores the temperature information for each hour in a 24-hour day, and you reduce the number of needed requests to create the graph from 24 to 1.

- **Compound key pattern**   You use the values from the *RowKey* of two different types of entities for creating a new type of entity in which the *RowKey* is the join of the *RowKeys* of each entity type.

- **Log tail pattern**   By default, values returned by the Table Storage service are sorted by *PartitionKey* and *RowKey*. This pattern returns the *n* most recently added entities to the table by using the *RowKey*.

- **High-volume delete pattern**   You can delete a high volume of data by storing all the entities that you want to delete in a separate table. Then you only need to delete the table that contains the entities that you want to delete.

- **Wide entities pattern**   If you need to create entities with more than 252 properties, you can split logical entities between several physical entities.

- **Large entities pattern**   If you need to store entities that are bigger than 1MB, you can use the blob storage service for storing the extra information and save a pointer to the blob as a property of the entity.

> *NEED MORE REVIEW?*   **TABLE DESIGN PATTERNS**
>
> You can find detailed information about how to implement table design patterns in the Table Design Patterns section of the article "Azure Storage Table Design Guide: Designing Scalable and Performant Tables" at *https://docs.microsoft.com/en-us/azure/cosmos-db/table-storage-design-guide#table-design-patterns*.

Skill 3.2: Develop solutions that use Cosmos DB storage

Cosmos DB is a premium storage service that Azure provides for satisfying your need for a globally distributed, low-latency, highly responsive, and always-online database service. Cosmo DB has been designed with scalability and throughput in mind. One of the most significant differences between Cosmos DB and other storage services offered by Azure is how easily you can scale your CosmoDB solution across the globe by simply clicking a button and adding a new region to your database.

Another essential feature that you should consider when evaluating this type of storage service is how you can access this service from your code and how hard it would be to migrate your existing code to a Cosmos DB–based storage solution. The good news is that Cosmos DB offers different APIs for accessing the service. The best API for you depends on the type of data that you want to store in your Cosmos DB database. You store your data using Key-Value, Column-Family, Documents, or Graph approaches. Each of the different APIs that Cosmos DB offers allows you to store your data with different schemas. Currently, you can access Cosmos DB using SQL, Cassandra, Table, Gremlin, and MongoDB APIs.

Create, read, update, and delete data by using the appropriate APIs

When you are planning how to store the information that your application needs to work, you need to consider the structure that you need to use for storing that information. You will find that some parts of your application need to store information using a Key-Value structure, while others may need a more flexible, schemaless structure in which you need to save the information into documents. Maybe one fundamental characteristic of your application is that you need to store the relationship between entities, and you need to use a graph structure for storing your data.

Cosmos DB offers a variety of APIs for storing and accessing your data, depending on the requirements that your application has:

- **SQL** This is the core and default API for accessing your data in your Cosmos DB account. This core API allows you to query JSON objects using SQL syntax, which means you don't need to learn another query language. Under the hood, the SQL API uses the JavaScript programming model for expression evaluation, function invocations, and typing system. You use this API when you need to use a data structure based on documents.

- **Table** You can think of the Table API as the evolution of the Azure Table Storage service. This API benefits from the high performance, low latency, and high scalability features of Cosmos DB. You can migrate from your current Azure Table Storage service with no code modification in your application. Another critical difference between Table API for Cosmos DB and Azure Table Storage is that you can define your own indexes in your tables. In the same way that you did with the Table Storage service, Table API allows you to store information in your Cosmos DB account using a data structure based on documents.

- **Cassandra** Cosmos DB implements the wire protocol for the Apache Cassandra database into the options for storing and accessing data in the Cosmos DB database. This allows you to forget about operations and performance-management tasks related to managing Cassandra databases. In most situations, you can migrate your application from your current Cassandra database to Cosmos DB using the Cassandra API by simply changing the connection string. Cassandra is a column-based database that stores information using a key-value approach.

- **MongoDB**   You can access your Cosmos DB account by using the MongoDB API. This NoSQL database allows you to store the information for your application in a document-based structure. Cosmos DB implements the wire protocol compatible with MongoDB 3.2. This means that any MongoDB 3.2 client driver that implements and understands this protocol definition can connect seamlessly with your Cosmos DB database using the MongoDB API.

- **Gremlin**   Based on the Apache TinkerPop graph transversal language or Gremlin, this API allows you to store information in Cosmos DB using a graph structure. This means that instead of storing only entities, you store:

  - **Vertices**   You can think of a vertex as in an entity in other information structures. In a typical graph structure, a vertex could be a person, a device, or an event.

  - **Edges**   These are the relationships between vertices. A person can know another person, a person might own a type of device, or a person may attend an event.

  - **Properties**   These are each of the attributes that you can assign to a vertex or an edge.

Beware that you cannot mix these APIs in a single Cosmos DB account. You need to define the API that you want to use for accessing your Cosmos DB account when you are creating the account. Once you have created the account, you won't be able to change the API for accessing it.

Azure offers SDKs for working with the different APIs that you can use for connecting to Cosmos DB. Supported languages are .NET, Java, Node.js, and Python. Depending on the API that you want to use for working with Cosmos DB, you can also use other languages like Xamarin, Golang, or PHP. In this section, you can review an example of each API and learn how to create, read, update, and delete data using the different APIs.

Before starting with the examples, you need to create a Cosmos DB account for storing your data. The following procedure shows how to create a Cosmos DB account with the SQL API. You can use this same procedure for creating accounts with the other APIs we have reviewed in this skill:

1. Sign in to the management portal (*http://portal.azure.com*).

2. In the top left corner in the Azure Portal, click Create A Resource.

3. On the New panel, under the Azure Marketplace column, click Databases. On the Featured column, click Azure Cosmos DB.

4. On the Create Azure Cosmos DB Account blade, in the Resource Group dropdown, click the Create New link below the drop-down menu. In the pop-up dialog, type a name for the new Resource Group. Alternatively, you can select an existing Resource Group from the drop-down menu.

5. In the Instance Details section, type an Account Name.

6. In the API drop-down menu, ensure that you have selected the option Core (SQL), as shown in Figure 3-3.

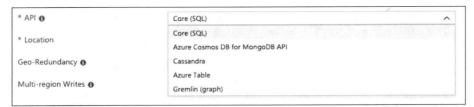

FIGURE 3-3 Selecting a Cosmos DB API

7. On the Location drop down menu, select the region most appropriate for you. If you are using App Services or virtual machines, you should select the same region in which you deployed those services.

8. Leave Geo-Redundancy and Multi-Region Write disabled.

9. In the bottom-left corner of the Create Azure Cosmos DB Account blade, click the Review + Create button.

10. In the bottom-left corner of the Review + Create tab, click the Create button to start the deployment of your Cosmos DB account.

> **NOTE   AZURE COSMOS DB EMULATOR**
>
> You can use the Azure Cosmos DB emulator during the development stage of your application. You should bear in mind that there are some limitations when working with the emulator instead of a real Cosmos DB account. The emulator is only supported on Windows platforms. You can review all characteristics of the Cosmos DB emulator at *https://docs.microsoft.com/ en-us/azure/cosmos-db/local-emulator*.

Once you have your Cosmos DB account ready, you can start working with the different examples. The following example shows how to create a console application using .NET Core. The first example uses Cosmos DB SQL API for creating, updating, and deleting some elements in the Cosmos DB account:

1. Open Visual Studio Code and create a directory for storing the example project.

2. Open the Terminal, switch to the project's directory, and type following command:

   ```
   dotnet new console
   ```

3. Install the NuGet package for interacting with your Cosmos DB account using the SQL API. Type following command in the Terminal:

   ```
   dotnet add package Microsoft.Azure.DocumentDB.Core
   ```

4. Change the content of the *Program.cs* file using the content provided in Listing 3-9. You need to change the namespace according to your project's name.

5. Sign in to the management portal (*http://portal.azure.com*).

6. In the Search box at the top of the Azure Portal, type the name of your Cosmos DB account and click the name of the account.

7. On your Cosmos DB Account blade, in the Settings section, click Keys.

8. On the Keys panel, copy the URI and Primary Keys values from the Read-Write Keys tab. You need to provide these values to the *EndpointUri* and *Key Constants* in the code shown in Listing 3-9. (The most important parts of the code are shown with bold format.)

LISTING 3-9 Cosmos DB SQL API example

```csharp
//C# .NET Core. Program.cs

using System.Collections.Immutable;
using System.Xml.Linq;
using System.Diagnostics;
using System.Runtime.CompilerServices;
using System;

using System.Linq;
using Microsoft.Azure.Documents;
using Microsoft.Azure.Documents.Client;
using System.Threading.Tasks;
using ch3_2_2_SQL.Model;
using System.Net;

namespace ch3_2_2_SQL
{
    class Program
    {
        private const string EndpointUri = "<INSERT_YOUR_COSMOS_DB_URI_HERE>";
        private const string Key = "<INSERT_YOUR_KEY_HERE>";
        private DocumentClient client;

        static void Main(string[] args)
        {

            try
            {
                Program demo = new Program();
                demo.StartDemo().Wait();
            }
            catch (DocumentClientException dce)
            {
                Exception baseException = dce.GetBaseException();
                System.Console.WriteLine($"{dce.StatusCode} error ocurred: {dce.Message},
                Message: {baseException.Message}");
            }
            catch (Exception ex)
            {
                Exception baseException = ex.GetBaseException();
                System.Console.WriteLine($"Error ocurred: {ex.Message}, Message:
                {baseException.Message}");
            }

        }
```

```
private async Task StartDemo()
{
    Console.WriteLine("Starting Cosmos DB SQL API Demo!");

    //Create a new demo database
    string databaseName = "demoDB_" + Guid.NewGuid().ToString().Substring(0, 5);

    this.SendMessageToConsoleAndWait($"Creating database {databaseName}...");

    this.client = new DocumentClient(new Uri(EndpointUri), Key);
    Database database = new Database { Id = databaseName };
    await this.client.CreateDatabaseIfNotExistsAsync(database);

    //Create a new demo collection inside the demo database.
    //This creates a collection with a reserved throughput.
    //This operation has pricing implications.
    string collectionName = "collection_" + Guid.NewGuid().ToString().
    Substring(0, 5);

    this.SendMessageToConsoleAndWait($"Creating collection demo
    {collectionName}...");

    DocumentCollection documentCollection = new DocumentCollection { Id =
    collectionName };
    Uri databaseUri = UriFactory.CreateDatabaseUri(databaseName);
    await this.client.CreateDocumentCollectionIfNotExistsAsync(databaseUri,
    documentCollection);

    //Create some documents in the collection
    Person person1 = new Person
    {
        Id = "Person.1",
        FirstName = "Santiago",
        LastName = "Fernandez",
        Devices = new Device[]
        {
            new Device { OperatingSystem = "iOS", CameraMegaPixels = 7,
            Ram = 16, Usage = "Personal"},
            new Device { OperatingSystem = "Android", CameraMegaPixels = 12,
            Ram = 64, Usage = "Work"}
        },
        Gender = "Male",
        Address = new Address
        {
            City = "Seville",
            Country = "Spain",
            PostalCode = "28973",
            Street = "Diagonal",
            State = "Andalucia"
        },
        IsRegistered = true
    };
```

```
await this.CreateDocumentIfNotExistsAsync(databaseName, collectionName,
person1);

Person person2 = new Person
{
    Id = "Person.2",
    FirstName = "Agatha",
    LastName = "Smith",
    Devices = new Device[]
    {
        new Device { OperatingSystem = "iOS", CameraMegaPixels = 12,
        Ram = 32, Usage = "Work"},
        new Device { OperatingSystem = "Windows", CameraMegaPixels = 12,
        Ram = 64, Usage = "Personal"}
    },
    Gender = "Female",
    Address = new Address
    {
        City = "Laguna Beach",
        Country = "United States",
        PostalCode = "12345",
        Street = "Main",
        State = "CA"
    },
    IsRegistered = true
};

await this.CreateDocumentIfNotExistsAsync(databaseName, collectionName,
person2);

//Make some queries to the collection
this.SendMessageToConsoleAndWait($"Getting documents from the collection
{collectionName}...");

FeedOptions queryOptions = new FeedOptions { MaxItemCount = -1 };

Uri documentCollectionUri = UriFactory.CreateDocumentCollectionUri
(databaseName, collectionName);

//Find documents using LINQ
IQueryable<Person> personQuery = this.client.CreateDocumentQuery<Person>
(documentCollectionUri, queryOptions)
    .Where(p => p.Gender == "Male");

System.Console.WriteLine("Running LINQ query for finding people...");
foreach (Person foundPerson in  personQuery)
{
    System.Console.WriteLine($"\tPerson: {foundPerson}");
}

//Find documents using SQL
IQueryable<Person> personSQLQuery = this.client.CreateDocumentQuery<Person>
(documentCollectionUri,
```

```
            "SELECT * FROM Person WHERE Person.Gender = 'Female'",
            queryOptions);

    System.Console.WriteLine("Running SQL query for finding people...");
    foreach (Person foundPerson in  personSQLQuery)
    {
        System.Console.WriteLine($"\tPerson: {foundPerson}");
    }
    Console.WriteLine("Press any key to continue...");
    Console.ReadKey();

    //Update documents in a collection
    this.SendMessageToConsoleAndWait($"Updating documents in the collection
    {collectionName}...");
    person2.FirstName = "Mathew";
    person2.Gender = "Male";

    Uri documentUri = UriFactory.CreateDocumentUri(databaseName, collectionName,
    person2.Id);
    await this.client.ReplaceDocumentAsync(documentUri, person2);
    this.SendMessageToConsoleAndWait($"Document modified {person2}");

    //Delete a single document from the collection
    this.SendMessageToConsoleAndWait($"Deleting documents from the collection
    {collectionName}...");

    documentUri = UriFactory.CreateDocumentUri(databaseName, collectionName,
    person1.Id);
    await this.client.DeleteDocumentAsync(documentUri);
    this.SendMessageToConsoleAndWait($"Document deleted {person1}");

    //Delete created demo database and all its children elements
    this.SendMessageToConsoleAndWait("Cleaning-up your Cosmos DB account...");

    await this.client.DeleteDatabaseAsync(databaseUri);
}
private void SendMessageToConsoleAndWait(string message)
{
    Console.WriteLine(message);
    Console.WriteLine("Press any key to continue...");
    Console.ReadKey();
}

private async Task CreateDocumentIfNotExistsAsync(string database,
string collection, Person person)
{
    try
    {
        Uri documentUri = UriFactory.CreateDocumentUri(database, collection,
        person.Id);
        await this?.client.ReadDocumentAsync(documentUri);
        this.SendMessageToConsoleAndWait($"Document {person.Id} already exists
        in collection {collection}");
    }
```

```
            catch (DocumentClientException dce)
            {
                if (dce.StatusCode == HttpStatusCode.NotFound)
                {
                    Uri collectionUri = UriFactory.CreateDocumentCollectionUri(database,
                    collection);
                    await this?.client.CreateDocumentAsync(collectionUri, person);
                    this.SendMessageToConsoleAndWait($"Created new document {person.Id}
                    in collection {collection}");
                }
            }
        }
    }
}
```

When you work with the SQL API, notice that you need to construct the correct URI for accessing the element that you want to work with. SQL API provides you with the *UriFactory* class for creating the correct URI for the object type. When you need to create a Database or a Document Collection, you can use *CreateDatabaseIfNotExistsAsync* or *CreateDocumentCollection IfNotExistsAsync*, respectively. These *IfNotExists* methods automatically check to determine whether the Document Collection or Database exists in your Cosmos DB account; if they don't exist, the method automatically creates the Document Collection or the Database. However, when you need to create a new document in the database, you don't have available this type of *IfNotExists* methods, so you need to check whether the document already exists in the collection. If the document doesn't exist, then you will create the actual document, as shown in the following fragment from Listing 3-9. (The code in bold shows the methods that you need to use for creating a document and getting the URI for a Document Collection.)

```
try
        {
            Uri documentUri = UriFactory.CreateDocumentUri(database, collection,
            person.Id);
            await this?.client.ReadDocumentAsync(documentUri);
            this.SendMessageToConsoleAndWait($"Document {person.Id} already exists
            in collection {collection}");
        }
        catch (DocumentClientException dce)
        {
            if (dce.StatusCode == HttpStatusCode.NotFound)
            {
                Uri collectionUri = UriFactory.CreateDocumentCollectionUri(database,
                collection);
                await this?.client.CreateDocumentAsync(collectionUri, person);
...
```

You need to do this verification because you will get a *DocumentClientException* with StatusCode 409 (Conflict) if you try to create a document with the same *Id* of an already existing document in the collection. Similarly, you get a *DocumentClientException* with StatusCode 404 (Not Found) if you try to delete a document that doesn't exist in the collection using the

DeleteDocumentAsync method or if you try to replace a document that doesn't exist in the collection using the *ReplaceDocumentAsync method*.

When you create a document, you need to provide an *Id* property of type *string* to your document. This property needs to uniquely identify your document inside the collection. If you don't provide this property, Cosmo DB automatically adds it to the document for you, using a GUID string.

As you can see in the example code in Listing 3-9, you can query your documents using LINQ or SQL sentences. In this example, I have used a pretty simple SQL query for getting documents that represent a person with the male gender. However, you can construct more complex sentences like a query that returns all people who live in a specific country; using the *WHERE Address.Country = 'Spain'* expression, or people that have an Android device using the *WHERE ARRAY_CONTAINS(Person.Devices, { 'OperatingSystem': 'Android'}, true)* expression.

NEED MORE REVIEW? **SQL QUERIES WITH COSMOS DB**

You can review all the capabilities and features of the SQL language that Cosmo DB implements by reviewing these articles:

- **SQL Language Reference for Azure Cosmos DB** *https://docs.microsoft.com/en-us/azure/cosmos-db/sql-api-query-reference*

Once you have modified the *Program.cs* file, you need to create some additional classes that you use in the main program for managing documents. You can find these new classes in Listings 3-10 to 3-12.

1. In the Visual Studio Code window, create a new folder named **Model** in the project folder.

2. Create a new C# class file in the *Model* folder and name it **Person.cs**.

3. Replace the content of the *Person.cs* file with the content of Listing 3-10. Change the namespace as needed for your project.

4. Create a new C# class file in the *Model* folder and name it **Device.cs**.

5. Replace the content of the *Device.cs* file with the content of Listing 3-11. Change the namespace as needed for your project.

6. Create a new C# class file in the *Model* folder and name it **Address.cs**.

7. Replace the content of the *Address.cs* file with the content of Listing 3-12. Change the namespace as needed for your project.

8. At this point, you can run the project by pressing F5 in the Visual Studio Code window. Check to see how your code is creating and modifying the different databases, document collections, and documents in your Cosmos DB account. You can review the

changes in your Cosmos DB account using the Data Explorer tool in your Cosmos DB account in the Azure Portal.

LISTING 3-10 Cosmos DB SQL API example: Person.cs

```csharp
//C# .NET Core.
using Newtonsoft.Json;

namespace ch3_2_2_SQL.Model
{
    public class Person
    {
        [JsonProperty(PropertyName="id")]
        public string Id { get; set; }
        public string FirstName { get; set; }
        public string LastName { get; set; }
        public Device[] Devices { get; set; }
        public Address Address { get; set; }
        public string Gender { get; set; }
        public bool IsRegistered { get; set; }
        public override string ToString()
        {
            return JsonConvert.SerializeObject(this);
        }
    }
}
```

LISTING 3-11 Cosmos DB SQL API example: Device.cs

```csharp
//C# .NET Core.

namespace ch3_2_2_SQL.Model
{
    public class Device
    {
        public int Ram { get; set; }
        public string OperatingSystem { get; set; }
        public int CameraMegaPixels { get; set; }
        public string Usage { get; set; }
    }
}
```

LISTING 3-12 Cosmos DB SQL API example. Address.cs

```csharp
//C# .NET Core.

namespace ch3_2_2_SQL.Model
{
    public class Address
    {
        public string City { get; set; }
        public string State { get; set; }
        public string PostalCode { get; set; }
        public string Country { get; set; }
        public string Street { get; set; }
    }
}
```

Working with Cosmos DB using the Table API is not too different from what you already did in the Azure Table Storage example in Listings 3-3 to 3-7. You need only make some slight modifications to make that example run using Cosmos DB Table API instead of using Azure Table Storage. Remember, to run this example, you need to create an Azure Cosmos DB Account using the Table API. Once you have created the account, copy the Connection String found in the Connection String panel under the Settings section of your Cosmo DB Account blade.

Use the following steps to adapt the examples in Listings 3-3 to 3-7 to work with the Cosmos DB Table API:

1. Make a copy of your Azure Table Storage project folder example and rename it.

2. Change the content in the *AppSettings.json* file with the following content:

```
{
    "ConnectionString": "<PUT_YOUR_CONNECTION_STRING_HERE>"
}
```

3. In the *AppSettings.cs* file, remove the *SASToken* and *StorageAccountName* properties and add a new property using the following code:

```
public string ConnectionString { get; set; }
```

4. In the *Common.cs* file, change the method *CreateStorageAccountFromSASToken* to:

```
public static CloudStorageAccount CreateStorageAccountFromConnectionString(string
connectionString)
```

5. In the *Common.cs* file, in the *CreateStorageAccountFromConnectionString* method, change

```
try
{
    //We required that the communication with the storage service uses HTTPS.
    bool useHttps = true;
    StorageCredentials storageCredentials = new StorageCredentials(SASToken);
    storageAccount = new CloudStorageAccount(storageCredentials, accountName,
null, useHttps);
}
```

To

```
try
{
    storageAccount = CloudStorageAccount.Parse(connectionString);
}
```

6. In the *Common.cs* file, in the *CreateTableAsync* method, change

```
AppSettings appSettings = AppSettings.LoadAppSettings();
string storageConnectionString = appSettings.SASToken;
string accountName = appSettings.StorageAccountName;

CloudStorageAccount storageAccount = CreateStorageAccountFromSASToken(storage
ConnectionString, accountName);
```

To

```
AppSettings appSettings = AppSettings.LoadAppSettings();
string cosmosDBConnectionString = appSettings.ConnectionString;
CloudStorageAccount storageAccount = CreateStorageAccountFromConnectionString
(cosmosDBConnectionString);
```

7. In the Visual Studio Code window, press F5 to run the project. You can connect to your Cosmos DB account and review the tables and entities in your account.

As you can see in this example, you can migrate from Azure Table Storage service to a Cosmos DB Table API account by making minimal changes to your code. You can migrate your data from Azure Table Storage to Cosmos DB using azCopy. See *https://docs.microsoft.com/ en-us/azure/storage/common/storage-use-azcopy*.

Working with the MongoDB API for Cosmos DB is as easy as working with any other Mongo DB library. You only need to use the connection string that you can find in the Connection String panel under the Settings section in your Azure Cosmos DB account.

The following example shows how to use Cosmos DB in your MongoDB project. For this example, you are going to use MERN (MongoDB, Express, React, and Node), which is a full-stack framework for working with MongoDB and NodeJS. Also, you need to meet following requirements:

- You must have the latest version of NodeJS installed on your computer.
- You must have an Azure Cosmos DB account configured for using MongoDB API. Remember that you can use the same procedure we saw earlier for creating a Cosmos DB with the SQL API to create an Azure Cosmos DB account with the MongoDB API. You only need to select the correct API when you are creating your CosmosDB account.
- You need one of the connection strings that you can find in the Connection String panel in your Azure Cosmos DB account in the Azure Portal. You need to copy one of these connection strings because you need to use it later in the code.

Use the following steps to connect a MERN project with Cosmos DB using the MongoDB API:

1. Create a new folder for your project.

2. Open the terminal and run the following commands:

```
git clone https://github.com/Hashnode/mern-starter.git
cd mern-starter
npm install
```

3. Open your preferred editor and open the *mern-starter* folder. Don't close the terminal window that you opened before.

4. In the *mern-starter* folder, in the *server* subfolder, open the *config.js* file and replace the content of the file with the following code:

```
const config = {
  mongoURL: process.env.MONGO_URL || '<YOUR_COSMOSDB_CONNECTION_STRING>',
  port: process.env.PORT || 8000,
};
export default config;
```

5. On the terminal window, run the command *npm start*. This command starts the NodeJS project and creates a Node server listening on port 8000.

6. Open a web browser and navigate to *http://localhost:8000*. This opens the MERN web project.

7. Open a new browser window, navigate to the Azure Portal, and open the Data Explorer browser in your Azure Cosmos DB account.

8. In the MERN project, create, modify, or delete some posts. Review how the document is created, modified, and deleted from your Cosmos DB account.

> **NEED MORE REVIEW?**   **GREMLIN AND CASSANDRA EXAMPLES**
>
> As you can see in the previous examples, integrating your existing code with Cosmos DB doesn't require too much effort or changes to your code. For the sake of brevity, we decided to omit the examples of how to connect your Cassandra or Gremlin applications with Cosmos DB. You can learn how to do these integrations by reviewing the following articles:
>
> - **Quickstart: Build a .NET Framework or Core application Using the Azure Cosmos DB Gremlin API account** *https://docs.microsoft.com/en-us/azure/cosmos-db/create-graph-dotnet*
> - **Quickstart: Build a Cassandra App with .NET SDK and Azure Cosmos DB** *https://docs.microsoft.com/en-us/azure/cosmos-db/create-cassandra-dotnet*

Implement partitioning schemes

When you save data to your Cosmos DB account—independently of the API that you decide to use for accessing your data—Azure places the data in different servers to accommodate the performance and throughput that you require from a premium storage service like Cosmos DB. The storage services use partitions to distribute the data. Cosmos DB slices your data into smaller pieces called partitions that are placed on the storage server. There are two different types of partitions when working with Cosmos DB:

- **Logical**   You can divide a Cosmos DB container into smaller pieces based on your criteria. Each of these smaller pieces are logical partitions.
- **Physical**   These partitions are a group of replicas of your data that are physically stored on the servers. Azure automatically manages this group of replicas or replica sets. A physical partition can contain one or more logical partitions.

By default, any logical partition has a limit of 10 GB for storing data. When you are configuring a new collection, as shown in Figure 3-4, you need to decide whether you want your collection to be stored in a single logical partition and keep it under the limit of 10 GB or allow it to grow over that limit and span across different logical partitions. If you need your container to split over several partitions, Cosmos DB needs some way to know how to distribute your data across the different logical partitions. This is where the partition key comes into play. Use the following procedure to create a new collection in your Cosmos DB account. This procedure could be slightly different depending on the API that you use for your Cosmos DB account. In this procedure, you use a Cosmos DB account configured with the MongoDB API:

1. Sign in to the management portal (*http://portal.azure.com*).

2. In the Search box at the top of the Azure Portal, type the name of your Cosmos DB account and click the name of the account.

3. On your Cosmos DB account blade, click Data Explorer.

4. On the Data Explorer blade, click the New Container icon in the top-left corner of the blade.

5. On the Add Container panel, shown in Figure 3-4, provide a name for the new database. If you want to add a container to an existing database, you can select the database by clicking the Use Existing radio button.

6. Provide a name for the collection.

7. Select the Storage Capacity by selecting Fixed (10GB) or Unlimited. Bear in mind that the partition key only makes sense for partitions bigger that 10GB.

8. Enter a Shard Key. This is the partition key that Cosmos DB uses for distributing your data across different partitions.

9. Enter a Thorughput Limit and click OK.

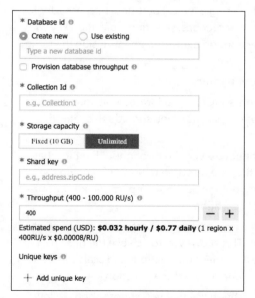

FIGURE 3-4 Creating a new Collection

One of the main differences between Azure Table Storage and Table API for Cosmos DB is whether you can choose the partition key. Azure Table Storage allows you to use the *PartitionKey* system property for selecting the partition key; Cosmos DB allows you to select the attribute that you want to use as the partition key, as shown in Figure 3-4. Bear in mind that this partition key is immutable, which means you cannot change the property that you want to use as the partition key once you have selected it.

Selecting the appropriate partition key for your data is crucial because of the effect it has on the performance of your application. If you select a partition key that has a lot of possible values, you will end up with many partitions, and each partition might contain only a few documents. This configuration can be beneficial when your application usually performs read workloads and uses parallelization techniques for getting the data. On the other hand, if you select a partition key with just a few possible values, you can end with "hot" partitions. A "hot" partition is a partition that receives most of the requests when working with your data. The main implication for these "hot" partitions is that they usually reach the throughput limit for the partition, which means you will need to provision more throughput. Another potential drawback is that you can reach the limit of 10GB for a single logical partition. Because a logical partition is the scope for efficient multi-document transactions, selecting a partition key with a few possible values allows you to execute transactions on many documents inside the same partition.

Use the following guidelines when selecting your partition key:

- The storage limit for a single logical partition is 10GB. If you foresee that your data would require more space for each value of the partition, you should select another partition key.

- The requests to a single logical partition cannot exceed the throughput limit for that partition. If your requests reach that limit, they are throttled to avoid exceeding the limit. If you reach this limit frequently, you should select another partition key because there is a good chance that you have a "hot" partition.

- Choose partition keys with a wide range of values and access patterns that can evenly distribute requests across logical partitions. This allows you to achieve the right balance between being able to execute cross-document transactions and scalability. Using timestamp-based partition keys is usually a lousy choice for a partition key.

- Review your workload requirements. The partition key that you choose should allow your application to perform well on reading and writing workloads.

- The parameters that you usually use on your requests are good candidates for a partition key.

NEED MORE REVIEW? **PARTITIONING**

You can review more information about how partitioning works viewing the following video at *https://azure.microsoft.com/en-us/resources/videos/azure-documentdb-elastic-scale-partitioning/.*

Set the appropriate consistency level for operations

One of the main benefits offered by Cosmos DB is the ability to have your data distributed across the globe with low latency when accessing the data. This means that you can configure Cosmos DB for replicating your data between any of the available Azure regions while achieving minimal latency when your application accesses the data from the nearest region. If you need to replicate your data to an additional region, you only need to add to the list of regions in which your data should be available.

This replication across the different regions has a drawback—the consistency of your data. To avoid corruption, your data needs to be consistent between all copies of your database. Fortunately, the Cosmos DB protocol offers five levels of consistency replication. Going from consistency to performance, you can select how the replication protocol behaves when copying your data between all the replicas that are configured across the globe. These consistency levels are region agnostic, which means the region that started the read or write operation or the number of regions associated with your Cosmos DB account doesn't matter, even if you configured a single region for your account. You configure this consistency level at the Cosmos DB level, and it applies to all databases, collections, and documents stored inside the same account. You can choose between the consistency levels shown in Figure 3-5. Use the following procedure to select the consistency level:

1. Sign in to the management portal (*http://portal.azure.com*).

2. In the Search box at the top of the Azure Portal, type the name of your Cosmos DB account and click the name of the account.

3. On your Cosmos DB account blade, click Default Consistency in the Settings section.

4. On the Default Consistency blade, select the desired consistency level. Your choices are Strong, Bounded Staleness, Session, Consistent Prefix, and Eventual.

5. Click the Save icon in the top-left corner of the Default Consistency blade.

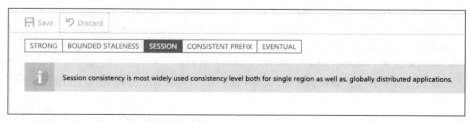

FIGURE 3-5 Selecting the consistency level

- **Strong** The read operations are guaranteed to return the most recently committed version of an element; that is, the user always reads the latest committed write. This consistency level is the only one that offers a linearizability guarantee. This guarantee comes at a price. It has higher latency because of the time needed to write operation confirmations, and the availability can be affected during failures.

- **Bounded Staleness** The reads are guaranteed to be consistent within a pre-configured lag. This lag can consist of a number of the most recent (K) versions or a time interval (T). This means that if you make write operations, the read of these operations happens in the same order but with a maximum delay of K versions of the written data or T seconds since you wrote the data in the database. For reading operations that happen within a region that accepts writes, the consistency level is identical to the Strong consistency level. This level is also known as "time-delayed linearizability guarantee."

- **Session** Scoped to a client session, this consistency level offers the best balance between a strong consistency level and the performance provided by the eventual consistency level. It best fits applications in which write operations occur in the context of a user session.

- **Consistent Prefix** This level guarantees that you always read data in the same order that you wrote the data, but there's no guarantee that you can read all the data. This means that if you write "A, B, C" you can read "A", "A, B" or "A, B, C" but never "A, C" or "B, A, C."

- **Eventual** There is no guarantee for the order in which you read the data. In the absence of a write operation, the replicas eventually converge. This consistency level offers better performance at the cost of the complexity of the programming. Use this consistency level if the order of the data is not essential for your application.

> **NOTE CUSTOM SYNCHRONIZATION**
>
> If none of the consistency levels shown in this section fit your needs, you can create a custom consistency level by implementing a custom synchronization mechanism. You can review how to implement a custom synchronization by reviewing this article: "How to Implement Custom Synchronization to Optimize for Higher Availability and Performance at *https://docs.microsoft. com/en-us/azure/cosmos-db/how-to-custom-synchronization.*

The best consistency level choice depends on your application and the API that you want to use to store data. As you can see in the different consistency levels, your application's requirements regarding data read consistency versus availability, latency, and throughput are critical factors that you need to consider when making your selection.

You should consider the following points when you use SQL or Table API for your Cosmos DB account:

- The recommended option for most applications is the level of session consistency.

- If you are considering the strong consistency level, we recommend that you use the bonded staleness consistency level because it provides a linearizability guarantee with a configurable delay.

- If you are considering the eventual consistency level, we recommend that you use the consistent prefix consistency level because it provides comparable levels of availability and latency with the advantage of guaranteed read orders.

- Carefully evaluate the strong and eventual consistency levels because they are the most extreme options. In most situations, other consistency levels can provide a better balance between performance, latency, and data consistency.

> **NEED MORE REVIEW?**   **CONSISTENCY LEVELS TRADEOFF**
>
> Each consistency level comes at a price. You can review the implications of choosing each consistency level by reading the article: "Consistency, Availability, and Performance Tradeoffs" at *https://docs.microsoft.com/en-us/azure/cosmos-db/consistency-levels-tradeoffs*.

When you use Cassandra or MongoDB APIs, Cosmos DB maps the consistency levels offered by Cassandra and MongoDB to the consistency level offered by Cosmos DB. The reason for doing this is because when you use these APIs, neither Cassandra or MongoDB offers a well-defined consistency level. Instead, Cassandra provides write or read consistency levels that map to the Cosmos DB consistency level in the following ways:

- **Cassandra write consistency level**   This level maps to the default Cosmos DB account consistency level.

- **Cassandra read consistency level**   Cosmos DB dynamically maps the consistency level specified by the Cassandra driver client to one of the Cosmos DB consistency levels.

On the other hand, MongoDB allows you to configure the following consistency levels: Write Concern, Read Concern, and Master Directive. Similar to the mapping of Cassandra consistency levels, Cosmos DB consistency levels map to MongoDB consistency levels in the following ways:

- **MongoDB write concern consistency level**   This level maps to the default Cosmos DB account consistency level.

- **MongoDB read concern consistency level**   Cosmos DB dynamically maps the consistency level specified by the MongoDB driver client to one of the Cosmos DB consistency levels.

- **Configuring a master region**   You can configure a region as the MongoDB "master" by configuring the region as the first writable region.

> **NEED MORE REVIEW?**   **CASSANDRA AND MONGODB CONSISTENCY LEVEL MAPPINGS**
>
> You can review how the different consistency levels map between Cassandra and MongoDB and Cosmos DB consistency levels in the article "Consistency Levels and Azure Cosmos DB APIs" at *https://docs.microsoft.com/en-us/azure/cosmos-db/consistency-levels-across-apis*.

Skill 3.3: Develop solutions that use a relational database

NoSQL databases have many desirable features that make them an excellent tool for some scenarios, but there is no one-size-fits-all tool for solving all your data needs. There might be times when you need to use relational databases, such as when you need to migrate an on-premises application to the cloud or write an application that requires strong enforcement of data integrity and transaction support.

Azure offers the SQL Database service, which is a database-as-a-service (DBaaS) platform that allows you to implement your relational database requirements directly in the cloud without worrying about the details of installing, configuring, and managing your instance of SQL Server. Azure SQL Database also provides to you out-of-the-box high availability, scalability, monitoring, and tuning features.

> **This skill covers how to:**
> - Provision and configure relational databases
> - Configure elastic pools for Azure SQL Database
> - Create, read, update, and delete data tables by using code

Provision and configure relational databases

Azure SQL Database offers different deployment models or deployment options to better fit your needs. The base code for all these deployment options is the same Microsoft SQL Server database engine that you can find in any installation of the latest version of SQL Server. Because of the cloud-first strategy, Microsoft includes the newest capabilities and features in the SQL Database cloud version and then adds it to the SQL Server itself.

As we mentioned, you can choose between the following three deployment options:

- **Single database** You assign a group of resources to your database. The SQL Database service manages these resources for you, and you only need to connect to your database for working with your data. A single database is similar to contained databases in SQL Server 2017.

- **Elastic pool** You configure a group of resources that the SQL Database service manages for you. You can deploy several databases that share these resources. This deployment option is appropriate when you have several databases that have an unpredictable workload or whose workload is predictable but not always stable (peak and valley usage patterns). You can move single databases in and out of elastic pools.

- **Managed instance** This is similar to installing your SQL Server in an Azure Virtual Machine with the advantage of not needing to provision or manage the VM. This deployment option is appropriate when you need to move an on-premises environment to the cloud, and your application depends on features available only for SQL instance. Bear in mind that this deployment option is different from deploying a SQL Server on Azure Virtual Machines.

NEED MORE REVIEW?   **AZURE SQL VERSUS SQL SERVER**

You can review a side-by-side comparison of features available in each version of the SQL service by consulting the article "Feature Comparison: Azure SQL Database versus SQL Server," at *https://docs.microsoft.com/en-us/azure/sql-database/sql-database-features*.

When you are planning to deploy an SQL Database, you should consider the purchasing model that best fits your needs. Azure SQL Database offers two purchasing models:

- **DTU-based**   Resources are grouped into bundles or service tiers—basic, standard, and premium. A DTU (Database Transaction Unit) is a grouping of computing, storage, and IO resources assigned to the database that allows you to measure the resources assigned to a single database. If you need to work with elastic pools, then you need to apply a similar concept—the elastic Database Transaction Unit or eDTU. You cannot use DTU or eDTU with managed instances.

- **vCore-based**   You have more fine-grained control over the resources that you want to assign to your single database, elastic pool, or managed instance. You can choose the hardware generation that you want to use with your databases. This pricing model offers two service tiers—general purpose and business critical. For single databases, you can also choose the additional service tier, hyperscale. When you use this pricing model, you pay for the following:

  - **Compute**   You configure the service tier, the number of vCores, amount of memory, and the hardware generation.

  - **Data**   You configure the amount of space reserved for your databases and log information.

  - **Backup storage**   You can configure Read Access Geo-Redundant Storage.

In general, if your single database or elastic pool is consuming more than 300 DTU, you should consider moving to a vCore pricing model. You can make this pricing model conversion with no downtime by using the Azure Portal or any of the available management APIs.

NEED MORE REVIEW?   **SQL DATABASE PRICING MODEL**

If you want to know more about the Azure SQL Database pricing model, you can review the Microsoft Docs article "Azure SQL Database Purchasing Models" at *https://docs.microsoft.com/en-us/azure/sql-database/sql-database-purchase-models*.

When you deploy a single database or an elastic pool, you need to use an Azure SQL Database server. This server is the parent resource for any single database or elastic pool, and it is the entry point for your databases. The SQL Database server controls important aspects, such as user logins, firewall and auditing rules, thread detection policies and failover groups. When you create your first database or elastic pool, you need to create an SQL Database server and provide an admin username and password for managing the server. This first administrator user has control over the master database on the server and all new databases created on the server.

You should not confuse this SQL Database server with an on-premises server or a managed instance server. The SQL Database server does not provide any instance-level features to you. It also does not guarantee the location of the databases that the server manages. This means that you can have your databases or elastic pools located in a region different from the region in which you deployed your SQL Database server. Also, this SQL Database server is different from a managed instance server because, in the case of the managed instance server, all databases are located in the same region in which you deployed the managed instance databases.

Use the following procedure for creating a single database with a new SQL Database server:

1. Sign in to the management portal (*http://portal.azure.com*).

2. In the top-left corner of the Azure Portal, click Create A Resource.

3. On the New panel, under the Azure Marketplace column, click Databases. In the Featured column, click SQL Database.

4. On the Create SQL Database blade, in the Resource Group, click the Create New Link below the drop-down menu. In the pop-up dialog, type a name for the new Resource Group. Alternatively, you can select an existing Resource Group from the drop-down menu.

5. In the Database Details section, type a name for the new database in the Database Name text box.

6. In the Server Option section, click the Create New link below the Select A Server drop-down menu to open the New Server panel.

7. In the New Server panel, shown in Figure 3-6, provide a name for the new SQL Database Server.

8. Leave the Allow Azure Services To Access Server option selected.

FIGURE 3-6 Creating a new SQL Database server

9. In the New Server panel, provide values for the Admin Username, Password, and Confirm Password fields.

10. Leave the Location drop-down menu with the default value.

11. At the bottom of the New Server panel, click the Select button.

12. On the Create SQL Database blade, in the Database Details section, ensure that the Want To Use SQL Elastic Pool? option is set to No. You only use this option when configuring an elastic pool.

13. In the Compute + Storage section, select the Standard S0 service tier.

14. Click the Next: Additional settings >> button at the bottom of the Create SQL Database blade.

15. On the Additional Settings tab, in the Data Source section, ensure that the None option is selected. Alternatively, you can create a database from an existing backup in your subscription. You can also create the AdventureWorksLT database with sample data.

16. In the database collation section, leave the SQL_Latin1_General_CP1_CI_AS option selected. In this section, you can configure any other collation that your database or application may require.

17. Click the Review + Create button at the bottom of the Create SQL Database blade.

18. On the Review + Create tab, make sure that all settings are correct and click the Create button at the bottom of the blade.

Once you have created your database, you need to configure a server-level firewall rule. You need to do this because when you create a SQL Database server, Azure doesn't allow any external clients to connect to the server. You need to allow the connections from your computer's IP to access your database. Because you kept the Allow Azure Services To Access Server option selected during the Azure SQL Database server creation, you don't need to explicitly grant access to any Azure service, such as App Services or Azure Functions that may need to access this database. You can create the appropriate client-side firewall rule using Azure Portal or Azure Data Studio. Use the following procedure for creating a server-side firewall rule for any network or host address:

1. Sign in to the management portal (*http://portal.azure.com*).

2. In the Search box at the top of the Azure Portal, type the name of your SQL Database.

3. On the Overview panel of your SQL Database, click the Set Server Firewall button on the top side of the blade.

4. On the Firewall Settings blade, click the Add Client IP button located on the top bar of the blade to add the IP address from which you are connected to the Azure Portal.

5. Click the Save button at the top of the blade.

Once you have created the server-side firewall rule, you can connect to your SQL Database, using your preferred SQL management tool or IDE, such as Azure Data Studio, SQL Server Management Studio, Visual Studio, or Visual Studio Code.

Another exciting feature that you should consider when working with the SQL Database service is the ability to create backups of your databases automatically. The retention period of these backups goes from 7 to 35 days, depending on the purchase model and the service tier that you choose for your database. You can configure this retention policy at the SQL Database server level. Use the following procedure for configuring the retention policy for your SQL Database server:

1. Sign in to the management portal (*http://portal.azure.com*).
2. In the Search box at the top of the Azure Portal, type the name of your SQL Database server.
3. In the Settings section, click the Manage Backups option.
4. On the Manage Backups panel, click the Configure Retention button in the top-left corner of the panel.
5. On the Configure Policies panel, in the Point In Time Restore Configuration drop-down menu, select the number of days that you want to keep your Point In Time Restore (PITR) backups.
6. Click the Apply button at the bottom of the Configure Policies panel.

> **NEED MORE REVIEW?**   **LONG-TERM BACKUPS**
>
> The retention time offered by the automatically created point-in-time restore backups may be not sufficient for your company. In those situations, you can configure long-term retention policies for storing full backups of the databases in a separate Storage Account for up to ten years. You can review how to configure these long-term backups by consulting the article "Store Azure SQL Database backups for up to 10 years" at *https://docs.microsoft.com/en-us/azure/sql-database/sql-database-long-term-retention*.

> **NEED MORE REVIEW?**   **RESTORE A DATABASE**
>
> You can use the point-in-time restore backups for restoring a previous version of your databases or restore a database that you deleted by accident. You can review the different options for restoring your databases in the article "Recover an Azure SQL Database Using Automated Database Backups." See *https://docs.microsoft.com/en-us/azure/sql-database/sql-database-recovery-using-backups*.

Configure elastic pools for Azure SQL Database

When you configure a single database in the SQL Database service, you reserve a group of resources for your database. If you deploy several databases, you reserve independent groups of resources, one for each database. This approach could lead to a waste of resources if the workload for your database is unpredictable. If you provide too many DTUs for the peak usage of your database, you can waste resources when your database is in the valley usage periods. If you decide to provide fewer resources to your database, you can face a situation in which your database doesn't have enough resources to perform correctly.

A solution to this problem is to use elastic pools. This deployment option allows you to allocate elastic Database Transaction Units (eDTUs) or vCore and to put several databases in the elastic pool. When you add a database to the elastic pool, you configure a minimum and maximum amount of resources for the database. The advantage of using a database in an elastic pool is that the database consumes resources based on its real usage. This means that if the database is under a heavy load, it can consume more resources; if the database is under a low load, it consumes fewer resources. This also means that if the database is not being used at all, it doesn't consume any resources. The real advantage of the elastic pool comes when you put more than one database in the elastic pool.

You can add or remove resources for your database in an elastic pool with no downtime of the database (unless you need to add more resources to the elastic pool). If you need to change service tiers, then you might experience a little downtime because SQL Database service creates a new instance on the new service tier. Then the SQL Database service copies all the data to the new instance. Once the data is completely synced, the service switches the routing of the connections from the old instance to the new one.

You can use the following procedure for creating a new elastic pool and adding an existing database to your elastic pool:

1. Sign in to the management portal (*http://portal.azure.com*).

2. In the top-left corner of the Azure Portal, click Create A Resource.

3. On the New panel, in the Search The Marketplace text box, type **ql elas** and select SQL Elastic Database Pool from the list of results.

4. On the SQL Elastic Database Pool panel, click the Create button.

5. On the Elastic Pool panel, type a name for the elastic pool in the Name text box.

6. In the Resource Group property drop-down control, click the Create New link. In the pop-up dialog, type a name for the new Resource Group. Alternatively, you can select an existing Resource Group from the drop-down menu.

7. From the Server Property drop-down menu, select the SQL Database server that you created in the previous procedure.

8. Click the Configure Pool property to open the Configure Panel, as shown in Figure 3-7, where you can select the service tier for this elastic pool.

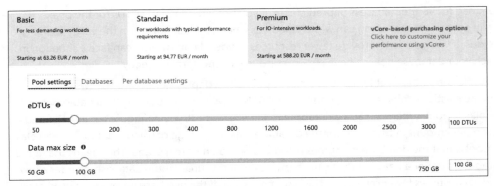

FIGURE 3-7 Configuring elastic pool service tier

9. Click the Databases tab and then click the Add Databases button.

10. In the Add Databases panel, select the database that you want to add to this elastic pool. It should appear in the list of databases that you created in the previous procedure.

11. Click the Apply button at the bottom of the Add Databases panel.

12. Click the Apply button at the bottom of the Configure panel.

13. Click the Create button at the bottom of the Elastic Pool panel.

Once you have created your elastic pool, you can configure the upper and lower limits of the resources that you want to assign to each database in the elastic pool. You must configure this limit for all databases together; you may not configure this limit per database. This means that if you set a lower limit of 10 DTUs and an upper limit of 20 DTUs, these limits apply to all databases in the elastic pool. Use the following procedure for configuring the per-database limit in your elastic pool:

1. Sign in to the management portal (*http://portal.azure.com*).

2. In the Search box at the top of the Azure Portal, type the name of your SQL Elastic Database Pool.

3. On the SQL Elastic Pool blade, click the Configure option under the Settings section.

4. On the Configure panel, click the Per Database Settings tab.

5. Move the slider control to adjust your Per Database limits. Move the left side to adjust the Minimum limit and use the right side to select the Maximum limit.

6. Click the Save button on the top-left side of the Configure panel.

Create, read, update, and delete data tables by using code

Working with an SQL Database from your code works the same way as you do with any other database hosted in an on-premises SQL Server instance. You can use the following drivers for SQL for accessing the database from your code: ADO.NET, ODBC, JDBC, and PDO (PHP). You can also work with Object-Relational Mapping frameworks like Entity Framework/Entity Framework Core or Java Hibernate. The following example shows how to connect to your SQL Database from your .NET Core code using ADO.NET. To run this example, you need:

- **Visual Studio 2017 installation** You can also use a Visual Studio Code installation.
- **SQL Database** You can use a single database or a database included in an elastic pool.

For the sake of simplicity, this example uses ADO.NET. Using other ORM frameworks like Entity Framework doesn't require any special consideration. You only need to use the connection string copied from your SQL Database:

1. Sign in to the management portal (*http://portal.azure.com*).
2. In the Search box at the top of the Azure Portal, type the name of your SQL Database.
3. Click the Properties option in the Settings section.
4. On the Properties panel, click the Show Databases Connection Strings link.
5. On the Databases Connection Strings panel, copy the connection string that appears on the ADO.NET tab. You will use this connection string later in the code.
6. Open your Visual Studio 2017 installation.
7. Click File > New > Project.
8. On the New Project window, on the navigation tree at the left, select Installed > Visual C# > .NET Core.
9. In the template list in the middle of the window, select Console App (.NET Core).
10. At the bottom of the window, type a name for the project and a name for the solution.

11. Select the location in which you want to save your solution.

12. Click the OK button in the bottom-right corner of the window.

13. On the Visual Studio window, click Tools > NuGet Package Manager > Manage NuGet Packages For Solution.

14. On the NuGet tab, click the Browse tab.

15. In the Search box, type **System.Data.SqlClient** and press the Enter key to install the *System.Data.SqlClient* NuGet package.

16. Replace the contents of the *Program.cs* file with the contents in Listing 3-13.

LISTING 3-13 Connect to your SQL Database. Program.cs

```
//C# .NET Core.

using System;
using System.Data.SqlClient;

namespace ch3_3_3
{
    class Program
    {
        static void Main(string[] args)
        {
            Console.WriteLine("SQL Database connection Demo!");
            try
            {
                Program p = new Program();
                p.StartADOConnectionDemo();
            }
            catch (Exception ex)
            {
                Console.WriteLine(ex.ToString());
            }
        }

        private void StartADOConnectionDemo()
        {
            try
            {
                string your_username = "<your_db_admin_username>";
                string your_password = "<your_db_admin_password>";
                string connectionString = $"<your_ADO.NET_connection_string>";
                using (var connection = new SqlConnection(connectionString))
                {
                    connection.Open();

                    Console.WriteLine("Creating tables with ADO");
                    using (var command = new SqlCommand(ADO_CreateTables(), connection))
                    {
                        int rowsAffected = command.ExecuteNonQuery();
                        Console.WriteLine($"Number of rows affected: {rowsAffected}");
                    }
```

```csharp
    Console.WriteLine("========================");
    Console.WriteLine("Press any key to continue");
    Console.ReadLine();

    Console.WriteLine("Adding data to the tables with ADO");
    using (var command = new SqlCommand(ADO_Inserts(), connection))
    {
        int rowsAffected = command.ExecuteNonQuery();
        Console.WriteLine($"Number of rows affected: {rowsAffected}");
    }
    Console.WriteLine("========================");
    Console.WriteLine("Press any key to continue");
    Console.ReadLine();

    Console.WriteLine("Updating data with ADO");
    using (var command = new SqlCommand(ADO_UpdateJoin(), connection))
    {
        command.Parameters.AddWithValue("@csharpParmDepartmentName",
        "Accounting");
        int rowsAffected = command.ExecuteNonQuery();
        Console.WriteLine($"Number of rows affected: {rowsAffected}");
    }
    Console.WriteLine("========================");
    Console.WriteLine("Press any key to continue");
    Console.ReadLine();

    Console.WriteLine("Deleting data from tables with ADO");
    using (var command = new SqlCommand(ADO_DeleteJoin(), connection))
    {
        command.Parameters.AddWithValue("@csharpParmDepartmentName",
        "Legal");
        int rowsAffected = command.ExecuteNonQuery();
        Console.WriteLine($"Number of rows affected: {rowsAffected}");
    }
    Console.WriteLine("========================");
    Console.WriteLine("Press any key to continue");
    Console.ReadLine();

    Console.WriteLine("Reading data from tables with ADO");
    using (var command = new SqlCommand(ADO_SelectEmployees(),
    connection))
    {
        using (SqlDataReader reader = command.ExecuteReader())
        {
            while (reader.Read())
            {
                Console.WriteLine($"{reader.GetGuid(0)} , " +
                    $"{reader.GetString(1)} , " +
                    $"{reader.GetInt32(2)} , " +
                    $"{reader?.GetString(3)} ," +
                    $"{reader?.GetString(4)}");
            }
        }
    }
```

```
                Console.WriteLine("=======================");
                Console.WriteLine("Press any key to continue");
                Console.ReadLine();
            }
        }
        catch (SqlException ex)
        {
            Console.WriteLine(ex.ToString());
        }

}

static string ADO_CreateTables()
{
    return @"
        DROP TABLE IF EXISTS tabEmployee;
        DROP TABLE IF EXISTS tabDepartment;  -- Drop parent table last.

        CREATE TABLE tabDepartment
        (
            DepartmentCode   nchar(4)          not null    PRIMARY KEY,
            DepartmentName   nvarchar(128)     not null
        );

        CREATE TABLE tabEmployee
        (
            EmployeeGuid     uniqueIdentifier  not null  default NewId()
            PRIMARY KEY,
            EmployeeName     nvarchar(128)     not null,
            EmployeeLevel    int               not null,
            DepartmentCode   nchar(4)                 null
            REFERENCES tabDepartment (DepartmentCode)  -- (REFERENCES would be
            //disallowed on temporary tables.)
        );
    ";
}

static string ADO_Inserts()
{
    return @"
        -- The company has these departments.
        INSERT INTO tabDepartment (DepartmentCode, DepartmentName)
        VALUES
            ('acct', 'Accounting'),
            ('hres', 'Human Resources'),
            ('legl', 'Legal');

        -- The company has these employees, each in one department.
        INSERT INTO tabEmployee (EmployeeName, EmployeeLevel, DepartmentCode)
        VALUES
            ('Alison'  , 19, 'acct'),
            ('Barbara' , 17, 'hres'),
            ('Carol'   , 21, 'acct'),
            ('Deborah' , 24, 'legl'),
```

```
                    ('Elle'     , 15, null);
        ";
    }

    static string ADO_UpdateJoin()
    {
        return @"
            DECLARE @DName1  nvarchar(128) = @csharpParmDepartmentName;
            --'Accounting';

            -- Promote everyone in one department (see @parm...).
            UPDATE empl
            SET
                empl.EmployeeLevel += 1
            FROM
                tabEmployee    as empl
            INNER JOIN
                tabDepartment as dept ON dept.DepartmentCode = empl.DepartmentCode
            WHERE
                dept.DepartmentName = @DName1;
        ";
    }

    static string ADO_DeleteJoin()
    {
        return @"
            DECLARE @DName2  nvarchar(128);
            SET @DName2 = @csharpParmDepartmentName;   --'Legal';

            -- Right size the Legal department.
            DELETE empl
            FROM
                tabEmployee    as empl
            INNER JOIN
                tabDepartment as dept ON dept.DepartmentCode = empl.DepartmentCode
            WHERE
                dept.DepartmentName = @DName2

            -- Disband the Legal department.
            DELETE tabDepartment
                WHERE DepartmentName = @DName2;
        ";
    }

    static string ADO_SelectEmployees()
    {
        return @"
            -- Look at all the final Employees.
            SELECT
                empl.EmployeeGuid,
                empl.EmployeeName,
                empl.EmployeeLevel,
                empl.DepartmentCode,
                dept.DepartmentName
```

```
        FROM
            tabEmployee     as empl
        LEFT OUTER JOIN
            tabDepartment as dept ON dept.DepartmentCode = empl.DepartmentCode
        ORDER BY
            EmployeeName;
        ";
    }
  }
}
```

As you can see in this example, the code that you use for connecting to your Azure SQL Database is the same that you use for connecting to a database hosted in an on-premises SQL Server instance. Migrating your code for connecting from your on-premises database to a cloud-based SQL database is a straightforward process.

> **NEED MORE REVIEW?** **AUTHENTICATION**
>
> In the previous example, you connected to your Azure SQL Database using SQL authentication. Also, Azure SQL Database services allow you to authenticate using Azure Active Directory users. You can review how to configure the integration between Azure SQL Database and Azure Active Directory by consulting the Microsoft Docs article "Tutorial: Secure a Single or Pooled Database" at *https://docs.microsoft.com/en-us/azure/sql-database/sql-database-security-tutorial*.

Skill 3.4: Develop solutions that use blob storage

Storing information in SQL or NoSQL databases is a great way to save that information when you need to save schemaless documents or if you need to guarantee the integrity of the data. The drawback of these services is that they are relatively expensive for storing data that doesn't have such requirements.

Azure blob storage allows you to store information that doesn't fit the characteristics of SQL and NoSQL storage in the cloud. This information can be images, videos, office documents, or more. The Azure Blob Storage still provides high availability features that make it an ideal service for storing a large amount of data but at a lower price compared to the other data storage solutions that we reviewed earlier in this chapter.

This skill covers how to:

- Move blob storage items between Storage Accounts or containers
- Set and retrieve properties and metadata
- Implement blob leasing
- Implement data archiving and retention

Move items in Blob storage between Storage Accounts or containers

When you are working with Azure Blob storage, there can be situations in which you may need to move blobs from one Storage Account to another or between containers. For particular situations, you can use the azCopy command-line tool for performing these tasks. This tool is ideal for doing incremental copy scenarios or copying an entire account into another account. You can use the following command for copying blob items between containers in different Storage Accounts:

```
azcopy copy <URL_Source_Item><Source_SASToken> <URL_Target_Container><Target_SASToken>
```

Although using the azCopy command may be appropriate for some situations, you may need to get more fine-grained control of the items that you need to move between containers or event-Storage Accounts. The following example written in .NET Core shows how to move a blob item between two containers in the same Storage Account and how to move a blob item between two containers in different Storage Accounts. Before you can run this example, you need to create two Storage Accounts with two blob containers. For the sake of simplicity, you should create the two containers with the same name in the two different Storage Accounts. Also, you need to upload two control files as blob items to one of the containers in one Storage Account:

1. Open Visual Studio Code and create a folder for your project.
2. In the Visual Studio Code Window, open a new terminal.
3. Use the following command to install NuGet packages:
   ```
   dotnet add package <NuGet_package_name>
   ```
4. Install the following NuGet packages:
   - *Microsoft.Azure.Storage.Blob*
   - *Microsoft.Azure.Storage.Common*
   - *Microsoft.Extensions.Configuration*
   - *Microsoft.Extensions.Configuration.Binder*
   - *Microsoft.Extensions.Configuration.Json*
5. In the project folder, create a new JSON file and name it **AppSettings.json**. Copy the content from Listing 3-14 to the JSON file.
6. Create a C# class file and name it **AppSettings.cs**.
7. Replace the contents of the *AppSettings.cs* file with the contents of Listing 3-15. Change the name of the namespace to match your project's name.
8. Create a C# class file and name it **Common.cs**.
9. Replace the contents of the *Common.cs* file with the contents of Listing 3-16.
10. Change the name of the namespace to match your project's name.

11. Replace the contents of the *Programm.cs* file with the contents of Listing 3-17. Change the name of the namespace to match your project's name.

12. Edit your *.csproj* project file and add the following code inside the *ItemGroup* section:

```
<None Update="AppSettings.json">
    <CopyToOutputDirectory>PreserveNewest</CopyToOutputDirectory>
</None>
```

13. At this point, you can set some breakpoints in the *Program.cs* file to see, step by step, how the code moves the blob items between the different containers and Storage Accounts.

14. In the Visual Studio Window, press F5 to build and run your code. You can use the Azure Portal or the Microsoft Azure Storage Explorer desktop application to review how your blob items change their locations.

LISTING 3-14 AppSettings.json configuration file

```json
{
    "SourceSASToken": "<SASToken_from_your_first_storage_account>",
    "SourceAccountName": "<name_of_your_first_storage_account>",
    "SourceContainerName": "<source_container_name>",
    "DestinationSASToken": "<SASToken_from_your_second_storage_account>",
    "DestinationAccountName": "<name_of_your_second_storage_account>",
    "DestinationContainerName": "<destination_container_name>"
}
```

LISTING 3-15 AppSettings.cs C# class

```csharp
//C# .NET Core

using Microsoft.Extensions.Configuration;

namespace ch3_4_1
{
    public class AppSettings
    {
        public string SourceSASToken { get; set; }
        public string SourceAccountName { get; set; }
        public string SourceContainerName { get; set; }
        public string DestinationSASToken { get; set; }
        public string DestinationAccountName { get; set; }
        public string DestinationContainerName { get; set; }

        public static AppSettings LoadAppSettings()
        {
            IConfigurationRoot configRoot = new ConfigurationBuilder()
                .AddJsonFile("AppSettings.json",false)
                .Build();
            AppSettings appSettings = configRoot.Get<AppSettings>();
            return appSettings;
        }
    }
}
```

LISTING 3-16 Common.cs C# class

```
//C# .NET Core

using System;
using Microsoft.Azure.Storage;
using Microsoft.Azure.Storage.Auth;
using Microsoft.Azure.Storage.Blob;

namespace ch3_4_1
{
    public class Common
    {
        public static CloudBlobClient CreateBlobClientStorageFromSAS(string SAStoken,
        string accountName)
        {
            CloudStorageAccount storageAccount;
            CloudBlobClient blobClient;
            try
            {
                bool useHttps = true;
                StorageCredentials storageCredentials =
                new StorageCredentials(SAStoken);
                storageAccount = new CloudStorageAccount(storageCredentials,
                accountName, null, useHttps);
                blobClient = storageAccount.CreateCloudBlobClient();
            }
            catch (System.Exception)
            {
                throw;
            }

            return blobClient;

        }
    }
}
```

In the following Listing, portions of the code that are significant to the process of working with the Azure Blob Storage service are shown in bold.

LISTING 3-17 Program.cs C# class

```
//C# .NET Core

using System.Threading.Tasks;
using System;
using Microsoft.Azure.Storage;
using Microsoft.Azure.Storage.Blob;

namespace ch3_4_1
{
    class Program
    {
```

```csharp
static void Main(string[] args)
{
    Console.WriteLine("Move items between Containers Demo!");
    Task.Run(async () => await StartContainersDemo()).Wait();
    Console.WriteLine("Move items between Storage Accounts Demo!");
    Task.Run(async () => await StartAccountDemo()).Wait();
}

public static async Task StartContainersDemo()
{
    string sourceBlobFileName = "<first_control_filename>";
    AppSettings appSettings = AppSettings.LoadAppSettings();

    //Get a cloud client for the source Storage Account
    CloudBlobClient sourceClient = Common.CreateBlobClientStorageFromSAS
    (appSettings.SourceSASToken, appSettings.SourceAccountName);

    //Get a reference for each container
    var sourceContainerReference = sourceClient.GetContainerReference
    (appSettings.SourceContainerName);
    var destinationContainerReference = sourceClient.GetContainerReference
    (appSettings.DestinationContainerName);

    //Get a reference for the source blob
    var sourceBlobReference = sourceContainerReference.GetBlockBlobReference
    (sourceBlobFileName);
    var destinationBlobReference = destinationContainerReference.GetBlockBlob
    Reference(sourceBlobFileName);

    //Move the blob from the source container to the destination container
    await destinationBlobReference.StartCopyAsync(sourceBlobReference);
    await sourceBlobReference.DeleteAsync();
}

public static async Task StartAccountDemo()
{
    string sourceBlobFileName = "<second_control_filename>";
    AppSettings appSettings = AppSettings.LoadAppSettings();

    //Get a cloud client for the source Storage Account
    CloudBlobClient sourceClient = Common.CreateBlobClientStorageFromSAS
    (appSettings.SourceSASToken, appSettings.SourceAccountName);
    //Get a cloud client for the destination Storage Account
    CloudBlobClient destinationClient = Common.CreateBlobClientStorageFromSAS
    (appSettings.DestinationSASToken, appSettings.DestinationAccountName);

    //Get a reference for each container
    var sourceContainerReference = sourceClient.GetContainerReference(appSettings.
    SourceContainerName);
    var destinationContainerReference = destinationClient.GetContainerReference
    (appSettings.DestinationContainerName);

    //Get a reference for the source blob
    var sourceBlobReference = sourceContainerReference.GetBlockBlobReference
    (sourceBlobFileName);
```

```
        var destinationBlobReference = destinationContainerReference.
        GetBlockBlobReference(sourceBlobFileName);

        //Move the blob from the source container to the destination container
        await destinationBlobReference.StartCopyAsync(sourceBlobReference);
        await sourceBlobReference.DeleteAsync();
      }
    }
}
```

In this example, you made two different movements—one between containers in the same Storage Account and another between containers in different Storage Accounts. As you can see in the code shown previously in Listing 3-17, the high-level procedure for moving blob items between containers is

1. Create a *CloudBlobClient* instance for each Storage Account that is involved in the blob item movement.

2. Create a reference for each container. If you need to move a blob item between containers in a different Storage Account, you need to use the **CloudBlobClient** object that represents each Storage Account.

3. Create a reference for each blob item. You need a reference to the source blob item because this is the item that you are going to move. You use the destination blob item reference for performing the actual copy operation.

4. Once you are done with the copy, you can delete the source blob item by using the *DeleteAsync()* method.

Although this code is quite straightforward, it has a critical problem that you can solve in the following sections. If someone else modifies the source blob item while the write operation is pending, the copy operation fails with an HTTP status code 412.

> **NEED MORE REVIEW?   CROSS-ACCOUNT BLOB COPY**
>
> You can review the details of how the asynchronous copy between Storage Accounts works by reading this MSDN article: "Introducing Asynchronous Cross-Account Copy Blob" at *https://blogs.msdn.microsoft.com/windowsazurestorage/2012/06/12/introducing-asynchronous-cross-account-copy-blob/*.

Set and retrieve properties and metadata

When you work with Azure Storage services, you can work with some additional information assigned to your blobs. This additional information is stored in the form of system properties and user-defined metadata:

- **System properties**   This is information that the Storage services automatically adds to each storage resource. You can modify some of these system properties, while others are read-only. Some of these system properties correspond with some HTTP headers.

You don't need to worry about maintaining these system properties because the Azure Storage client libraries automatically make any needed modification for you.

- **User-defined metadata**   You can assign key-value pairs to an Azure Storage resource. These metadata are for your own purposes and don't affect the behavior of the Azure Storage service. You need to take care of updating the value of these metadata according to your needs.

Listing 3-18 shows how to create a new container and get a list of some system properties assigned automatically to the container when you create it.

LISTING 3-18 Getting system properties from a storage resource

```
//C# .NET Core
using System;
using System.Threading.Tasks;
using Microsoft.Azure.Storage.Blob;

namespace ch3_4_2
{
    class Program
    {
        static void Main(string[] args)
        {
            Console.WriteLine("Getting System properties Demo!");

            AppSettings appSettings = AppSettings.LoadAppSettings();

            //Create a CloudBlobClient for working with the Storage Account
            CloudBlobClient blobClient = Common.CreateBlobClientStorageFromSAS
            (appSettings.SASToken, appSettings.AccountName);

            //Get a container reference for the new container.
            CloudBlobContainer container = blobClient.
            GetContainerReference("container-demo");

            //Create the container if not already exists
            container.CreateIfNotExistsAsync();

            //You need to fetch the container properties before getting their values
            container.FetchAttributes();
            Console.WriteLine($"Properties for container {container.StorageUri.
            PrimaryUri.ToString()}");
            System.Console.WriteLine($"ETag: {container.Properties.ETag}");
            System.Console.WriteLine($"LastModifiedUTC: {container.Properties.
            LastModified.ToString()}");
            System.Console.WriteLine($"Lease status: {container.Properties.LeaseStatus.
            ToString()}");
            System.Console.WriteLine();
        }
    }
}
```

As you can see in the previous code in Listing 3-18, you need to use the *FetchAttributes()* or *FetchAttributesAsync()* before you can read the properties from the container, stored in the *Properties* property of the *CloudBlobContainer* or *CloudBlockBlob* objects. If you get null values for *system* properties, ensure that you called the *FetchAttributes()* method before accessing the *system* property.

Working with user-defined metadata is quite similar to working with *system* properties. The main difference is that you can add your custom key-pairs to the storage resource. These user-defined metadata are stored in the *Metadata* property of the storage resource. Listing 3-19 extends the example in Listing 3-18 and shows how to set and read user-defined metadata in the container that you created in Listing 3-18.

LISTING 3-19 Setting user-defined metadata

```
//C# .NET Core
//Add some metadata to the container that we created before
          container.Metadata.Add("department", "Technical");
          container.Metadata["category"] = "Knowledge Base";
          container.Metadata.Add("docType", "pdfDocuments");

          //Save the containers metadata in Azure
          container.SetMetadata();

          //List newly added metadata. We need to fetch all attributes before being
          //able to read if not, we could get nulls or weird values
          container.FetchAttributes();

          System.Console.WriteLine("Container's metadata:");
          foreach (var item in container.Metadata)
          {
              System.Console.WriteLine($"\tKey: {item.Key}");
              System.Console.WriteLine($"\tValue: {item.Value}");
          }
```

You can find a complete list of system properties in the Microsoft.Azure.Storage.Blob .NET client reference at *https://docs.microsoft.com/en-us/dotnet/api/microsoft.azure.storage.blob. blobcontainerproperties*. The *BlobContainerProperties* and *BlobProperties* classes are responsible for storing the system properties for the storage resources in a Blob Storage account.

You can also view and edit system properties and user-defined metadata by using the Azure Portal, using the Properties and Metadata sections in the Settings section of your container, or clicking on the ellipsis next to the blob item and selecting the Blob Properties option in the contextual menu.

Implement blob leasing

When you are working with the Blob Storage service—in which several users or process can simultaneously access the same Storage Account—you can face a problem when two users or processes are trying to access the same blob. Azure provides a leasing mechanism for solving this kind of situation. A lease is a short block that the blob service sets on a blob or container item for granting exclusive access to that item. When you acquire a lease to a blob, you get exclusive write and delete access to that blob. If you acquire a lease in a container, you get exclusive delete access to the container.

When you acquire a lease for a storage item, you need to include the active lease ID on each write operation that you want to perform on the blob with the lease. You can choose the duration for the lease time when you request it. This duration can last from 15 to 60 seconds or forever. Each lease can be in one of the following five states:

- **Available**   The lease is unlocked, and you can acquire a new lease.
- **Leased**   There is a lease granted to the resource and the lease is locked. You can acquire a new lease if you use the same ID that you got when you created the lease. You can also release, change, renew, or break the lease when it is in this status.
- **Expired**   The duration configured for the lease has expired. When you have a lease on this status, you can acquire, renew, release, or break the lease.
- **Breaking**   You have broken the lease, but it's still locked until the break period expires. In this status, you can release or break the lease.
- **Broken**   The break period has expired, and the lease has been broken. In this status, you can acquire, release, and break a lease. You need to break a lease when the process that acquired the lease finished suddenly, such as when network connectivity issues or any other condition results in the lease not being released correctly. In these situations, you may end up with an orphaned lease, and you cannot write or delete the blob with the orphaned lease. In this situation, the only solution is to break the lease. You may also want to break a lease when you need to force the release of the lease manually.

You use the Azure Portal for managing the lease status of a container or blob item, or you use it programmatically with the Azure Blob Storage client SDK. In the example shown in Listings 3-14 to 3-17, in which we reviewed how to move items between containers or Storage Accounts, we saw that if some other process or user modifies the blob while our process is copying the data, we get an error. You can avoid that situation by acquiring a lease for the blob that you want to move. Listing 3-20 shows the modification that you need to add to the code in Listing 3-17 so that you can acquire a lease for the blob item.

LISTING 3-20 Program.cs modification

```
//C# .NET Core

//Add lines in bold to StartContainersDemo method on Listing 3-18
public static async Task StartContainersDemo()
        {
            string sourceBlobFileName = "prueba.pdf";
            AppSettings appSettings = AppSettings.LoadAppSettings();

            //Get a cloud client for the source Storage Account
```

```
CloudBlobClient sourceClient = Common.CreateBlobClientStorageFromSAS
(appSettings.SourceSASToken, appSettings.SourceAccountName);

//Get a reference for each container
var sourceContainerReference = sourceClient.GetContainerReference
(appSettings.SourceContainerName);
var destinationContainerReference = sourceClient.GetContainerReference
(appSettings.DestinationContainerName);

//Get a reference for the source blob
var sourceBlobReference = sourceContainerReference.GetBlockBlobReference
(sourceBlobFileName);
var destinationBlobReference = destinationContainerReference.GetBlockBlob
Reference(sourceBlobFileName);

//Get the lease status of the source blob
await sourceBlobReference.FetchAttributesAsync();
System.Console.WriteLine($"Lease status: {sourceBlobReference.Properties.
LeaseStatus}" +
        $"\tstate: {sourceBlobReference.Properties.LeaseState}" +
        $"\tduration: {sourceBlobReference.Properties.LeaseDuration}");

//Acquire an infinite lease. If you want to set a duration for the lease use
//TimeSpan.FromSeconds(seconds). Remember that seconds should be a value
//between 15 and 60.
//We need to save the lease ID automatically generated by Azure for release
//the lease later.
string leaseID = Guid.NewGuid().ToString();
await sourceBlobReference.AcquireLeaseAsync(null, leaseID);

await sourceBlobReference.FetchAttributesAsync();
System.Console.WriteLine($"Lease status: {sourceBlobReference.Properties.
LeaseStatus}" +
        $"\tstate: {sourceBlobReference.Properties.LeaseState}" +
        $"\tduration: {sourceBlobReference.Properties.LeaseDuration}");

//Move the blob from the source container to the destination container
await destinationBlobReference.StartCopyAsync(sourceBlobReference);
await sourceBlobReference.DeleteAsync();
await sourceBlobReference.ReleaseLeaseAsync(AccessCondition.
GenerateLeaseCondition(leaseID));

await sourceBlobReference.FetchAttributesAsync();
System.Console.WriteLine($"Lease status: {sourceBlobReference.Properties.
LeaseStatus}" +
        $"\tstate: {sourceBlobReference.Properties.LeaseState}" +
        $"\tduration: {sourceBlobReference.Properties.LeaseDuration}");

}
```

As you can see in the previous example, you use the *AcquireLeaseAsync()* method to acquire the lease for the blob. In this case, you create an infinite lease, so you need to release the lease using *ReleaseLeaseAsync* method.

> **NEED MORE REVIEW?** **LEASING BLOBS AND CONTAINERS**
>
> You can review the details of how leasing works for blobs and containers by consulting the following articles:
>
> - **Lease Blob** *https://docs.microsoft.com/en-us/rest/api/storageservices/lease-blob*
>
> - **Lease Container** *https://docs.microsoft.com/en-us/rest/api/storageservices/ lease-container*

Implement data archiving and retention

When you are working with data, the requirements for accessing the data changes during the lifetime of the data. Data that has been recently placed on your storage system usually will be accessed more frequently and requires faster access than older data. If you are using the same type of storage for all your data, that means you are using storage for data that is rarely accessed. If your storage is based on SSD disk or any other technology that provides proper performance levels, this means that you can be potentially wasting expensive storage for data that is rarely accessed. A solution to this situation is to move less-frequently accessed data to a cheaper storage system. The drawback of this solution is that you need to implement a system for tracking the last time data has been accessed and moving it to the right storage system.

Azure Blob Storage provides to you with the ability to set different levels of access to your data. These different access levels, or tiers, provide different levels of performance when accessing the data. Each different access level has a different price. Following are the available access tiers:

- **Hot** You use this tier for data that you need to access more frequently. This is the default tier that you use when you create a new Storage Account.

- **Cool** You can use this tier for data that is less frequently accessed and is stored for at least 30 days.

- **Archive** You use this tier for storing data that is rarely accessed and is stored for at least 180 days. This access tier is available only at the blob level. You cannot configure a Storage Account with this access tier.

The different access tiers have the following performance and pricing implications:

- Cool tier provides slightly lower availability, reflected in the service-level agreement (SLA) because of lower storage costs; however, it has higher access costs.

- Hot and cool tiers have similar characteristics in terms of time-to-access and throughput.

- Archive storage is offline storage. It has the lowest storage cost rates but has higher access costs.
- The lower the storage costs, the higher the access costs.
- You can use storage tiering only on General Purpose v2 (GPv2) Storage Accounts.
- If you want to use storage tiering with a General Purpose v1 (GPv1) Storage Account, you need to convert to a GPv2 Storage Account.

Moving between the different access tier is a transparent process for the user, but it has some implications in terms of pricing. In general, when you are moving from a warmer tier to a cooler tier—hot to cool or hot to archive—you are charged for the write operations to the destination tier. When you move from a cooler tier to a warmer tier—from the archive to cold or from cold to hot—you are charged for the read operations from the source tier. Another essential thing to bear in mind is how the data is moved when you change your data tier from archive to any other access tier. Because data in the archive tier is saved into offline storage, when you move data out of the access tier, the storage service needs to move the data back to online storage. This process is known as blob rehydration and can take up to 15 hours.

If you don't manually configure the access tier for a blob, it inherits the access from its container or Storage Account. Although you can change the access tier manually using the Azure Portal, this process creates an administrative overload that could also lead to human errors. Instead of manually monitoring the different criteria for moving a blob from one tier to another, you can implement policies that make that movement based on the criteria that you define. You use these policies for defining the lifecycle management of your data. You can create these lifecycle management policies by using the Azure Portal, Azure PowerShell, Azure CLI, or REST API.

A lifecycle management policy is a JSON document in which you define several rules that you want to apply to the different containers or blob types. Each rule consists of a filter set and an action set.

- **Filter set**   The filter set limits the actions to only a group of items that match the filter criteria.
- **Action set**   The action sets define the actions that are performed on the items that matched the filter.

The following procedure for adding a new policy using the Azure Portal:

1. Sign in to the management portal (*http://portal.azure.com*).
2. In the Search box at the top of the Azure Portal, type the name of your Storage Account.
3. On the Blob service section, click Lifecycle Management.
4. Copy the content from Listing 3-21 and paste it into the Lifecycle Management panel.
5. Click the Save button on the top-left corner of the panel.

LISTING 3-21 Lifecycle management policy definition

```json
{
    "rules": [
        {
            "enabled": true,
            "name": "rule1",
            "type": "Lifecycle",
            "definition": {
                "actions": {
                    "baseBlob": {
                        "tierToCool": {
                            "daysAfterModificationGreaterThan": 30
                        },
                        "tierToArchive": {
                            "daysAfterModificationGreaterThan": 90
                        },
                        "delete": {
                            "daysAfterModificationGreaterThan": 2555
                        }
                    },
                    "snapshot": {
                        "delete": {
                            "daysAfterCreationGreaterThan": 90
                        }
                    }
                },
                "filters": {
                    "blobTypes": [
                        "blockBlob"
                    ],
                    "prefixMatch": [
                        "container-a"
                    ]
                }
            }
        }
    ]
}
```

The previous policy applies to all blobs under the container named *container-a*, as stated by the *prefixMatch* in the *filters* section. In the *actions* sections, you can see the following things:

- Blobs that are not modified in 30 days or more will be moved to the cool tier.
- Blobs that are not modified in 90 days or more will be moved to the archive tier.
- Blobs that are not modified in 2,555 days or more will be deleted from the Storage Account.

Snapshots that are older than 90 days will be also deleted. The lifecycle management engine process the policies every 24 hours. This means that it is possible that you won't see your changes reflected on your Storage Account until several hours after you made the changes.

Chapter summary

- Azure Table Storage provides a NoSQL schemaless storage system, which allows your applications to work with documents called entities.
- Each entity can have up to 253 properties.
- Entities are stored in tables.
- You can use the Table API for Cosmos DB for accessing Azure Table Storage and Cosmos DB services.
- The *PartitionKey* system property defines the partition where the entity will be stored.
- Choosing the correct *PartitionKey* is critical for achieving the right performance level.
- You cannot create additional indexes in an Azure Table.
- You can bypass the custom index creating limitation by implementing some partitioning patterns.
- Cosmos DB is a premium storage service that provides low-latency access to data distributed across the globe.
- You can access Cosmo DB using different APIs: SQL, Table, Gremlin (Graph), MongoDB, and Cassandra.
- You can create your custom indexes in Cosmos DB.
- You can choose the property that is used as the partition key.
- You should avoid selecting partition keys that create too many or too few logical partitions.
- A logical partition has a limit of 10GB of storage.
- Consistency levels define how the data is replicated between the different regions in a Cosmos DB account.
- There are five consistency levels: strong, bounded staleness, session, consistent prefix, and eventual.
- Strong consistency level provides a higher level of consistency but also has a higher latency.
- Eventual consistency level provides lower latency and lower data consistency.

- Azure SQL Database offers a managed relational storage solution for your application.

- You can purchase resources for your database using two different purchase models: DTU-based and vCore-based.

- You can save money by putting several databases with unpredictable workloads into an elastic pool.

- If you need to migrate an on-premises SQL Server database, you can achieve a seamless migration using SQL Database–managed instances.

- You can move blob items between containers in the same account storage or containers in different account storages.

- Azure Blob Storage service offers three different access tiers with different prices for storage and accessing data.

- You can move less frequently accessed data to cool or archive access tiers to save money.

- You can automatically manage the movement between access tiers by implementing lifecycle management policies.

Thought experiment

In this thought experiment, you can demonstrate your skills and knowledge about the topics covered in this chapter. You can find the answers to this thought experiment in the next section.

You are developing a web application that needs to work with information with a structure that can change during the lifetime of the development process. You need to query this information using different criteria. You need to ensure that your application returns the results of the queries as fast as possible. You don't require your application to be globally available.

With this information in mind, answer the following questions:

1. Which technology should you use? You should select the most cost-effective solution.

2. How many indexes should you create in your storage system?

Thought experiment answers

This section contains the solutions to the thought experiment.

1. You should use Azure Table Storage for your application. This is a cost-effective solution that allows you to work with schemaless documents, allowing you to change the structure of your documents during the development process and minimizing the impact on your data.

2. Because you should use Azure Table Storage, you cannot define your custom indexes. You can bypass this limitation by using partitioning and implementing the Index Entities pattern.

## CHAPTER 4

Implement Azure security

Regardless of the application, most of them have a standard requirement—protect the information that it manages. When we talk about security, we need to think in the five dimensions of information security awareness: integrity, availability, confidentiality, authorization, and no-repudiation. Each of these dimensions is useful for evaluating the different risks and the countermeasures that you need to implement for mitigating the associated risks.

Implementing the appropriate security mechanism on your application can be tedious and potentially error prone. Azure offers several mechanisms for adding security measures to your applications, controlling the different security aspects for accessing your data, and controlling the services that depend on your applications.

Skills covered in this chapter:

- Skill 4.1: Implement authentication
- Skill 4.2: Implement access control
- Skill 4.3: Implement secure data solutions

Skill 4.1: Implement authentication

When a user wants to access your application, the user needs to prove that she is who she claims to be. Authentication is the action that the user performs to prove his or her identity. The user proves his or her identity using information known only to the user. An authentication system needs to address how to protect that information so only the appropriate user can access it while nobody else—not even the authorization system—can access it. A solution for this problem is to allow the user to access his or her data by using two different mechanisms for proving his or her identity— information that only the user knows and showing something, a token, only the user has. The approach is known as multifactor authentication.

Azure provides a secure mechanism for integrating authentication into your applications. You can use single-factor or multifactor authentication systems without worrying about the intricate details of implementing this kind of system.

Implement authentication by using certificates, forms-based authentication, or tokens

The authentication process requires the user to provide evidence that the user is who he or she claims to be. In the real world, you can find multiple examples of authentication; for example, every time that you show your driver's license to a police officer, you are actually authenticating against the police officer. In the digital world, this authentication happens by providing some information that only you know, such as a secret word (a password), a digital certificate, or any kind of token that only you possess.

You have a range of options for implementing such an authentication mechanism in your application. Each implementation has its pros and cons, and the appropriate authentication mechanism depends on the level of security that you require for your application.

The most basic way of authenticating a user is form-based authentication. When you use this mechanism, you need to program a web form that asks the user for a username and a password. Once the user submits the form, the information in the form is compared to the values stored in your storage system. This storage system can be a relational database, a NoSQL database, or even a simple file with different formats stored on a server. If the information provided by the user matches the information stored in your system, the application sends a cookie to the user's browser. This cookie stores a key or some type of ID for authenticating subsequent requests to access your application without repeatedly asking the user for his or her username and password.

The main drawback of using this authentication method for your application is that data travels from the user's browser to the server in plain text, meaning other malicious users could intercept the communications and get the password quickly. You can mitigate this risk by forcing your application and users to use HTTPS only. The following example shows how to implement form-based authentication. The example uses the template provided in Visual Studio for deploying an MVC ASP.NET application:

1. Open Visual Studio 2017 on your computer.
2. Click on File > New > Project.

3. In the New Project window, in the tree control on the left side of the window, navigate to Installed > Visual C# > Web.

4. In the list of templates in the center of the New Project window, select the template ASP. NET Web Application (.NET Framework).

5. On the bottom side of the New Project window, provide a name for the project and the solution. Also, choose a location for storing the project.

6. Click the OK button in the bottom-right corner of the New Project window.

7. In the New ASP.NET Web Application window, select MVC from the list of templates in the center of the window.

8. Ensure that the MVC option is checked under Add Folders And Core References For located below the templates.

9. Click the Change Authentication button at the middle-right of the window.

10. In the Change Authentication window, select Individual User Accounts.

11. Click OK.

12. On the New ASP.NET Web Application window, click OK.

At this point, you have created a basic ASP.NET Web Application configured for using form-based authentication. Also, this web application has configured other authentication mechanisms that we are going to review later in this section.

Now you can check how the authentication in this application works:

1. Press F5 to run the project.

2. In the top-right corner of your application's web browser, click Register.

3. On the Register form, enter an email address and password.

4. Click on the Register button at the bottom of the form.

5. Once you have registered, you are automatically logged on, and you can log off and log in again to ensure everything works properly.

This example is based on the ASP.NET Identity framework. This library allows you to quickly implement different authorization methods and control other essential aspects of the identity management operations that you need to perform on your application.

When you need to implement form-based authentication, you need to deal with three key components:

- **Authentication forms**   You need to provide the user with the appropriate web form, not only for providing the user's credentials but also for resetting the user's password in case the user forgot it. You might also need a form that allows new users to register to your application.

- **Credentials storage**   You need to store the passwords of your registered users. You use the password provided by the user to compare with your stored password. If the values match, then the user is authenticated.

- **Credentials management** This is the piece of your code that makes the comparison between the value provided by the user and the value that you have stored in the application's credential storage. You usually never store the user's password in plain text. Instead, you use one of the available hashing algorithms for storing the hashed value of the real password. This component performs all these hashing operations, as well as password resets and new user registration.

Because you implemented the Model-View-Controller pattern in this example, as you selected the MVC template in step 7 of the previous procedure, you need to use views for creating the different forms that you need for presenting the necessary information to the user. The general operations that the user needs to perform are logging in, registering, and recovering a lost password. You use the following views for providing these functionalities to the users:

- **Login** Managed by the *Login.cshtml* view.
- **Register** Managed by the *Register.cshtml* view.
- **Forgot the password** Managed by the *ForgotPassword.cshtml* view.

You can review the content of these views in the Visual Studio Solution Explorer; navigate to the Views > Accounts folder inside your project folder. Listing 4-1 shows the content of the *Login.cshtml* view. You can review this listing to see how to construct the login form to provide the necessary information to the controller. The bold parts in Listing 4-1 show the significant code for implementing the login form:

LISTING 4-1 Login.cshtml

```
// C#. ASP.NET.
@using ch4_1_1.Models
@model LoginViewModel
@{
    ViewBag.Title = "Log in";
}

<h2>@ViewBag.Title.</h2>
<div class="row">
    <div class="col-md-8">
        <section id="loginForm">
            @using (Html.BeginForm("Login", "Account", new { ReturnUrl = ViewBag.
            ReturnUrl }, FormMethod.Post, new { @class = "form-horizontal", role =
            "form" }))
            {
                @Html.AntiForgeryToken()
                <h4>Use a local account to log in.</h4>
                <hr />
                @Html.ValidationSummary(true, "", new { @class = "text-danger" })
                <div class="form-group">
                    @Html.LabelFor(m => m.Email, new { @class = "col-md-2 control-label" })
                    <div class="col-md-10">
                        @Html.TextBoxFor(m => m.Email, new { @class = "form-control" })
                        @Html.ValidationMessageFor(m => m.Email, "", new { @class =
                        "text-danger" })
```

```
                    </div>
                </div>
                <div class="form-group">
                    @Html.LabelFor(m => m.Password, new { @class = "col-md-2 control-
                    label" })
                    <div class="col-md-10">
                        @Html.PasswordFor(m => m.Password, new { @class = "form-control" })
                        @Html.ValidationMessageFor(m => m.Password, "", new { @class =
                        "text-danger" })
                    </div>
                </div>
                <div class="form-group">
                    <div class="col-md-offset-2 col-md-10">
                        <div class="checkbox">
                            @Html.CheckBoxFor(m => m.RememberMe)
                            @Html.LabelFor(m => m.RememberMe)
                        </div>
                    </div>
                </div>
                <div class="form-group">
                    <div class="col-md-offset-2 col-md-10">
                        <input type="submit" value="Log in" class="btn btn-default" />
                    </div>
                </div>
                <p>
                    @Html.ActionLink("Register as a new user", "Register")
                </p>
                @* Enable this once you have account confirmation enabled for password
                reset functionality
                    <p>
                        @Html.ActionLink("Forgot your password?", "ForgotPassword")
                    </p>*@
            }
        </section>
    </div>
    <div class="col-md-4">
        <section id="socialLoginForm">
            @Html.Partial("_ExternalLoginsListPartial", new ExternalLoginListViewModel
            { ReturnUrl = ViewBag.ReturnUrl })
        </section>
    </div>
</div>
@section Scripts {
    @Scripts.Render("~/bundles/jqueryval")
}
```

When you review the code in Listing 4-1, you need to focus on some key points. You used model binding for sending the information to the web application. In this example, the *LoginViewModel* model is used:

```
@model LoginViewModel
```

Another important point is where the information is sent when the user submits the form. In your code, you set the action URL or the route that is going to process the form when the user submits it, by providing the appropriate values to the *BeginForm* method:

```
Html.BeginForm("Login", "Account", new { ReturnUrl = ViewBag.ReturnUrl }, FormMethod.
Post, new { @class = "form-horizontal", role = "form" })
```

This method creates an HTML form tag where the attribute action is */Account/Login* and where *Account* is the controller that manages the *Login* action. This method also sets *HTTP POST* as the method for sending the information to the application. Because you are using model binding, you bind the value of the input forms to the properties of the *LoginViewModel*, as you can see in the following lines highlighted in Listing 4-1:

```
@Html.TextBoxFor(m => m.Email, new { @class = "form-control" })
@Html.PasswordFor(m => m.Password, new { @class = "form-control" })
@Html.CheckBoxFor(m => m.RememberMe)
```

When the user submits the information for creating a new login account, the application saves this information in the storage system. In this example, you use an SQL Server Express LocalDB database for storing the entities that your application needs. Your application uses the *ApplicationUser* class for managing the users who can access your application. This class, shown in Listing 4-2, inherits from the *IdentityUser* class defined in the ASP.NET Identity framework.

LISTING 4-2 ApplicationUser class

```
// C#. ASP.NET. IdentityModels.cs
public class ApplicationUser : IdentityUser
    {
        public async Task<ClaimsIdentity> GenerateUserIdentityAsync(UserManager
        <ApplicationUser> manager)
        {
            // Note the authenticationType must match the one defined in
            // CookieAuthenticationOptions.AuthenticationType
            var userIdentity = await manager.CreateIdentityAsync(this,
            DefaultAuthenticationTypes.ApplicationCookie);
            // Add custom user claims here
            return userIdentity;
        }
    }
```

ASP.NET Identity uses the Entity Framework for managing the models needed by your application. The default entities provided by ASP.NET Identity are:

- **Users** This entity stores the users registered in your application. The entity stores the username, email, the hashed password, and a security stamp for controlling any changes in the user credentials.

- **User Claims** This entity stores different statements about the user and associates it with the user entity.

- **User Logins** This entity stores information about external authentication providers, such as Twitter, a Microsoft Account, or Facebook.

- **Roles** This entity represent groups of users who have specific access privileges to your application, like "Admin" or "User" roles.

When you run the example application for the first time, the Entity Framework creates all the necessary tables for your application, as shown in Figure 4-1. You can view the users registered in your application by right-clicking the *AspNetUsers* table and clicking View Data in the contextual menu.

FIGURE 4-1 Tables for storing entities for a form-based authentication

The Identity Framework uses the *UserManager<T>* class for managing all the operations related to your application users. Because of the way the Identity Framework works, the *UserManager* class sends the information to the *UserStore* class that is in charge of persisting the information in the database. In your example, you can see how the *UserManager* class uses the *CreateAsync* method for persisting the newly created user in the database by reviewing the *Register* method in the *AccountController.cs* file. Listing 4-3 shows how you should use the *CreateAsync* method for creating new users in your database.

LISTING 4-3 Persisting a new user in the database

// C#. ASP.NET. AccountController.cs

```
// POST: /Account/Register
    [HttpPost]
    [AllowAnonymous]
    [ValidateAntiForgeryToken]
    public async Task<ActionResult> Register(RegisterViewModel model)
    {
        if (ModelState.IsValid)
        {
            var user = new ApplicationUser { UserName = model.Email, Email = model.
            Email };
            var result = await UserManager.CreateAsync(user, model.Password);
            if (result.Succeeded)
            {
                await SignInManager.SignInAsync(user, isPersistent:false,
                rememberBrowser:false);
```

```
                return RedirectToAction("Index", "Home");
            }
            AddErrors(result);
        }
        // If we got this far, something failed, redisplay form return View(model);
    }
```

Because the Entity Framework is the base for the storage system of your user's credentials and identities, you can easily change the underlying storage and use other systems, such as Azure Storage Table, or other relational databases engines, such as SQL Server.

> **NEED MORE REVIEW?** **EXTENDING THE PROFILE INFORMATION**
>
> By default, the *ApplicationUser* class that you use in the previous example only contains two properties: email and password. You can extend these properties by taking advantage of the Entity Framework. The following articles show how to extend the default user identity:
>
> Customizing profile information in ASP.NET Identity in VS 2013 templates: *https://devblogs.microsoft.com/aspnet/customizing-profile-information-in-asp-net-identity-in-vs-2013-templates/*
>
> Add, download, and delete custom user data to Identity in an ASP.NET Core project: *https://docs.microsoft.com/en-us/aspnet/core/security/authentication/add-user-data*

When the users of your application submit the information for login or registering in your application, their web browsers send that information to your application, and then your application processes the request for creating the user in the database or authenticating the user. In a form-based authentication mechanism, the authentication process is performed by your code; it compares the value of the hashed password stored in your database with the hashed value of the password provided by the user on your web form. Your application also needs to ensure that any request made to the application needs to be authenticated before serving the content to the user. To avoid having the application prompt the user for credentials every single time the user tries to access to a protected section of your application, you need to save the credentials into a cookie that the user's browser provides to your application. The application usually encrypts the content of this cookie, so no malicious user or process can easily guess the username and password of a valid user of your application.

Fortunately, the Identity Framework takes care of most of these operations for you, and you only need to correctly configure it to your needs. This configuration consists of two different steps:

- Configuring the form-based authentication
- Configuring the middleware filtering

By using the MVC pattern to configure middleware filtering, you ensure that all requests to your application are evaluated before sending the information to the controllers. You configure your application to require authentication for all actions in your controllers. The middleware sits between the request and the controller to enforce this requirement.

This example uses the Open Web Interface for .NET (OWIN) specification for managing the interaction between the code and the web server. OWIN is an open-source specification that decouples the code from the implementation of the web server on which your code is supposed to run. OWIN can do this by running as a middleware in your application. This means you need to make the configurations to your code in the *Startup* class instead of using *Global.asax.cs*.

You configure the Identity Framework for managing the authentication of your application by using two different files—*Startup.Auth.cs* and *IdentityConfig.cs*. You use the *Startup.Auth.cs* class for making the basic configuration of the authorization features that you want to enable in your application. We saw that one of the characteristics of the form-based authentication is that you need to store the user and passwords needed to grant access to the application. You can use different storage solutions for this credential storage system, but you would typically use a relational database like SQL Server. Although the Identity Framework allows you to abstract from the storage details, you still need to provide some configuration for storing users and passwords. In the *Startup.Auth.cs* file, this line attaches the database connection, defined in the *connectionStrings* sections in the *Web.config* file, to your code:

```
app.CreatePerOwinContext(ApplicationDbContext.Create);
```

In this example, the *ApplicationDbContext* class inherits from the *IdentityDbContext* that provides the persistence layer to the *UserManager* class.

Once you added the persistence layer to the application, you need to add the *UserManager* and *SignInManager* classes, as shown in the following lines in the *Startup.Auth.cs* file:

```
app.CreatePerOwinContext<ApplicationUserManager>(ApplicationUserManager.Create);
app.CreatePerOwinContext<ApplicationSignInManager>(ApplicationSignInManager.Create);
```

The *ApplicationUserManager* class that inherits from the *UserManager* class manages all the operations related with the user, like creating new users, deleting old users, or checking the features that are enabled for the user. Remember that the *UserManager* class does not persist any information to the database by itself. It provides the needed information to the *UserStore* class that uses the *IdentityDbContext* for persisting the information in the database. You use this class in the *AccountController* class for registering new users in your application.

The *ApplicationSignInManager* that inherits from the *SignInManager* class performs the actual signing process of the user in the application. You use this class in your *AccountController* class for logging users in and out of your application.

Once you added the needed basic components for the authentication, you can now configure the type of authentication that you need for your application. In this example, you used form-based or cookie-based authentication. Remember that one of the parts of the form-based authentication is to provide the authenticated user with a cookie that stores some information that allows the user to access the application without needing to type his or her credentials each time the browser makes a request to the web server. You configure form-based authentication in the OWIN middleware by using the following lines:

```
app.UseCookieAuthentication(new CookieAuthenticationOptions
        {
            AuthenticationType = DefaultAuthenticationTypes.ApplicationCookie,
            LoginPath = new PathString("/Account/Login"),
            Provider = new CookieAuthenticationProvider
            {
                // Enables the application to validate the security stamp when the
                // user logs in. This is a security feature which is used when you
                // change a  password or add an external login to your account.
                OnValidateIdentity = SecurityStampValidator.OnValidateIdentity
                <ApplicationUserManager, ApplicationUser>(
                    validateInterval: TimeSpan.FromMinutes(30),
                    regenerateIdentity: (manager, user) =>
                    user.GenerateUserIdentityAsync(manager))
            }
        });
```

As you can see in the code above, you add the cookie authentication to the middleware and configure some essential points for the authentication:

- **AuthenticationType** You use this property for setting the identifier for the authentication type. You use different values of this property for using the same authentication middleware type more than once in the pipeline.

- **LoginPath** If your user tries to access a protected resource, he or she gets a 401 Unauthorized status code. The middleware changes the 401 status code into a 302 redirection to the path provided by this property.

- **Provider** The middleware makes calls to the authentication provider to give the application control when events occur in the pipeline, such as during the sign-in sign-out process. If you don't provide an instance of an authentication provider, then Katana provides an empty authentication provider.

Once you have configured the authentication methods for your application, you need to configure the *UserManager* class. You use this configuration to set the properties for the password length or complexity. You made this configuration in the *IdentityConfig.cs* file when you define the *IdentityUserManager* class. This class implements the method *Create*, shown in Listing 4-4, which handles the configuration of features for your users and passwords. We intentionally omitted portions of the code in Listing 4-4.

LISTING 4-4 Create method from *ApplicationUserManager*

// C#. ASP.NET. IdentityConfig.cs

```csharp
public static ApplicationUserManager Create(IdentityFactoryOptions<ApplicationUser
Manager> options, IOwinContext context)
        {
            var manager = new ApplicationUserManager(new UserStore<ApplicationUser>
            (context.Get<ApplicationDbContext>()));
            // Configure validation logic for usernames
            manager.UserValidator = new UserValidator<ApplicationUser>(manager)
            {
                AllowOnlyAlphanumericUserNames = false,
                RequireUniqueEmail = true
            };

            // Configure validation logic for passwords
            manager.PasswordValidator = new PasswordValidator
            {
                RequiredLength = 6,
                RequireNonLetterOrDigit = true,
                RequireDigit = true,
                RequireLowercase = true,
                RequireUppercase = true,
            };

            // Configure user lockout defaults
            manager.UserLockoutEnabledByDefault = true;
            manager.DefaultAccountLockoutTimeSpan = TimeSpan.FromMinutes(5);
            manager.MaxFailedAccessAttemptsBeforeLockout = 5;

            return manager;
        }
```

Once you have configured the authentication method for your application, you can implement how to create the actual user authentication and registration in the corresponding endpoints defined in the *AccountController.cs* file.

When you configured the cookie authentication, you set the *LoginPath* property to the value */Account/Login*. Now you can review the *Login* method shown in Listing 4-5, in the *AccountController*. You use the *PasswordSignInAsync()* method for authenticating a user with the with the username and password values provided by the form shown in Listing 4-1.

LISTING 4-5 Login method for the Account Controller

```
// C#. ASP.NET. AccountController.cs
//
      // POST: /Account/Login
      [HttpPost]
      [AllowAnonymous]
      [ValidateAntiForgeryToken]
      public async Task<ActionResult> Login(LoginViewModel model, string returnUrl)
      {
          if (!ModelState.IsValid)
          {
              return View(model);
          }

          // This doesn't count login failures towards account lockout
          // To enable password failures to trigger account lockout, change to
          // shouldLockout: true
          var result = await SignInManager.PasswordSignInAsync(model.Email, model.
          Password, model.RememberMe, shouldLockout: false);
          switch (result)
          {
              case SignInStatus.Success:
                  return RedirectToLocal(returnUrl);
              case SignInStatus.LockedOut:
                  return View("Lockout");
              case SignInStatus.RequiresVerification:
                  return RedirectToAction("SendCode", new { ReturnUrl = returnUrl,
                  RememberMe = model.RememberMe });
              case SignInStatus.Failure:
              default:
                  ModelState.AddModelError("", "Invalid login attempt.");
                  return View(model);
          }
      }
}
```

As you can see in Listing 4-5, you use the *SignInManager* for authenticating the user by using the *PasswordSignInAsync* method and providing the parameters to the method based on the values that you got from the form and that are stored in the *LoginViewModel*. If you review Listing 4-1, you can see that you configured the form for sending the information by using the *POST* method. This means that you need to use the *HttpPost* attribute for telling the MVC that it should run this method when it receives a request to the */Account/Login* route using the *POST* method. Another interesting attribute that you should consider is the *AllowAnonymous* attribute. Because you configured the authentication for all requests to your application in the *Startup.Auth.cs* file, you need to specify manually which routes accept requests without requiring authentication. At this point, the user is not authenticated yet, so you need to allow the user to access this route without requiring authentication. The *CaludateAntiForgeryToken* is also essential because it provides an additional security level by checking if the requests come from a valid user and preventing a malicious user from copying the authentication cookie from a valid user and reusing it for authentication to your application.

One of the most significant drawbacks of using form-based authentication is the authentication mechanism's dependency on cookies. Another inconvenience is that this is stateful, which requires that your server keeps an authentication session for tracking the activity between the server and the client. This makes it more difficult to scale solutions using form-based authentication. One additional point to consider is that cookies don't work well (or it's challenging to work with them) on mobile apps. Fortunately, there are alternatives to form-based authentication that are more suitable for the requirements that have Mobile or IoT scenarios; also, there are alternatives that can improve the scalability of your web application.

Token-based authentication is the most extended authentication mechanism for environments and scenarios that require high scalability or do not support the usage of cookies. Token-based authentication consists of a signed token that your application uses for authenticating requests and granting access to the resources in your application. The token does not contain the username and password of your user. Instead, the token stores some information about the authenticated user that your server can use for granting access to your application's resources.

When you use token-based authentication, you follow a workflow similar to the one shown in Figure 4-2:

1. An unauthenticated user connects to your web application.

2. Your web application redirects the user to the login page. This login page can be provided by your web application acting as a security server or by an external security server.

3. The security server validates the information provided by the user—typically, the username and password—and generates a JWT token.

4. The security server sends the JWT token to the user. The browser or mobile app that the user used to connect to your application is responsible for storing this JWT token for reusing it in the following requests.

5. The browsers or mobile app provides the JWT token to your web application on each following request.

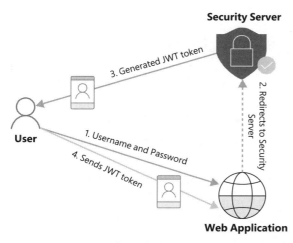

FIGURE 4-2 Basic workflow of token-based authentication

There are several token implementations, but the most extended one is JSON Web Token or JWT. A JWT token consists of:

- **Header** The header contains the name of the algorithm used for signing the token.

- **Body or Payload** The body or payload contains different information about the token and the purpose of this token. The body contains several standard fields or claims that are defined in the RFC 7519 and any other custom field that you may need for your application.

- **Cryptographic signature** This is a string that validates your token and ensures that the token was not corrupted or incorrectly manipulated.

One of the main advantages of using token-based authentication is that you can delegate the process of managing the identity of the users to external security servers. This means you can abstract from the implementation of managing and storing JWT tokens and usernames and passwords. That is what you do when you want to allow your users to access your application by using their Facebook, Google, or Twitter accounts. Your application trusts the identification and authentication processes made by these external security servers or identity managers, and you grant access to your application based on the information stored in the JWT token provided by the security server. You still need to store some information about the user, but there is no need to know anything about the password or any other information that the user needed to provide to the security server for authentication.

Using the Identity Framework, you can add token-based authentication to your application. As we mentioned before, you can implement your own token-based authentication or use an external authentication provider that performs the verification of the user's login and password. The following steps show how to enable Google authentication in the web application that you created in the previous example. You can use a similar procedure for enabling another social login to your application, such as Facebook, Twitter, or Microsoft accounts.

1. In Visual Studio, open the example that we reviewed in Listings 4-1 to 4-5.

2. On the Solution Explorer window, click on the project's name and press F4 for opening the Properties tab of the project.

3. On the Development Server section, change the value of the SSL Enabled setting to be True.

4. Copy the SSL URL below the SSL Enabled setting and close the Properties window.

5. In the Solution Explorer, right-click the project's name and click Properties at the bottom of the contextual menu. This opens your project's *csproj* file in a new tab.

6. On your project's *csproj* file tab, select the Web tab and paste the SSL URL in the Project Url text box in the Servers section.

7. Open the *HomeController.cs* file and add the *RequireHttps* attribute to the *HomeController* class:

```
[RequireHttps]
public class HomeController : Controller
{
    public ActionResult Index()
```

8. Create a Google Project for integrating your web application with Google's authentication platform. You need a Google account for these steps:

   a. Log in to your Google account.

   b. Navigate to *https://developers.google.com/identity/sign-in/web/devconsole-project*.

   c. Click Configure A Project.

   d. On the Configure A Project For Google Sign-In dialog box, select Create A New Project from the drop-down menu.

   e. Enter a name for your project and click Next at the bottom-left corner of the dialog box.

   f. On the Configure Your OAuth Client dialog box, type the name of your web application. This name will be shown in the consent window that appears to the user during login.

   g. On the Configure Your OAuth Client dialog box, select Web Server in the Where Are You Calling From? drop-down menu.

   h. In the Authorized Redirect URIs text box, use the URL SSL that you copied in step 4 and create a redirect URI with this structure:
   <YOUR_URL_SSL>/signin-google
   Use the following example for your reference:
   https://localhost:44397/signin-google

   i. Click Create in the bottom-left corner of the dialog box.

   j. On the You're All Set! dialog box, click the Download Client Configuration button. Alternatively, you can copy the Client ID and Client Secret fields. You will use these values later.

   k. Click the API Console link at the bottom of the dialog box.

   l. On the left side of the Google Console, click Library.

   m. In the Search For APIs & Services textbox, type **Google+**.

   n. In the result list, click Google+ API.

   o. In the Google+ API window, click the Enable button.

9. In the *App_Start/Startup.Auth.cs* file, in the *ConfigureAuth* method, uncomment the following lines:

```
app.UseGoogleAuthentication(new GoogleOAuth2AuthenticationOptions()
{
    ClientId = "",
    ClientSecret = ""
});
```

10. Use the Client ID and Client Secret values that you copied in step 8.j and assign the value to the correspondent variable in the code above. (Note that these items are placed inside quotation marks.)

11. Press F5 for running the application.

12. Click Log In in the top-left corner of the web application.

13. Under the Use Another Service To Log In option on the left side of the page, click the Google button.

14. Log in using your Google account.

15. Click the Register button. Once you are logged in with Google, you are redirected to the web application. Because your Google account does not exist on your application's database, you get a registration form.

16. Now you are registered and logged in to your application using a Google account.

Once you have logged in to the application using your Google account, you can review the database and look for the new login information. You can see in the *AspNetUser* table that there is a new entry for your new Google account login, but the *PasswordHash* field is empty. You can also review the *AspNetUserLogins* table. This table contains all the logins from external authorization providers, such as Google, that have been registered in your application.

In the same way that you configured the form-based authentication in the *Startup.Auth.cs* file, you configure the external authentication in the same file. Once you have configured the *DbContext*, *UserManager*, and *SignInManager* for your application, you add the external cookie management middleware, using this line:

```
app.UseExternalSignInCookie(DefaultAuthenticationTypes.ExternalCookie);
```

You need this for managing the information that comes from the third party's authentication providers. Finally, you register the authentication provider by providing the client ID and client secrets that allow your application to connect to the external authentication provider and get the token information.

If you run this example and review the headers in the different requests, you can see that the web browser still provides authentication information by using cookies. The token-based authentication on this example comes from the fact that you use an external authorization provider that uses OpenID Connect for authenticating your users. In the following sections, we review how to implement your own fully token-based authentication web API.

When the user is providing the credentials to your web application, you need to consider whether the authentication method that you are using transmits the username and password in plain text over the Internet. This is especially true for form-based authentication or basic authentication. In these situations, you can solve the problem by sending the authentication information through an encrypted SSL channel using digital certificates.

Using SSL certificates, you encrypt the communication channel between the client and server, and while you are authenticating the client, the client is also authenticating the server to which it is connecting. This server authentication is then performed automatically by the browser by checking that a trusted certification authority signs the server certificate, the certificate is not expired, and that the certificate is issued to the same host to which you are connecting.

You can also use SSL certificates for authenticating the clients for your application. Using that kind of authentication, you issue a certificate to your clients. When your client tries to connect to your web application, the web server asks the web browser to send an SSL certificate; then the web application checks whether the user provided a valid certificate and authenticates the connection without needing the user to provide a username and password. This authentication makes the communication between client and server more secure because you are authenticating both ends of the connection. However, it also is more complex to configure and manage in a production environment because you need to deploy a private-key infrastructure (PKI) and distribute the client certificates to the users in a secure way.

> **NEED MORE REVIEW?** **CONFIGURE TLS MUTUAL AUTHENTICATION FOR AZURE APP SERVICE**
>
> You can learn more about how to enable client certificate authentication by reviewing the Microsoft Docs article "Configure TLS mutual authentication for Azure App Service" at *https:// docs.microsoft.com/en-us/azure/app-service/app-service-web-configure-tls-mutual-auth*.

Implement multifactor or Windows authentication by using Azure AD

One commonality that you can observe in the examples in the previous section is that all users or identities are stored in a conventional storage system, such as a relational database. If you are developing an application for a company with hundreds or thousands of users, using a distinct storage system for managing the identities of the users who need to access the application may create undesirable administrative overhead. This type of organization usually uses some identity or directory service that centralizes and eases the administration of all users who have some kind of relationship with the company. For Microsoft-based deployment, companies use Microsoft Active Directory Domain Services (AD DS), which provides the authentication and authorization capabilities needed for the company.

With the evolution of the cloud, Microsoft released Azure Active Directory (Azure AD), which provides identity and access management services for managing the access to the different services and resources that Microsoft offers. You should not confuse Active Directory Domain Services, with Azure AD. They both provide identity and access management services, but they are not the same service, they provide different features, and they apply to different scenarios. You can connect an Azure AD tenant with an Active Directory Domain Services domain, but you need to remember that you mainly use Azure AD for cloud-based scenarios, while you typically use AD DS domain for on-premises scenarios.

Windows authentication is the type of authentication that you perform in an on-premises environment where there is an AD DS domain deployed. The NTLM and Kerberos protocols are the protocols that support client authentication in an AD DS domain environment. Neither of these protocols is well suited for the Internet, so you need to use alternative authentication protocols when you need to authorize your users to access your application. You use Windows

Authentication or Integrated Windows Authentication when your users are members of an AD DS domain and they are connecting to your application from a computer that is also joined to the same AD DS domain.

There are situations in which your company has both an AD DS domain and an Azure AD tenant. In that kind of scenario, it's very common to connect your domain and tenant. This means any new user you add to your AD DS domain is automatically added to the Azure AD tenant. This configuration also allows your users to authenticate to your AD DS domain or Azure AD tenant using the same credentials. You can make this connection using two different methods: Azure AD Connect or Active Directory Federation Services (AD FS).

> **NEED MORE REVIEW?** **HYBRID IDENTITY WITH AZURE AD**
>
> You have several options when you configure the connection between an Azure AD tenant and an AD DS domain. You can review the different options by consulting the article "What is hybrid identity with Azure Active Directory?" at *https://docs.microsoft.com/en-us/azure/active-directory/hybrid/whatis-hybrid-identity*.

If you are writing a desktop or mobile application that needs to use Azure AD authentication and your desktop or mobile devices are joined to your AD DS domain or Azure AD tenant, you can use the Microsoft Authentication Library for .NET (MSAL.NET). Using this library, you can request an Azure AD token by using Integrated Windows Authentication. The following example shows how to implement Integrated Windows Authentication using MSAL.NET. Before you can run this example, you need to consider the following requirements:

- You need to run the example from a computer that is a member of an Azure AD tenant or an AD DS domain. The Azure AD tenant and AD DS domain need to be connected using AD FS.

- Your user needs to exist on the AD DS domain. This AD DS and the Azure AD tenant need to connect using a federation service, such as AD FS. Using managed users—that is, users who only exist on the Azure AD tenant—is not valid for this scenario.

Because your application needs to connect to Azure AD to get the authentication token, you need to register the application in your Azure AD tenant before your application can access your tenant or AD DS domain. The following steps show how to register an application in your Azure AD tenant:

1. Sign in to the management portal (*http://portal.azure.com*).

2. On the left side of the Azure portal, in the list of your favorite resources, click Azure Active Directory.

3. On the Azure Active Directory blade, click App Registrations.

4. On the App Registrations blade, click the New Registration button in the top-left corner of the blade.

5. On the Register An Application blade, type a name for your application.

6. On the Supported Account Types radio button control, ensure that the Accounts In This Organization Only option is selected. This ensures that authentication is only valid for users in your organization.

7. Click the Register button at the bottom of the blade.

8. On your application blade, on the Overview panel, copy the Application (Client) and the Directory (Tenant) IDs.

9. On your application blade, click the Authentication option in the Manage section.

10. On the Authentication blade, in Advanced Settings, check the ID Tokens Implicit Grant option.

11. Set Treat Application As A Public Client setting to Yes.

12. Click the Save button at the top-left corner of the Authentication blade.

13. On your application blade, click API Permissions in the Manage section.

14. On the API Permissions blade, click the Add A Permission button.

15. On the Request API Permissions panel, click the Microsoft Graph button.

16. On the What Type Of Permissions Does Your Application Require? section, click Delegated Permissions.

17. In the Permission list, expand the User node, and select *User.ReadBasic.All*. You may need to scroll down to find the User node.

18. Click the Add Permissions button at the bottom of the Request API Permissions panel.

19. On the API Permissions blade, in the Grant Consent section, click the button Grant Admin Consent For <Your_Tenant's_Name>.

20. Click the Yes button on the confirmation dialog.

21. Clone the source code of this example:

    ```
    git clone https://github.com/Azure-Samples/active-directory-dotnet-iwa-v2.git
    ```

22. Open the solution in Visual Studio.

23. Edit the *appsettings.json* file and make the following changes:

    a. Set the *AadAuthrityuAudience* to the value *AzureAdMyOrg*.

    b. Inside the *Authentication* section, add a new key-value pair:

       i. key *TenantId*

       ii. value insert the tenant ID you copied in step 8

    c. Replace the value of the *ClientId* with the client ID that you copied in step 8.

24. Edit the *Program.cs* file and comment the following line:

    ```
    .WithAuthority(appConfig.AzureCloudInstance, AadAuthorityAudience.
    AzureAdMultipleOrgs)
    ```

25. Run the application.

This console application tries to log in to your Azure AD tenant using the username that runs the application. When you run the application, you should get the information stored in the AD DS domain about your user.

During the login flow, your application needs to contact your AD FS servers. If you try to run this example on a computer that is joined to an Azure AD tenant or that is not a member of an AD DS domain federated with an Azure AD tenant, you will get an error. You should bear in mind that the previous example does not work if you have configured Multifactor Authentication (MFA) for your users in the Azure AD tenant.

> **NEED MORE REVIEW?**   **ACTIVE DIRECTORY FEDERATION SERVICES**
>
> You can deploy a testing scenario for your experiments using virtual machines. You can review how to configure a federation trust between an AD DS domain and an Azure AD tenant by reviewing the article, "Azure AD Connect and federation," at *https://docs.microsoft.com/en-us/azure/active-directory/hybrid/how-to-connect-fed-whatis*.

When you work with MSAL, you need to start by creating a *PublicClientApplication* object. You use this object for managing the interactions with your Azure AD tenant. When you create this object, you need to provide some information stored in the *appsettings.json* file. You create this object in the *Program.cs* file, using the following lines of code:

```
SampleConfiguration config = SampleConfiguration.ReadFromJsonFile("appsettings.json");
var appConfig = config.PublicClientApplicationOptions;
var app = PublicClientApplicationBuilder.CreateWithApplicationOptions(appConfig).
Build();
```

In the previous example, the class *PublicAppUsingIntegratedWindowsAuthentication* performs the actual authentication with the Azure AD tenant. This class has two main methods:

- **AcquireATokenFromCacheOrIntegratedWindowsAuthenticationAsync**   This method gets information from the currently logged-in user and tries to get any cached token. If there is no cached token, then it calls the *GetTokenForWebApiUsingIntegrated-WindowsAuthenticationAsync* method for acquiring a new token.

- **GetTokenForWebApiUsingIntegratedWindowsAuthenticationAsync**   Uses the *AcquireTokenByIntegratedWindowsAuth* method for getting a token based on the information of the currently logged-in user.

> **NEED MORE REVIEW?**   **MICROSOFT IDENTITY PLATFORM AUTHENTICATION LIBRARIES**
>
> The Microsoft identity platform authentication libraries are available for different languages. You can use these libraries for adding authentication features in your applications for different platforms, such as web, Android, iOS, Windows Universal, or desktop applications. You can review the detail of these libraries using the following link *https://docs.microsoft.com/en-us/azure/active-directory/develop/reference-v2-libraries*.

Using Azure AD as your identity manager service has some advantages over implementing your own identity solution. One of these advantages is the implementation of Multifactor Authentication (MFA). The MFA means that a user needs to provide additional proof of his or her identity before the user can be authenticated. You can configure different verification methods for your user, such as using notifications or verification codes from a mobile app or calling or sending a text message to the user's phone. Microsoft provides the Microsoft Authenticator mobile app—available for Android, iOS, and Windows Phone platforms—for allowing your users to provide the verification needed.

When you enable the MFA feature that Microsoft offers in your Azure AD tenant, you can delegate the complexity of the MFA authentication to Azure. Use the following procedure for enabling MFA authentication in your Azure AD tenant:

1. Open the Azure Portal (*https://portal.azure.com*).
2. On the left side of the Azure Portal, click Azure Active Directory.
3. On the Azure Active Directory blade, click Users in the Manage section.
4. On the All Users blade, click the Multi-Factor Authentication button. This opens a new window where you can enable the MFA for your users.
5. On the Multi-Factor Authentication page shown in Figure 4-3, click the check box next to the display name of the user for whom you want to enable the MFA. (Note that Figure 4-3 has been intentionally blurred to protect the anonymity of the users.)

FIGURE 4-3 Enable multifactor authentication

6. On the Multi-Factor Authentication page, click the Enable link on the right side of the page.
7. On the About Enabling Multi-Factor Auth dialog box, click the Enable Multifactor Auth button.

Once you enable the MFA in your Azure AD tenant, your users need to use any of the additional verification methods when they authenticate to your application. Use the following steps for creating an example application that uses Azure AD authentication:

1. Open your Visual Studio 2017.
2. Create a new project by clicking File > New > Project.
3. On the left side of the New Project window, click Installed > Visual C# > Web.
4. On the New Project window, in the template area, click ASP.NET Core Web Application.
5. Type a name for your example application and click the OK button.
6. In the New ASP.NET Core Web Application window, select Web Application (Model-View-Controller).
7. Click the Change Authentication button.
8. On the Change Authentication window, select Work or School Accounts.
9. On the right side of the Change Authentication window, in the first drop-down menu, ensure that the Cloud – Single Organization value is selected. This drop-down menu allows you to configure whether only the users from your organization can log in to this application.
10. In the Domain drop-down menu, select the domain that you want to use for authenticating your users.
11. Leave the other options as is and click the OK button.
12. On the New ASP.NET Core Web Application window, click the OK button.
13. Press F5 to run your application.

When you run your application, the web browser would present the Azure AD login. Once you provide the credentials for your user and if you configured the MFA for this user in the previous steps, you need to provide the second authentication by using one of the configured validation methods.

> **NEED MORE REVIEW?**   **AZURE AD CONDITIONAL ACCESS**
>
> You can automatically configure the multifactor authentication for your organization's users depending on different conditions. For example, you can enable MFA only for certain users and applications. You can extend the information about conditional access in Azure AD by reviewing the following article: *https://docs.microsoft.com/en-us/azure/active-directory/ conditional-access/overview.*

Implement OAuth2 authentication

At the beginning of this chapter, we reviewed how to you can use third-party identity servers for authenticating users in your application, using the OAuth2 protocol. In this section, we are going to review how to create your own OAuth2 server. You usually add this type of authentication when you need these third-party applications to access some services or resources of your code. You can grant access to these applications by creating a token that authenticates the third-party application and grants access to specific parts of your HTTP service.

The OAuth protocol addresses the need to secure access to resources and information in your application by the third party's process. Without OAuth, if you want to grant access to an external application to the resources of your application, you need to use a username and password. If the third-party application is compromised, then the username and password are also compromised, and your resources are exposed. The OAuth protocol defines four different roles:

- **Resource owner**   This is the person or entity that can grant access to the resources. If the resource owner is a person, it can also be referred to as the user.

- **Resource server**   This is the server that hosts the resources that you want to share. This server needs to be able to accept and respond to the access codes used for accessing the resource.

- **Client**   This is the third-party application that needs to access the resource. The client makes the needed requests to the resource server on behalf of the resource owner. The term "client" does not necessarily imply any specific implementation, like a server, a desktop, or any other kind of device.

- **Authorization server**   This is the server that issues the access token to the client for accessing the resources. The client needs to be authenticated before it can get the correct token.

Figure 4-4 shows the basic authentication flow for OAuth.

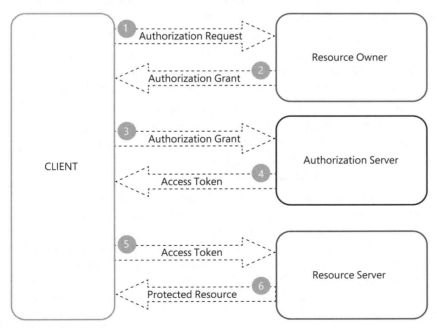

FIGURE 4-4 OAuth basic authentication flow

As you can see in Figure 4-4, the process of acquiring a token for accessing a protected resource consists of the following steps:

- **Authentication request**   The client requests access to the protected resource. The resource owner, based on the privileges of the client, grants access to the client for accessing the resource. The authentication of the client can be directly done by the resource owner or preferably by the authentication server.

- **Authentication grant**   When the resource owner grants client access to the resource, the client sends an authentication grant, which is is a code or credential that represents the permission to access the resource, which has been granted by the resource owner. The client uses this authentication grant credential to request an access token to the authorization server. There are four different mechanisms for handling this authentication:

  - **Authorization code**   The client instructs the resource owner to request authentication to the authentication server. Once the resource owner is authenticated, the authentication server creates an authorization code that the resource owner sends back to the client. The client uses this authorization code as the grant for requesting the access token.

  - **Implicit**   Using this authentication grant flow, the authentication server does not authenticate the client. Instead, the client gets the access token without needing to authenticate to the resource server using an authentication grant. This implicit flow is a simplified authorization code flow. To improve security in this flow, the resource server uses the redirect URI provided by the client.

  - **Resource owner credentials**   Instead of using an authorization code or implicit authentication, the client uses the credentials of the resource owner for authenticating against the resource server. This type of authentication grant should be used only when there is a high level of trust between the client and the resource owner.

  - **Client credentials**   The client provides his or her credentials for accessing the resource. This authentication grant is useful for scenarios in which the client needs access to resources that are protected by the same authorization server as the client and are under the control of the client. This is also useful if the resource server and the client arranged the same authorization for the resources and the client.

- **Access token**   The client requests an access token from the authorization server that allows the client to access the resource on the resource server. The client sends this access token to the resource server with each request to access the resource. This access token has an expiration date. Once the access token is expired, the token is invalid, and the client needs to request another access token. To ease the process of renewing the access token, the authentication server provides two different tokens—the actual access token and a refresh token. The client uses the refresh token when it needs to renew an expired access token.

- **Protected resource** This is the resource that the client wants to access. The resource server protects the resource. The client needs to send the access token to the resource server every time it needs to access the resource.

NEED MORE REVIEW? **THE OAUTH 2.0 AUTHORIZATION FRAMEWORK**

You can get more information about the details of how the OAuth 2.0 Authorization Framework works by reviewing the official RFC 6749 at *https://tools.ietf.org/html/rfc6749*.

The following example shows how to implement OAuth 2.0 authentication in your Web API application. In this example, you are going to create an authorization server, a resource server, and client that can request an access token before accessing the resource. For the sake of readability, we have split the steps for implementing this example into different parts. The following steps show how to create the authorization server:

1. Open Visual Studio.

2. Click File > New > Project.

3. In the New Project window, in the tree control on the left side, click Installed > Visual C# > Web.

4. Select the ASP.NET Web Application (.NET Framework) template.

5. Type a Name for your project.

6. Select the Location where you want to save your project.

7. Type a name for your Solution.

8. Click the OK button.

9. In the New ASP.NET Web Application window, click the MVC template.

10. Click the Change Authentication button on the right side of the window.

11. On the Change Authentication window, click the Individual User Accounts option.

12. On the New ASP.NET Web Application window, click the OK button.

13. In Visual Studio, open the file at App_Start > Startup.Auth.cs, and add the following line to the beginning of the file:

    ```
    using Microsoft.Owin.Security.OAuth;
    ```

14. Add the code shown in Listing 4-6 to the *Startup.Auth.cs* file. You need to add this code to the *ConfigureAuth()* method, after the line

    ```
    app.UseTwoFactorRememberBrowserCookie(DefaultAuthenticationTypes.
    TwoFactorRememberBrowserCookie);
    ```

15. Add also the following using statements to the *Startup.Auth.cs* file for avoiding compilation errors:

    - *using System;*
    - *using Microsoft.AspNet.Identity;*

- *using Microsoft.AspNet.Identity.Owin;*

- *using Owin;*

- *using Microsoft.Owin;*

- *using Microsoft.Owin.Security.Cookies;*

- *using Microsoft.Owin.Security.OAuth;*

- *using Microsoft.Owin.Security.Infrastructure;*

- *using AuthorizationServer.Constants;*

- *using System.Threading.Tasks;*

- *using System.Collections.Concurrent;*

- *using System.Security.Claims;*

- *using System.Security.Principal;*

- *using System.Linq;*

- *using <your_project's_name>.Models;*

LISTING 4-6 Adding OAuth Authorization Server

```
// C#. ASP.NET.

//Setup the Authorization Server
          app.UseOAuthAuthorizationServer(new OAuthAuthorizationServerOptions
          {
               AuthorizeEndpointPath = new PathString(Paths.AuthorizePath),
               TokenEndpointPath = new PathString (Paths.TokenPath),
               ApplicationCanDisplayErrors = true,
#if DEBUG
               AllowInsecureHttp = true,
#endif
               Provider = new OAuthAuthorizationServerProvider
               {
                    OnValidateClientRedirectUri = ValidateClientRedirectUri,
                    OnValidateClientAuthentication = ValidateClientAuthentication,
                    OnGrantResourceOwnerCredentials = GrantResourceOwnerCredentials,
                    OnGrantClientCredentials = GrantClientCredentials
               },

// The authorization code provider is the object in charge of creating and receiving the
// authorization code.
     AuthorizationCodeProvider = new AuthenticationTokenProvider
     {
          OnCreate = CreateAuthenticationCode,
          OnReceive = ReceiveAuthenticationCode,
     },

     // The refresh token provider is in charge in creating and receiving refresh token.
     RefreshTokenProvider = new AuthenticationTokenProvider
     {
          OnCreate = CreateRefreshToken,
```

```
          OnReceive = ReceiveRefreshToken,
    }
        });

        //Protect the resources on this server.
        app.UseOAuthBearerAuthentication(new OAuthBearerAuthenticationOptions
        {
        });
```

This code configures the OAuth Authentication Server by using the *UseOAuthAuthorization Server()* method. This method accepts an *OAuthAuthorizationServerOptions* object for configuring several useful endpoints:

- **AuthorizeEndpointPath**   The authorize endpoint is the path in the authorization server to which the client application redirects the user-agent to obtain the user or resource owner's consent to access the resource. With this consent, the client application can request an access token.

- **TokenEndpointPath**   This is the path in the authorization server that the client uses to obtain an access token. If the client is configured with a client secret, the client needs to provide this client secret on the request for obtaining a new token.

- **AllowInsecureHttp**   This setting allows the client to make requests to the authorize and token endpoints by using HTTP URIs instead of HTTPS URIs.

- **Provider**   Your authorization server application needs to provide the needed delegated methods for processing the different events that arise during the OAuth authorization flow. You can do this by implementing the *OAuthAuthorizationServerProvider* interface or using the default implementation provided by the *OAuthAuthorization-ServerProvider* object. In this example, you use the *OAuthAuthorizationServerProvider* object and provide four delegate functions for the different events. Listings 4-7 to 4-10 show the different delegate methods that you use for the events managed by this provider.

- **AuthorizationCodeProvider**   When the authorization server authenticates the client, the server needs to send an authorization code to the server. This provider manages the events that arise during the management of the authentication code. Listings 4-11 and 4-12 show the delegate methods that manage the events of creating or receiving a code.

- **RefreshTokenProvider**   This object controls the events that happen when the client requests a refresh of an access token. Listings 4-13 and 4-14 show the delegate methods that control the events of creating and receiving a request of refreshing an access token.

16. Add the content from Listings 4-6 to 4-13 to the *Startup.Auth.cs* file. Add these methods to the *Startup* class. The implementation for these delegates is not suitable for production environments. For example, the validation of the client redirect URI, and the authentication of the clients are based on a hard-coded value stored in the *Client* class. In a real-world scenario, you should have these entities stored in a database. In this example, the creation of the access token, shown in Listing 4-9, is stored in an in-memory dictionary. In a real-world scenario, you should save in a database the access tokens that you grant to the clients.

LISTING 4-7 *OnValidateClientRedirectUri* delegate

// C#. ASP.NET.

```
private Task ValidateClientRedirectUri(OAuthValidateClientRedirectUriContext context)
    {
        if (context.ClientId == Clients.Client1.Id)
        {
            context.Validated(Clients.Client1.RedirectUrl);
        }
        else if (context.ClientId == Clients.Client2.Id)
        {
            context.Validated(Clients.Client2.RedirectUrl);
        }
        return Task.FromResult(0);
    }
```

LISTING 4-8 *OnValidateClientAuthentication* delegate

// C#. ASP.NET.

```
private Task ValidateClientAuthentication(OAuthValidateClientAuthenticationContext
context)
    {
        string clientId;
        string clientSecret;
        if (context.TryGetBasicCredentials(out clientId, out clientSecret) ||
            context.TryGetFormCredentials(out clientId, out clientSecret))
        {
            if (clientId == Clients.Client1.Id && clientSecret == Clients.Client1.
            Secret)
            {
                context.Validated();
            }
            else if (clientId == Clients.Client2.Id && clientSecret == Clients.
            Client2.Secret)
            {
                context.Validated();
            }
        }
        return Task.FromResult(0);
    }
```

LISTING 4-9 *OnGrantResourceOwnerCredentials* delegate

```
// C#. ASP.NET.

private Task GrantResourceOwnerCredentials(OAuthGrantResourceOwnerCredentialsContext
context)
        {
                ClaimsIdentity identity = new ClaimsIdentity(new GenericIdentity(context.
                UserName, OAuthDefaults.AuthenticationType), context.Scope.Select(x => new
                Claim("urn:oauth:scope", x)));

                context.Validated(identity);

                return Task.FromResult(0);
        }
```

LISTING 4-10 *OnGrantClientCredentials* delegate

```
// C#. ASP.NET.

private Task GrantClientCredentials(OAuthGrantClientCredentialsContext context)
        {
                var identity = new ClaimsIdentity(new GenericIdentity(context.ClientId,
                OAuthDefaults.AuthenticationType), context.Scope.Select(x => new
                Claim("urn:oauth:scope", x)));

                context.Validated(identity);

                return Task.FromResult(0);
        }
```

LISTING 4-11 Authorization code for *OnCreate* delegate

```
// C#. ASP.NET.

private void CreateAuthenticationCode(AuthenticationTokenCreateContext context)
        {
                context.SetToken(Guid.NewGuid().ToString("n") + Guid.NewGuid().
                ToString("n"));
                _authenticationCodes[context.Token] = context.SerializeTicket();
        }
```

LISTING 4-12 Authorization code for *OnReceive* delegate

```
// C#. ASP.NET.

private void ReceiveAuthenticationCode(AuthenticationTokenReceiveContext context)
        {
                string value;
                if (_authenticationCodes.TryRemove(context.Token, out value))
                {
                        context.DeserializeTicket(value);
                }
        }
```

LISTING 4-13 Refresh token for *OnCreate* delegate

```csharp
// C#. ASP.NET.

private void CreateRefreshToken(AuthenticationTokenCreateContext context)
        {
            context.SetToken(context.SerializeTicket());
        }
```

LISTING 4-14 Refresh token for *OnReceive* delegate

```csharp
// C#. ASP.NET.

private void ReceiveRefreshToken(AuthenticationTokenReceiveContext context)
        {
            context.DeserializeTicket(context.Token);
        }
```

17. Add the following private property to the Startup class in the *Startup.Auth.cs* file:

```csharp
private readonly ConcurrentDictionary<string, string> _authenticationCodes =
                        new ConcurrentDictionary<string,
                        string>(StringComparer.Ordinal);
```

18. On the Solution Explorer window, add a new folder to your project called *Constants*.

19. In the *Constants* project, right-click the *Constants* folder and click Add > New Item.

20. On the New Item window, on the tree control on the left side of the window, click Installed > Visual C# Code.

21. Click the template named *Class*.

22. At the bottom of the Add New Item window, type **Clients.cs** in the Name text box.

23. Click the Add button in the bottom-right corner of the window.

24. Replace the content of the *Clients.cs* file with the content in Listing 4-15. Change the namespace to match your project's name.

LISTING 4-15 *Clients.cs*

```csharp
// C#. ASP.NET.

namespace <YOUR_PROJECT'S_NAME>.Constants
{
    public class Clients
    {
        public readonly static Client Client1 = new Client
        {
            Id = "123456",
            Secret = "abcdef",
            RedirectUrl = Paths.AuthorizeCodeCallBackPath
        };

        public readonly static Client Client2 = new Client
        {
            Id = "78901",
```

```
            Secret = "aasdasdef",
            RedirectUrl = Paths.ImplicitGrantCallBackPath
    };

}

    public class Client
    {
        public string Id { get; set; }

        public string Secret { get; set; }

        public string RedirectUrl { get; set; }
    }
}
```

25. On the Solution Explorer window, click your project's name and press F4.

26. On your project's properties window, change the value of SSL Enabled to True.

27. Copy the value of the SSL URL setting.

28. Right-click the project's name and click the Properties menu item at the bottom of the contextual menu.

29. On the project's properties tab in Visual Studio, click the Web element on the left side of the window.

30. In the Servers section, paste the SSL URL value that you copied in step 26 in the Project URL text box.

31. Add a new empty C# class and name it **Paths.cs**. You can repeat the steps 18–22 to create a new C# class.

32. Replace the content of the file *Paths.cs* with the code shown in Listing 4-16.

33. Paste the value of the SSL URL that you copied on step 26 on the following constants:

- *AuthorizationServerBaseAddress*

- *ResourceServerBaseAddress*

- *ImplicitGrantCallBackPath* Ensure that you don't delete the URI part. This constant should look like *<SSL URL>/Home/SignIn*.

- *AuthorizeCodeCallBackPath* Ensure that you don't delete the URI part. This constant should look like *<SSL URL>/Manage*.

LISTING 4-16 Paths.cs

```
// C#. ASP.NET.
namespace <YOUR_PROJECT'S_NAME>.Constants
{
    public class Paths
    {
        public const string AuthorizationServerBaseAddress = "https://localhost:44317";
        public const string ResourceServerBaseAddress = "https://localhost:44317";
```

```
        public const string ImplicitGrantCallBackPath = "https://localhost:44317/Home/
        SignIn";
        public const string AuthorizeCodeCallBackPath = "https://localhost:44317/
        Manage";

        public const string AuthorizePath = "/OAuth/Authorize";
        public const string TokenPath = "/OAuth/Token";
        public const string LoginPath = "/Account/Login";
        public const string LogoutPath = "/Account/Logout";
        public const string MePath = "/api/Me";
    }
}
```

At this point, you need to create the API Controller that manages the requests to the Authorize and Token endpoint. When you configured the Authentication Server, you used the following code snippet for setting the endpoints that the server uses for attending OAuth requests:

```
app.UseOAuthAuthorizationServer(new OAuthAuthorizationServerOptions
        {
                AuthorizeEndpointPath = new PathString(Paths.AuthorizePath),
                TokenEndpointPath = new PathString(Paths.TokenPath),
```

If you review the value of the parameters *AuthorizePath* and *TokenPath* in your Paths class, you can see that their values are /OAuth/Authorize and /OAuth/Token, respectively. Now, you need to create the controller that manages the requests to these endpoints.

34. On the Solution Explorer window, right-click the Controllers folders in your project, and then choose Add > Controller.

35. On the Add Scaffold window, choose MVC 5 Controller – Empty.

36. Click the Add button.

37. On the Add Controller window, type **OAuthController**.

38. Open the *OAuthController.cs* file and replace the content of the file with the code shown in Listing 4-17:

LISTING 4-17 *Startup.WebApi.cs*

```
// C#. ASP.NET.
using System.Security.Claims;
using System.Web;
using System.Web.Mvc;

namespace <your_project's_name>.Controllers
{
    public class OAuthController : Controller
    {

        // GET: OAuth/Authorize
        public ActionResult Authorize()
```

```
    {
        if (Response.StatusCode != 200)
        {
            return View("AuthorizeError");
        }

        var authentication = HttpContext.GetOwinContext().Authentication;
        var ticket = authentication.AuthenticateAsync("ApplicationCookie").Result;
        var identity = ticket != null ? ticket.Identity : null;
        if (identity == null)
        {
            authentication.Challenge("ApplicationCookie");
            return new HttpUnauthorizedResult();
        }

        var scopes = (Request.QueryString.Get("scope") ?? "").Split(' ');

        if (Request.HttpMethod == "POST")
        {
            if (!string.IsNullOrEmpty(Request.Form.Get("submit.Grant")))
            {
                identity = new ClaimsIdentity(identity.Claims, "Bearer", identity.
                NameClaimType, identity.RoleClaimType);
                foreach (var scope in scopes)
                {
                    identity.AddClaim(new Claim("urn:oauth:scope", scope));
                }
                authentication.SignIn(identity);
            }
            if (!string.IsNullOrEmpty(Request.Form.Get("submit.Login")))
            {
                authentication.SignOut("ApplicationCookie");
                authentication.Challenge("ApplicationCookie");
                return new HttpUnauthorizedResult();
            }
        }

        return View();
    }
    }
}
```

39. Right-click Views > OAuth, and then select Add > View.

40. On the Add View window, on the View Name field, type **Authorize**.

41. Click OK.

42. Replace the content of the file *Authorize.cshtml* with the code shown in Listing 4-18:

LISTING 4-18 *Authorize.cshtml*

```
// C#. ASP.NET.
@{
    ViewBag.Title = "Authorize";
}

@using System.Security.Claims
@using System.Web
@{
    var authentication = Context.GetOwinContext().Authentication;
    var ticket = authentication.AuthenticateAsync("ApplicationCookie").Result;
    var identity = ticket != null ? ticket.Identity : null;
    var scopes = (Request.QueryString.Get("scope") ?? "").Split(' ');
}
<!DOCTYPE html>
<html xmlns="http://www.w3.org/1999/xhtml">
<head>
    <title>@ViewBag.Title</title>
</head>
<body>
    <h1>Authorization Server</h1>
    <h2>OAuth2 Authorize</h2>
    <form method="POST">
        <p>Hello, @identity.Name</p>
        <p>A third party application wants to do the following on your behalf:</p>
        <ul>
            @foreach (var scope in scopes)
            {
                <li>@scope</li>
            }
        </ul>
        <p>
          <input type="submit" name="submit.Grant" value="Grant" />
          <input type="submit" name="submit.Login" value="Sign in as different user" />
        </p>
    </form>
</body>
</html>
```

43. Add another empty view named **AuthorizeError**.

44. Replace the content of the file *AuthorizeError.cshtml* with the code shown in Listing 4-19:

LISTING 4-19 *AuthorizeError.cshtml*

```
// C#. ASP.NET.
@{
    ViewBag.Title = "AuthorizeError";
}
@using System
@using System.Security.Claims
@using System.Web
@using Microsoft.Owin
@{
```

```
    IOwinContext owinContext = Context.GetOwinContext();
    var error = owinContext.Get<string>("oauth.Error");
    var errorDescription = owinContext.Get<string>("oauth.ErrorDescription");
    var errorUri = owinContext.Get<string>("oauth.ErrorUri");
}
<!DOCTYPE html>
<html xmlns="http://www.w3.org/1999/xhtml">
<head>
    <title>@ViewBag.Title</title>
</head>
<body>
    <h1>Katana.Sandbox.WebServer</h1>
    <h2>OAuth2 Authorize Error</h2>
    <p>Error: @error</p>
    <p>@errorDescription</p>
</body>
</html>
```

In this example, we only provide an implementation for the *Authorize* endpoint for the sake of simplicity. An authorized user in your application needs to grant access to the resources in your application explicitly. When the user grants those privileges, the application automatically creates an in-memory OAuth token that you can use to make a request to the protected resources. In a real-world scenario, this process should be separated in the two different endpoints—Authorize and Token. You should use the Token endpoint for creating or refreshing the access token issued by the authorization server.

Now that you have created and configure your authorization server, you can create the resource server. In this example, you are going to create the resource server on the same application where you implemented the authorization server. In a real-world scenario, you can use the same application, or you can use a different application deployed by a different server or Azure App Service.

1. On the Solution Explorer window, right-click the Controllers folder in your project and click Add > Controller.

2. On the Add Scaffold window, select the Web API 2 Controller – Empty template.

3. Click the Add button.

4. On the Add Controller window, type **MeController** and click the Add button.

5. Replace the content of the *MeController.cs* file with the code shown in Listing 4-20. This controller is quite simple and only returns the information stored in the token that you provide to the resource server when you try to access the resource.

LISTING 4-20 *MeController.cs*

```
// C#. ASP.NET.

using System.Collections.Generic;
using System.Linq;
using System.Security.Claims;
using System.Web.Http;
```

```
namespace <your_project's_name>.Controllers
{
    [Authorize]
    public class MeController : ApiController
    {
        // GET api/<controller>
        public IEnumerable<object> Get()
        {
            var identity = User.Identity as ClaimsIdentity;
            return identity.Claims.Select(c => new
            {
                Type = c.Type,
                Value = c.Value
            });
        }
    }
}
```

6. On the Solution Explorer window, in the *App_Start* folder, rename the file *WebApiConfig.cs* to *Startup.WebApi.cs*.

7. In the Visual Studio window, click Tools > NuGet Package Manager > Manage NuGet Packages For Solution.

8. On the NuGet Package Manager tab, click Browse.

9. Type **Microsoft asp.net web api 2.2 owin** and press Enter.

10. Click the *Microsoft.AspNet.WebApi.Owin* package.

11. On the right side of the NuGet Manager tab, click the checkbox beside your project.

12. Click the Install button.

13. On the Preview Changes window, click OK.

14. On the License Acceptance, click the I Accept button.

15. Open the *Startup.WebApi.cs* file and change the content of the file with the content shown in Listing 4-21:

LISTING 4-21 *Startup.WebApi.cs*

```
// C#. ASP.NET.
using Microsoft.Owin.Security.OAuth;
using Owin;
using System.Web.Http;

namespace <your_project's_name>
{
    public partial class Startup
    {
        public void ConfigureWebApi(IAppBuilder app)
        {
            var config = new HttpConfiguration();
            // Web API configuration and services
            // Configure Web API to use only bearer token authentication.
```

```
            config.SuppressDefaultHostAuthentication();
            config.Filters.Add(new HostAuthenticationFilter(OAuthDefaults.
            AuthenticationType));

            // Web API routes
            config.MapHttpAttributeRoutes();

            config.Routes.MapHttpRoute(
                name: "DefaultApi",
                routeTemplate: "api/{controller}/{id}",
                defaults: new { id = RouteParameter.Optional }
            );

            app.UseWebApi(config);
        }
    }
}
```

16. Open the *Startup.cs* file and add the following line at the end of the *Configuration()* method:

```
ConfigureWebApi(app);
```

Once you have implemented the resource server in your application, you should be able to make requests to the authorization server to get access to the resource published by the resource server. As you saw in the OAuth workflow, you need to get authenticated by the authorization server before you can get an access token. This means that you need to be logged in to the application before being able to make any requests to the */OAuth/Authorize* endpoint.

Now you can create your client application that makes requests to the authorization server and resource server. That client application can be the same application that you used for implementing the authorization and resource servers. We are going to modify the default MVC template for making requests to the Authorization and Resource servers.

1. In the Visual Studio window, click Tools > NuGet Package Manager > Manage NuGet Packages For Solution.

2. In the NuGet Package Manager tab, click Browse.

3. Type **DotNetOpenAuth.OAuth2.Client** and press enter.

4. Click the *DotNetOpenAuth.OAuth2.Client* package. This NuGet package eases the interaction with OAuth servers.

5. On the right side of the NuGet Manager tab, click the checkbox beside your project.

6. Click the Install button.

7. On the Preview Changes window, click OK.

8. Open the *ManageController.cs* file.

9. Add the following *using* statements to the *ManageController.cs* file:

- *using System;*

- *using System.Linq;*

- *using System.Threading.Tasks;*

- *using System.Web;*

- *using System.Web.Mvc;*

- *using Microsoft.AspNet.Identity;*

- *using Microsoft.AspNet.Identity.Owin;*

- *using Microsoft.Owin.Security;*

- *using AuthorizationServer.Models;*

- *using AuthorizationServer.Constants;*

- *using DotNetOpenAuth.OAuth2;*

- *using System.Net.Http;*

10. Replace the *Index()* method with the code shown in Listing 4-22:

LISTING 4-22 Index method in *ManageController.cs*

```
// C#. ASP.NET.
public async Task<ActionResult> Index(ManageMessageId? message)
        {
            ViewBag.StatusMessage =
                message == ManageMessageId.ChangePasswordSuccess ? "Your password has
                been changed."
                : message == ManageMessageId.SetPasswordSuccess ? "Your password has
                been set."
                : message == ManageMessageId.SetTwoFactorSuccess ? "Your two-factor
                authentication provider has been set."
                : message == ManageMessageId.Error ? "An error has occurred."
                : message == ManageMessageId.AddPhoneSuccess ? "Your phone number was
                added."
                : message == ManageMessageId.RemovePhoneSuccess ? "Your phone number was
                removed."
                : "";

            var userId = User.Identity.GetUserId();
            var model = new IndexViewModel
            {
                HasPassword = HasPassword(),
                PhoneNumber = await UserManager.GetPhoneNumberAsync(userId),
                TwoFactor = await UserManager.GetTwoFactorEnabledAsync(userId),
                Logins = await UserManager.GetLoginsAsync(userId),
                BrowserRemembered = await AuthenticationManager.TwoFactorBrowserRemember
                edAsync(userId)
            };
```

```
ViewBag.AccessToken = Request.Form["AccessToken"] ?? "";
ViewBag.RefreshToken = Request.Form["RefreshToken"] ?? "";
ViewBag.Action = "";
ViewBag.ApiResponse = "";

InitializeWebServerClient();
var accessToken = Request.Form["AccessToken"];
if (string.IsNullOrEmpty(accessToken))
{
    var authorizationState = _webServerClient.ProcessUserAuthorization(Request);
    if (authorizationState != null)
    {
        ViewBag.AccessToken = authorizationState.AccessToken;
        ViewBag.RefreshToken = authorizationState.RefreshToken;
        ViewBag.Action = Request.Path;
    }
}

if (!string.IsNullOrEmpty(Request.Form.Get("submit.Authorize")))
{
    var userAuthorization = _webServerClient.PrepareRequestUserAuthorization
    (new[] { "bio", "notes" });
    userAuthorization.Send(HttpContext);
    Response.End();
}
else if (!string.IsNullOrEmpty(Request.Form.Get("submit.Refresh")))
{
    var state = new AuthorizationState
    {
        AccessToken = Request.Form["AccessToken"],
        RefreshToken = Request.Form["RefreshToken"]
    };
    if (_webServerClient.RefreshAuthorization(state))
    {
        ViewBag.AccessToken = state.AccessToken;
        ViewBag.RefreshToken = state.RefreshToken;
    }
}
else if (!string.IsNullOrEmpty(Request.Form.Get("submit.CallApi")))
{
    var resourceServerUri = new Uri(Paths.ResourceServerBaseAddress);
    var client = new HttpClient(_webServerClient.CreateAuthorizingHandler
    (accessToken));
    var body = client.GetStringAsync(new Uri(resourceServerUri, Paths.
    MePath)).Result;
    ViewBag.ApiResponse = body;
}

return View(model);
}
```

11. Add the following property to the *ManageController* class:

```
private WebServerClient _webServerClient;
```

12. Add the following helper method to the *ManageController* class:

```
private void InitializeWebServerClient()
{
    var authorizationServerUri = new Uri(Paths.AuthorizationServerBaseAddress);
    var authorizationServer = new AuthorizationServerDescription
    {
        AuthorizationEndpoint = new Uri(authorizationServerUri, Paths.
        AuthorizePath),
        TokenEndpoint = new Uri(authorizationServerUri, Paths.TokenPath)
    };
    _webServerClient = new WebServerClient(authorizationServer, Clients.Client1.
    Id, Clients.Client1.Secret);
}
```

13. On the *Application_Start()* method in the *Global.asax.cs* file, add the following line:

```
AntiForgeryConfig.SuppressXFrameOptionsHeader = true;
```

14. Add the following *using* statement to the *Global.asax.cs* file:

```
using System.Web.Helpers;
```

15. In the Solution Explorer window, click Views > Manage > Index.cshtml.

16. Add the code shown in Listing 4-23 after the section *Two-Factor Authentication* in the *Index.cshtml* file.

LISTING 4-23 Authorization Code Grant section

```
// C#. ASP.NET.

<dt>Authorization Code Grant Client:</dt>
    <dd>
        <form id="form1" action="@ViewBag.Action" method="POST">
            <div>
                Access Token<br />
                <input id="AccessToken" name="AccessToken" width="604" type="text"
                value="@ViewBag.AccessToken" />
                <input id="Authorize" name="submit.Authorize" value="Authorize"
                type="submit" />
                <br />
                <br />
                Refresh Token<br />
                <input id="RefreshToken" name="RefreshToken" width="604" type="text"
                value="@ViewBag.RefreshToken" />
                <input id="Refresh" name="submit.Refresh" value="Refresh"
                type="submit" />
                <br />
                <br />
                <input id="CallApi" name="submit.CallApi" value="Access Protected
                Resource API" type="submit" />
            </div>
            <div>
```

```
            @ViewBag.ApiResponse
        </div>
    </form>
</dd>
```

At this point, your example application is ready for testing the implementation of the different actors that take part in the OAuth workflow. The following steps show how to test your OAuth implementation to ensure that it works correctly:

1. Open the example project in Visual Studio and press F5 to run the project.

2. Open the web application in a web browser and click the Register link located on the top-left corner of the page.

3. On the Register page, add an email address and password and confirm the password. Then click the Register button. You are going to use this user to grant privileges to OAuth client for making requests to the */OAuth/Me* endpoint.

4. Once you have registered the new user, you are automatically logged on and redirected to the Home page.

5. On the Home page, click your user's email link at the top-left corner of the Home page.

6. On the Manage page, click the Authorize button, which redirects you to the Authorization Server page.

7. On the Authorization Server page, review the information provided and click the Grant button. After you grant access to the OAuth client application, you get the access and refresh token shown in Figure 4-5, which is needed to make requests to the resource server.

8. Click the Access Protected Resource API to make a request to the */OAuth/Me* endpoint. You should get all information stored in the identity claim that you use for making this request, including the scopes *bio* and *notes*.

FIGURE 4-5 OAuth Access and Refresh Token

Implement Managed Service Identity (MSI)/Service Principal authentication

When you are designing your application, you usually identify the different services or systems on which your application depends. For example, your application may need to connect to an Azure SQL Database for storing data or may need to connect to Azure Event Hub for reading messages from other services. In all these situations, there is a common need to authenticate with the service before you can access it. In the Azure SQL Database case, you need to use a connection string; if you need to connect to an Azure Event Hub, you need to use a combination of event publishers and Shared Access Signature (SAS) tokens.

The drawback with this approach is that you need to store a security credential, token, or password to be able to authenticate to the service that you want to access. This is a drawback because you might find that this information is stored on developers' computers or is checked in to the source control by mistake. You can address most of these situations by using the Azure Key Vault, but your code still needs to authenticate to Azure Key Vault to get the information for accessing the other services.

Fortunately, Azure Active Directory (Azure AD) provides the Managed Identities for Azure resources (formerly known as Managed Service Identity) that removes the need of using credentials for authenticating your application to any Azure service that supports Azure AD authentication. This feature automatically creates a managed identity that you can use for authenticating to any service that supports Azure AD authentication, without needing to provide any credential.

When you work with Managed Identities, you can work with two different types:

- **System-assigned managed identities** These are identities that Azure automatically enables when you create an Azure service instance, like an Azure Virtual Machine or an Azure Data Lake Store. Azure creates an identity associated with the new instance and stores it to the Azure AD tenant associated with the subscription where you created the service instance. If you decide to delete the service instance, then Azure automatically deletes the managed instance associated with the service instance stored in the Azure AD tenant.

- **User-assigned managed identities**   You can create your managed identities in the Azure AD tenant associated with your Azure subscription. You can associate this type of managed identity to one or more service instances. The lifecycle of the managed identity is independent of the service instance. This means that if you delete the service instance, the user-assigned managed identity remains in the Azure AD tenant. You need to remove the managed identity manually.

Usually, you use the system-assigned managed identities when your workload is contained within the same Azure resource or you need to independently identify each of the service instances, like Virtual Machines. On the other hand, if you need to grant access to a workload that is distributed across different resources or you need to pre-authorize a resource as part of a provisioning flow, you should use user-assigned managed identities.

When you work with Managed Identities, you need to bear in mind three concepts:

- **Client ID**   This is a unique identifier generated by Azure AD. This ID associates the application and the service principal during its initial provisioning.

- **Principal ID**   This is the ID of the service principal associated with the managed identity. A service principal and a managed identity are tightly coupled, but they are different objects. The service principal is the object that you use to grant role-based access to an Azure resource.

- **Azure Instance Metadata Service (IMDS)**   When you use Managed Identities in an Azure VM, you can use the IMDS for requesting OAuth Access Token from your application deployed within the VM. The IMDS is a REST endpoint that you can access from your VM using a non-routable IP address (169.254.169.254).

The following example shows how to create a system-assigned identity in an Azure App Service and how to use this managed identity from your code for accessing an Azure Key Vault. For this example, you need to have an empty Azure App Service, an Azure Key Vault, and at least one item on the Azure Key Vault. You also need to have your Visual Studio connected to the Azure Subscription where you have configured the Azure Key Vault.

1. Open the Azure portal at *https://portal.azure.com*.

2. In the search text box on top of the Azure portal, type the name of your Azure Web App. If you don't have an Azure Web App, you can create a new Azure Web App by using the procedure at *https://docs.microsoft.com/en-in/azure/app-service/app-service-web-get-started-dotnet*.

3. On the Azure Web App Service blade, click the Identity menu item in the Settings section.

4. On the Status switch control, click the On option.

5. Click the Save button.

6. In the Enable System Assigned Managed Identity dialog box, click the Yes button.

7. Once you enable the system-assigned managed identity, you get the Principal or Object ID, as shown in Figure 4-6.

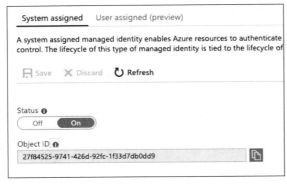

FIGURE 4-6 System assigned managed identity

8. In the Visual Studio window, click New > Project.

9. In the New Project window, in the tree control on the left side of the window, click Installed > Visual C# > Cloud.

10. Select the ASP.NET Web Application (.NET Framework) template.

11. At the bottom of the New Project window, type a Name and a Solution Name for the project.

12. Select the Location where you want to save your code.

13. Click the OK button at the bottom-left corner of the window.

14. In the New ASP.NET Web Application, select the MVC template.

15. Click the OK button.

16. In the Visual Studio window, click Tools > NuGet Package Manager > Manage NuGet Packages For Solution.

17. In the NuGet Package Manager tab, click Browse.

18. Type **Microsoft.Azure.Services.AppAuthentication** and press Enter.

19. Click the *Microsoft.Azure.Services.AppAuthentication* package.

20. At the right side of the NuGet Manager tab, click on the checkbox beside your project.

21. Click the Install button.

22. In the Preview Changes window, click OK.

23. On the License Acceptance page, click the I Accept button.

24. Repeat steps 11 to 23 and install the *Microsoft.Azure.KeyVault* package.

25. Open the Controllers > *HomeController.cs* file.

26. Add the following statements to the *HomeController.cs* file:

    - *using Microsoft.Azure.KeyVault;*
    - *using Microsoft.Azure.Services.AppAuthentication;*

27. Replace the content of the *Index()* method with the content of Listing 4-24. The important pieces of code related to accessing the Azure Key Vault are highlighted in bold.

LISTING 4-24 Getting a secret from the key vault

```
// C#. ASP.NET.
string keyVaultName = "<PUT_YOUR_KEY_VAULT_NAME_HERE>";
string secretName = "<PUT_YOUR_SECRET_NAME_HERE>";

//Get a token for accessing the Key Vault.
var azureServiceTokenProvider = new AzureServiceTokenProvider();

//Create a Key Vault client for accessing the items in the vault.
var keyVault = new KeyVaultClient(new KeyVaultClient.AuthenticationCallback(azureService
TokenProvider.KeyVaultTokenCallback));

var secret = Task.Run(async () =>  await keyVault.GetSecretAsync($"https://
{keyVaultName}.vault.azure.net/secrets/{secretName}")).GetAwaiter().GetResult();

ViewBag.KeyVaultName = keyVaultName;
ViewBag.keyName = secretName;
ViewBag.secret = secret.Value;

return View();
```

Before you can access the Azure Key Vault, you need to get an OAuth token by using the *AzureServiceTokenProvider* class. Then you can create your Azure Key Vault client and get any item stored in the vault. When you create the Azure Key Vault client, make sure you provide the *KeyVaultTokenCallback*. Even if you get a valid access token, you still need to grant access to your Azure App Service application in the Azure Key Vault.

28. Open the Views > Home > *Index.cshtml* file.

29. Append the content of Listing 4-25 to the end of the file.

LISTING 4-25 Adding secret information to the home page

```
// C#. ASP.NET.
<div class="row">
    <div class="col-lg-12">
        <dl class="dl-horizontal">
            <dt>Key Vault Name: </dt>
            <dd>@ViewBag.keyVaultName</dd>
            <dt>Key Name: </dt>
            <dd>@ViewBag.keyName</dd>
            <dt>Key Secret: </dt>
            <dd>@ViewBag.secret</dd>
        </dl>

    </div>
</div>
```

At this point, you could run your project and see the results. Depending on the access policies defined in your Azure Key Vault, your Azure user may already have access to the secrets stored in the key vault. In that case, you should be able to access the secret stored in the Azure Key Vault. If you get an exception when running the web application, there are good chances that you don't have access to the Azure Key Vault. The following steps show how to grant access to your Azure App Service application in the Azure Key Vault.

1. Open the Azure Portal.
2. Type the name of your Azure Key Vault in the search text box at the top of the Azure Portal. If you don't already have an Azure Key Vault and need to create a new one, you can use the procedure at *https://docs.microsoft.com/en-us/azure/key-vault/quick-create-portal.*
3. On your Azure Key Vault blade, click Access Policies in the Settings section.
4. On the Access Policies blade, click Add New.
5. On the Add Access Policy page, select Secret Management in the Configure From Template drop-down menu.
6. Click the Select Principal control.
7. In the Principal panel, type the name of your Azure App Service in the Select text box. Your Azure App Service should appear on the list below the text box.
8. Click your App Service name in the list below the Select text box.
9. Click the Select button at the bottom of the panel.
10. Click the OK button at the bottom of the Add Access Policy blade.
11. Click the Save button at the top of the Access Policies blade.
12. In the Visual Studio window, right click your project's name in the Solution Explorer window.
13. In the contextual menu, click Publish.
14. In the Pick A Publish Target window, ensure that App Service is selected on the left side of the window.
15. In the Azure App Service section, click Select Existing.
16. Click the Publish button at the bottom-right corner of the window.
17. In the App Service window, in the tree view at the bottom of the window, look for your App Service and click it.
18. Click the OK button.

At this point, Visual Studio starts publishing your web application to the selected Azure App Service. When the publishing operation finishes, you should be able to see your web application showing the content of the secret stored in your Key Vault.

Skill 4.2: Implement access control

Authentication is only the first step in the process of securing access to the resources managed by your application. Once you successfully authenticate the user for accessing your application, you need to grant access to the different areas of your application. Not all users need to access the same kind of information. You can grant access to your resources based on the actions that a user needs to do in your application. Or you could grant user access to your application based on information the user provides when he or she tries to access some information.

Granting access based on the group of actions that a user needs to do in your application is knowns as Role-Based Access Control. If you control the access to your application based on the information that the user provides, then you are performing Claims-Based Access Control.

This skill covers how to:

- Implement CBAC (Claims-Based Access Control) authorization
- Implement RBAC (Role-Based Access Control) authorization
- Create shared access signatures

Implement CBAC (Claims-Based Access Control) authorization

When you need to control the access to your application, one of the mechanisms that you can use to make the distinction between users who can access a resource, those who can't is CBAC (Claims-Based Access Control) authorization. Those who cannot access are referred to as claims. When we talk about claims, you should think about a property associated with the user. Once the user has been authenticated, the object that represents the user in your application can have attached some attributes, such as email address, birthdate, department membership, or nearly any other attribute. In general terms, a claim represents a fact about the authenticated identity. An authenticated identity can be a real user or an application.

Using claims-based access control means that you use one or more of these attributes—represented as a key/value pair—for restricting or granting access to the resources managed by your application. For example, you could grant access to users that are of legal age by using the birthdate claim, or you could use the department membership claim for granting access to the contract documents stored in your application only to the members of the legal department. You can also create complex access control rules by using several claims in the access control.

When you work with claims, you are very dependent on the identity management service that you use for providing authentication. If you relay the authentication to external identity management services, such as Azure AD, Google, or Facebook, you are limited to the claims that those providers add to the access token. A solution for that limitation could be adding your claims to the identity once the users have been authenticated. In that case, you need to extend the identity model to store the values of your application's claims and add those claims programmatically to the identity when the user is authenticated. On the other hand, if you decide to implement your authorization server, you have the flexibility of adding the claims that your application needs to work.

In both cases, you need to follow the same pattern for implementing claims-based access control. You can control the access to your application at the controller or actions within the controller level. You use the *AuthorizeAttribute* applied to the correct level. Before you can work with the claims in your controllers, you need to define a policy in your code. Using that policy, you define the conditions that the identity should meet. For example, you can define a policy for ensuring that the *EmployeeID* claim is present in the user's identity, or you can check whether the user is of legal age by checking the birthdate claim. The following example shows how to check the claims for a user and make claims-based access control. For the sake of simplicity, you are going to use Azure AD authentication in this example.

1. Open Visual Studio 2017.
2. Click File > New > Project.
3. On the New Project window, in the tree control on the left side of the window, click Installed > Visual C# > Cloud.
4. Select the ASP.NET Core Web Application template.
5. Type a Name for your project.
6. Select the Location where your project will be stored.
7. Click the OK button.
8. In the New ASP.NET Core Web Application window, select the Web Application (Model-View-Controller) template.
9. Click the Change Authentication button.
10. On the Change Authentication window, select the Work or School Accounts option on the left side of the window.
11. On the right side of the window, select Cloud – Single Organization from the first drop-down menu.
12. In the Domain drop-down menu, select your Azure AD tenant's domain.

13. In the Directory Access Permissions, check the Read Directory Data option. Your window should look similar to Figure 4-7.

14. Click the OK button.

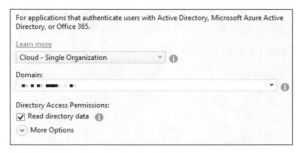

FIGURE 4-7 Configuring Authentication

15. In the New ASP.NET Core Web Application window, click the OK button.

16. Open the *Startup.cs* file.

17. Add the following code snippet after the line that starts with

```
.AddAzureAD:
services.AddAuthorization(options =>
        {
            options.AddPolicy("RequireMFA", policy => policy.
            RequireClaim("http://schemas.microsoft.com/claims/
            authnmethodsreferences", "mfa"));
        });
```

The previous code snippet creates a policy named *RequireMFA*. You use this policy to control the access to resources in your application. When you define the policy, you use the *RequireClaim()* method for setting which claims you require to be present in a user's identity to access your resources. In this example, you only allow access to the protected resources to users who have enabled the Multifactor Authentication feature.

18. In the Solution Explorer window, right-click the Controllers folder. In the contextual menu, click Add > Controller.

19. In the Add Scaffold window, select the MVC Controller – Empty template.

20. Click the Add button.

21. In the Add Empty MVC Controller, type **SecureController**.

22. In the Solution Explorer window, right click on the Views folder. In the contextual menu, click Add > New Folder.

23. Type **Secure** as the new folder's name.

24. In the Solution Explorer window, right-click the Secure folder. In the contextual menu, click Add > View.

25. In the Add MVC View window, type **Index** in the View Name textbox.

26. Click the Add button.

27. Open the *Index.cshtml* file in the Views > Secure folder.

28. Replace the content of the *Index.cshtml* file with the following code:

```
@{
    ViewData["Title"] = "Secure access";
}
<h1>Your user has MFA enabled</h1>
```

29. Open the Views > Home > *Index.cshtml* file.

30. Replace the content of the file with the code shown in Listing 4-26:

LISTING 4-26 Showing claims in the home page

```
// C#. ASP.NET.
@using System.Security.Claims;

@{
    ViewData["Title"] = "Home Page";
}
<div class="text-center">
    <h1 class="display-4">Welcome</h1>
    <p>Learn about <a href="https://docs.microsoft.com/aspnet/core">building Web apps
    with ASP.NET Core</a>.</p>
    <p>Access <a asp-action="Index" asp-controller="Secure">secure</a> content</p>
</div>
<div>
    <table class="table-hover claim-table">
        <tr>
            <th>Claim Type</th>
            <th>Claim Value</th>
        </tr>
        <tbody>
            @foreach (Claim claim in User.Claims)
            {
            <tr>
                <td>@claim.Type</td>
                <td>@claim.Value</td>
            </tr>
            }
        </tbody>
    </table>
</div>
```

At this point, if you run your application and you log in using any user account existing in the tenant that you configured on step 12, your home page should show you the list of the claims provided by Azure AD attached to the logged-in user's identity. If you click the Secure link on top of the list of claims, you should be able to see the secured page with the message *Your user has MFA enabled*. You can see this page using any Azure AD user because you didn't protect the access to this resource yet. The following steps show how to protect the access to these resources by only allowing users who have the MFA feature enabled to access them.

1. Open the *SecureController.cs* file.

2. Add the following class attribute to the class. You should put this code snippet before the declaration of the class:

```
[Authorize(Policy = "RequireMFA")]
```

3. Run your code again and log in to the application using a user who does not have the MFA feature enabled. When you try to access the Secure page, you get an *AccessDenied* error. If you use a user with the MFA feature enabled, you should be able to access the Secure page and see the *Your user has MFA enabled* message.

NOTE   **ACCESS ERROR**

In this example, when you get the *AccessDenied* error, you actually get a *NotFound HTTP ERROR 404*. The reason for this is that you didn't implement the error control and your code is redirecting you to the route that should show the *AccessDenied* error. For the sake of brevity, we decided not to implement that error control. In a real-world application, you should implement the appropriate error control.

NEED MORE REVIEW?   **CLAIMS-BASED AUTHORIZATION IN ASP.NET CORE**

You can find more information about how to create more complex policies for protecting your resources by reviewing the following articles:

- Claims-based authorization in ASP.NET Core: *https://docs.microsoft.com/en-us/aspnet/core/security/authorization/claims*
- Policy-based authorization in ASP.NET Core: *https://docs.microsoft.com/en-us/aspnet/core/security/authorization/policies*

Implement RBAC (Role-Based Access Control) authorization

In the previous section, we reviewed how to control the access to your application based on properties of the user, such as birthdate or if the user has Multifactor Authentication enabled. In this section, we are going to review how to control the access to your application based on the actions that your user is allowed to do in your application. For example, a user could have permission to delete data from your application. Another user could update data related to prices in an online shopping application. Or another user could perform all possible actions in the web application. You can also group the available actions in your application into groups of actions, or roles.

A role represents the group actions or permissions that your users have for doing things in your application. For example, a user with the Administrator role would have full access to all areas in your application. In the online shopping application, the administrator could create new products, add a new currency, or configure a new payment gateway. Using the same online shopping application, a user with the Contributor role could add, update, or remove products but not configure currencies or payment gateways.

When you are developing your web application, you can implement Role-Based Access Control by defining which roles are meaningful for your application and adding the needed constraints to your code. Azure Active Directory allows you to define your custom roles in the manifest of your application registered in the Azure AD tenant. Once you have defined your roles, you can use these roles in your code for making the appropriate access control. The following example shows how to define and implement a Role-Based Access Control (RBAC) using Azure AD app roles. These roles are sent to your application as role claims inserted in your user's identity.

1. Open a command-line window.

2. Change your working directory to the path where you want to save the project. For example:

   ```
   cd c:\az2013_examples
   ```

3. Clone the repository with the source code for this example:

   ```
   git clone https://github.com/Azure-Samples/microsoft-identity-platform-aspnetcore-
   webapp-tutorial.git
   ```

4. Open Visual Studio 2017.

5. Open the solution in the *5-WebApp-AuthZ\5-1-Roles* folder, which is located in the folder where you cloned the project.

Once you have the code of the example, you need to register an application in your Azure AD Tenant before you can authenticate users in the application:

6. Open the Azure Portal (*https://portal.azure.com*).

7. On the left side of the portal, click the Azure Active Directory item.

8. On the Azure Active Directory blade, in the Manage section, click App Registrations.

9. In the App Registrations blade, click the New Registration button.

10. In the Register An Application blade, type a name for your application.

11. In the Supported Account Types radio button control, ensure that the selected option is Accounts In this Organizational Directory Only.

12. Click the Register button at the bottom of the blade.

13. In your registered application's blade, copy the Application (Client) ID and Directory (Tenant) ID values from the Overview panel. You need these values later, so be sure to copy them.

14. In the Manage section, shown in Figure 4-8, click Manifest.

FIGURE 4-8 Manage section in a registered application

15. In the Manifest panel, change the value of the setting *groupMembershipClaims* to *SecurityGroup*. This setting should look like the following code snippet:

```
"groupMembershipClaims": "SecurityGroup",
```

16. In the next step, you are going to add the roles that your application needs for performing the Role-Based Access Control. You need to provide a valid GUID for each application role that you add to your application's manifest. You can generate new GUIDs using the *New-Guid* PowerShell cmdlet, the *uuidgen* command for Linux and MacOSX or any of the existing online GUID generators.

17. When you define new application roles, you need to ensure that the *Value* property matches exactly with the role name that you configure in your application.

18. In the Manifest panel, add the JSON code shown in Listing 4-27 to the *appRoles* section.

LISTING 4-27 JSON Application Roles definition

```
"appRoles": [
    {
        "allowedMemberTypes": [
            "User"
        ],
        "description": "User readers can read basic profiles of all users in the
        directory",
        "displayName": "UserReaders",
        "id": "a816142a-2e8e-46c4-9997-f984faccb625",
        "isEnabled": true,
        "lang": null,
        "origin": "Application",
        "value": "UserReaders"
    },
    {
```

```
            "allowedMemberTypes": [
                "User"
            ],
            "description": "Directory viewers can view objects in the whole directory.",
            "displayName": "DirectoryViewers",
            "id": "72ff9f52-8011-49e0-a4f4-cc1bb26206fa",
            "isEnabled": true,
            "lang": null,
            "origin": "Application",
            "value": "DirectoryViewers"
        }
    ],
```

19. In the Manifest panel, click the Save button.

20. In the navigation menu on the left side of your application's blade, click Certificates & Secrets.

21. On the Certificates & Secrets panel, click the New Client Secret button.

22. Type a Description for the client secret. This description is only for your reference.

23. Click the Add button.

24. In the Client Secrets lists, copy the value of the new client secret. You are going to use it in a later step, so you should copy this value now. Once you leave the Certificates & Secrets blade, you won't be able to see the value of any client secret.

25. In the navigation menu on the left side of your application's blade, click Authentication.

26. On the Redirect URIs section, add a new redirect URI. Ensure that the selected type is Web.

27. On the Redirect URI textbox, type **https://localhost:44321/signing-oidc.**

28. On the Advanced settings, in the Logout URL setting, type **https://localhost:44321// signout-callback-oidc**.

29. In the Implicit Grant section, check the ID Tokens option.

30. At the top of the Authentication blade, click the Save button.

31. In the Visual Studio 2017 window, on the Solution Explorer, open the *appsetings.json* file in the *WebApp-OpenIDConnect-DotNet* project.

32. In the *appsettings.json* file, replace the values of the following properties with the values that you copied in steps 13 and 22:

    ■ Domain   This is the domain name of your tenant and should be a DNS fully qualified name, such as contoso.com. You can find the name of your tenant at the top of the Overview blade of your Azure Active Directory tenant in the Azure Portal.

    ■ TenantId   You got this value in step 13.

    ■ ClientId   You got this value in step 13.

    ■ ClientSecret   You got this value in step 22.

At this point, you should be able to run the example application in Visual Studio. Because you didn't assign any of the application roles to any of your Azure AD users, in order for users to access protected items, you need to assign application roles to your Azure AD users. The next steps show how to assign an application role to any of your Azure AD users. For this example, you should use two different users to test the different application roles.

1. Open the Azure Portal (*https://portal.azure.com*).
2. In the navigation menu on the left side of the portal, click Azure Active Directory.
3. On the Azure Active Directory blade, in the Manage section on the navigation menu, click Enterprise Applications.
4. On the Enterprise Applications blade, look for your application's name in the list of applications and click it.
5. On your application's blade, on the Manage section in the navigation menu, click Users And Groups.
6. On the Users And Groups panel, click the Add User button.
7. On the Add Assignment panel, click the Users And Groups item.
8. On the Users And Groups panel, look for the user to whom you want to assign a role.
9. Click each user for whom you want to assign the application role.
10. Click the Select button.
11. On the Add Assignment panel, click the Select Role item.
12. On the Select Role panel, shown in Figure 4-9, select the role that you want to assign to your users.
13. Click the Select button.
14. In the Add Assignment panel, click the Assign button.

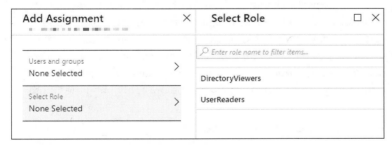

FIGURE 4-9 Assigning an application role

15. Repeat steps 5-12 for any additional role assignment.
16. In Visual Studio, rebuild your solution by clicking Build > Rebuild Solution.
17. Press F5 to run your solution.

18. When you log in the first time to your application using your Azure AD user, Azure AD should ask your consent to access your Azure AD tenant information. On the Permissions Requested page, check the Consent On Behalf Of Your Organization option.

19. Click the Accept button.

20. On the application's home page, click the List All Users In The Tenant (You Need To Be A Member Of The 'UserReaders' Role) link. If you assigned your user the *UserReaders* role, you should be able to see a list of all users in your Azure AD tenant.

21. On the application's home page, click the link List All The Groups And Roles The Signed In User Is A Member Of (You Need To Be A Member Of The 'DirectoryViewers' Role). If you assigned your user the *DirectoryViewers* role, you should be able to see a list of all roles and groups that your user is a member of.

If you get a Denied Access error, review the role that you assigned to the user who you are using for login to the application.

During the configuration of this example, we reviewed how to create your custom application roles. Now we are going to review how to use those application roles in your code for controlling the access to the different parts of your application.

You configure the role-based authentication in the *ConfigureService()* method in the *Startup.cs* file. In this example, your code extracts the role membership based on the claims contained in the JWT token. For this reason, you need to tell your code which claims contain the roles. You do this by using the following code snippet:

```
services.Configure<OpenIdConnectOptions>(AzureADDefaults.OpenIdScheme, options =>
    {
        // The claim in the Jwt token where App roles are available.
        options.TokenValidationParameters.RoleClaimType = "roles";
    });
```

When your code extracts and maps the claims from the JWT token, it uses the default claims mapping. The drawback of using this default mapping is that the claims are mapped using the old format for accommodating old SAML applications. This means that using the default mapping, the name of the claim that contains the role membership of your user would be *http://schemas.microsoft.com/ws/2008/06/identity/claims/role* instead of just "roles." You can change this behavior by adding the following line of code before configuring the OAuth authentication:

```
JwtSecurityTokenHandler.DefaultMapInboundClaims = false;
```

Once you have configured your code for extracting the roles from the JWT token, you need to configure the access control on each controller for which you need to restrict the access. In this example, you use the *AppRoles* helper class for storing the different application roles, which is shown in the following code snippet:

```
/// <summary>
/// Contains a list of all the Azure Ad app roles this app works with
/// </summary>
```

```
public static class AppRoles
{
    public const string UserReaders = "UserReaders";
    public const string DirectoryViewers = "DirectoryViewers";
}
```

Bear in mind that the strings defined for the properties of this class match exactly with the *Value* property of each application role that you configured in the application's manifest.

You control which role is allowed to access a resource in your application by using the *Authorize* attribute on each *action* method that you want to protect. The following code snippets show how to protect the *Groups()* action in the *Account* controller and the *Users()* action in the *Home* controller:

```
//Allow access only to users with the DirectoryViewers role.
[Authorize(Roles = AppRoles.DirectoryViewers)]
public async Task<IActionResult> Groups()
{

//Allow access only to users with the UserReaders role.
[Authorize(Roles = AppRoles.UserReaders )]
public async Task<IActionResult> Users()
{
```

EXAM TIP

Role-Based Access Control grants access to the different resources of your application based on the actions that the user is allowed to perform in your application. Claims-Based Access Control grants access to the resource based on the information that the user has; for example, this information could be the birthdate or if Multifactor Authentication option is enabled for the user. You should not confuse the RBAC roles that you can define for your application with the built-in RBAC roles available for managing the access to the Azure Resources.

Create shared access signatures

Until now, all the protection and access control mechanisms that we have reviewed in this section had to do with protecting the information managed directly by your application. These mechanisms are good if your application manages and presents the information to the user, but they are not appropriate for other services that can also store information managed by your application. If your application uses Azure Storage accounts for storing some reports, images, or documents in a table, and you want to grant access to third parties to that information, none of the mechanisms we already reviewed are appropriate for this scenario.

Azure provides you with the ability to control the access to information stored in Azure Storage Accounts without needing to grant access to external user accounts to the Azure Storage Account or sharing the Access Keys with third parties. This mechanism is the Shared Access Signature.

A Shared Access Signature (SAS) is a special token that you can use for granting granular access to only specific parts of your Azure Storage Account. When you create an SAS token, you define which service (blobs, files, queues, or tables) can access the user, and which operation the user can perform in that service. You can define an SAS at different levels:

- **Service** You grant access to all containers and elements related to the same service. For example, if you define an SAS for the Blob service, the user has access to all containers and blobs in the Azure Blob storage account.

- **Container** You grant access only to all elements stored in a single container inside a storage service. For example, if you define an SAS for the blob container test, the user can access any blob created in the test container.

- **Element** You grant access only to specific elements in a container. You can only create SAS tokens for blobs and files. For example, you can create an SAS for a file in a file share or a blob in a blob container.

The following example shows how to create a Shared Access Signature for a blob in a blob container. For this example, you need an Azure Storage Account with a blob container that is configured with a private access level and a blob stored in the blob container:

1. Open the Azure Portal (*https://portal.azure.com*).

2. In the search text box on the top of the Azure Portal, type the name of your Azure Storage Account.

3. In the Results list, click the name of your Azure Storage Account.

4. On your Azure Storage Account's blade, click *StorageExplorer* (preview) in the navigation menu on the left side of the blade.

5. On the Storage Explorer (preview) panel shown in Figure 4-10, expand the Blob Containers node and click on the container that stores the blob to which you need to grant access.

FIGURE 4-10 Storage services in the Storage Explorer (preview)

6. In the Blob Containers panel, right-click the blob and click Get Share Access Signature on the contextual menu.

7. In the Shared Access Signature panel shown in Figure 4-11, configure the Start Time, Expiry Time, and Permissions that you want to grant to the SAS token.

8. Click the Create button at the bottom of the panel.

FIGURE 4-11 Creating a Shared Access Signature

9. On the Shared Access Signature panel, copy the URL of the newly generated SAS. You can share this SAS URL with any third party who needs to access this specific blob.

You can use these same steps for creating an SAS for a container. Right-click on the container for which you want to create the SAS and click Get Shared Access Signature in the contextual menu.

As you can imagine, one drawback of using this approach is that anyone who has access to the SAS URL can access the information protected by that SAS. You can improve the security of the SAS tokens by creating an Access Policy and attaching the policy to the SAS token. In the "Design and Implement Policies for Tables" section in Chapter 3, we reviewed how Access Policy works for Azure tables. The same concepts that you reviewed in that section apply to the rest of services available in the Azure Storage Account.

Skill 4.3: Implement secure data solutions

In the previous skills, we reviewed how to protect the access to the data by authenticating and authorizing users who try to access the information managed in your application. This protection is only a portion of the mechanisms that you should put in place for protecting your data. You also need to ensure that your data is unreadable by non-authorized users while the data is traveling from the server to your users' application or browser and vice-versa. You should also ensure that once your users don't need to work with your application data, this data is securely stored on your servers. You can achieve both objectives by applying encryption techniques to your data while they are traveling over the internet (encryption in transit) or while they are stored in your server (encryption at rest).

When you encrypt your data, you need to use encryption and decryption keys or secrets for accessing and protecting the data. Storing these secrets and encryption keys is as important as encrypting the data. Losing an encryption or decryption key is similar to losing the keys to your house. The Azure Key Vault allows you to securely store these encryption/decryption keys as well as other secrets or certificates that your applications may require in a secured encryption store in Azure. In conjunction with Managed Identities, the Azure Key Vault services allow you to securely store your secrets without needing to store a password, certificate, or any kind of credentials for accessing your secrets.

> **This skill covers how to:**
> - Encrypt and decrypt data at rest and in transit
> - Create, read, update, and delete keys, secrets, and certificates by using the KeyVault API

Encrypt and decrypt data at rest and in transit

When you access an Azure service, you are sending and receiving information that travels over the Internet. If that information is not protected, a malicious user could steal that information. The solution for protecting your information while it is traveling over the Internet is to encrypt that information before it is sent from the source and decrypt it when it arrives at the destination. This process is known as encryption in transit. Azure offers different techniques for applying encryption in transit to your communications with the Azure services:

- **SSL/TLS** Microsoft uses TLS for encrypting the connections between Azure services and its customers. TLS is a well-known protocol for encrypting connections. This protocol is the base for other secure protocols like HTTPS or RDP. Microsoft also uses the Perfect Forward Secrecy (PFS) feature for ensuring the uniqueness of the keys used for the encryption in the TLS protocol.

- **SAS** When you configure a Shared Access Signature for your storage account, you have the option to enforce the use of the HTTPS protocol. This means you ensure that your data is encrypted in transit while it is traveling from or to the Azure datacenter.

- **SMB 3.0** You can use the SMB 3.0 protocol for accessing data in your Azure File Storage or your Windows Server 2012 or newer Azure Virtual Machines. This protocol supports encryption that is enabled by default for Azure File Storage. If you want to use

SMB 3.0 in your Azure VMs, you need to enable the encryption on the file shares. Azure only allows encrypted connections to the Azure Files from outside the region or datacenter if SMB 3.0 encryption is enabled.

- **RDP**   You can access your IaaS Windows Virtual Machines by using the Remote Desktop Protocol (RDP). This protocol uses TLS for encrypting the connection from your Windows, Linux, or MacOSX RDP client to your Azure VM.

- **SSH**   You can access your IaaS Linux Virtual Machines by using the Secure Shell protocol (SSH). The SSH protocol encrypts all the communications between the client and the server. You can use a public/private key pair for authentication, eliminating the need for using usernames and passwords.

- **VPN**   The Virtual Private Network (VPN) allows you to establish a secure connection with your Azure Virtual Networks using different secure and well-known protocols, such as IPSec/IKE or SSTP (based on HTTPS connections). You can even use your internal Public Key Infrastructure (PKI) for using your internal certificates for authenticating Point-to-Site VPN clients.

Use the following procedure for enforcing HTTPS connections on your Azure App Service application:

1. Open the Azure Portal (*https://portal.azure.com*).

2. In the search textbox at the top of the Azure Portal, type the name of your Azure App Service application.

3. In the result list, click your Azure App Service application.

4. On your Azure App Service application's blade, on the navigation menu at the left side of the blade, click TLS/SSL Settings in the Settings section.

5. On the TLS/SSL Settings panel shown in Figure 4-12, click the HTTPS Only switch control and set this control to On.

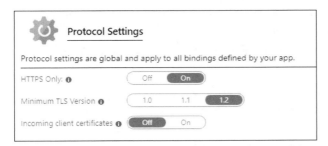

FIGURE 4-12 Configuring HTTPS options in an Azure App Service

Encryption at rest is the capability that Azure offers of encrypting your data while it is stored in any of the services offered by Azure. When encryption at rest is enabled on Azure services, such as Azure Storage, Azure SQL Database, Azure Data Lake, or Azure Cosmos DB, the data is encrypted when it is committed to the storage system, and it is decrypted when you need to access it. Microsoft takes care of the encryption keys for these services.

Azure uses symmetric cryptography for encrypting and decrypting a large amount of data using a Data Encryption Key (DEK). This data can be partitioned. In that case, Azure uses different encryption keys for different partitions. Azure stores the encryption keys in a secure location with identity-based access control and audit policies. Azure uses asymmetric keys, or Key Encryption Keys (KEK), for encrypting the symmetric key on the secure location. Using that asymmetric key enhances the security level when storing the encryption key used for your data. When you plan to enable encryption at rest, you should consider three different data encryption models:

- **Server-side encryption using Service-Managed keys**   In this model, the Azure service provides and manages the encryption keys. The Azure Resource Provider performs all the encryption and decryption operations.

- **Server-side encryption using Customer-Managed keys in Azure Vault**   In this model, the customer provides and manages the encryption keys. The encryption keys are stored in an Azure Key Vault managed by the customer. The Azure Resource Provider performs all the encryption and decryption operations.

- **Server-side encryption using Customer-Managed keys on customer-controller hardware**   In this model, the customer provides and manages the encryption keys. The encryption keys are stored using specialized hardware controlled by the customer. The Azure Resource Provider performs all the encryption and decryption operations. Not all Azure services support this type of integration with external services.

- **Customer-side encryption**   The customer encrypts the data before uploading it to the Azure service and decrypts the data after downloading from the Azure service. In this model, the Azure service cannot see the decrypted data. The encryption keys are managed by the customer, using on-premises or cloud-based keys stores.

The following example shows how to ensure that encryption at rest is enabled for an Azure SQL Database:

1. Open the Azure Portal (*https://portal.azure.com*).

2. Type the name of your SQL Database in the search text box at the top of the Azure Portal.

3. On the Azure SQL Database blade of your database, click Transparent Data Encryption on the Security section on the navigation menu.

4. On the Transparent Data Encryption blade shown in Figure 4-13, ensure that the Data Encryption switch is set to On.

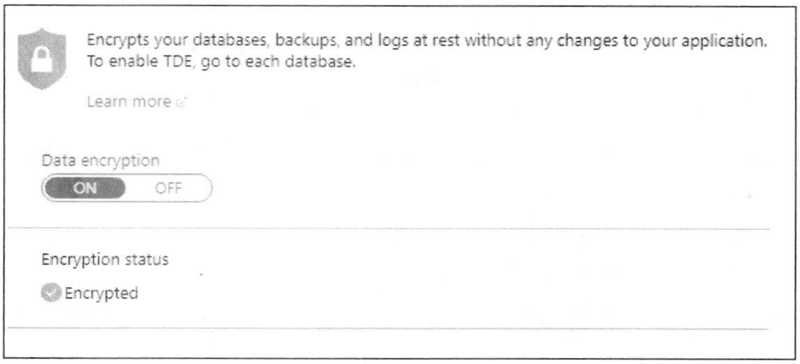

FIGURE 4-13 Transparent Data Encryption

> **NEED MORE REVIEW?** AZURE ENCRYPTION-AT-REST
>
> You can find more information about how Encryption at Rest works by reviewing the article at *https://docs.microsoft.com/en-us/azure/security/azure-security-encryption-atrest*.
>
> You can also extend your information about the different encryption options available in Azure by reviewing the article at *https://docs.microsoft.com/en-us/azure/security/security-azure-encryption-overview*.

Create, read, update, and delete keys, secrets, and certificates by using the KeyVault API

Azure Key Vault is the service provided by Microsoft for securely storing secret keys and certificates in a centralized, secure store. By using Azure Key Vault, your developers no longer need to store this sensitive information on their computers while they are developing an application. Thanks to the identity-based access control, you only need to configure a policy for granting access to the needed service or user principals to the secure store. Another advantage is that you can apply fine-grained access control, allowing access to specific secrets only to the needed application or user.

The next example shows how to use the KeyVault API for creating, reading, updating, or deleting the different elements that you can store in the Azure Key Vault. You need an empty Azure App Service and an Azure Key Vault configured in your Azure subscription to run this example.

1. Open the Azure portal at *https://portal.azure.com*.
2. In the search text box on top of the Azure portal, type the name of your Azure Web App. Click the name of your Azure Web App.
3. On the Azure Web App Service blade, click on the Identity menu item in the Settings section.

4. In the Status switch control, click the On option.

5. Click Save.

6. In the Enable System Assigned Managed Identity dialog box, click Yes.

7. Once you enable the system-assigned managed identity, you get the Principal or Object ID associated with your Azure App Service.

8. In the search text box at the top of the Azure portal, type the name of your Azure Key Vault. Click the name of your Azure Key Vault.

9. On the Key Vault blade, click Access Policies in the Settings section in the navigation menu.

10. On the Access Policies blade, click Add New.

11. On the Add Access Policy panel, click the Configure From Template drop-down menu and select the Key, Secret, and Certificate Management option.

12. Click Select Principal.

13. On the Principal panel, type the name of your Azure App Service in the Select textbox.

14. In the results list, click the name of your Azure App Service.

15. Click the Select button.

16. On the Add Access Policy panel, click OK.

17. On the Access Policies blade, click Save.

18. Repeat steps 10 to 17 and add the user account that you use for accessing your Azure subscription. You need to add this policy to be able to debug your code using Visual Studio. You need to ensure that you add the policy for granting access to the same user account that you use accessing your Azure subscription from Visual Studio.

19. Open Visual Studio 2017.

20. Click File > New > Project.

21. On the New Project window, on the navigation menu on the left of the window, click Installed > Visual C# > Cloud.

22. In the template list, select ASP.NET Web Application (.NET Framework).

23. At the bottom of the window, type a Name for the project.

24. Select the Location where this project will be saved.

25. Click OK.

26. On the New ASP.NET Web Application window, select the MVC template.

27. Click OK.

28. In the Visual Studio window, click Tools > NuGet Package Manager > Manage NuGet Packages For Solution.

29. On the NuGet Package Manager tab, click Browse.

30. Type **Microsoft.Azure.Services.AppAuthentication** and press Enter.

31. Click the *Microsoft.Azure.Services.AppAuthentication* package.

32. On the right side of the NuGet Manager tab, click the checkbox next to your project.

33. Click the Install button.

34. In the Preview Changes window, click OK.

35. In the License Acceptance window, click the I Accept button.

36. Repeat steps 27 to 34 and install the *Microsoft.Azure.KeyVault* package.

37. Open the *HomeController.cs* file.

38. Replace the content of the *Index()* method with the content of Listing 4-28. You may need to add the following namespaces to the *HomeController.cs* file:

   ■ *Microsoft.Azure.KeyVault*

   ■ *Microsoft.Azure.KeyVault.Models*

   ■ *Microsoft.Azure.Services.AppAuthentication*

   ■ *System.Threading*

   ■ *System.Threading.Tasks*

LISTING 4-28 Creating, deleting, updating, and reading Key Vault items

```
// C#. ASP.NET.
public ActionResult Index()
        {
            string keyVaultName = "<YOUR_VAULT's_NAME>";
            string vaultBaseURL = $"https://{keyVaultName}.vault.azure.net";


            //Get a token for accessing the Key Vault.
            var azureServiceTokenProvider = new AzureServiceTokenProvider();

            //Create a Key Vault client for accessing the items in the vault;
            var keyVault = new KeyVaultClient(new KeyVaultClient.AuthenticationCallback(
            azureServiceTokenProvider.KeyVaultTokenCallback));

            // Manage secrets in the Key Vault.
            // Create a new secret
            string secretName = "secret-az203";
            Task.Run(async () => await keyVault.SetSecretAsync(vaultBaseURL, secretName,
            "This is a secret testing value")).Wait();
            var secret = Task.Run(async () => await keyVault.GetSecretAsync
            ($"{vaultBaseURL}/secrets/{secretName}")).GetAwaiter().GetResult();
            // Update an existing secret
            Task.Run(async () => await keyVault.SetSecretAsync(vaultBaseURL, secretName,
            "Updated the secret testing value")).Wait();
            secret = Task.Run(async () => await keyVault.
            GetSecretAsync($"{vaultBaseURL}/secrets/{secretName}")).GetAwaiter().
            GetResult();
            // Delete the secret
            Task.Run(async () => await keyVault.DeleteSecretAsync(vaultBaseURL,
            secretName)).Wait();

            // Manage certificates in the Key Vault
```

```
string certName = "cert-az203";
// Create a new self-signed certificate
var policy = new CertificatePolicy
{
    IssuerParameters = new IssuerParameters
    {
        Name = "Self",
    },
    KeyProperties = new KeyProperties
    {
        Exportable = true,
        KeySize = 2048,
        KeyType = "RSA"
    },
    SecretProperties = new SecretProperties
    {
        ContentType = "application/x-pkcs12"
    },
    X509CertificateProperties = new X509CertificateProperties
    {
        Subject = "CN=AZ203KEYVAULTDEMO"
    }
};

Task.Run(async () => await keyVault.CreateCertificateAsync(vaultBaseURL,
certName, policy, new CertificateAttributes { Enabled = true })).Wait();
// When you create a new certificate in the Key Vault it takes some time
// before is ready.
// We added some wait time here for the sake of simplicity.
Thread.Sleep(10000);
var certificate = Task.Run(async () => await keyVault.GetCertificateAsync
(vaultBaseURL, certName)).GetAwaiter().GetResult();

// Update properties associated with the certificate.
CertificatePolicy updatePolicy = new CertificatePolicy
{
    X509CertificateProperties = new X509CertificateProperties
    {
        SubjectAlternativeNames = new SubjectAlternativeNames
        {
            DnsNames = new[] { "az203.examref.testing" }
        }
    }
};


Task.Run(async () => await keyVault.UpdateCertificatePolicyAsync(vaultBase
URL, certName, updatePolicy)).Wait();
Task.Run(async () => await keyVault.CreateCertificateAsync(vaultBaseURL,
certName)).Wait();
Thread.Sleep(10000);

certificate = Task.Run(async () => await keyVault.GetCertificateAsync(vaultB
aseURL, certName)).GetAwaiter().GetResult();
```

```
Task.Run(async () => await keyVault.UpdateCertificateAsync(certificate.
CertificateIdentifier.Identifier, null, new CertificateAttributes { Enabled
= false })).Wait();
Thread.Sleep(10000);

// Delete the self-signed certificate.
Task.Run(async () => await keyVault.DeleteCertificateAsync(vaultBaseURL,
certName)).Wait();


// Manage keys in the Key Vault
string keyName = "key-az203";
NewKeyParameters keyParameters = new NewKeyParameters
{
    Kty = "EC",
    CurveName = "SECP256K1",
    KeyOps = new[] { "sign", "verify" }
};
Task.Run(async () => await keyVault.CreateKeyAsync(vaultBaseURL, keyName,
keyParameters)).Wait();
var key = Task.Run(async () => await keyVault.GetKeyAsync(vaultBaseURL,
keyName)).GetAwaiter().GetResult();

// Update keys in the Key Vault
Task.Run(async () => await keyVault.UpdateKeyAsync(vaultBaseURL, keyName,
null, new KeyAttributes { Expires = DateTime.UtcNow.AddYears(1)})).Wait();
key = Task.Run(async () => await keyVault.GetKeyAsync(vaultBaseURL,
keyName)).GetAwaiter().GetResult();

// Delete keys from the Key Vault
Task.Run(async () => await keyVault.DeleteKeyAsync(vaultBaseURL, keyName)).
Wait();


    return View();
}
```

At this point, you should be able to run the example. Because we didn't make any modifications to any view, you should not be able to see any changes in your Azure Key Vault. To be able to see how this code creates, reads, modifies, and deletes the different item types in your Azure Key Vault, you should set some breakpoints:

1. Add a breakpoint to the following lines:
   - string secretName = "secret-az203";
   - string certName = "cert-az203";
   - string keyName = "key-az203";

2. Open your Azure Key Vault in the Azure Portal, as shown in step 8 of the previous procedure.

3. On your Azure Key Vault blade, click Secrets in the Settings section in the navigation menu.

4. In Visual Studio, press F5 to debug your project.

5. When you hit the breakpoint, press F10 and go back to the Azure Portal to see the results. You should use the Refresh button to see the changes in your Azure Key Vault.

> **NOTE FORBIDDEN ACCESS**
>
> If you get a Forbidden Access Error while you are debugging your application in Visual Studio, ensure that you created an Access Policy for the user account that you have configured in your Visual Studio for connecting with your Azure subscription. You need to ensure that the Access Policy grants all the needed privileges to the different object types in the Azure Key Vault.

When you work with the KeyVault API, you need to create a *KeyVaultClient* object that is responsible for the communication with the Azure Key Vault services. As we saw in the example shown in the "Implement Managed Service Identity (MSI)/Service Principal authentication" section, you need to get an access token for authenticating your service or user principal to the Azure Key Vault. The following code snippet shows how to perform this authentication:

```
var azureServiceTokenProvider = new AzureServiceTokenProvider();
var keyVault = new KeyVaultClient(new KeyVaultClient.AuthenticationCallback(azureService
TokenProvider.KeyVaultTokenCallback));
```

Now you can use the *keyVault* variable for working with the different item types. The KeyVault API provides specialized methods for each item type. This way, you should use the *SetSecretAsync()* method for creating a new secret in your Azure Key Vault. The following code snippet shows how to create a new secret:

```
Task.Run(async () => await keyVault.SetSecretAsync(vaultBaseURL, secretName, "This is a
secret testing value")).Wait();
```

If you try to create a new secret, key, or certificate using the same name of an object that already exists in the vault, you are creating a new version of that object, as shown in Figure 4-14. You can click on each version to review the properties of the object for that version.

FIGURE 4-14 A secret object with different versions

Most of the methods in the KeyVault API that work with items require the vault URL and the name of the item that you want to access. In this example, you define a variable with the correct value at the beginning of the *Index()* method, as shown in the following code snippet:

```
string keyVaultName = "<YOUR_VAULT's_NAME>";
string vaultBaseURL = $"https://{keyVaultName}.vault.azure.net";
```

These methods are usually overloaded for accepting an object identifier instead of the vault base URL and the object's name. The identifier has the following form:

https://{keyvault-name}.vault.azure.net/{object-type}/{object-name}/{object-version}

Where:

- **Keyvault-name** This is the name of the key vault where the object is stored.
- **Object-type** This is the type of object that you want to work with. This value can be secrets, keys, or certificates.
- **Object-name** This is the name that you give the object in the vault.
- **Object-version** This is the version of the object that you want to access.

Creating a key or certificate uses a slightly different approach from the one that you used for creating a secret. Keys and certificates are more complex objects and require some additional configuration for creating them. The following code snippet extracted from Listing 4-28 shows how to create a new self-signed certificate in the Azure Key Vault:

```
// Create a new self-signed certificate
var policy = new CertificatePolicy
{
    IssuerParameters = new IssuerParameters
    {
        Name = "Self",
    },
    KeyProperties = new KeyProperties
    {
        Exportable = true,
        KeySize = 2048,
        KeyType = "RSA"
    },
    SecretProperties = new SecretProperties
    {
        ContentType = "application/x-pkcs12"
    },
    X509CertificateProperties = new X509CertificateProperties
    {
        Subject = "CN=AZ203KEYVAULTDEMO"
    }
};
Task.Run(async () => await keyVault.CreateCertificateAsync(vaultBaseURL, certName,
policy, new CertificateAttributes { Enabled = true })).Wait();
```

You need to create a *CertificatePolicy* object before you can create the certificate. A certificate policy is an object that defines the properties of how to create a certificate and any additional version associated with the certificate object. You use this certificate policy object as a parameter of the *CreateCertificateAsync()* method. If you need to modify any property of an existing certificate, you need to define a new certificate policy, update the policy using the *UpdateCertificatePolicyAsync()* method, and create a new certificate version using the *CreateCertificateAsync()* method, as shown in the following code snippet:

```
// Update properties associated with the certificate.
CertificatePolicy updatePolicy = new CertificatePolicy
{
    X509CertificateProperties = new X509CertificateProperties
    {
        SubjectAlternativeNames = new SubjectAlternativeNames
        {
            DnsNames = new[] { "az203.examref.testing" }
        }
    }
};

Task.Run(async () => await keyVault.UpdateCertificatePolicyAsync(vaultBaseURL, certName,
updatePolicy)).Wait();
Task.Run(async () => await keyVault.CreateCertificateAsync(vaultBaseURL, certName)).
Wait();
```

Deleting an object from the key vault is quite straightforward; you only need to provide the vault base URL and the object's name to the *DeleteSecretAsync()*, *DeleteCertificateAsync()*, or *DeleteKeyAsync()* method. Azure Key Vault also supports soft-delete operations on the protected objects or the vault itself. This option is not enabled by default. When you soft delete an object or a vault, the Azure Key Vault provider automatically marks them as deleted but holds the object or vault for a default period of 90 days. This means you can recover the deleted object later if needed.

NEED MORE REVIEW? **MORE DETAILS ABOUT KEYS, SECRETS, AND CERTIFICATES**

You can find more information about the details of the different object types that are available in the Azure Key Vault service by reviewing this article: *https://docs.microsoft.com/en-us/azure/key-vault/about-keys-secrets-and-certificates*.

Chapter summary

- Authentication is the act of proving that a user is who he or she claims claims to be.
- A user authenticates by providing some information that the user only knows.
- There are several mechanisms of authentication that provide different levels of security.

- Some of the authentication mechanisms are form-based, token-based, or certificate-based.

- Using form-based authentication requires your application to store your users' passwords.

- Form-based authentication requires HTTPS to make the authentication process more secure.

- Using token-based authentication, you can delegate the authorization to third-party authentication providers.

- You can add social logins to your application by using token-based authentication.

- Certificate-based authentication requires that the user send a valid digital certificate for authenticating to the server.

- Multifactor Authentication is an authentication mechanism that requires the users to provide more than one more piece of information that only the user knows.

- You can easily implement Multifactor Authentication by using Azure Active Directory.

- There are four main actors in OAuth authentication: client, resource server, resource owner, and authentication server.

- The resource owner needs to authenticate the client before sending the Authorization Grant.

- The access token grants access to the resource hosted on the resource server.

- The authorization grant or authorization code grants the client the needed rights to request an Access Token to the Authorization Server.

- The client uses the refresh token to get a new access token when it expires without needing to request a new authorization code.

- The JSON web token is the most extended implementation of OAuth tokens.

- Claim-based access control authorization controls the access to your application based on properties of the users.

- The identity manager adds claims to the user's identity.

- You need to define a policy in your code for asking for the presence of a claim or the accepted values for a claim.

- Role-Based Access Control (RBAC) authorization controls the access to your application based on the actions that a user can do in your application.

- You need to modify the manifest of your application registered in Azure AD for creating your custom application roles.

- Application roles are attached to the user's identity as role claims.

- Shared access signature tokens provide fine-grained access control to your Azure storage accounts.

- You can create an SAS token for service, container, and item levels.
- Azure provides encryption features for protecting the information on your service instances.
- Azure encrypts the information while it is traveling over a virtual network or the Internet by using encryption in transit.
- Azure encrypts the information when it is stored and not accessed by using encryption at rest.
- Data stored with encryption at rest enabled is encrypted and decrypted when the user needs to access the data.
- Azure Key Vault allows you to store three types of objects: keys, secrets, and certificates.
- You should use Managed Service Identity authentication for accessing the Azure Key Vault.
- You need to define a certificate policy before creating a certificate in the Azure Key Vault.
- If you import a certificate into the Azure Key Vault, a default certificate policy is automatically created for you.

Thought experiment

In this thought experiment, demonstrate your skills and knowledge of the topics covered in this chapter. You can find answers to this thought experiment in the next section.

You are developing a web application for your company. The application is in the early stages of development. This application is an internal application that will be used only by the employees of the company. Your company uses Office 365 connected with your company's Active Directory domain. Answer the following questions about the security implementation of this application:

1. The employees need to be able to access the application using the same username and password they use for accessing Office 365. What type of authentication should you use?

2. Some parts of the application manage sensitive information. The security policy of the company requires users who need to access this information to use Multifactor Authentication. How should you implement the access control to these sensitive areas?

3. You are using Azure App Services for developing the application. You need to ensure that the web application can access other Azure services without using credentials in your code. What should you do?

Thought experiment answers

This section contains the solution to the thought experiment. Each answer explains why the answer choice is correct.

1. You should use OAuth authentication with Azure Active Directory (Azure AD). When you connect Office 365 with an Active Directory (AD) domain, users in the AD domain can authenticate to Office 365 using the same username and password they use in the AD domain. Office 365 uses an Azure AD tenant for managing the identities of the users in the subscription. Your organization already has configured the synchronization between AD and Office 365 and Azure AD. By using OAuth authentication with Azure AD, your users should be able to access your application using the same username and passwords that they use in the AD domain.

2. You should implement a Claims-Based Access Control (CBAC) authentication. You need to control the access to sensitive parts of the application based on a feature of the user that is trying to get access. In this situation, the user needs to have configured the Multifactor Authentication (MFA) feature. You use CBAC authentication when you need to control the access based on properties of the user. You should not use Role-Based Access Control (RBAC) authentication for this scenario because you cannot guarantee that the user in the role has the MFA feature enabled.

3. You should use the Managed Service Identity (MSI) authentication. Using the feature, Azure authenticates services based on a service principal configured in a service instance. You can use MSI authentication with services that support Azure AD authentication, like Azure Key Vault or Azure SQL Databases. You need to enable a system-assigned or user-assigned managed identity on your Azure App Service. Using MSI, the Azure SQL Database authenticates the identity assigned to your Azure App Service without needing to provide any password.

CHAPTER 5

Monitor, troubleshoot, and optimize Azure solutions

Providing a good experience to your users is one of the key factors for the success of your application. Several factors affect the user's experience, such as a good user interface design, ease of use, good performance, and low failure rate. You can ensure that your application will perform well by assigning more resources to your application, but if there are not enough users using your application, you might be wasting resources and money.

To ensure that your application is working correctly, you need to deploy a monitoring mechanism that helps you to get information about your application's behavior. This is especially important during peak usage periods or failures. Azure provides several tools that help you to monitor, troubleshoot, and improve the performance of your application.

Skills covered in this chapter:

- Skill 5.1: Develop code to support scalability of apps and services
- Skill 5.2: Integrate caching and content delivery within solutions
- Skill 5.3: Instrument solutions to support monitoring and logging

Skill 5.1: Develop code to support scalability of apps and services

Azure provides several out-of-the-box high-availability and fault-tolerance features. Although these Azure features improve the resiliency of your application, you need to understand when taking advantage of these features is necessary. Just adding more resources to an application doesn't mean that your application will perform better, and adding more resources won't increase performance or resiliency if the application is not aware of these changes.

You usually add more resources when your application is at peak usage or you remove resources from your application when the usage is low. To be efficient, you can configure Azure resources to automatically add or remove resources based on schedules or conditions that you can configure.

Implement autoscaling rules and patterns

One of the biggest challenges you face when deploying your application in a production environment is ensuring that you provide enough resources, so that your application performs as expected. Determining the number of resources you should allocate is the big question when it comes to configuring the resources for your application. If you allocate too many resources, your application will perform well during usage peaks, but you are potentially wasting resources. If you allocate fewer resources, you are saving resources, but your application may not perform well during usage peaks. Also, anticipating heavy usage peaks is very difficult. This is especially true for applications that have unpredictable usage patterns.

Fortunately, Azure allows you to dynamically assign more resources to your application when you need them. Autoscaling is the action of automatically adding or removing resources to an Azure service and providing needed computing power for your application in each situation. An application can scale in two different ways:

- **Vertically** You add more computing power by adding more memory, CPU resources, and IOPS to the application. At the end of the day, your application runs on a virtual machine. It doesn't matter if you use an IaaS (Infrastructure as a Service) virtual machine, Azure App Service, or Azure Service Fabric; you are using virtual machines under the hood. Vertically scaling an application means moving from a smaller VM to a larger VM size and adding more memory, CPU, and IOPS. Vertically scaling requires stopping the system while the VM is resizing. This type of scaling is also known as "scaling up and down."

- **Horizontally** You can also scale your application by creating or removing instances of your application. Each instance of your application is executed in a virtual machine that is part of a virtual machine scale set. The corresponding Azure service automatically manages the virtual machine scale set for you. All these instances of your application work together to provide the same service. The advantage of scaling horizontally is that the availability of your application is not affected because there is no need to reboot all the instances of your application that provide the service. This type of scaling is also known as "scaling out and in."

When we work with autoscaling, we refer to horizontally scaling because vertical scaling requires the service interruption while the Azure Resource Manager is changing the size of the virtual machine. For that reason, vertical scaling is not suitable for autoscaling.

You configure autoscaling based on criteria your application should meet to provide a good performance level. You configure these criteria in Azure by using autoscaling rules. A rule defines which metric Azure Monitor should use to perform the autoscaling. When that metric reaches the configured condition, Azure automatically performs the action configured for that rule. In addition to adding or removing virtual machines from the scale set, the rule can perform other actions, such as sending an email or making an HTTP request to a webhook. You can configure three different types of rules when working with the autoscaling rules:

- **Time-based**   Azure Monitor executes the autoscaling rule based on a schedule. For example, if your application requires more resources during the first week of the month, you can add more instances and reduce the number of resources for the rest of the month.

- **Metric-based**   You configure the threshold for standard metrics, such as the usage of the CPU, the length of the HTTP queue, or the percentage of memory usage, as shown in Figure 5-1.

- **Custom-based**   You can create your own metrics in your application, expose them using Application Insight, and use them for autoscaling rules.

FIGURE 5-1 Configuring a metric-based autoscale rule

You can only use the built-in autoscaling mechanism with a limited group of Azure resource types:

- **Azure virtual machines**   You can apply autoscaling by using virtual machine scale sets. All the virtual machines in a scale set are treated as a group. By using autoscaling, you can add virtual machines to the scale set or remove virtual machines from it.

- **Azure Service Fabric**   When you create an Azure Service Fabric cluster, you define different node types. A different virtual machine scale set supports each node type that you define in an Azure Service Fabric cluster. You can apply the same type of autoscaling rules that you use in a standard virtual machine scale set.

- **Azure App Service**   This service has built-in autoscaling capabilities that you can use for adding or removing instances to the Azure App Service. The autoscale rules apply to all apps inside the Azure App Service.

- **Azure Cloud Services**   This service has built-in autoscaling capabilities that allow you to add or remove resources to or from the roles in Azure Cloud Service.

When you work with the autoscale feature in one of the supported Azure services, you define a profile condition. A profile condition defines the rule that you configure to add or remove resources. You can also define the default, minimum, and maximum allowed instances for this profile. When you define a minimum and maximum, your service cannot decrease or grow beyond the limits you define in the profile. Also, you can configure the profile for scaling based on a schedule or based on the values of built-in or custom metrics. Use the following procedure to add a metric-based autoscaling rule to an Azure App Service. This rule will add an instance to the Azure App Service plan when the average percentage of CPU usage is over 80 percent more than 10 minutes:

1. Open the Azure Portal (*https://portal.azure.com*).

2. In the search text box at the top of the Azure Portal, type the name of your Azure App Service.

3. Click the name of your Azure App Service in the results list.

4. On the Azure App Service blade, in the navigation menu on the left side of the blade, click the Scale-out (App Service Plan) option in the Settings section.

5. On the Scale-Out (App Service Plan) blade, on the Configure tab, click the Enable Autoscale button. Autoscale rules are available only for the App Service plans that are Standard size or bigger.

6. On the Scale-Out (App Service Plan) blade, on the Configure tab, in the Default Auto Created Scale Condition window shown in Figure 5-2, click the Add A Rule link.

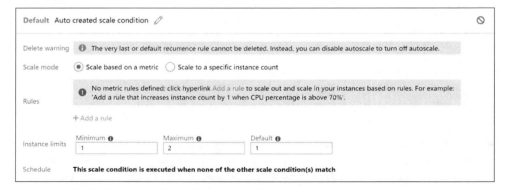

FIGURE 5-2 Configuring a metric-based autoscale rule

7. On the Scale rule panel, in the Criteria section, ensure that CPU Percentage is selected in the Metric Name drop-down menu.

8. Ensure that the Greater Than value is selected from the Operator drop-down menu.

9. Type the value **80** in the Threshold text box.

10. In the Action section, ensure that the Instance count value is set to **1**.

11. Click the Add button at the bottom of the panel.

12. On the Scale-Out (App Service Plan) blade, in the Default Profile condition, set the Maximum Instance Limit to **3**.

13. Click the Save button at the top-left corner of the blade.

> **NOTE SCALE-OUT / SCALE-IN**
>
> The previous procedure shows how to add an instance to the App Service plan (it is scaling out the App Service plan) but doesn't remove the additional instance once the CPU percentage falls below the configured threshold. You should add a Scale-In rule for removing the additional instances once they are not needed. You configure a Scale-In rule in the same way you did it if for the Scale-Out rule. Just set the Operation drop-down menu to the Decrease Count To value.

You can use different common autoscale patterns, based on the settings that we have reviewed so far:

- **Scale Based On CPU**   You scale your service (Azure App Service, VM Scale Set, or Cloud Service) based on your CPU. You need to configure a Scale-Out and a Scale-In rule for adding and removing instances to the service. In this pattern, you also set a minimum and a maximum number of instances.

- **Scale Differently On Weekdays vs. Weekends**   You use this pattern when you expect that the main usage of your application will happen on weekdays. You configure the default profile condition with a fixed number of instances, and then you configure another profile condition for reducing the number for instances on the weekends.

- **Scale Differently During Holidays**   You use the Scale Based On CPU pattern, but you add a profile condition to add additional instances during holidays or days that are important to your business.

- **Scale Based On Custom Metrics**   You use this pattern with a web application composed of three layers: front end, back end, and API tiers. The front end of an API tier communicates with the back-end tier. You define your custom metrics in the web application and expose them to the Azure Monitor by using Application Insights. Then you can use these custom metrics to add more resources to any of the three layers.

Implement code that handles transient faults

Developing applications for the cloud means that your application depends on the resources in the cloud to run your code. As we already reviewed in previous chapters, these resources provide out-of-the-box high availability and fault-tolerant features that make your application more resilient. Azure Cloud Services use redundant hardware and load balancers. Although you are guaranteed not to suffer big breakdowns, there can be situations that can temporarily affect your application, such as performing automatic failovers or load balancing operations. Usually, recovery from that kind of transient situation is as simple as retrying the operation your application was performing. For example, if your application was reading a record from a database and you get a timeout error because of a temporary overload of the database, you can retry the read operation to get the needed information.

Dealing with these transient faults leads you to deal with some interesting challenges. Your application needs to respond to these challenges to ensure that it offers a reliable experience to your users. These challenges are:

- **Detect and classify faults** Not all the faults that may happen during the application execution are transient. Your application needs to identify whether the fault is transient, long-lasting, or a terminal failure. Even the term "long-lasting failure" is dependent on the logic of your application because the amount of time that you consider "long-lasting" depends on the type of operations your application performs. Your application also needs to deal with the different responses that come from different services types.

An error occurring while reading data from a storage system is different than an error occurring while writing data.

- **Retry the operation when appropriate**   Once your application determines that it's dealing with a transient fault, the application needs to retry the operation. It also needs to keep track of the number of retries of the faulting operation.

- **Implement an appropriate retry strategy**   Indefinitely retrying the operation could lead to other problems, such as performance degradation or the resource being blocked. To avoid those performance problems, your application needs to set a retry strategy that defines the number of retries, sets the delay between each retry, and sets the actions that your application should take after a failed attempt. Setting the correct number of retries and the delay between them is a complex task that depends on factors such as the type of resources, the operating conditions, and the application itself.

You can use the following guidelines when implementing a suitable transient fault mechanism in your application:

- **Use existing built-in retry mechanism**   When working with SDKs for specific services, the SDK usually provides a built-in retry mechanism. Before thinking of implementing your retry mechanism, you should review the SDK that you are using to access the services on which your application depends and use the built-in retry mechanism. These built-in retry mechanisms are tailored to the specific features and requirements of the target service. If you still need to implement your retry mechanism for a service—such as a storage service or a service bus—you should carefully review the requirements of each service to ensure that you correctly manage the faulting responses.

- **Determine whether the operation is suitable for retrying**   When an error is raised, it usually indicates the nature of the error. You can use this information to determine whether the error is a transient fault. Once you determine your application is dealing with a transient fault, you need to determine whether retrying the operation can succeed. You should not retry operations that indicate an invalid operation, such as a service that suffered a fatal error or continuing to look for an item after receiving an error indicating the item does not exist in the database. You should implement operation retries if the following conditions are met:

    - You can determine the full effect of the operation.

    - You fully understand the conditions of the retry.

    - You can validate these conditions.

- **Use the appropriate retry count and interval**   Setting the wrong retry count could lead your application to fail or could lock resources that can affect the health of the application. If you set the retry count too low, your application may not have enough time to recover from the transient fault and will fail. If you set the retry count to a value that is too high or too short, you can lock resources that your application is using, such as threads, connections, or memory. This high-resource consumption can affect the health of your application. When choosing the appropriate retry count and interval, you need to consider the type of operation that suffered the transient fault. For example, if the transient fault happens during an operation that is part of user interaction, you should use a short retry interval and count, which avoids having your user wait too long for your application to recover from the transient fault. On the other hand, if the fault happens during an operation that is part of a critical workflow, setting a longer retry count and interval makes sense if restarting the workflow is time-consuming or expensive. Following are some of the most common strategies for choosing the retry interval:

- **Exponential back-off**   You use a short time interval for the first retry, and then you exponentially increase the interval time for subsequent retries. For example, you set the initial interval to 3 seconds and then use 9, 27, 81 for the subsequent retries.

- **Incremental intervals**   You set a short time interval for the first retry, then you incrementally increase the interval time for the subsequent retries. For example, you set the initial interval to 3 seconds and then use 5, 8, 13, 21 for the subsequent retries.

- **Regular intervals**   You use the same time interval for each retry. This strategy is not appropriate in most cases. You should avoid using this strategy when accessing services or resources in Azure. In those cases, you should use the exponential back-off strategy with a circuit breaker pattern.

- **Immediate retry**   You retry as soon as the transient fault happens. You should not use this type of retry more than once. The immediate retries are suitable for peak faults, such as network package collisions or spikes in hardware components. If the immediate retry doesn't recover from the transient fault, you should switch to another retry strategy.

- **Randomization**   If your application executes several retries in parallel—regardless of the retry strategy—using the same retry values for all the retries can negatively affect your application. In general, you should use random starting retry interval values with any of the previous strategies. This allows you to minimize the probability that two different application threads start the retry mechanism at the same time in the event of a transient fault.

- **Avoid anti-patterns**   When implementing your retry mechanism, there are some patterns you should avoid:

  - Avoid implementing duplicated layers of retries. If your operation is made of several requests to several services, you should avoid implementing retries on every stage of the operation.

  - Never implement endless retry mechanisms. If your application never stops retrying in the event of a transient fault, the application can cause resource exhaustion or connection throttling. You should use the circuit breaker pattern or a finite number of retries.

  - Never use immediate retry more than once.

- **Test the retry strategy and implementation**   Because of the difficulties when selecting the correct retry count and interval values, you should thoroughly test your retry strategy and implementation. You should pay special attention to heavy load and high-concurrency scenarios. You should test this by injecting transient and non-transient faults into your application.

- **Manage retry policy configuration**   When you are implementing your reply mechanism, you should not hardcode the values for the retry count and intervals. Instead, you can define a retry policy that contains the retry count and interval as well as the mechanism that determines whether a fault is transient or non-transient. You should store this retry policy in configuration files so that you can fine-tune the policy. You should also implement this retry policy configuration so that your application stores the values in memory instead of continuously re-reading the configuration file. If you are using Azure App Service, you should consider using the service configuration shown in Figure 5-3.

+ New application setting	⊙ Show values	✎ Advanced edit	▽ Filter		
Name		Value		deployment...	
AzureSearchAdminKey		⊙ Hidden value. Click show values button above to view		🗑	✎
AzureSearchName		⊙ Hidden value. Click show values button above to view		🗑	✎
DefaultAnswer		⊙ Hidden value. Click show values button above to view		🗑	✎
PrimaryEndpointKey		⊙ Hidden value. Click show values button above to view		🗑	✎
QNAMAKER_EXTENSION_VERSION		⊙ Hidden value. Click show values button above to view		🗑	✎
SecondaryEndpointKey		⊙ Hidden value. Click show values button above to view		🗑	✎
UserAppInsightsAppId		⊙ Hidden value. Click show values button above to view		🗑	✎
UserAppInsightsKey		⊙ Hidden value. Click show values button above to view		🗑	✎
UserAppInsightsName		⊙ Hidden value. Click show values button above to view		🗑	✎

FIGURE 5-3 Configuring a metric-based autoscale rule

- **Log transient and non-transient faults**   You should include a log mechanism in your application every time a transient or non-transient fault happens. A single transient fault doesn't indicate an error in your application. If the number of the transient faults is increasing, this can be an indicator of a bigger potential failure or that you should increase the resources assigned to the faulting service. You should log transient faults as warning messages instead of errors. Using the Error Log Level could lead to triggering false alerts in your monitoring system. You should also consider measuring and logging the overall time taken by your retry mechanism when recovering a faulty operation. This allows you to measure the overall impact of transient faults on user response times, process latency, and efficiency of the application.

NEED MORE REVIEW?   **MANAGING TRANSIENT FAULTS**

You can review some general guidelines for implementing a transient fault-handling mechanism by reviewing the following articles:

- *https://docs.microsoft.com/en-us/azure/architecture/best-practices/transient-faults*
- *https://docs.microsoft.com/en-us/aspnet/aspnet/overview/developing-apps-with-windows-azure/building-real-world-cloud-apps-with-windows-azure/transient-fault-handling*

Skill 5.2: Integrate caching and content delivery within solutions

Any web application that you implement delivers two types of content—dynamic and static.

- Dynamic content is the type of content that changes depending on user interaction. An example of dynamic content would be a dashboard with several graphs or a list of user movements in a banking application.

- Static content is the same for all application users. Images and PDFs are examples of static content (as long as they are not dynamically generated) that users can download from your application.

If the users of your application access it from several locations across the globe, you can improve the performance of the application by delivering the content from the location nearest to the user. For static content, you can improve the performance by copying the content to different cache servers distributed across the globe. Using this technique, users can retrieve the static content from the nearest location with lower latency, which improves the performance of your application.

For dynamic content, you can use cache software to store most accessed data. This means your application returns the information from the cache, which is faster than reprocessing the data or getting it from the storage system.

> **This skill covers how to:**
> - Store and retrieve data in Azure Redis Cache
> - Develop code to implement CDN's in solutions
> - Invalidate cache content (CDN or Redis)

Store and retrieve data in Azure Redis Cache

Redis is an open-source cache system that allows you to work as an in-memory data structure store, database cache, or message broker. The Azure Redis Cache or Azure Cache for Redis is a

Redis implementation managed by Microsoft. Azure Redis Cache has three pricing layers that provide you with different levels of features:

- **Basic**   This is the tier with the fewest features and less throughput and higher latency. You should use this tier only for development or testing purposes. There is no Service Level Agreement (SLA) associated with the Basic tier.

- **Standard**   This tier offers a two-node, primary-secondary replicated Redis cache that is managed by Microsoft. This tier has associated a high-availability SLA of 99.9 percent.

- **Premium**   This is an enterprise-grade Redis cluster managed by Microsoft. This tier offers the complete group of features with the highest throughput and lower latencies. The Redis cluster is also deployed on more powerful hardware. This tier has a high-availability SLA of 99.9 percent.

> **NOTE   SCALING THE AZURE REDIS CACHE SERVICE**
>
> You can scale up your existing Azure Redis cache service to a higher tier, but you cannot scale down your current tier to a lower one.

When you are working with Azure Cache for Redis, you can use different implementation patterns that solve different issues, depending on the architecture of your application:

- **Cache-Aside**   In most situations, your application stores the data that it manages in a database. Accessing data in a database is a relatively slow operation because it depends on the time to access the disk storage system. A solution would be to load the database in memory, but this approach is costly; in most cases, the database simply doesn't fit on the available memory. One solution to improve the performance of your application in these scenarios is to store the most-accessed data in the cache. When the back-end system changes the data in the database, the same system can also update the data in the cache, which makes the change available to all clients.

- **Content caching**   Most web applications use web page templates that use common elements, such as headers, footers, toolbars, menus, stylesheets, images, and so on. These template elements are static elements (or at least don't change often). Storing these elements in Azure Cache for Redis relieves your web servers from serving these elements and improves the time your servers need to generate dynamic content.

- **User session caching**   This pattern is a good idea if your application needs to register too much information about the user history or data that you need to associate with cookies,. Storing too much information in a session cookie hurts the performance of your application. You can save part of that information in your database and store a pointer or index in the session cookie that points that user to the information in the database. If you use an in-memory database, such as Azure Cache for Redis, instead of a traditional database, your application will benefit from the faster access times to the data stored in memory.

- **Job and message queuing** You can use Azure Cache for Redis to implement a distributed queue that executes long-lasting tasks that may negatively affect the performance of your application.
- **Distributed transactions** A transaction is a group of commands that need to complete or fail together. Any transaction needs to ensure that the data is always in a stable state. If your application needs to execute transactions, you can use Azure Cache for Redis for implementing these transactions.

You can work with Azure Cache for Redis using different languages, such as ASP.NET, .NET, .NET Core, Node.js, Java, or Python. Before you can add caching features to your code using Azure Redis Cache, you need to create your Azure Cache for Redis database using the following procedure:

1. Open the Azure Portal (*https://portal.azure.com*).
2. On the navigation menu at the left side of the Azure Portal, click Create A Resource.
3. On the New blade, click Databases on the navigation menu on the left side of the blade.
4. In the list of Database services, shown in Figure 5-4, click the Azure Cache For Redis item.

FIGURE 5-4 Creating a new Azure Cache for Redis resource

5. On the New Redis Cache blade, type a DNS Name for your Redis resource.
6. Select the Subscription, Resource Group, and Location from the appropriate drop-down menu that best fits your needs.
7. In the Pricing tier drop-down menu, select the Basic C0 tier.
8. Click the Create button at the bottom of the New Redis Cache blade.

The deployment of your new Azure Cache for Redis takes a few minutes to complete. Once the deployment is complete, you need to get the access keys for your instance of the Azure Cache for Redis. You use this information in your code to connect the Redis service in Azure.

If you are using any of the .NET languages, you can use the *StackExchange.Redis* client for accessing your Azure Cache for Redis resource. You can also use this Redis client for accessing other Redis implementations. When reading or writing values in the Azure Cache for Redis, you need to create a *ConnectionMultiplexer* object. This object creates a connection to your Redis server. The *ConnectionMultiplexer* class is designed to be reused as much as possible.

For this reason, you should store this object and reuse it across all your code, whenever it is possible to reuse. Creating a connection is a costly operation. For this reason, you should not create a *ConnectionMultiplexer* object for each read or write operation to the Redis cache. Once you have created your *ConnectionMultiplexer* object, you can use any of the available operations in the *StackExchange.Redis* package. Following are the basic operations that you can use with Redis:

- **Use Redis as a database**   You get a database from Redis, using the *GetDatabase()* method, for writing and reading values from the database. You use the *StringSet()* or *StringGet()* methods for writing and reading.
- **Use Redis as a messaging queue**   You get a subscriber object from the Redis client, using the *GetSubscriber()* method. Then you can publish messages to a queue, using the Publish() method, and read messages from a queue, using the Subscribe() method. Queues in Redis are known as "channels."

The following procedure shows how to connect to an Azure Cache for Redis database and read and write data to and from the database using an ASP.NET application:

1. Open Visual Studio 2017.
2. In the Visual Studio 2017 window, click File > New > Project.
3. On the New Project window, in the navigation menu on the left side of the window, select Installed > Visual C# > Cloud.
4. Select the ASP.NET Web Application (.NET Framework) template.
5. Type a Name and Solution Name for your project.
6. Select the Location for your project.
7. Click OK.
8. On the New ASP.NET Web Application, select the MVC template.
9. Click OK.
10. On the Visual Studio 2017 window, click Tools > NuGet Package Manager > Manage NuGet Packages For Solution.
11. On the NuGet – Solution tab, click Browse.
12. On the Search text box control type **StackExchange.Redis**.
13. Select the *StackExchange.Redis* NuGet package.
14. On the right side of the NuGet tab, select the checkbox beside your project's name and click the Install button.

15. On the Preview Changes window, click OK.

16. Open the Azure Portal (*https://portal.azure.com*).

17. On the search text box in the top-middle of the portal, type the name of your Azure Cache for Redis that you created in the previous example.

18. Click your Azure Cache for Redis in the results list.

19. On the Azure Cache for Redis blade, click Access Keys in the Settings section in the navigation menu on the left side of the blade.

20. On the Access Keys blade, copy the value of the Primary Connection String (*StackExchange.Redis*). You need this value on the next steps.

21. On the Visual Studio 2017 window, open the *Web.config* file

22. On the *<appSettings>* section, add the following code:

```
<add key="CacheConnection " value="<value_copied_in_step_20>"/>
```

> **NOTE   SECURITY BEST PRACTICE**
>
> In real-world development, you should avoid putting connection strings and secrets on files that could be checked with the rest of your code. To avoid this, you can put the *<appSettings>* section with the keys containing the sensible secrets or connection strings in a separate file outside the source code control folder. Then add the file parameter to the *<appSettings>* tag pointing to the external *appSettings* file path.

23. Open the *HomeController.cs* file in the Controllers folder.

24. Add the following using statements to the *HomeController.cs* file:

- *using System.Configuration;*
- *using StackExchange.Redis;*

25. Add the code in Listing 5-1 to the *HomeController* class.

LISTING 5-1 *HomeController* RedisCache method

```
// C#. ASP.NET.
public ActionResult RedisCache()
{
    ViewBag.Message = "A simple example with Azure Cache for Redis on ASP.NET.";

    var lazyConnection = new Lazy<ConnectionMultiplexer>(() =>
{
    string cacheConnection = ConfigurationManager.AppSettings["CacheConnection"].
    ToString();
    return ConnectionMultiplexer.Connect(cacheConnection);
});
    // You need to create a ConnectionMultiplexer object for accessing the Redis cache.
    // Then you can get an instance of a database.
    IDatabase cache = lazyConnection.Value.GetDatabase();
```

```
    // Perform cache operations using the cache object...

    // Run a simple Redis command
    ViewBag.command1 = "PING";
    ViewBag.command1Result = cache.Execute(ViewBag.command1).ToString();

    // Simple get and put of integral data types into the cache
    ViewBag.command2 = "GET Message";
    ViewBag.command2Result = cache.StringGet("Message").ToString();

    // Write a new value to the database.
    ViewBag.command3 = "SET Message \"Hello! The cache is working from ASP.NET!\"";
    ViewBag.command3Result = cache.StringSet("Message", "Hello! The cache is working
    from ASP.NET!").ToString();

    // Get the message that we wrote on the previous step
    ViewBag.command4 = "GET Message";
    ViewBag.command4Result = cache.StringGet("Message").ToString();

    // Get the client list, useful to see if connection list is growing...
    ViewBag.command5 = "CLIENT LIST";
    ViewBag.command5Result = cache.Execute("CLIENT", "LIST").ToString().Replace(" id=",
    "\rid=");

    lazyConnection.Value.Dispose();

    return View();
}
```

26. On the Solution Explorer, right-click the Views > Home folder and click Add > View on the contextual menu.

27. On the Add View window, type **RedisCache** for the View Name.

28. Click the Add button.

29. Open the *RedisCache.cshtml* file.

30. Replace the content of the *RedisCache.cshtml* file with the content of Listing 5-2.

LISTING 5-2 RedisCache View

```
// C#. ASP.NET.
@{
    ViewBag.Title = "Azure Cache for Redis Test";
}

<h2>@ViewBag.Title.</h2>
<h3>@ViewBag.Message</h3>
<br /><br />
<table border="1" cellpadding="10">
    <tr>
        <th>Command</th>
        <th>Result</th>
    </tr>
    <tr>
        <td>@ViewBag.command1</td>
```

```
        <td><pre>@ViewBag.command1Result</pre></td>
    </tr>
    <tr>
        <td>@ViewBag.command2</td>
        <td><pre>@ViewBag.command2Result</pre></td>
    </tr>
    <tr>
        <td>@ViewBag.command3</td>
        <td><pre>@ViewBag.command3Result</pre></td>
    </tr>
    <tr>
        <td>@ViewBag.command4</td>
        <td><pre>@ViewBag.command4Result</pre></td>
    </tr>
    <tr>
        <td>@ViewBag.command5</td>
        <td><pre>@ViewBag.command5Result</pre></td>
    </tr>
</table>
```

31. Now press F5 to run your project locally.

32. In the web browser running your project, append the */Home/RedisCache* URI to the URL. Your result should look like Figure 5-5.

Command	Result
PING	PONG
GET Message	
SET Message "Hello! The cache is working from ASP.NET!"	True
GET Message	Hello! The cache is working from ASP.NET!
CLIENT LIST	id=9774 addr=127.0.0.1:35187 fd=8 name=PORTAL_CONSOLE age=152 id=9853 addr=83.56.0.194:61343 fd=18 name=DEV-CS age=1 idle=0 id=9854 addr=83.56.0.194:61344 fd=14 name=DEV-CS age=1 idle=1

FIGURE 5-5 Example results

EXAM TIP

You can use Azure Cache for Redis for static content and for the most-accessed dynamic data. You can use it for in-memory databases or message queues using a publication/ subscription pattern.

Develop code to implement CDNs in solutions

A Content Delivery Network (CDN) is a group of servers distributed in different locations across the globe that can deliver web content to users. Because the CDN has servers distributed in several locations, when a user makes a request to the CDN, the CDN delivers the content from the nearest server to the user.

The main advantage of using Azure CDN with your application is that Azure CDN caches your application's static content. When a user makes a request to your application, the CDN stores the static content, such as images, documents, and stylesheet files. When a second user from the same location as the first user accesses your application, the CDN delivers the cached content, relieving your web server from delivering the static content. You can use third-party CDN solutions such as Verizon or Akamai with Azure CDN.

To use Azure CDN with your solution, you need to configure a profile. This profile contains the list of endpoints in your application that would be included in the CDN. The profile also configures the behavior of content delivery and access of each configured endpoint. When you configure an Azure CDN profile, you need to choose between using Microsoft's CDN or using CDNs from Verizon or Akamai.

You can configure as many profiles as you need for grouping your endpoints based on different criteria, such as Internet domain, web application, or any other criteria. Bear in mind that Azure CDN pricing tiers are applied at the profile level, so you can configure different profiles with different pricing characteristics. The following procedure shows how to create an Azure CDN profile with one endpoint for caching content from a web application:

1. Open the Azure Portal (*https://portal.azure.com*).
2. In the navigation menu on the left side of the portal, click Create A Resource.
3. On the New blade, in the Search The Marketplace text box, type **CDN**.
4. In the result list, click CDN.
5. On the CDN blade, click the Create button.
6. On the CDN profile blade, type a Name for the profile.
7. Select an existing Resource Group in the drop-down menu. Alternatively, you can create a new resource group by clicking the Create New link below the Resource Group drop-down menu.
8. In the Pricing Tier drop-down menu, select Standard Microsoft.

9. Click the Create button at the bottom of the CDN profile blade.

10. In the search text box on the middle-top side of the Azure Portal, type the name for your CDN profile.

11. In the result list, click the name of your CDN profile.

12. On the CDN profile blade, shown in Figure 5-6, click the Endpoint button.

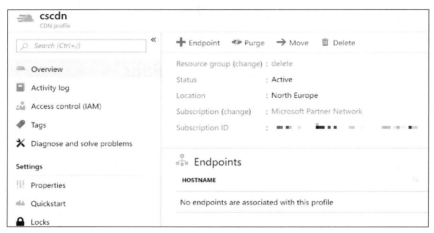

FIGURE 5-6 CDN profile

13. On the CDN Profile blade's Overview panel, click the Endpoint button.

14. In the Add An Endpoint panel, type a Name for the endpoint. Bear in mind that this name needs to be globally unique.

15. In the Origin Type drop-down menu, select Web App.

16. In the Origin Hostname drop-down menu, select the name of your web application.

17. In the Origin Path text box, type the path to the application you need to include in the CDN.

18. Leave the Origin Host header value as is. The Origin Host header value should match the Origin Hostname value.

19. Leave the other options as is.

20. Click the Add button.

The propagation of the content through the CDN depends on the type of CDN that you configured. For Standard Microsoft CDN, the propagation usually completes in 10 minutes. Once the propagation of the CDN completes, you can access your web application by using the endpoint that you configured in the previous procedure: *https://<your_endpoint's_name>. azureedge.net*

Once you have configured the endpoint, you can apply some advanced options to adjust the CDN to your needs:

- **Custom DNS domain** By default, when using the CDN, your users access your application by using the URL *https://<your_endpoint's_name>.azureedge.net*. This URL would not be appropriate for your application. You can assign more appropriate DNS domains to the CDN endpoint, such as *https://app.contoso.com*, which allows your users to access your web application using a URL related to your business and your DNS domain name.

- **Compression**   You can configure the CDN endpoint to compress some MIME types. This compression is made on the fly by the CDN when the content is delivered from the cache. Compressing the content allows you to deliver smaller files, improving the overall performance of the application.

- **Caching rules**   You can control how the content is stored in the cache by setting different rules for different paths or content types. By configuring a cache rule, you can modify the cache expiration time, depending on the conditions you configure. Caching rules are only available for profiles from Verizon's Azure CDN Standard and Akamai's Azure CDN Standard.

- **Geo-filtering**   You can block or allow a web application's content to certain countries across the globe.

- **Optimization**   You can configure the CDN for optimizing the delivery of different types of content. Depending on the type of profile, you can optimize your endpoint for:
  - General web delivery
  - Dynamic site acceleration
  - General media streaming
  - Video-on-demand media streaming
  - Large file downloads

> *NOTE*   **DYNAMIC SITE ACCELERATION**
>
> Although Dynamic Site Acceleration is part of the features provided by the Azure CDN, this is not strictly a cache solution. If you need to use Dynamic Site Acceleration with Microsoft Azure services, you should use Azure Front Door Service instead of Azure CDN.

If you need to dynamically create new CDN profiles and endpoints, Microsoft provides the Azure CDN Library for .NET and Azure CDN Library for Node.js. Using these libraries, you can automate most of the operations that we reviewed in this section.

> *NEED MORE REVIEW?*   **HOW CACHING WORKS**
>
> Caching web content involves working with HTTP headers, setting the appropriate expiration times, or deciding which files should be included in the cache. You can review the details of how caching works by reading the article at *https://docs.microsoft.com/en-us/azure/cdn/cdn-how-caching-works*.

EXAM TIP

Content Delivery Networks (CDN) are appropriate for caching static content that changes infrequently. Although Azure CDN from Akamai and Azure CDN from Verizon include Dynamic Site Acceleration (DSA), this feature is not the same as a cache system. You should not confuse Azure CDN DSA optimization with Azure CDN cache.

Invalidate cache content (CDN or Redis)

When you work with cached content, you need to control the lifetime or validity of that content. Although static content usually has a low rate of change, this kind of content *can* change. For example, if you are caching the logo of your company and the logo is changed, your users won't see the change in the application until the new logo is loaded in the cache. In this scenario, you can simply purge or remove the old logo from the cache, and the new image will be loaded into the cache as soon as the first user accesses the application.

This mechanism of manually purging the cache could be appropriate for a very specific scenario, but in general terms, you should consider using an automatic mechanism for having the freshest content in your cache system. When you add content to a CDN cache, the system automatically assigns a TimeToLive (TTL) value to the content file instead of continuously comparing the file in the cache with the original content on the web server. The cache system checks whether the TTL is lower than the current time. If the TTL is lower than the current time, the CDN considers the content to be fresh and keeps the content in the cache. If the TTL expires, the CDN marks the content as stale or invalid. When the next user tries to access the invalid content file, the CDN compares the cached file with the content in the web server. If both files match, the CDN updates the version of the cached file and makes the file valid again by resetting the expiration time. If the files in the cache and the web server don't match, the CDN removes the file from the cache and updates the content with the freshest content file on the web server.

The cached content can become invalid by deleting the content from the cache or by reaching the expiration time. You can configure the default TTL associated to a site by using the Cache-Control HTTP Header. You set the value for this header in different ways:

- **Default CDN configuration** If you don't configure any value for the TTL, the Azure CDN automatically configures a default value of seven days.
- **Caching rules** You can configure TTL values globally or by using custom matching rules. Global caching rules affect all content in the CDN. Custom caching rules control the TTL for different paths or files in your web application. You can even disable the caching for some parts of your web application.
- **Web.config files** You use the *web.config* file to set the expiration time of the folder. You can even configure *web.config* files for different folders by setting different TTL values. Use the following XML code to set the TTL:

```
<configuration>
    <system.webServer>
```

```
    <staticContent>
        <clientCache cacheControlMode="UseMaxAge" cacheControlMaxAge=
        "3.00:00:00" />
    </staticContent>
</system.webServer>
</configuration>
```

■ **Programmatically** If you work with ASP.NET, you can control the CDN caching
behavior by setting the *HttpResponse.Cache* property. You can use the following code to
set the expiration time of the content to five hours:

```
// Set the caching parameters.
Response.Cache.SetExpires(DateTime.Now.AddHours(5));
Response.Cache.SetCacheability(HttpCacheability.Public);
Response.Cache.SetLastModified(DateTime.Now);
```

Use the following procedure to create caching rules in your Azure CDN. Bear in mind that
you can only configure caching rules for Azure CDN for Verizon and Azure CDN for Akamai
profiles:

1. Open the Azure Portal (*https://portal.azure.com*).
2. In the navigation menu on the left side of the portal, click Create A Resource.
3. On the New blade, in the Search The Marketplace text box, type **CDN**.
4. In the result list, click CDN.
5. On the CDN blade, click the Create button.
6. On the CDN profile blade, type a Name for the profile.
7. Select an existing Resource Group from the drop-down menu. Alternatively, you can
    create a new resource group by clicking the Create New link below the Resource Group
    drop-down menu.
8. On the Pricing Tier drop-down menu, select Standard Akamai.
9. Check the Create A New CDN Endpoint Now check box.
10. Type a name for the endpoint in the CDN Endpoint Name text box.
11. In the Origin Type drop-down menu, select Web App.
12. In the Origin Hostname drop-down menu, select the name of your web application.
13. Click the Create button at the bottom of the CDN Profile blade.
14. In the search text box on the middle-top side of the Azure Portal, type the name of your
    CDN profile.
15. In the result list, click your CDN profile's name.
16. On the Overview panel, on the CDN profile blade, in the Endpoints list, click the existing
    endpoint.
17. On the Endpoint blade, click Caching Rules in the Settings section of the navigation
    menu.
18. On the Caching Rules panel, shown in Figure 5-7, set the Caching Behavior drop-down
    menu to Override in the Global Caching Rules section.

19. Set the Cache Expiration Duration to 15 days.

20. On the Custom Caching Rules list, create a new custom rule. Set the Match Condition drop-down menu to File Extension(s).

21. In the Match Value(s) text box, type **png**.

22. In the Caching Behaviour drop-down menu, select Override.

23. In the Days column, type **4**.

24. In the top-left corner of the panel, click the Save button.

FIGURE 5-7 Configuring Caching Rules

When you work with Azure Cache for Redis, you can also set the TTL for the different values stored in the in-memory database. If you don't set a TTL for the key/value pair, the entry in the the cache won't expire. When you create a new entry in the in-memory database, you set the TTL value as a parameter of the *StringSet()* method. The following code snippet shows how to set a TTL of 5 hours to a *String* value:

```
_cache.StringSet(key, Serialize(value), new TimeSpan(5, 0, 0));
```

Apart from invalidating the content of the cache by the expiration of the content, you can manually invalidate the content by removing it directly from the CDN or Redis Cache. You can remove a key from the Azure Cache for Redis in-memory database. You can use the following methods:

- **KeyDelete() method** Use this method for removing a single key from the database. You need to use this method with a database instance.

- **FlushAllDatabases() method** Use this method to remove all keys from all databases in the Azure Cache for Redis.

For Azure CDN, you can invalidate part or the entire content of the CDN profile by using the Purge option available in the Azure Portal. Use the following procedure for purging content from your Azure CDN profile:

1. Open the Azure Portal (*https://portal.azure.com*).

2. In the search text box on the middle-top side of the Azure Portal, type the name of your CDN profile.

3. On the Overview panel, in your CDN profile blade, click the Purge button.

4. On the Purge panel, shown in Figure 5-8, select the Endpoint you want to purge from the drop-down menu control.

FIGURE 5-8 Purging content from the cache

5. In the Content Path text box, type the path that you want to purge from the cache. If you want to purge all the content from the cache, you need to check the Purge All checkbox.

> **NOTE   PURGE ALL AND WILDCARDS IN AZURE CDN FOR AKAMAI**
>
> At the time of this writing, the Purge All and Wildcard options are not available for Akamai CDNs.

Skill 5.3: Instrument solutions to support monitoring and logging

Knowing how your application behaves during normal operation is important, especially for production environments. You need to get information about the number of users, resource consumption, transactions, and other metrics that can help you to troubleshoot your application if an error happens. Adding custom metrics to your application is also important when creating alerts that warn you when your application is not behaving as expected.

Azure provides features for monitoring the consumption of resources assigned to your application. Also, you can monitor the transactions and any other metrics that you may need, which allows you to fully understand how your application behaves under conditions that are usually difficult to simulate or test. You can also use these metrics for efficiently creating autoscale rules to improve the performance of your application, as we reviewed in Skill 5.1.

Configure instrumentation in an app or service by using Application Insights

Microsoft provides you with the ability to monitor your application while it is running by using Application Insights. This tool integrates with your code, allowing you to monitor what is happening inside your code while it is executing in a cloud, on-premises, or hybrid environment. You can also enable Application Insights for applications that are already deployed in Azure without modifying the already deployed code.

By adding a small instrumentation package, you can measure several aspects of your application. These measures, known as telemetry, are automatically sent to the Application Insight component deployed in Azure. Based on the information sent from the telemetry streams from your application to the Azure Portal, you can analyze your application's performance and create alerts and dashboards, which help you better understand how your application is behaving. Although Application Insight needs to be deployed in the Azure Portal, your application can be executed in Azure, in other public clouds, or in your on-premises infrastructure. When you deploy the Application Insight instrumentation in your application, it monitors the following points:

- **Request rates, response times, and failure rates**   You can view which pages your users request more frequently, distributed across time. You may find that your users tend to visit certain pages at the beginning of the day while others are more visited at the end of the day. You can also monitor the time that your server takes for delivering the requested page or even if there were failures when delivering the page. You should monitor the failure rates and response times to ensure that your application is performing correctly and your users have a good experience.

- **Dependency rates, response times, and failure rates**   If your application depends on external services (such as Azure Storage Accounts), Google or Twitter security services for authenticating your users, or any other external service, you can monitor how these external services are performing and how they are affecting your application.

- **Exceptions**   The instrumentation keeps track of the exceptions raised by servers and browsers while your application is executing. You can review the details of the stack trace for each exception via the Azure Portal. You can also view statistics about exceptions that arise during your application's execution.

- **Page views and load performance**   Measuring the performance of your server's page delivery is only part of the equation. Using Application Insights, you can also get information about the page views and load performance reported from the browser's side.

- **AJAX calls**   This measures the time taken by AJAX calls made from your application's web pages. It also measures the failure rates and response time.

- **User and session counts**   You can keep track of the number of users who are connected to your application. Just as the same user can initiate multiple sessions, you can track the number of sessions connected to your application. This allows you to clearly measure the threshold of concurrent users supported by your application.

- **Performance counters**   You can get information about the performance counters of the server machine (CPU, memory, and network usage) from which your code is executing.

- **Hosts diagnostics**   Hosts diagnostics can get information from your application if it is deployed in a Docker or Azure environment.

- **Diagnostic trace logs**   Trace log messages can be used to correlate trace events with the requests made to the application by your users.

- **Custom events and metrics**   Although the out-of-the-box instrumentation offered by Application Insights offers a lot of information, there are some metrics that are too specific to your application that cannot be generalized and included in the general telemetry. For those cases, you can create custom metrics to monitor your server and client code. This allows you to monitor user actions, such as shopping cart checkouts or game scoring.

Application Insights are not limited to .NET languages. There are instrumentation libraries available for other languages, such as Java, JavaScript, or Node.js. There are also libraries available for other platforms like Android or iOS. You can use the following procedure to add Application Insight instrumentation to your ASP.NET application. To run this example, you need to meet these requisites:

- An Azure Subscription.

- Visual Studio 2017/2019. If you don't have Visual Studio, you can download the Community edition for free from *https://visualstudio.microsoft.com/free-developer-offers/*.

- Install the following workloads in Visual Studio:

    - ASP.NET and web development, including the optional components.

    - Azure development.

For this example, we are going to create a new MVC application from a template, and then we will add the Application Insight instrumentation. You can use the same procedure to add instrumentation to any of your existing ASP.NET applications:

1. Open Visual Studio 2019.

2. In the home window in Visual Studio, click the Create A New Project button in the section Get Started on the right side of the window.

3. In the Create A New Project window, on the search box, type **MVC**.

4. Select the ASP.NET Web Application (.NET Framework) template.

5. Click the Next button in the bottom-right corner of the window.

6. Type a name for your project and solution in the Project Name and Solution Name boxes, respectively.

7. Select the Location where your project will be stored.

8. Click the Create button at the bottom-right corner of the window.

9. On the Create A New ASP.NET Web Application window, select the MVC template.

10. Click the Create button at the bottom-right corner of the window.

11. In the Solution Explorer window, right-click the name of your project.

12. In the contextual menu, shown in Figure 5-9, click Add > Application Insights Telemetry.

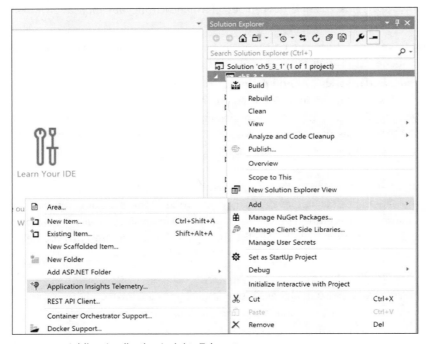

FIGURE 5-9 Adding Application Insights Telemetry

13. On the Application Insights Configuration page, click the Get Started button at the bottom of the page.

14. On the Register Your App With Application Insights page, ensure that the correct Azure Account and Azure Subscription are selected in the drop-down menus.

15. Click the Configure Settings link below the Resource drop-down menu.

16. In the Application Insights Configuration dialog box, select the Resource Group and Location where you want to create the new Application Insight resource.

17. Click the Register button.

18. On the Application Insights Configuration tab, click the Collect Traces From System. Diagnostics button at the bottom of the tab. Enabling this option allows you to send a log message directly to Application Insights.

At this point, Visual Studio starts adding the needed packages and dependencies to your project. Visual Studio also automatically configures the Instrumentation Key, which allows your application to connect to the Application Insight resource created in Azure. Now your project is connected with the instance of the Application Insights deployed in Azure. As soon as you run your project, the Application Insight instrumentation starts sending information to Azure. You can review this information in the Azure Portal or your Visual Studio. Use the following steps to access the Application Insight from Visual Studio and Azure Portal:

1. From the Visual Studio window, in the Solution Explorer window, navigate to your project's name and choose Connected Services > Application Insights.

2. Right-click Application Insights.

3. On the contextual menu, click Search Live Telemetry. The Application Insights Search tab will appear in Visual Studio.

4. In the Solution Explorer, right-click Application Insights to open the Azure Portal Application Insights from Visual Studio.

5. On the contextual menu, click Open Application Insights Portal.

Apart from the standard metrics that come out-of-the-box with the default Application Insight instrumentation, you can also add your custom events and metrics to your code. Using custom events and metrics, you can analyze and troubleshoot logic and workflows that are specific to your application. The following example shows how to modify the MVC application that you created on the previous example for adding custom events and metrics:

1. Open the project that you created in the previous example.

2. Open the *HomeController.cs* file.

3. Add the following using statement at the beginning of the file:

```
using Microsoft.ApplicationInsights;
using System.Diagnostics;
```

4. Replace the content of the *HomeController* class in the *HomeController.cs* file with the content in Listing 5-3.

LISTING 5-3 *HomeController* class

```
// C#. ASP.NET.
public class HomeController : Controller
    {
        private TelemetryClient telemetry;
        private double indexLoadCounter;

        public HomeController()
        {
            //Create a TelemetryClient that can be used during the life of the Controller.
            telemetry = new TelemetryClient();
```

```
        //Initialize some counters for the custom metrics.
        //This is a fake metric just for demo purposes.
        indexLoadCounter = new Random().Next(1000);
    }

    public ActionResult Index()
    {
        //This example is trivial as ApplicationInsights already register the load
        of the page.
        //You can use this example for tracking different events in the application.
        telemetry.TrackEvent("Loading the Index page");

        //Before you can submit a custom metric, you need to use the GetMetric
        //method.
        telemetry.GetMetric("CountOfIndexPageLoads").TrackValue(indexLoadCounter);

        //This trivial example shows how to track exceptions using Application
        //Insights.
        //You can also send trace message to Application Insights.
        try
        {
            Trace.TraceInformation("Raising a trivial exception");
            throw new System.Exception("Trivial Exception for testing Tracking
            Exception feature in Application Insights");
        }
        catch (System.Exception ex)
        {
            Trace.TraceError("Capturing and managing the trivial exception");
            telemetry.TrackException(ex);
        }

        //You need to instruct the TelemetryClient to send all in-memory data to the
        //ApplicationInsights.
        telemetry.Flush();
        return View();
    }

    public ActionResult About()
    {
        ViewBag.Message = "Your application description page.";

        //This example is trivial as ApplicationInsights already register the load
        //of the page.
        //You can use this example for tracking different events in the application.
        telemetry.TrackEvent("Loading the About page");

        return View();
    }

    public ActionResult Contact()
    {
        ViewBag.Message = "Your contact page.";

        //This example is trivial as ApplicationInsights already register the load
        //of the page.
```

```
        //You can use this example for tracking different events in the application.
        telemetry.TrackEvent("Loading the Contact page");

        return View();
    }
}
```

5. In the Solution Explorer, open the *ApplicationInsights.config* file.

6. In the *<Add Type="Microsoft.ApplicationInsights.Extensibility.PerfCounterCollector.
   PerformanceCollectorModule, Microsoft.AI.PerfCounterCollector">* XML item, add the
   following child XML item:

   ```
   <EnableIISExpressPerformanceCounters>true</EnableIISExpressPerformanceCounters>
   ```

> **NOTE CONTROLLERS CONSTRUCTORS**
>
> In the previous example, we used a private property in the constructor for creating and
> initializing a *TelemetryClient* object. In a real-world application, you should use dependency
> injection techniques for properly initializing the *Controller* class. There are several frameworks,
> like Unity, Autofac, or Ninject, that can help you in implementing the dependency injection
> pattern in your code.

At this point, you can press F5 and run your project and see how your application is sending
information to Application Insights. If you review the Application Insight Search tab, you can
see the messages, shown in Figure 5-10, that your application is sending to Application Insights.

FIGURE 5-10   Application Insights messages

You send messages to Application Insights by using the *TelemetryClass* class. This class
provides you with the appropriate methods for sending the different types of messages to

Application Insights. You can send custom events by using the *TrackEvent()* method. You use this method for tracking meaningful events to your application, such as the user created a new shopping cart in an eCommerce web application or the user won a game in a mobile App.

If you need to keep track of the value of certain variables or properties in your code, you can use the combination of *GetMetric()* and *TrackValue()* methods. The *GetMetric()* method retrieves a metric from the *azure.applicationinsight* namespace. If the metric doesn't exist on the namespace, Application Insight library automatically creates a new one. Once you have a reference to the correct metric, you can use the *TrackValue()* method to add a value to that metric. You can use these custom metrics for setting alerts or autoscale rules. Use the following steps for viewing the custom metrics in the Azure Portal:

1. From the Visual Studio window, in the Solution Explorer window, navigate to your project's name and choose Connected Services > Application Insights.

2. Right-click Application Insights.

3. In the contextual menu, click Open Application Insights Portal.

4. On the Application Insights blade, click Metrics in the Monitoring section of the navigation menu on the left side of the blade.

5. On the Metrics blade, on the toolbar above the empty graph, on the Metric Namespace drop-down menu, select *azure.applicationsight*.

6. On the Metric drop-down menu, select *CoutOfIndexPageLoad*. This is the custom metric that we defined in the previous example.

7. On the Aggregation drop-down menu, select Count. The values for your graph will be different but should look similar to Figure 5-11.

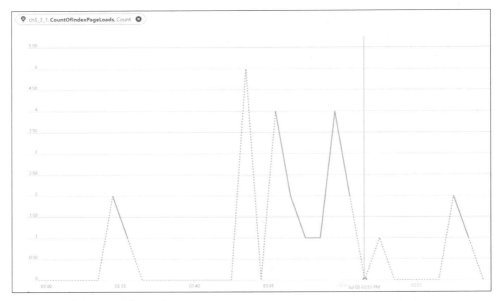

FIGURE 5-11 Custom metric graph

You can also send log messages to Application Insights by using the integration between *System.Diagnostics* and Application Insights. Any message sent to the diagnostics system using the *Trace* class appears in the Application Insights as a Trace message. In this same line, use the *TraceException()* method for sending the stack trace and the exception to Application Insights. The advantage of doing this is that you can easily correlate exceptions with the operations that were performing your code when the exception happened.

Analyze and troubleshoot solutions by using Azure Monitor

Azure Monitor is a tool composed of several elements that help you monitor and better understand the behavior of your solutions. Application Insights is a tool for collecting information from your solutions. Once you have the collected information, you can use the Analyze tools for reviewing the data and troubleshooting your application. Depending on the information that you need to analyze, you can use Metric Analytics or Log Analytics.

You can use Metric Analytics for reviewing the standard and custom metrics sent from your application. A metric is a numeric value that is related to some aspect at a particular point in time of your solution. CPU usage, free memory, and number of requests are all examples of metrics; also, you can create your own custom metrics. Because metrics are lightweight, you can use them to monitor scenarios in near real-time. You analyze metric data by representing the values of the metrics in a time interval using different types of graphs. Use the following steps for reviewing graphs:

1. Open the Azure Portal (*https://portal.azure.com*).
2. On the navigation menu on the left side of the Azure Portal, click Monitor.
3. On the Monitor blade, click Metrics on the navigation menu on the left side of the blade.
4. On the Metrics blade, click the Select A Resource button.

5. On the Select A Resource panel, on the Resource Group drop-down menu, select all the resource groups that contain the Azure App Service containing the metrics you want to add to the graph.

6. In the Resource Type drop-down menu, select only the App Service Plans and App Service resource types.

7. On the list of filtered resources, click the resource that you want to add to the graph.

8. Click the Apply button at the bottom of the panel.

9. On the Metrics blade, select the Average Response Time metric in the Metric drop-down menu.

10. Click the Add Metric button at the top of the graph. You can add several metrics to the same graph, which means you can analyze different metrics that are related between them.

11. Repeat steps 4 to 10 for adding the Connections metric. Figure 5-12 shows the metrics added to the graph.

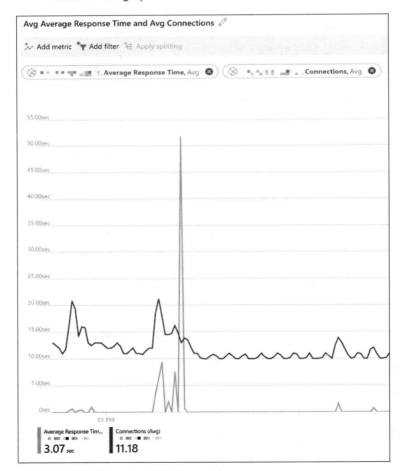

FIGURE 5-12 Configuring metrics for a graph.

You use Log Analytics for analyzing the trace, logs, events, exceptions, and any other message sent from your application. Log messages are more complex than metrics because they can contain much more information than a simple numeric value. You can analyze log messages by using queries for retrieving, consolidating, and analyzing the collected data. Log Analytics for Azure Monitor uses a version of the Kusto query language. You can construct your queries to get information from the data stored in Azure Monitor. To do so, complete the following steps:

1. Open the Azure Portal (*https://portal.azure.com*).

2. In the navigation menu on the left side of the Azure Portal, click Monitor.

3. On the Monitor blade, click Logs in the navigation menu on the left side of the blade.

4. On the Logs blade, type **Event | search "error"** in the text area.

5. Click the Run button.

6. You can review the result of your query in the section below the query text area.

This simple query returns all error events stored in the default workspace. You can use more complex queries for getting more information about your solution. The available fields for the queries depend on the data loaded in the workspace. These fields are managed by the data schema. Figure 5-13 shows the schema associated with a workplace that stores data from Application Insights.

FIGURE 5-13 Workspace schema

Once you get the results from a query, you can easily refine the results of the query by adding *where* clauses to the query. The easiest way to add new filtering criteria is to expand one of the records in the table view in the results section below the query text area. If you move your mouse over each of the fields in a record, you can see two small plus and minus sign icons. If you click the plus sign, you add the value of the field as an inclusive *where* clause. If you click the minus sign beside the name of the field, you add the value of the field as an exclusive *where* clause. Based on the example that we reviewed in the previous section, the following query would get all traces sent from the application except those with the message *"Raising a trivial exception"*.

```
traces | where message <> "Raising a trivial exception"
```

You can review the results of this query in both table and chart formats. Using the different visualization formats, you can get a different insight into the data. Figure 5-14 shows how the results from the previous query are plotted into a pie chart.

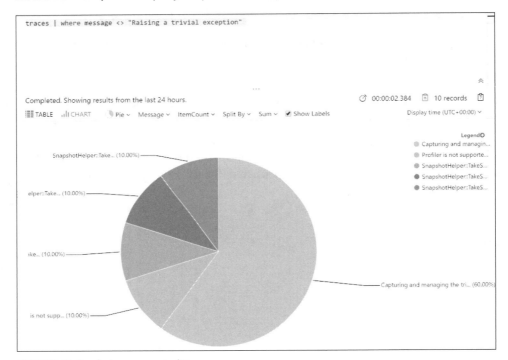

FIGURE 5-14 Rendering query results

NEED MORE REVIEW? **CREATING LOG QUERIES**

Creating the appropriate query for your need greatly depends on the details of your solution. You can review the details about the Kusto query language and how to create complex queries by reviewing the following articles:

- Kusto Query Language: *https://docs.microsoft.com/en-us/azure/kusto/query/*
- Azure Monitor log queries: *https://docs.microsoft.com/en-us/azure/azure-monitor/log-query/query-language*

Implement Application Insights Web Test and Alerts

As a result of analyzing the data sent from your application to the Azure Monitor using Application Insights, you may find some situations that you need to monitor more carefully. Using Azure Monitor, you can set alerts based on the value of different metrics or logs. For example, you can create an alert to receive a notification when your application generates an HTTP return code 502.

You can also configure Application Insights for monitoring the availability of your web application. You can configure different types of tests for checking the availability of your web application:

- **URL ping test** This is a simple test for checking whether your application is available by making a request to a single URL for your application.

- **Multi-step web test** Using Visual Studio Enterprise, you can record the steps that you want to use as the verification for your application. You use this type of test for checking complex scenarios. The process of recording the steps in a web application generates a file with the recorded steps. Using this generated file, you can create a web test in Application Insights; then you upload the recording file.

- **Custom Track Availability Test** You can create your own availability test in your code using the *TrackAvailability()* method.

When creating a URL ping test, you can check not only the HTTP response code but also the content returned by the server. This way, you can minimize the possibility of false positives. These false positives can happen if the server returns a valid HTTP response code, but the content is different due to configuration errors. Use the following procedure for creating an URL ping test on your Application Insights that checks the availability of your web application:

1. Open the Azure Portal (*https://portal.azure.com*).

2. In the navigation menu on the left side of the Azure Portal, click Monitor.

3. On the Monitor blade, click Applications in the Insights section.

4. On the Applications blade, click the Application Insight resource where you want to configure the alert.

5. On the Applications Insights blade, click Availability in the Investigate section of the navigation menu on the left side of the blade.

6. On the Availability blade, click Add Test on the top-left corner of the blade.

7. On the Create Test blade, shown in Figure 5-15, type a name for the test in the Test Name text box.

Create test

∧ Basic Information

* Test name

Give your test a name

Learn more about configuring tests against applications hosted behind a firewall

Test type

URL ping test ⌄

* URL ❶

Parse dependent requests ❶
☐

Enable retries for availability test failures. ❶
☑

Test frequency ❶

5 minutes ⌄

⌄ Test locations
   5 location(s) configured

⌄ Success criteria
   HTTP response: 200, Test Timeout: 120 seconds

⌄ Alerts
   Enabled

FIGURE 5-15 Creating a URL test

8. Ensure that URL Ping Test is selected in the Test Type drop-down menu.

9. In the URL text box, type the URL of the application you want to test.

10. Expand the Test Location section. Select the locations from which you want to perform the URL ping test.

11. Leave the other options as is.

12. Click the Create button at the bottom of the panel.

When you configure the URL ping test, you cannot configure the Alert directly during the creation process. You need to finish the creation of the test and then you can edit the Alert for defining the actions that you want to perform when the alert fires. Use the following procedure for configuring an alert associated with the URL ping test that you configured previously:

1. On the Availability blade, click the ellipsis beside the newly created alert.

2. In the contextual menu, click Edit Alert.

3. On the alert blade, in the Actions section, click the Add button. You are going to configure an action for sending an email when the URL ping test fails.

4. On the Configured Actions panel, click the Create Action Group button.

5. On the Add Action Group panel, type a name in the Action Group Name text box. Bear in mind that an action group appears as a resource in the Resource Group. This means that the name that you choose for this action group needs to be unique to the resource group.

6. Type a name in the Short Name text box. This name is used in the email and SMS communications for identifying the source action group that sent the message.

7. Select a resource group in the Resource Group drop-down menu.

8. In the Actions section, type a name in the Action Name text box.

9. In the Action Type drop-down menu, select Email/SMS/Push/Voice.

10. On the Email/SMS/Push/Voice panel, select the Email checkbox.

11. Type an email address in the text box below the Email checkbox.

12. Click the OK button at the bottom of the panel.

13. On the Add Action Group panel, click the OK button at the bottom of the panel.

14. On the Configured Actions panel, click the Done button at the bottom of the panel.

15. On the alert blade, click the Save button on the top-left corner of the blade.

Now you can test whether the URL ping test is working correctly by temporarily shutting down your testing application. After five minutes, you should receive an email message at the email address you configured in the alert action associated with the URL ping test.

EXAM TIP

Remember that you need a Visual Studio Enterprise license for creating multi-step web tests. You use the Visual Studio Enterprise for the definition of the steps that are part of the test, and then you upload the test definition to Azure Application Insights.

NEED MORE REVIEW? **AZURE MONITOR ALERTS**

Apart from creating alerts when a web test fails, you can also create alerts based on other conditions that depend on the events information stored in the Application Insights. You can review the details about how to create these alerts by reviewing the article:
https://docs.microsoft.com/en-us/azure/azure-monitor/platform/alerts-log

Chapter summary

- Horizontal scaling or In-Out scaling is the process of adding or removing instances of an application.
- Vertical scaling or Up-Down scaling is the process of adding or removing resources to the same virtual machine that hosts your application.
- Scale In/Out doesn't affect the availability of the application.

- Vertical scaling affects the availability of the application because the application needs to be deployed in a virtual machine with the new resources assignment.
- You can add and remove resources to your applications by using autoscale rules.
- You can apply autoscale only to some Azure Resource types.
- Autoscale depends on Azure virtual machine scale sets.
- Your application needs to be aware of the changes in the resources assignment.
- Your application needs to be able to manage transient faults.
- You need to determine the type of fault before retrying the operation.
- You should not use immediate retry more than once.
- You should use random starting values for the retry periods.
- You should use built-in SDK mechanism when available.
- You should test your retry count and interval strategy.
- You should log transient and non-transient faults.
- You can improve the performance of your application by adding cache to your application.
- Azure Cache for Redis allows the caching of dynamic content.
- Using Azure Cache for Redis, you can create in-memory databases to cache the most-used values.
- Azure Cache for Redis allows you to use messaging queue patterns.
- Content Deliver Networks (CDNs) store and distribute static content in servers distributed across the globe.
- CDNs reduce the latency by serving the content from the server nearest to the user.
- You can invalidate the content of the cache by setting a low TTL (Time-To-Live).
- You can invalidate the content of the cache by removing all or part of the content from the cache.
- Application Insights gets information from your application and sends it to Azure.
- You can use Application Insights with different platforms and languages.
- Application Insights is part of the Azure Monitor service.
- Application Insights generates two types of information: metrics, and logs.
- You can use Log Analyze and Metric Analyze to troubleshoot your application.
- Application Insights allows you to create web tests to monitor the availability of your application.
- You can configure alerts and trigger different actions associated with web tests.

Thought experiment

In this thought experiment, demonstrate your skills and knowledge of the topics covered in this chapter. You can find answers to this thought experiment in the next section.

Your company has a Line-of-Business (LOB) application that has been developed by your team. This LOB application is an eCommerce application that has more usage during holiday periods. This application is deployed on several Azure virtual machine scale sets. You are receiving some complaints about the stability and the performance of the application. Answer the following questions about the troubleshooting and the performance of the application:

1. You need to ensure that the application has enough resources for providing good performance. You decide to configure autoscaling rules. Which type of autoscale rules should you configure?

2. After reviewing the metrics of your application in the Azure Monitor, you find that you don't have enough detail about the performance of the internal application workflows. What should you do to get information about the internal workflows?

3. You need to ensure that the purchase process is working correctly. You decide to configure a web test in Application Insights. Which type of test should you configure?

Thought experiment answers

This section contains the solution to the thought experiment. Each answer explains why the answer choice is correct.

1. You should configure schedule-based and metric-based autoscale rules.

   ■ You configure the schedule-based rule for ensuring that the application has enough resources during the holiday period.

   ■ You also need to configure a metric-based autoscale rule to ensure that you assign more resources if the application goes over a certain threshold of CPU or memory usage that could affect the performance of the application.

2. You should integrate Application Insights instruments with your code. Once you integrate the Application Insights with your code, you can track custom events in your code. You can define operations inside your code to track complex operations compounds of several tasks. This allows you to get more information about the internal workflows executed in the application. Performing Application Insight agent-based monitoring doesn't provide enough information.

3. The process of a purchase in a web application is a complex testing scenario. In this scenario, you need to use a multi-step web test. Using Visual Studio Enterprise, you need to record the steps needed for performing a purchase in your web application. Once you have generated the file with the recorded steps, you can create a web test in Application Insights to monitor the purchase process.

## CHAPTER 6

Connect to and consume Azure services and third-party services

N owadays, companies use different systems for different tasks that are usually performed by different departments. Although these separate systems work for solving a specific need, they usually act as independent actors in a big scenario. These independent actors manage information about the company that can potentially be duplicated by other independent actors.

When a company realizes that independent actors are managing their data, they usually try to make all the independent actors or systems work together and share information between them. This situation is independent of using cloud services or on-premises services. To make the independent actors work together, you need to make connections between each actor or service that needs to communicate with the other.

You can use different services and techniques to achieve this interconnection. Azure provides some useful services that allow different services to work together without making big changes to the interconnected services.

Skills covered in this chapter:

- Skill 6.1: Develop an App Service Logic App
- Skill 6.2: Integrate Azure Search within solutions
- Skill 6.3: Establish API Gateways
- Skill 6.4: Develop event-based solutions
- Skill 6.5: Develop message-based solutions

Skill 6.1: Develop an App Service Logic App

Exchanging information between different applications is a goal for most companies. Sharing the information enriches the internal process and creates more insight into the information itself. By using the App Service Logic App, you can create workflows that interconnect different systems, based on conditions and rules and easing the process of sharing information between them. Also, you can also take advantage of the Logic Apps features to implement business process workflows.

Create a Logic App

Before you can interconnect two separate services, you need to fully understand which information you need to share between the services. Sometimes the information needs to undergo some transformations before it can be consumed by a service. You could write code for making this interconnection, but this is a time-consuming and error-prone task.

Azure offers the App Service Logic Apps that allows the interconnection of two or more services that share information between them. This interconnection between different services is defined by a business process. Azure Logic Apps allows you to build complex interconnection scenarios by using some elements that ease the work:

- **Workflows**   Define the source and destination of the information. Workflows connect to different services by using connectors. A workflow defines the steps or actions that the information needs to take to deliver the information from the source to the correct destination. You use a graphical language to visualize, design, build, automate, and deploy a business process.

- **Managed Connectors**   A connector is an object that allows your workflow to access data, services, and systems. Microsoft provides some prebuilt connectors to the Microsoft services. These connectors are managed by Microsoft and provide the needed triggers and action objects to work with those services.

- **Triggers**   Triggers are events that fire when certain conditions are met. You use a trigger as the entry or starting point of a workflow. For example, when a new message arrives at your company's purchases mailbox, it can start a workflow that can access information from the subject and body of the message and create a new entry in the ERP system.

- **Actions**   Actions are each of the steps that you configure in your workflow. Actions happen only when the workflow is executed. The workflow starts executing when a new trigger fires.

- **Enterprise Integration Pack**   If you need to perform more advanced integrations, the Enterprise Integration Pack provides you with BizTalk Server capabilities.

You can use Azure Logic Apps for different purposes. The following procedure shows how to create an Azure Logic App workflow that writes a message in the Microsoft Teams app when a new build completes in Azure DevOps. For this procedure, you need an Azure DevOps account with a configured project that you can build. You also need a Microsoft Office 365 subscription with access to the Microsoft Teams application. Let's start by creating and config- uring the Azure Logic App:

1. Open the Azure Portal (*https://portal.azure.com*).
2. Click Create A Resource in the navigation menu on the left side of the Azure Portal.
3. On the New blade, on the Azure Marketplace list at the left side of the blade, click Integration.
4. In the Featured column on the right side of the blade, click Logic App.
5. On the Create Logic App blade, type a name in the Name text box.
6. In the Resource group text box, type a name for a new resource group. Alternatively, you can use a new resource group, selecting it from the drop-down menu.
7. Select a location from the Location drop-down menu.
8. Click the Create button at the bottom of the blade.
9. A dialog box appears in the top-right corner of the Azure Portal once the Azure Logic App is created. Click the Go To Resource button in the dialog box.
10. On the Logic Apps blade, on the Logic App Designer, click the Blank Logic App in the Templates section.
11. On the Logic Apps Designer, on the Search Connectors And Triggers text box, type **Azure DevOps**.
12. Click the Azure DevOps icon on the Results panel.
13. On the Triggers tab, select the trigger named When A Build Completes.
14. Click the Sign In button on the Azure DevOps element. At this point, you connect your Azure Subscription with your Azure DevOps account. If you don't already have an Azure DevOps account, you can configure one now by using the guide at *https://docs.microsoft.com/en-us/ azure/devops/user-guide/sign-up-invite-teammates?view=azure-devops*.
15. On the panel for the When A Build Completes trigger, shown in Figure 6-1, select your Azure DevOps account's name from the Account Name drop-down menu.

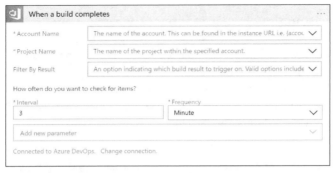

FIGURE 6-1 Configuring an Azure Logic Apps trigger

16. On the panel for the When A Build completes trigger, shown in Figure 6-1, select a project in your Azure DevOps account from the Project Name drop-down menu. If you don't have a project in Azure DevOps, you can review the article at *https://docs.microsoft.com/en-us/azure/devops/organizations/projects/create-project?view=azure-devops*.

17. Click the New Step button below the trigger panel.

18. On the Choose An Action panel, type **Teams** in the Search Connectors And Actions text box.

19. On the Actions tab, click the Post A Message (V3) action.

20. On the Post A Message (V3) action panel, select a team from the Team drop-down menu.

21. Select General from the Channel drop-down menu.

22. In the Message text area, type **The**.

23. In the Dynamic Content dialog, shown in Figure 6-2, on the right side of the Message text area, click the See More link. This link shows the list of dynamic attributes that you can add to your message.

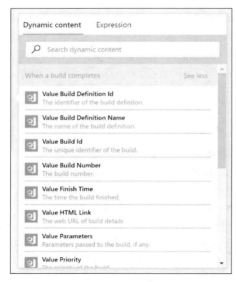

FIGURE 6-2 Dynamic content from a connector trigger

24. Choose Value Build Definition Name.

25. Type **build finished with status** in the message area next to the dynamic attribute.

26. Click Value Status.

27. Click the Save button in the top-left corner of the Azure Logic Apps Designer blade.

28. Click the Run button in the top left corner of the Azure Logic Apps Designer blade.

29. At this point, the Azure Logic Apps start listening for the configured trigger in Azure DevOps. When a new build finishes in Azure DevOps, Azure Logic Apps sends a message to your configured team's General Channel in your Microsoft Teams account. Now, you are going to create a pipeline in Azure DevOps to build an example project. Once the build finishes, you will receive a new message in the Microsoft Teams channel:

30. Navigate to the GitHub example at *https://github.com/MicrosoftDocs/ pipelines-dotnet-core*, and sign in to your account. If you don't have a GitHub account, you can create a new one for free by visiting *https://github.com/join*.

31. At the top-right corner of the project's page, click the Fork button.

32. Open your Azure DevOps account (*https://dev.azure.com*).

33. Click the Project name that you configured in step 16.

34. Click the Pipelines element on the navigation bar on the left side of the project's page.

35. Click the New Pipeline button.

36. On the New Pipeline window, click GitHub.

37. Sign in to your GitHub account.

38. On the Authorize Azure Pipelines (OAuth) window, click Authorize AzurePipelines at the bottom of the page.

39. In your Azure DevOps account, on the Select A Repository page, click the *pipelines-dotnet-core project*.

40. On the GitHub Approve & Install Azure Pipelines page, click the Approve & Install button at the bottom of the page.

41. In your Azure DevOps account, on the Configure Your Pipeline page, click ASP.NET Core.

42. Click the Save And Run button in the top-right corner of the page.

43. On the Save and Run panel, click the Save And Run button on the bottom of the panel.

At this point, the Azure DevOps agent is building the sample project. Once the build finishes, you will receive a new message in your Microsoft Teams channel, as shown in Figure 6-3.

Santiago Fernández Muñoz 19:45
The santifdezmunoz.pipelines-dotnet-core build finished with status completed

FIGURE 6-3 A message in Microsoft Teams from Azure DevOps

> *NEED MORE REVIEW?* **CONTROL WORKFLOW**
>
> In a regular workflow, you need to run different actions based on the input values or based on certain conditions. You can run these different actions using control workflow. To learn more about control flow and other connectors that you can use in Azure Logic Apps, see *https:// docs.microsoft.com/en-us/azure/logic-apps/logic-apps-control-flow-conditional-statement*.

Create a custom connector for Logic Apps

Microsoft provides more than 200 built-in connectors that you can use in your Azure Logic Apps workflow. Despite this number of connectors, there are opportunities that you need some specific features that are not provided by the built-in connectors, or you want to create a connector for your company's application.

You can create custom connectors for Microsoft Flow, PowerApps, and Azure Logic Apps. Although you cannot share Azure Logic Apps connectors with Microsoft Flow and PowerApps connectors, the principle for creating custom connectors is the same for all three platforms. A custom connector is basically a wrapper for a REST or SOAP API. This wrapper allows Azure Logic Apps to interact with the API of the application. The application that you want to include in the custom connector can be a public application, such as Amazon Web Services, Google Calendar, or the API of your application published to the Internet. Using the on-premises data gateway, you can also connect the custom connector with an on-premises application deployed in your data center. Every custom connector has the following lifecycle:

1. **Build your API**   You can wrap any REST or SOAP API in a custom connector. If you are creating your API, you should consider using Azure Functions, Azure Web Apps, or Azure API Apps.

2. **Secure your API**   You need to authenticate the access to your API. If you are implementing your application using Azure Functions, Azure Web Apps, or Azure API Apps, you can enable the Azure Active Directory authentication in the Azure Portal for your application. Also, you can enforce authentication directly on your API's code. You can use any of the following authentication mechanisms:

    - Generic OAuth 2.0
    - OAuth 2.0 for specific services, like Azure Active Directory, Dropbox, GitHub, or SalesForce
    - Basic Authentication
    - API Key

3. **Describe the API and define the custom connector**   You need to provide a description of your API's endpoints. Azure Logic Apps supports two different language-agnostic and machine-readable document formats that you can use for documenting this description: OpenAPI (formerly known as Swagger) or Postman collections. You can create a custom connector from the OpenAPI or Postman collection documentation.

4. **Use the connector in an Azure Logic Apps**   Once you have created the custom connector, you can use it as a regular managed built-in connector in your workflow. You need to create a connection to your API using your custom connector. Then you can use the triggers and actions that you configured in your custom connector.

5. **Share your connector**   Once you have created your custom connector, you can share it with other users in your organization. This step is optional.

6. **Certify your connector**   If you want to share your custom connector with other users outside your organization, you need to send the custom connector to Microsoft. Then Microsoft can review your custom connector to ensure that it works correctly. Once the connector is reviewed and validated, Microsoft certifies it, and you can share with users outside your organization.

The following steps show how to create a custom connector following the previous lifecycle. For the sake of brevity, we are using an Azure Cognitive Services API for creating this custom connector. For this example, you need to create an Azure Cognitive Services account that uses the Text Analytics API. You can sign up for a Text Analytics API at *https://docs.microsoft.com/en-us/azure/cognitive-services/text-analytics/how-tos/text-analytics-how-to-signup*.

1. Open the Azure Portal (*https://portal.azure.com*).

2. Click Create A Resource in the top-left corner of the Azure Portal.

3. Type **logic apps** on the Search The Marketplace text box.

4. Click Logic Apps Custom Connector in the results list.

5. Click the Create button.

6. On the Create Logic Apps Custom Connector panel, type a Name for your custom connector.

7. Select a Subscription and Location from their respective drop-down menus.

8. Type a name for the new Resource Group. Alternatively, you can click the Use Existing control and select an existing resource group from the drop-down menu.

9. Click the Create button at the bottom of the panel.

10. Type the name of your Azure Text Analytics API in the search text box at the top of the Azure Portal.

11. Click the name of your Azure Text Analytics API in the results list.

12. On the Overview blade of your Text Analytics account, copy the Endpoint value. You will need this value in a later step.

13. On the Overview blade, click the Show Access Keys link.

14. On the Keys blade, copy one of the two available keys. You will need this value in step 27 to create a workflow using this custom connector.

15. Download the OpenAPI definition of Azure Cognitive Services at *https://procsi.blob.core.windows.net/docs/SentimentDemo.openapi_definition.json*. You will need this file in step 20.

16. Type the name of your Azure Logic Apps Custom Connector on the search text box at the top of the Azure Portal.

17. Click the name of your Azure Logic Apps Custom Connector in the results list.

18. Click the Edit button on the Custom Connector's Overview blade.

19. On the Edit Logic Apps Custom Connector blade, click the Import button on the How Do You Want To Create Your Connector panel, shown in Figure 6-4.

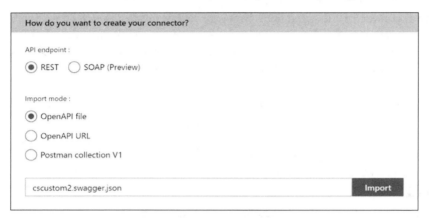

FIGURE 6-4 Importing the OpenAPI definition of a REST API

20. Choose the JSON file that you downloaded in step 15.

21. In the General Information section, below the Custom Connectors section, change the value of the Host parameter to the hostname of your Azure Text Analytics endpoint. You copied this value in step 12. You only need to use the host part of the URL.

> **NOTE BASE URL**
>
> In this example, the endpoint definition already contains the correct base URL in the endpoint definition. If you change the default Base URL property in the General Information section in your Azure Logic Apps Custom Connector, you will receive a 404 error every time that you try to use your custom connector in an Azure Logic Apps workflow.

22. Click the Security link on top of the page. (You can also find a Security link at the bottom-left corner of the page, and either of these links will take you to the Security section.)

23. Review the options on the Security page. For this custom connector, you are using API Key authentication. This authentication means that you need to provide an API Key when you use this connector in a workflow. Leave all settings in this page as they are.

24. Click the Definition link on top of the page. (You can also find a Definition link at the bottom-left corner of the page, and either of these links will take you to the Definition section.)

25. Review the settings on the Definition page. On this page, you will find all the endpoints that have been defined in the OpenAPI JSON file that you imported in step 19. These endpoints translate into Actions or Triggers, depending on the definition in the JSON file. You can also manually add new Actions and Triggers as needed using this page. Leave all settings on this page unchanged.

26. Click the Update Connector link at the top-right corner of the Edit Logic Apps Custom Connector blade.

At this point, you have successfully created your Azure Logic Apps Custom Connector. In the following steps, you are going to create a workflow for testing your new custom connector. This workflow gets the content from files in an Azure Blob Storage account, sends the content of the files to the Azure Cognitive Services, and sends the sentiment score of the content to a Microsoft Teams channel:

1. Open the Azure Portal (*https://portal.azure.com*).

2. Click Create A Resource in the top-left corner of the Azure Portal.

3. Type **logic apps** in the Search The Marketplace text box.

4. Click Logic App in the results list.

5. Click the Create button.

6. On the Create Logic App panel, type a Name for your Azure Logic App.

7. Select the appropriate Subscription and Location from their respective drop-down menus.

8. In the Resource Group text box, type the name of the new resource group. Alternatively, you can use an existing resource group by clicking the Use Existing option and selecting a resource group from the drop-down menu.

9. Click the Create button at the bottom of the panel.

10. Navigate to the newly created Azure Logic App.

11. On the Logic Apps Designer blade, choose the Blank Logic App template. If you don't see the Logic Apps Designer blade as soon as you open your Azure Logic App, click Logic App Designer on the navigation menu on the left side of your Azure Logic App.

12. In the Search Connectors and Triggers text box, type **Azure Blob**.

13. In the Triggers section, click the When A Blob Is Added Or Modified (Properties Only) trigger.

14. On the When A Blob Is Added Or Modified (Properties Only) panel, type a name for the connection with the Azure Blob Storage service. If you don't have an Azure Blob Storage account, you can learn how to create a new Azure Blob Storage account and a new container at *https://docs.microsoft.com/en-us/azure/storage/blobs/storage-quickstart-blobs-portal*.

15. Select a storage account from the available list of storage accounts.

16. On the When A Blob Is Added Or Modified (Properties Only) panel, click the folder icon next to the Select A Container text box, shown in Figure 6-5, and select the container that contains the files we used in this example.

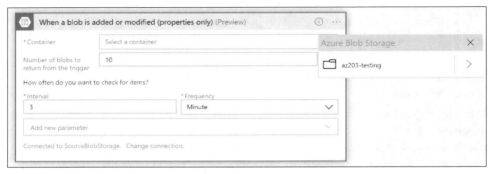

FIGURE 6-5 Selecting a container for an Azure Blob Storage connector trigger

17. Click the New Step button below the trigger dialog box.
18. On the Choose An Action panel, click the Azure Blob Storage icon in the Recent section.
19. Click the Get Blob Content action in the Actions section.
20. Click the Specify The Blob text box.
21. Click the List Of Files Id in the dialog box with the Dynamic Content list. Leave the Infer Content Type setting as is.
22. Click the New Step button.
23. On the Choose An Action panel, click Custom. Your Azure Logic Apps Custom Connector should appear in this section.
24. Click your Azure Logic Apps Custom Connector.
25. Click the Returns A Numeric Score Representing The Sentiment Detected action.
26. On the Returns A Numeric Score Representing The Sentiment Detected action panel, type a Connection Name for the connection with your Azure Cognitive Services Text Analytics API.
27. On the API Key text box, paste the value of the Text Analytics API key that you copied in step 14; doing so creates an Azure Logic Apps Custom Connector.
28. Click the Create button.
29. Click inside the Documents ID – 1 text box.
30. In the list of Dynamic Content, select List Of Files Id.
31. Click inside the Documents Text -1 text box.
32. In the list of Dynamic Content, select File Content from the Get Blob Content section.
33. Click the New Step button.
34. Type **Microsoft Teams** in the Search Connectors And Actions text box on the Choose An Action panel.

35. Click the Microsoft Teams icon.

36. Click the Post A Message (V3) action.

37. Grant access to your Microsoft Teams account.

38. On the Post A Message (V3) action panel, select an existing team from the Team drop-down menu.

39. Select the General channel in the Add Teams Channel ID drop-down menu.

40. Click inside the Message text box.

41. In the Dynamic Content dialog box, click the See More link in the Get Blob Content section.

42. In the Get Blob Content section, click File Content.

43. In the Message text area, type **Sentiment score:** . (Note that you need to add a space after the colon.)

44. In the Dynamic Content dialog box, click the See More link in the Returns A Numeric Score Representing The Sentiment section.

45. In the Returns A Numeric Score Representing The Sentiment section, click the Documents Score item.

46. Click the Save button in the top-left corner of the Logic Apps Designer blade.

47. Click the Run button.

At this point, you should be ready to test your new Azure Logic Apps Custom Connector. Now you can simply create one text file containing a positive sentence, such as **Today is a great day.** Then upload that file to the Azure Blob Storage container that you configured previously. If everything went well, you should get a new message in the selected team's General channel, and the output of the workflow should look similar to Figure 6-6.

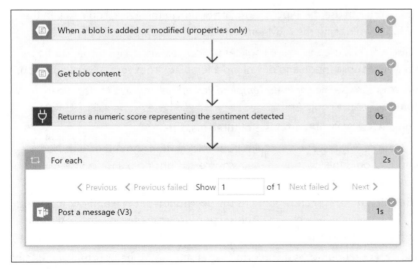

FIGURE 6-6 Workflow execution result

Create a custom template for Azure Logic Apps

Once you have created an Azure Logic App, you can reuse it in other Azure subscriptions or share with other colleagues. You can create a template from your working Azure Logic App to automate deployment processes. When you create a template, you are converting the definition of your Azure Logic App into an Azure Resource Manager (ARM) template. Using ARM templates allows you to take advantage of the flexibility of the ARM platform by separating the definition of the Azure Logic App from the values used in the logic app. When you deploy a new Azure Logic App from a template, you can provide a parameter file in the same way that you do with other ARM templates. Azure also provides some prebuilt Logic App templates. You can use these templates as a base for creating your own templates.

You can download an Azure Logic Apps template using several mechanisms:

- **Azure Portal**   You can use the Export Template option in the Azure Logic App in the Azure Portal for downloading the ARM template.
- **Visual Studio**   You can use the Azure Logic Apps Tools extension for Visual Studio to connect your Azure Subscription and download a template from your Azure Logic Apps.
- **PowerShell**   You can use the *LogicAppTemplate* PowerShell module to download a template from your Azure Logic App.

A Logic App template is a JSON file comprises of three main areas:

- **Logic App resource**   This section contains basic information about the Logic App itself. This information is the location of the resource, the pricing plans, and the workflow definition.
- **Workflow definition**   This section contains the description of the workflow, including the triggers and action in your workflow. This section also contains how the Logic App runs these triggers and actions.
- **Connections**   This section stores the information about the connectors that you use in the workflow.

Use the following procedure to create a template from your Azure Logic App using Visual Studio:

1. Download the Azure Logic Apps Tool extension for Visual Studio 2019 at *https://aka.ms/ download-azure-logic-apps-tools-visual-studio-2019*.

2. Install the Azure Logic Apps Tool extension.

3. Open Visual Studio 2019.

4. In the Visual Studio 2019 welcome window, click the Continue Without Code link below the Get Started section.

5. In the Visual Studio window, click View > Cloud Explorer.

6. In the Cloud Explorer window, shown in Figure 6-7, click the user icon to open the Account Manager.

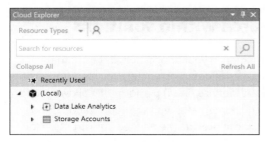

FIGURE 6-7 Cloud Explorer window

7. Click the Manage Accounts link.

8. In the All Accounts section, click the Sign In link.

9. Sign in with an account that has privileges to access your Azure subscription.

10. Ensure that your Azure subscription appears in the list of subscriptions in the Cloud Explorer window.

11. Click the Apply button.

12. In the Cloud Explorer tree control, navigate to Your Subscription > Logic Apps.

13. Right-click the Logic App that you want to convert to a template.

14. In the contextual menu shown in Figure 6-8, click Open With Logic App Editor.

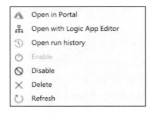

FIGURE 6-8 Logic App tool contextual menu

15. On the Logic App Editor tab, click the Download button.

16. Select a location to which you want to download the JSON file.

At this point, you can edit and customize your template. Once you are done with the modifications to your template, you can create a parameters file for deploying this template.

NEED MORE REVIEW? **LOGIC APP TEMPLATES**

You can learn more by reading the following articles about Logic App templates:

- **Create Logic App Templates** *https://docs.microsoft.com/en-us/azure/logic-apps/ logic-apps-create-deploy-template*
- **Deploy Logic App Templates** *https://docs.microsoft.com/en-us/azure/logic-apps/ logic-apps-create-deploy-azure-resource-manager-templates*

Skill 6.2: Integrate Azure Search within solutions

If you want to add the ability to search for information in your application, indexing that information can be difficult if your app manages a lot of data. Fortunately, Microsoft offers the Azure Search service. Azure Search is a Search-as-a-Service (SaaS) platform that allows you to index information from different data sources, and it integrates with your application using a REST API or a .NET SDK. Using Azure Search, you can provide the needed infrastructure for storing the indexes and all other components needed by the search engine.

This skill covers how to:
- Create an Azure Search index
- Import searchable data
- Query the Azure Search index

Create an Azure Search index

The Azure Search service provides an API that you can use to add search capabilities to your solution. You can access the Azure Service by using a REST API or a .NET SDK. Using the API or the SDK, you can extrapolate the details from and the complexity of retrieving information from the indexes.

You can think of an index as a database that contains the information that you want to be available for searching. That information is stored in the index as a document, which is a searchable entity or unit. For example, if your application manages data from devices, a document is the structure that represents each of the devices managed by your application. Another example of a document would be each of the articles of a news company. Indexes and documents are conceptually equivalent to tables and rows in a database.

Azure Search creates physical structures to store the indexes that you upload or add to the service. These physical structures depend on the index schema that you provide. Before you can create an Azure Search index, you need to create an Azure Search service instance. Use the following procedure to create an Azure Search service instance:

1. Open the Azure Portal (*https://portal.azure.com*).
2. Click Create A Resource on the navigation menu at the left side of the portal.
3. Click Web in the New blade's Azure Marketplace column.
4. Click Azure Search in the New blade's Featured column.
5. On the New Search Service blade, select a resource group from the Resource Group drop-down menu. Alternatively, you can create a new resource group by clicking the Create New link below the Resource Group drop-down menu.
6. In the Instance Details section, type a name for your service instance in the URL text box.
7. Click the Change Pricing Tier link.
8. Select the Free offering in the Select Pricing Tier panel.
9. Click the Select button at the bottom of the panel.
10. On the New Search Service blade, click the Review + Create button at the bottom of the blade.
11. Once the validation of your settings finishes successfully, click the Create button at the bottom of the blade.

Once you have created an Azure Search service instance, you can create indexes and import data. You can create indexes by using the Azure Portal, or you can create them programmatically using C#, PowerShell, Postman, or Python. Creating an index is usually an iterative process that requires several iterations before you get the appropriate index definition for your application. Because of this iterative process and the fact that the index schema is tightly coupled with the physical storage, each time you need to make significant changes to an existing field definition, you need to rebuild the entire index. During the development stage of your index, you will use the following recommended workflow for creating a basic index:

1. **Create an initial index in the portal** You can create the first initial version of your index by using the Azure Portal. You should also review whether any of your data sources are compatible with the indexer tool. If you are using supported data sources, you can speed up the prototyping and loading steps by using the Import Data wizard.
2. **Download the index schema** Once you have created the initial definition of your index in the portal, you can download the index definition by using the Get Index REST API method. You can use any web testing tool, such as Postman, to complete this step. In this step, you get a JSON representation of your index definition that you can use to make modifications and to fine-tune without needing to create the entire definition in the portal on every iteration.
3. **Load your modified index** If you made any modifications to your index definition, you could upload them in this step. If you made any modifications to the definition of your index, you should also upload some data to your index in this step. You can upload data to your index using JSON documents in the payload of a REST API request.

4. **Query your index**   Now it's time to check your index by querying the Azure Search API. You can use Postman or Search Explorer for this purpose.

5. **Use code for the following iterations**   If you need to make modifications to your index definition, you should use the modification-by-code approach because you cannot make modifications to an existing index. This means you need to rebuild the entire index. Using the Azure Portal, this rebuild process means that you need to create all the fields in your index every time the index needs to be modified. Using the modification-by-code approach is much more effective because you only need to modify an existing JSON definition that you can upload on every rebuild.

> **NOTE   SIZE OF THE DATASET**
>
> During the development of an index, you should consider using only a subset of your entire data-set because you usually need to make modifications to the index definition. Every time that you modify the index definition, you need to rebuild the entire index. Using a subset of your dataset makes this rebuilding process faster because you aren't loading as much data in your index.

Use the following procedure to create your index by using the Azure Portal. (Once you create the first definition of your index, we will review how to make modifications to an existing index using some code.)

1. Open the Azure Portal (*https://portal.azure.com*).

2. In the Azure Portal search text box, type the name of your Azure Search service instance.

3. Click the name of your Azure Search service instance in the results list.

4. On the Overview blade of your Azure Search service instance, click the Add Index button in the top-left corner of the blade.

5. On the Add Index blade, shown in Figure 6-9, type a name for the index. This name must start and end with alphanumeric characters and may contain only lowercase letters, digits, or dashes.

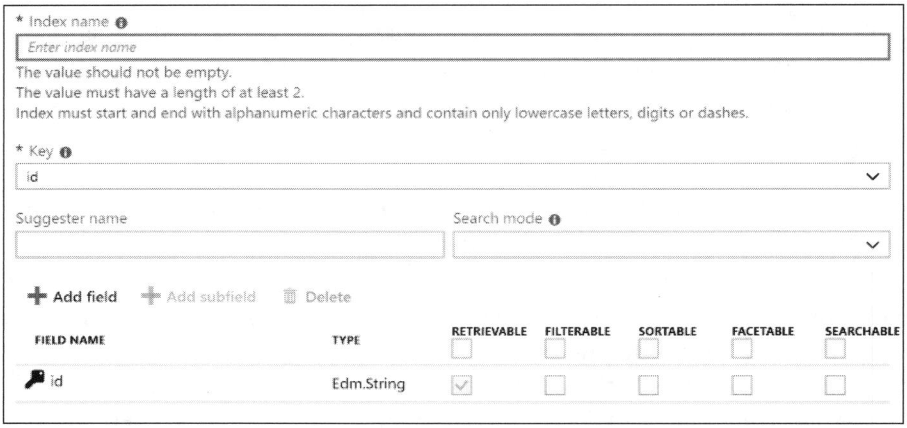

FIGURE 6-9 Creating a new index

6. Click the Add Field button.

7. Type a name for the new field.

8. In the Type drop-down menu, select the appropriate type for the field.

9. Select the appropriate field attributes. For example, you can create a field to store customer surnames:

    - **Field Name**   This should be the name of the field; in this example, it should be *surname.*

    - **Type**   Because this field stores customer surnames, the type should be *Edm.String.*

    - **Retrievable**   Checked. You should include this field in the search results.

    - **Filterable**   Not checked. When you search strings by using filters, you look for exact matches by using Boolean operations. Filters are case sensitive and more strict than using search queries.

    - **Sortable**   Checked. You may want to get your results ordered by this field.

    - **Facetable**   Not checked. If your application does not use navigation trees for constructing filters, you should not check this attribute.

    - **Searchable**   Checked. You want to search for people by their surnames. Using this option, you get the full power of the full-text search engine.

10. Click the Create button at the bottom of the blade.

11. Click Keys in the navigation menu on the left side of your Azure Search service instance.

12. On the Keys blade, copy the Primary Admin Key. You will need this value in a later step.

13. Open Postman or your favorite web analysis tool. (You can download Postman from *https://www.getpostman.com*.)

14. On the Postman's welcome window, click Request in the Building Blocks section.

15. In the Save Request dialog box, type a name for the request.

16. Click the Create Collection link.

17. Type a name for your new collection and press Enter.

18. Click the Save button on the bottom-right corner of the dialog box.

19. In the Requests Definition window, use the following URL for accessing your index: *https://[service name].search.windows.net/indexes/[index name]?api-version=2019-05-06*

    - [service name]   This should be the name of your Azure Search service instance that you created at the beginning of this section.

    - [index-name]   This should be the name of the index that you provided in step 5 of this procedure.

20. In the Request Definition window, click the Headers tab, below the request's URL text box.

21. Add the following headers:

    - *Content-type*   application/json

    - *api-key*   Paste the value that you copied on step 12

22. Click the Send button beside the request's URL. At this point, you should get the JSON definition of your index, as shown in Figure 6-10. You can download this JSON definition by clicking the Download button in the top-right corner of the results window.

FIGURE 6-10 Downloading an index definition using Postman

At this point, you can modify your index definition by changing the JSON file with your index definition that you just downloaded in the previous procedure. When you are creating and updating the definition of your index and its fields, there are some concepts that you should bear in mind:

- **Fields** Your index is composed of a list of fields that define the data contained in the index. You can find the definition of the fields grouped as a collection in the JSON file. Each field has some attributes that control the behavior of the field. Each field has the following properties that you need to provide:
  - **Name** This is the name of the field.
  - **Type** This sets the kind of data that the field stores.
  - **Attributes** This is an attribute of a field that defines the behavior of the field in the index. For example, you can assign the *searchable* attribute to a field. That attribute marks the field as full-text searchable. Another important attribute that you need to consider is the *Key* attribute. Every index that you define must have one—and only one—field configured with the *Key* attribute. This field must be of type *Edm.String*. Table 6-1 shows a list of the available attributes that you can configure for your fields.
- **Suggesters** You use this section to define which fields should be used to auto-complete the search feature. This feature presents some suggestions for search terms as the user is typing.

- **Scoring Profiles** By assigning scores to the items, you can influence which items should appear higher in the search results. You need to define scoring profiles that are made up of functions and fields so you can automatically assign the scores to the items in the search results. The scoring profiles are transparent to the users.

- **Analyzers** Configure the language analyzer for a field. When you configure a field as searchable, you need to set the language that this field contains to make the appropriate analysis.

- **CORS** You configure which JavaScript client-side code can make API calls to the Search API. By default, CORS is disabled, so your solutions cannot query the Search API from the client side.

- **Encryption key** You can configure your Azure Search service instance to encrypt the indexes using customer manager keys instead of the default Microsoft managed keys.

TABLE 6-1 List of field attributes

Attribute	Description
Key	Every index must have one—and only one—field marked as the key of the index. This field needs to be of type *Edm.String*.
Retrievable	The field is included in a search result.
Filterable	You can use this field in the list of filters when querying the index.
Sortable	You can use this field as a sorting criterion for the results of a search.
Facetable	You can use the field for creating a faceted navigation structure. This type of structure helps the user to create self-directed filtering.
Searchable	Marks the field as full-text searchable. When you mark a field as searchable, you need to define the analyzer for that field.

Once you are happy with the first definition of your index, you can upload data to your index and make queries to ensure that the index is performing as you need. You can repeat these steps as many times as you need to achieve the best results. In the following sections, we review how to upload data to your index and how to query your indexes.

EXAM TIP

You cannot make modifications or edits to an existing index using the Azure Portal. Because the definition of an index is an iterative process, you should make the first index definition using the Azure Portal and then download the index definition using any web analyzing tool, such as Postman. Once you have the JSON definition, you can make updates to the index and upload it to your Azure Search service instance.

Import searchable data

Once you have made a definition of your index, you need to import data to it before you can get results from the API. Importing data to the index depends on the type of data source that you are using for your data. You can define empty search indexes, but you cannot query those empty indexes until you fill them with some data.

There are two ways to import data into an index or search index:

- **Push**   Using this method; you are actually uploading data to your index. You need to provide JSON documents to the index and you programmatically upload the content to the index. The advantage of this import data method is that it is very flexible, and there are no restrictions regarding the type of data source that you use for your data as long as you convert the data to JSON documents that you upload to the search index.

- **Pull**   The data is not stored in the index itself; instead, it is stored in one of the supported data sources. Using the indexers that you can configure for your search index, you can connect data stored in the following Azure services: Azure Blob storage, Azure Table storage, Azure Cosmos DB, Azure SQL database, and SQL Server deployed on Azure VMs. The Azure Search service connects your search index with one of the supported indexers, and then, the indexer maps the fields defined in your index with the fields stored in the documents in the data source. The indexer automatically converts your data stored in the data source to a JSON document that can be used in the search index.

Because the push mechanism stores the information directly in the search index, it provides the lowest latency, making this method the most appropriate for applications that are sensitive to latency.

The following procedure shows how to upload content to your index by using Postman. Before you can start uploading data to the Azure Search service, you need to create the *hotels* index:

1. Open the Postman desktop application.

2. Create a new *PUT* request. Using the *PUT* or *POST* methods, the Azure Search API creates the index if it doesn't exist. If the index already exists, then the index is updated with the new definition.

3. Use the following URL to create the *hotels* index:

   https://[service name].search.windows.net/indexes/hotels?api-version=2019-05-06

4. Click the Headers tab below the request's URL.

5. Create the following headers:

   - *Content-type*   application/json

   - *api-key*   You can find this value in the Keys blade of your Azure Search service instance.

6. Click the Body tab below the request's URL.

7. Select the raw option below the Body tab. Ensure that the JSON (application/json) option is selected in the drop-down menu.

8. Open the index JSON definition. You can find this definition in the *hotels/ Hotels_IndexDefinition.json* file in the Azure Search sample dataset.

9. Copy the content of the *Hotels_IndexDefinition.json* file into the text area in the Body tab of your request in Postman, as shown in Figure 6-11.

FIGURE 6-11 Creating a new index using Postman

10. Click the Send button next to the request's URL.

At this point, you have created a new index called *hotels* in your Azure Search service instance. The next step is to import data into the new index. In this section, we review how to import data by using push and pull methods.

You upload (or push) data to your Azure Search service instance by using the REST API or by using the .NET SDK. Using the REST API is quite similar to the procedure that we previously used for creating an index. You need to use the *POST HTTP* method and use the URL *https:// [service name].search.windows.net/indexes/[index name]/docs/index?api-version=2019-05-06*. For this example, the index name should be *hotels*. You need to use the content of the *HotelsData_toAzureSearch.json* file to upload the information to your Azure Search service instance.

When you are pushing data to your Azure Search service instance, you can control each action you want to perform on each document in the index. By setting the *@search.action* property in the JSON file, you can control the action performed on each document. The following list shows the available operations you can apply to the documents:

- **upload**   If the document doesn't exist on the index, it uploads the new document. If the document already exists, it updates the document. When updating a document, any existing field in the document that is not specified in the request will be automatically set to *null*.

- **merge**   This action updates an existing document with the value of the fields specified in the request. The value set in the Request For field replaces the value of that field in the existing document in the index. If the document doesn't exist in the index, the request fails.

- **mergeOrupload**   This action is similar to the *merge* action, but if the document doesn't exist in the index, the action behaves as the *upload* action and creates a new document.

- **delete**   This action removes the specified document from the index.

For each action type, you at least need to provide a value for the *key* field to locate the correct document in the index. The other fields are optional, depending on the type of action that you want to perform on the document. Complete the following steps to push data to your index by using the .NET SDK:

1. Open Visual Studio 2019.
2. On the welcome window, click Create A New Project.
3. Select the Console App (.NET Core) template.
4. Click the Next button at the bottom-right corner of the Create A New Project window.
5. In the Configure Your New Project window, type a name for your project.
6. Select a Location for your solution.
7. Click the Create button in the bottom-right corner of the window.
8. Click Tools > NuGet Package Manager > Manage NuGet Packages For Solution.
9. In the NuGet – Solution tab, click Browse.
10. In the Search text box, type **Microsoft.Azure.Search**.
11. Click *Microsoft.Azure.Search* in the results list.
12. On the right side of the NuGet – Solution tab, click the name of your project.

13. Click the Install button.

14. In the Preview Changes window, click the OK button.

15. In the License Acceptance window, click the I Accept button.

16. Repeat steps 10 to 15 and install the *Microsoft.Extensions.Configuration.Json* NuGet Package.

17. In the Solution Explorer window, right-click your project's name.

18. In the contextual menu, click Add > New Item.

19. In the Add New Item dialog box, type **json** in the Search text box.

20. Click the JSON File template.

21. Type **appsettings.json** in the Name text box.

22. Click the Add button in the bottom-right corner of the window.

23. In the Solution Explorer window, click the *appsettings.json* file.

24. In the properties window, set the Copy To Output Directory setting to Copy Always.

25. Open the *appsettings.json* file and replace the content of the file with the content of Listing 6-1. You can get the admin key from the Key blade in your Azure Search service instance.

LISTING 6-1 *appsetting.json* file

```
{
  "JSONDocumentsFile": "HotelsData_toAzureSearch.json",
  "SearchIndexName": "hotels",
  "SearchServiceAdminApiKey": "<Your_admin_key>",
  "SearchServiceName": "<Your_search_service_name>"
}
```

26. Copy the *HotelsData_toAzureSearch.json* file from the sample data folder to your solution's folder.

27. In the Solution Explorer, right-click your project's name.

28. In the contextual menu, click Add > Existing Item.

29. In your solution's folder, click the *HotelsData_toAzureSearch.json* file and click the Add button.

30. On the Solution Explorer, click the *HotelsData_toAzureSearch.json*.

31. On the file's properties window, set the Copy To Output Directory setting to Copy Always.

32. Open the *HotelsData_toAzureSearch.json* file.

33. Remove the *value* property. Ensure that the JSON file starts with the *[* character.

34. Remove the last line of the file. Ensure that the JSON file ends with the *]* character.

35. Add a new empty C# class file and name it **Hotel.cs**.

36. Replace the content of the *Hotel.cs* file with the content of Listing 6-2.

LISTING 6-2 *Hotel.cs* file

```
// C# .NET

using Microsoft.Azure.Search;
using Microsoft.Azure.Search.Models;
using System;
using System.Collections.Generic;
using System.Text;
using Newtonsoft.Json;

namespace <your_project_name>
{
    public partial class Hotel
    {
        [System.ComponentModel.DataAnnotations.Key]
        [IsFilterable]
        public string HotelId { get; set; }

        [IsSearchable, IsSortable]
        public string HotelName { get; set; }

        [IsSearchable]
        [Analyzer(AnalyzerName.AsString.EnMicrosoft)]
        public string Description { get; set; }

        [IsSearchable]
        [Analyzer(AnalyzerName.AsString.FrLucene)]
        [JsonProperty("Description_fr")]
        public string DescriptionFr { get; set; }

        [IsSearchable, IsFilterable, IsSortable, IsFacetable]
        public string Category { get; set; }

        [IsSearchable, IsFilterable, IsFacetable]
        public string[] Tags { get; set; }

        [IsFilterable, IsSortable, IsFacetable]
        public bool? ParkingIncluded { get; set; }

        [IsFilterable, IsSortable, IsFacetable]
        public DateTimeOffset? LastRenovationDate { get; set; }

        [IsFilterable, IsSortable, IsFacetable]
        public double? Rating { get; set; }

        public Address Address { get; set; }
    }
}
```

The *Hotel* class represents a document stored in the JSON file. As you can see in Listing
6-2, each of the properties has assigned a property attribute, such as *IsFilterable*, *IsSortable*,
IsFacetable, and *IsSearchable*, which matches the attributes in the definition of a search index
field. When you work with the .NET Azure Search SDK, you need to explicitly add the property attribute to the properties that define your document. You cannot depend only on the
definition of the index fields. This is different from using REST API, where you don't need to

add that explicit definition to the JSON document. Also, pay attention to the *HotelID* property. This property has also assigned the *System.ComponentModel.DataAnnotations.Key* property attribute which means it is the *Key* attribute for this document. You also use property attributes for configuring the *Analyzer* for those properties that have the *IsSearchonable* attribute.

37. Add a new empty C# class file and name it **Hotel.Methods.cs**.

38. Replace the content of the *Hotel.Methods.cs* file with the content of Listing 6-3.

LISTING 6-3 Hotel.Methods.cs file

```csharp
// C# .NET
using System;
using System.Collections.Generic;
using System.Text;

namespace <your_project_name>
{
    public partial class Hotel
    {
        public override string ToString()
        {
            var builder = new StringBuilder();

            if (!String.IsNullOrEmpty(HotelId))
            {
                builder.AppendFormat("HotelId: {0}\n", HotelId);
            }

            if (!String.IsNullOrEmpty(HotelName))
            {
                builder.AppendFormat("Name: {0}\n", HotelName);
            }

            if (!String.IsNullOrEmpty(Description))
            {
                builder.AppendFormat("Description: {0}\n", Description);
            }

            if (!String.IsNullOrEmpty(DescriptionFr))
            {
                builder.AppendFormat("Description (French): {0}\n", DescriptionFr);
            }

            if (!String.IsNullOrEmpty(Category))
            {
                builder.AppendFormat("Category: {0}\n", Category);
            }

            if (Tags != null && Tags.Length > 0)
            {
                builder.AppendFormat("Tags: [ {0} ]\n", String.Join(", ", Tags));
            }

            if (ParkingIncluded.HasValue)
            {
```

```
            builder.AppendFormat("Parking included: {0}\n", ParkingIncluded.Value ?
            "yes" : "no");
        }

        if (LastRenovationDate.HasValue)
        {
            builder.AppendFormat("Last renovated on: {0}\n", LastRenovationDate);
        }

        if (Rating.HasValue)
        {
            builder.AppendFormat("Rating: {0}\n", Rating);
        }

        if (Address != null && !Address.IsEmpty)
        {
            builder.AppendFormat("Address: \n{0}\n", Address.ToString());
        }

        return builder.ToString();
    }
  }
}
```

39. Add a new empty C# class file and name it **Address.cs**.

40. Replace the content of the *Address.cs* file with the content of Listing 6-4.

LISTING 6-4 *Address.cs* file
```
// C# .NET

using System;
using Microsoft.Azure.Search;
using Microsoft.Azure.Search.Models;
using Newtonsoft.Json;

namespace <your_project_name>
{
    public partial class Address
    {
        [IsSearchable]
        public string StreetAddress { get; set; }

        [IsSearchable, IsFilterable, IsSortable, IsFacetable]
        public string City { get; set; }

        [IsSearchable, IsFilterable, IsSortable, IsFacetable]
        public string StateProvince { get; set; }

        [IsSearchable, IsFilterable, IsSortable, IsFacetable]
        public string PostalCode { get; set; }

        [IsSearchable, IsFilterable, IsSortable, IsFacetable]
        public string Country { get; set; }
    }
}
```

41. Add a new empty C# class file and name it **Address.Methods.cs**.

42. Replace the content of the *Address.Methods.cs* file with the content of Listing 6-5.

LISTING 6-5 *Address.Methods.cs* file

```csharp
// C# .NET
using System;
using System.Collections.Generic;
using System.Text;
using Newtonsoft.Json;

namespace <your_project_name>
{
    public partial class Address
    {

        public override string ToString() =>
            IsEmpty ?
                string.Empty :
                $"{StreetAddress}\n{City}, {StateProvince} {PostalCode}\n{Country}";

        [JsonIgnore]
        public bool IsEmpty => String.IsNullOrEmpty(StreetAddress) &&
                               String.IsNullOrEmpty(City) &&
                               String.IsNullOrEmpty(StateProvince) &&
                               String.IsNullOrEmpty(PostalCode) &&
                               String.IsNullOrEmpty(Country);

    }
}
```

43. Open the *Program.cs* file and add the following using statements:

- *using System.Collections.Generic;*
- *using System.IO;*
- *using System.Linq;*
- *using Microsoft.Azure.Search;*
- *using Microsoft.Azure.Search.Models;*
- *using Microsoft.Extensions.Configuration;*
- *using Newtonsoft.Json;*

44. Replace the content of the *Main* method with the content in Listing 6-6.

LISTING 6-6 *Program.cs Main* method

```csharp
// C# .NET
IConfigurationBuilder builder = new ConfigurationBuilder().AddJsonFile("appsettings.
json");
IConfigurationRoot configuration = builder.Build();

string searchServiceName = configuration["SearchServiceName"];
string indexName = configuration["SearchIndexName"];
```

```
string adminApiKey = configuration["SearchServiceAdminApiKey"];
string jsonFilename = configuration["JSONDocumentsFile"];

SearchServiceClient serviceClient = new SearchServiceClient
(searchServiceName, new SearchCredentials(adminApiKey));

ISearchIndexClient indexClient = serviceClient.Indexes.GetClient(indexName);

//Batch documents import.
//Reading documents from the JSON file.
List<Hotel> actions;
using (StreamReader file = File.OpenText(jsonFilename))
{
    string json = File.ReadAllText(jsonFilename);
    actions = JsonConvert.DeserializeObject<List<Hotel>>(json);
}

//Create a batch object.
var batchActions = new List<IndexAction<Hotel>>();
foreach (var hotel in actions)
{
    var indexAction = new IndexAction<Hotel>(hotel);
    batchActions.Add(indexAction);
}
var batch = IndexBatch.New(batchActions.ToArray());

//Push the documents to the Azure Search service instance
try
{
    indexClient.Documents.Index(batch);
}
catch (IndexBatchException ex)
{
    Console.WriteLine($"Failed to index some documents: {String.Join(", ",
    ex.IndexingResults.Where(r => !r.Succeeded).Select(r => r.Key))}");
}
```

Now press F5 to execute the code. You can check whether the documents have been cor-rectly loaded into your index by reviewing the Overview blade in your Azure Search service instance, as shown in Figure 6-12. Depending on the size of your dataset, it can take several minutes to show the updated summary information in the Overview blade.

Usage	Monitoring	**Indexes**	Indexers	Data sources	Skillsets	
NAME			**DOCUMENT COUNT**		**STORAGE SIZE**	
hotels			50		82.27 kB	

FIGURE 6-12 List of indexes in an Azure Search service instance

Pushing data to your search index is one way of importing data. The other way is to pull data from a supported data source. By using indexers, Azure Search service can connect to

Azure Blobs, Azure Tables, Azure Cosmos DBs, Azure SQL Databases, or databases in SQL Servers deployed on Azure VMs, and the Azure Search service can extract information from those data sources. The indexer connects to a table, view, or equivalent structure in the data source, and it maps the columns or fields in the data source structure with the fields defined in the search index. Then the indexer converts the rowset into a JSON document that is loaded into the index. You can schedule the indexer to check at regular intervals for changes in the data source. You can configure an indexer by using the Azure Portal, the REST API, or the .NET Azure Search SDK. The following procedure shows how to import data from a Cosmos DB database to an index using Azure Portal:

1. Open the Azure Portal (*https://portal.azure.com*).

2. Click Create A Resource in the navigation menu on the left side of the Azure Portal.

3. Click Azure Cosmos DB on the Popular column in the New blade.

4. On the Create Azure Cosmos DB Account, select a Subscription from the drop-down menu.

5. Select an existing resource group from the Resource Group drop-down menu. Alternatively, you can create a new resource group by clicking the Create New link below the drop-down menu.

6. Type an Account Name in the Enter Account Name text box.

7. Ensure that the Core (SQL) value is selected in the API drop-down menu.

8. Leave other options as is and click the Review + Create button at the bottom of the blade.

9. On the Review + Create tab, click the Create button at the bottom of the blade.

10. On the Deployment Overview blade, click the Go To Resource button. This button appears when the new Cosmos DB is deployed successfully.

11. Click Data Explorer in the navigation bar on the left side of your newly created Azure Cosmos DB Account blade.

12. On the Data Explorer blade, click the New Container button.

13. On the Add Container panel, shown in Figure 6-13, type **hoteldb** as the Database id.

14. Type **HotelId** as the Container Id.

15. Type **Category** as the Partition Key. You don't need to add the / character at the beginning of the Partition Key, as the Azure Portal does it automatically for you.

16. Click the OK button at the bottom of the panel.

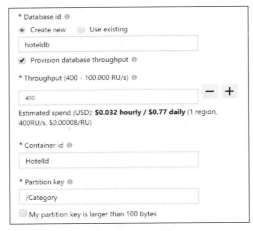

FIGURE 6-13 Creating a Cosmos DB database for Azure Search

17. On the Data Explorer blade, in the tree control on the left side of the blade, choose hoteldb > HotelId > Items.

18. Click the Upload Item icon at the top of the Items tab.

19. On the Upload Items panel, click the folder icon next to the text box.

20. In the Open file dialog box, look for the *HotelsData_toCosmosDB.json* file. Remember that you can get this file from the Azure Search sample dataset, which you can download from *https://azure.microsoft.com/en-us/resources/samples/azure-search-sample-data/.*

21. Click the Upload button at the bottom of the panel.

22. Click Keys on the navigation menu on the left side of the Azure Cosmos DB Account.

23. Copy the Primary Connection String. Ensure that the connection string has the *AccountEndpoint* and *AccountKey* parameters. You need this value for a later step.

24. In the Search Resources text box at the top of the Azure Portal, type the name of your Azure Search service instance.

25. Click your Azure Search service instance's name in the results list.

26. Click the Import Data button on the Overview blade.

27. On the Import Data blade, select the Cosmos DB in the Data Source drop-down menu control.

28. Type a Name for the data source.

29. Paste the connection string that you copied in step 23 into the Cosmos DB Account text box.

30. Select the *hoteldb* value in the Database drop-down menu.

31. In the Collection drop-down menu, select *HotelId*. Your blade should look like Figure 6-14.

FIGURE 6-14 Creating an Azure Search data source

32. Click the Add Cognitive Search (Optional) button at the bottom of the blade. When you click this button, the Import Data wizard automatically creates the configured data source.

33. On the Add Cognitive Search (Optional) tab, click the Skip To: Customize Target Index option at the bottom of the blade.

34. On the Customize Target Index tab, select HotelId in the Key drop-down menu.

35. On the fields definition table, click the checkbox in the Retrievable column, which will select this attribute for all fields.

36. Click the checkbox in the Searchable column, which will select this attribute for all fields of the *Edm.String* type.

37. In the Description field, select the English – Microsoft value in the Analyzer column.

38. In the Description_fr field, select the French – Microsoft value in the Analyzer column. Your index definition should look like Figure 6-15.

39. Click the Next: Create An Indexer button at the bottom of the blade.

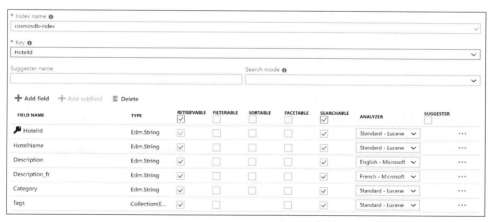

FIGURE 6-15 Creating an Azure Search search index

40. On the Create An Indexer tab, leave the Name as is. If you prefer, you can provide a different indexer name.

41. In the Schedule setting, click Hourly. This setting configures how often the indexer checks for changes on the data source.

42. Click the Submit button.

43. On the Overview blade of your Azure Search service instance, you can view the newly created index. Importing the new data can take several minutes.

When you are using the Import Data wizard in the Azure Portal, you can only associate data sources to new indexes created during the importing data process. If you need to associate a data source with an existing search index, you need to use the REST API or the .NET Azure Search SDK.

EXAM TIP

Using the Azure Portal when working with Azure Search index offers a limited set of features. The Azure Portal is the best tool for creating the initial definition of fields, data sources, and indexes. If you need to import data into your existing index or you need to make modifications to the definition of existing indexes, you should use the REST API or the .NET Azure Search SDK.

NEED MORE REVIEW? LOADING DATA INTO AZURE SEARCH

You learn more about complex scenarios by reviewing the following articles:

- Load Data *https://docs.microsoft.com/en-in/azure/search/search-what-is-data-import*
- Load Data with Indexers *https://docs.microsoft.com/en-in/azure/search/search-indexer-overview*
- Indexer Operations Using the Azure Search Service REST API *https://docs.microsoft.com/en-us/rest/api/searchservice/Indexer-operations*

NEED MORE REVIEW? USING COGNITIVE SERVICES WITH AZURE SEARCH SERVICE

You can take advantage of the several Azure Cognitive Services by integrating your Azure Search Service with Computer Vision (for image analysis) or Text Analytics (for entities recognition). This allows you to enrich the features available for Azure Services. You can review how to make these integrations at *https://docs.microsoft.com/en-in/azure/search/cognitive-search-attach-cognitive-services*.

Query the Azure Search index

Once you have defined your index and populated it with your dataset, you need to query the index to take advantage of the Azure Search service. You can make queries to your index by using different tools:

- **Search Explorer**   You can use the Search Explorer tool integrated into the Azure Portal for querying your index.

- **Web testing tools**   Use your favorite web testing tool, such as Fiddler or Postman, to make REST API calls.

- **.NET SDK**   Using the .NET Azure Search SDK, you can extrapolate from the details of implementing the REST API calls to the Azure Search service. You need to use the *SearchIdexClient* class for querying the index.

- **REST API**   You can make REST API calls using your favorite language and using the *GET* or *POST* methods on your index.

Whatever tool you decide to use for making queries to your index, you need to choose between two different query types—simple and full.

- **Simple**   The simple query type is used for typical queries. The behavior of the Azure Search when you use the simple query type is similar to other search engines like Google or Bing. This query type is faster and more effective for free-form text queries. The simple query syntax used in the simple query type contains operators like *AND*, *OR*, *NOT*, *phrase*, *suffix*, and *precedence* operators.

- **Full**   The full query type extends the features of the simple query type. While the simple query type uses the Simple Query Parser, the full query type uses the Lucene Query Parser. The Azure Search service is based on the Apache Lucene high-performance search engine developed by the Apache Software Foundation. Using the full query type, you can construct more complex queries by using regular expressions, proximity searches, or fuzzy and wildcard searches, among others. Using *queryType=full* in your request instructs the Azure Search to use the Lucene Query Parser instead of the default Simple Query Parser.

When constructing a query, you need to bear in mind the definition of your index. Depending on the attributes that you assigned to the fields of your index, you can use them for sorting and filtering the results based on a particular field (or if you can use a specific field for searching). The definition of the field also affects whether the field would be included in the results of the query. For example, in our previous hotel's index example in which you get the information from an Azure Cosmos DB database, you cannot sort by any field because we didn't configure any fields as sortable.

Another important distinction that you should bear in mind when querying your index is the difference between filtering and searching.

- **Searching**   Searching uses full-text search to look for a value in a string. During the lookup process in a full-text search, the Lucene engine removes stopwords (such as "the" or "and"), reduces the query term to the root of the word, lowercases the query term, and breaks composite words into their parts. Then the engine returns the list of matches.

- **Filtering**   On the other hand, filtering uses a Boolean expression that must evaluate *true* or *false*. You can use filtering with strings, but in those situations, you only get those results that exactly match your filter expression, including word casing.

The following procedure shows how to perform a search using the .NET Azure Search SDK. The procedure below is based on the procedure that you followed in "Import Searchable Data," earlier in this chapter, in which you learned how to push data into an Azure Search index. Please ensure that you have completed the procedure in Listings 6-1 to 6-6 before starting the following procedure:

1. Open the solution for the example you created in the "Import Searchable Data" section earlier in this chapter.

2. Open the *Program.cs* file.

3. Add the content of Listing 6-7 to the end of the *Main* method.

LISTING 6-7 *Program.cs Main* method

```
// C# .NET
//Querying the index
        SearchParameters parameters;
        DocumentSearchResult<Hotel> results;

        //Looking for hotels in Dallas.
        Console.WriteLine("Query 1: Search for term 'Atlanta'");
        parameters = new SearchParameters();
        results = indexClient.Documents.Search<Hotel>("Atlanta", parameters);
        WriteDocuments(results);

        //Looking for hotels in Dallas. Get only certain fields of the document.
        Console.WriteLine("Query 2: Search for term 'Atlanta'");
        Console.WriteLine("Get only properties: HotelName, Tags, Rating, and
        Address:\n");
        parameters = new SearchParameters()
        {
            Select = new[] {"HotelName", "Tags", "Rating", "Address"},
        };
        results = indexClient.Documents.Search<Hotel>("Atlanta", parameters);
        WriteDocuments(results);

        //Looking for hotels with restaurants and wifi. Get only the HotelName,
        //Description and Tags properties
        Console.WriteLine("Query 3: Search for terms 'restaurant' and 'wifi'");
        Console.WriteLine("Get only properties: HotelName, Description, and
        Tags:\n");
        parameters = new SearchParameters()
        {
```

```
            Select = new[] { "HotelName", "Description", "Tags" },
        };
        results = indexClient.Documents.Search<Hotel>("Dallas", parameters);
        WriteDocuments(results);

        //Use filtering instead of full text searches
        Console.WriteLine("Query 4: Filter on ratings greater than 4");
        Console.WriteLine("Returning only these fields: HotelName, Rating:\n");
        parameters =
            new SearchParameters()
            {
                Filter = "Rating gt 4",
                Select = new[] { "HotelName", "Rating" }
            };
        results = indexClient.Documents.Search<Hotel>("*", parameters);
        WriteDocuments(results);

        //Getting the two best scored hotels.
        Console.WriteLine("Query 5: Search on term 'boutique'");
        Console.WriteLine("Sort by rating in descending order, taking the top two
        results");
        Console.WriteLine("Returning only these fields: HotelId, HotelName,
        Category, Rating:\n");
        parameters =
            new SearchParameters()
            {
                //If you try to use a field that is not configured with the
                //IsSortable attribute, you will get an error
                OrderBy = new[] { "Rating desc" },
                Select = new[] { "HotelId", "HotelName", "Category", "Rating" },
                Top = 2
            };
        results = indexClient.Documents.Search<Hotel>("boutique", parameters);
        WriteDocuments(results);
```

4. Add the method shown in Listing 6-8 to the *Program* class.

LISTING 6-8 *Program.cs WriteDocuments helper* method

```
// C# .NET

//Helper method for printing the results of a query.
        private static void WriteDocuments(DocumentSearchResult<Hotel> searchResults)
        {
            foreach (SearchResult<Hotel> result in searchResults.Results)
            {
                Console.WriteLine(result.Document);
            }

            Console.WriteLine();
        }
```

Skill 6.3: Establish API Gateways

Most of the applications and solutions that you can find or develop nowadays offer an API for accessing the features available in the solution. In business environments, those solutions usually need to communicate with each other using their respective APIs. Sometimes, you need to expose your solutions to your clients to offer your services. In those situations, you need to ensure that you offer a consistent and secure API. It isn't easy to implement the necessary mechanism to achieve an enterprise-grade level of security, consistency, and flexibility. If you also need to publish several of your services under a common API, this task is even harder.

Microsoft provides the Azure API Management (APIM) service. This service allows you to create an enterprise-grade API for your existing back-end services. Using APIM, you can securely publish your back-end applications, providing your customers with a platform protected against DOS attacks or JWT token validations.

> **This skill covers how to:**
> - Create an APIM instance
> - Configure authentication for APIs
> - Define policies for APIs

Create an APIM instance

The API Management service allows you to expose a portion (or all) of the APIs offered by your back-end systems. By using the APIM service, you can unify all your back-end APIs in a common interface that you can offer to external users, such as clients or partners and internal or external developers. In general, the APIM service is a façade of the APIs that you configure in your APIM instance. Thanks to this façade feature, you can customize the front-end API offered by the APIM instance without changing the back-end API.

When exposing your back-end systems, you are not limited to REST API back ends. You can use a back-end service that uses a SOAP API and then publish this SOAP API as a REST API. This means you can update your older back-end systems without needing to modify the code and take advantage of the greater level of integration of the REST APIs.

Use the following procedure to create a new APIM instance:

1. Open the Azure Portal (*https://portal.azure.com*).
2. Click Create A Resource on the navigation bar on the left side of the Azure Portal.
3. On the New blade, click Integration in the Azure Marketplace column.
4. Click API Management in the Featured column. If the API Management service doesn't appear in the Featured column, you can use the Search The Marketplace text box and look for the API Management service.
5. On the API Management Service blade, type a Name for your new APIM instance.
6. Select a subscription from the Subscription drop-down menu.
7. Select a resource group from the Resource Group drop-down menu. Alternatively, you can create a new one by clicking the Create New link below the drop-down menu.
8. Select a location from the Location drop-down menu.
9. In the Organization Name text box, type the name of your organization. This name appears on the developer's portal and email notifications.
10. In the Administrator Email, type the name of the email account that should receive all notifications from the APIM instance. By default, the value associated with this property is the email address of the logged-in user.
11. In the Pricing Tier, leave the Developer tier selected.
12. Click the Create button at the bottom of the blade. The process of creating the APIM instance takes several minutes. When your new APIM instance is ready, you will receive a welcome email at the administrator email address that you configured in step 10.

> *NOTE* **PRICING TIERS**
>
> The Developer pricing tier is appropriate for testing and development environments, but you should not use it for production because the Developer tier does not offer high-availability features and can be affected by disconnections during the updates of the node. You can review the full offer and the features available on each tier at *https://azure.microsoft.com/en-us/pricing/details/api-management/*.

Once you have created your APIM instance, you can start adding APIs to your instance. In the following procedure, you are going to add two different APIs, using different methods. The first method is the OpenAPI specification. For the second API, you are going to create a blank API definition and add only those methods that are appropriate for you.

1. Open the Azure Portal (*https://portal.azure.com*).
2. Type the name of your APIM instance in the Search text box at the top of the portal.
3. Click the name your APIM instance in the results list.

4. Click APIs in the navigation menu on your APIM instance blade.

5. On the Add A New API blade, click OpenAPI.

6. On the Create From OpenAPI Specification dialog box, shown in Figure 6-16, copy the following URL from the OpenAPI specification text box: *https://conferenceapi.azurewebsites. net/?format=json*

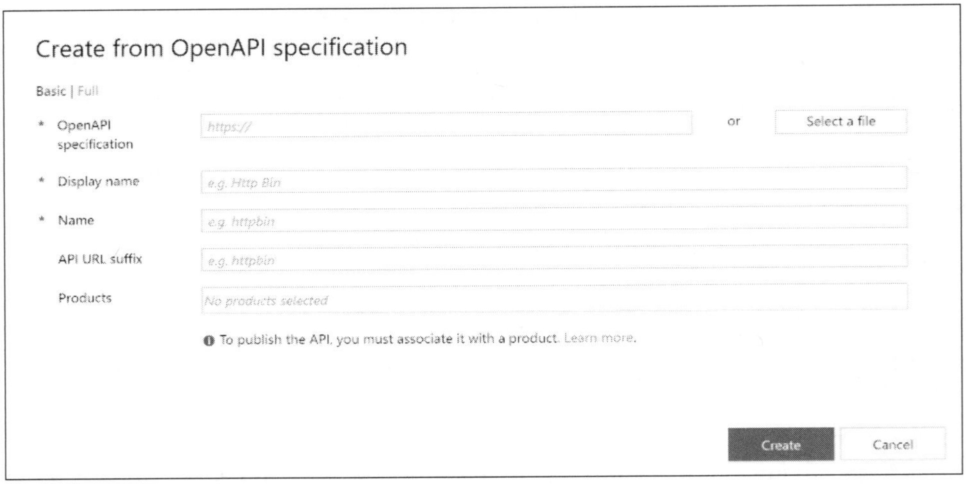

FIGURE 6-16 Adding a back-end API to an APIM instance

7. Azure automatically fills the the Display Name and Name properties text boxes; check them to ensure the entries are correct.

8. Type **conference** in the API URL Suffix field. If you are going to connect more than one back-end API to the APIM instance, you need to provide a suffix for each API. The APIM instance uses this suffix for differentiating between the different APIs that you connected to the instance.

9. Do not select any product for the Products property.

10. Click the Create button at the bottom of the dialog box.

At this point, you have added your first back-end API to the APIM instance by using the OpenAPI specification of your back-end API. In the following steps, you are going to add a back-end API without using any specification. Creating the front-end endpoints is useful if you need to connect only a few endpoints from your back-end API, or if you don't have the OpenAPI or SOAP specification of your API in any format:

1. Click APIs on the navigation menu in your APIM instance blade.

2. On the Add A New API blade, click Blank API.

3. On the Create A Blank API dialog box, type **Fake API** in the Display Name text box.

4. Leave the Name property with the default value.

5. Type **https://fakerestapi.azurewebsites.net** in the Web Service URL text box.

6. Type **fakeapi** in the API URL Suffix text box.

7. On the Design tab of the API blade with the newly added API selected, click Add Operation.

8. On the Add Operation editor, shown in Figure 6-17, type **GetActivities** in the Display Name text box.

9. In the URL HTTP Method drop-down menu, ensure that the *GET* method is selected.

10. In the URL text box, type **/api/activities**.

11. Click the Save button at the bottom of the editor.

Fake API > Add operation

Frontend

* Display name	GetActivities
* Name	getactivities
* URL	GET ∨ /api/activities
Description	
Tags	e.g. Booking

FIGURE 6-17 Adding an API operation to an API in an APIM instance

12. On the API blade, ensure that Fake API is selected.

13. Click the Test tab.

14. Click the *GetActivities* operation.

15. Click the Send button at the bottom of the *GetActivities* operation panel. Using this panel, you can test each of the operations that are defined in your API. Alternatively, you can also use the Developer Portal for testing your APIs and Applications. You can access the Developer Portal by clicking the appropriate button on the top side of the APIs blade.

At this point, you have two back-end APIs connected to your APIM instance. As you can see in the previous example, you don't need to expose the entire back-end API. By adding the appropriate operations, you can publish only those parts of the back-end API that are useful for you. Once you have created the APIs in your APIM instance, you can grant access to these APIs to your developers by using the Developer Portal. You can access the APIM Developer Portal at *https://<your_APIM_name>.developer.azure-api.net/*.

Bear in mind that you need to associate a Product to your API for publishing it. Because you didn't associate your APIs to any Product, your APIs won't be available to the external world. Bear in mind that you can associate an API to more than one Product. Use the following procedure to create a Product and associate it with your APIs:

1. Open the Azure Portal (*https://portal.azure.com*).

2. Type the name of your APIM instance in the Search text box on the top-middle of the portal.

3. Click the name of your APIM instance in the results list.

4. Click Products on the navigation menu in your APIM instance blade.

5. Click the Add button in the top-left corner of the Products blade.

6. Type a Name in the Display Name text box on the Add Product panel.

7. Leave the value in the ID text box as is.

8. Type a description in the Description text area.

9. Select the Published value in the State switch control. If you don't select this option at this time, you can publish later, or you can publish the Product using its panel.

10. Click the Select API button in the APIs section.

11. On the APIs blade, select Demo Conference and Fake APIs by clicking the checkbox next to the name of the API.

12. Click the Select button at the bottom of the panel.

13. Click the Create button at the bottom of the Add Product panel.

By default, when you create a new Product, only members of the Administrators built-in group can access the Product. You can configure this by using the Access Control section in the Product.

> **NEED MORE REVIEW?** **CUSTOMIZING THE DEVELOPERS PORTAL**
>
> You can customize the Developers Portal for your APIM instance by modifying the content of the pages, adding more pages, and so on. You can review the details about how to perform these customizations by consulting the article at *https://docs.microsoft.com/en-us/azure/api-management/api-management-customize-styles*.

> **NEED MORE REVIEW?** **REVISIONS AND VERSIONS**
>
> During the lifetime of your API, you may need to add to, update, or remove operations from your API. You can make these modifications without disrupting the usage of your API by using revisions and versions. You can review how to work with revisions and versions in your API by reading the article at *https://azure.microsoft.com/es-es/blog/versions-revisions/*.

Configure authentication for APIs

Once you have imported your back-end APIs, you need to configure the authentication for accessing these APIs. When you configure the security options in the APIM instance, the back-end API delegates the security to the APIM instance. This means that even though your API has implemented its own authentication mechanism, they are never used when the API is accessed through the APIM instance.

This ability to hide the authentication of the back-end APIs is useful for unifying your security using a consistent and unique authentication mechanism. You can manage the authentication options associated with a Product or API by using Subscriptions. A Subscription manages the keys a developer can use to access your API. If an HTTP request made to an API protected by a Subscription does not provide a valid subscription key, the request is immediately rejected by the APIM gateway without reaching your back-end API. When you define a Subscription, you can use three different scopes to apply this Subscription:

- **Product**   When a developer wants to use one of your Products, the developer connects to the Developers Portal of your APIM instance and submits a request to subscribe to the product he or she wants to use.

- **All APIs**   The developer can access all APIs in your APIM instance using the same subscription key.

- **Single API**   The developer can access a single API in your APIM instance using a subscription key. There is no need for the API to be part of a Product.

If you use the All APIs or Single API scopes, you don't need to associate the back-end API with an API. A Subscription using any of these two scopes allows access directly to the API. You can use the following procedure to create a Subscription and associate it with a Program:

1. Open the Azure Portal (*https://portal.azure.com*).
2. Type the name of your APIM instance in the Search text box at the top of the portal.
3. Click the name of your APIM instance in the results list.
4. Click Subscriptions in the navigation menu in your APIM instance blade.
5. Click the Add Subscription button in the top-left corner of the Subscriptions blade.
6. On the New Subscription panel shown in Figure 6-18, type a Name for the subscription. This name may only contain letters, numbers, and hyphens.

FIGURE 6-18 Creating a new API Management Subscription

7. In the Scope drop-down menu, select the Product value.

8. Click the Product property.

9. In the Products panel, click the name of the Product that you created in the previous section.

10. Click the Select button at the bottom of the panel.

11. Click the Save button at the bottom of the panel.

12. On the Subscription blade, click the ellipsis at the end of the row for your newly created subscription.

13. On the contextual menu, click Show/Hide keys. You can use either of these keys to access the APIs configured in the Product associated with the Subscription. You need to use the Header *Ocp-Apim-Subscription-Key* to provide the subscription key in your HTTP requests.

NEED MORE REVIEW? **OTHER AUTHENTICATION METHODS**

Using subscription and subscription keys is not the only mechanism for protecting access to your APIs. API Management allows you to use OAuth 2.0, client certificates, and IP whitelisting. You can use the following articles to review how to use other authentication mechanisms for protecting your APIs:

- IP whitelisting   *https://docs.microsoft.com/en-us/azure/api-management/ api-management-access-restriction-policies#RestrictCallerIPs*

- OAuth 2.0 authentication using Azure AD   *https://docs.microsoft.com/en-us/azure/ api-management/api-management-howto-protect-backend-with-aad*

- Mutual authentication using client certificates   *https://docs.microsoft.com/en-us/ azure/api-management/api-management-howto-mutual-certificates*

Define policies for APIs

When you publish a back-end API using the API Management service, all the requests made to your APIM instance are forwarded to the correct back-end API, and the response is sent back to the requestor. All of these requests or responses are altered or modified by default. But there could be some situations where you need to modify some requests and/or responses. An example of these modification needs could be transforming the format or a response from XML to JSON. Another example could be throttling the number of incoming calls from a particular IP or user.

A policy is a mechanism that you can use to change the default behavior of the APIM gateway. Policies are XML documents that describe a sequence of inbound and outbound steps or statements. Each policy is made of four sections:

- **Inbound** In this section, you can find any statement that applies to requests from the managed API clients.
- **Backend** This section contains the steps that need to be applied to the request that should be sent from the API gateway to the back-end API.
- **Outbound** This section contains statements or modifications that you need to apply to the response before it's sent to the requestor.
- **On-Error** In case there is an error on any of the other sections, the engine stops processing the remaining steps on the faulty section and jumps to this section.

When you are configuring or defining a policy, you need to bear in mind that you can apply it at different scope levels:

- **Global** The policy applies to all APIs in your APIM instance. You can configure global policies by using the code editor in the All APIs policy editor on the APIs blade of your APIM instance.
- **Product** The policy applies to all APIs associated with a Product. You can configure product policies on the Policies blade of the Product in your API instance.
- **API** The policy applies to all operations configured in the API. You can configure API-scoped policies by using the code editor in the All Operations option on the Design Tab of the API in your APIM instance.
- **Operation** The policy applies only to a specific operation in your API. You can configure operation-scoped policies by using the code editor in the specific operation.

Policies are a powerful and very flexible mechanism that allow you to do a lot of useful work, such as applying caching to the HTTP requests, performing monitoring on the request and responses, authenticating with your back-end API using different authentication mechanisms, or even interacting with external services. Use the following procedure to apply some transformations to the Demo Conference API that you configured in previous sections:

1. Open the Azure Portal (*https://portal.azure.com*).
2. Type the name of your APIM instance in the Search text box at the top of the portal.
3. Click the name of your APIM instance in the results list.
4. Click APIs in the navigation menu on your APIM instance blade.
5. Click Demo Conference API on the APIs blade.
6. Click the *GetSpeakers* operation.
7. Click the Test tab.
8. Click the Send button at the bottom of the tab. This will send a request to the Demo Conference API and get results similar to those shown in Figure 6-19. In this procedure, you transform the HTTP headers highlighted in Figure 6-19.

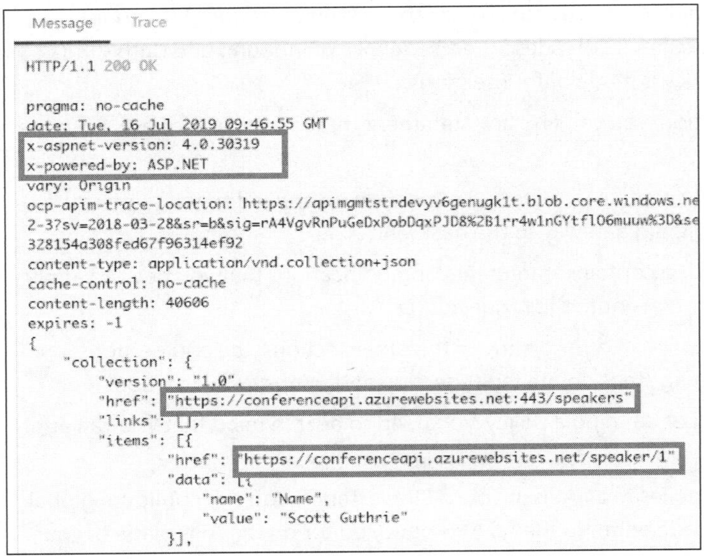

FIGURE 6-19 Testing an API operation

9. Click the Design tab.

10. Click All Operations in the list of available operations for this API.

11. Click the icon next to Policies in the Outbound Processing section.

12. In the Policy Editor, place the cursor before the *base* tag in the Outbound section and add a new line by pressing the Enter key.

13. Click the Insert Policy button in the top-left corner of the Policy Editor.

14. In the list of available policies on the right side of the Policy Editor, navigate to Transformation Policies.

15. Click the Set HTTP Header policy twice to insert the policies.

16. Modify the inserted policies with the following content:

```
<set-header name="X-Powered-By" exists-action="delete" />
<set-header name="X-AspNet-Version" exists-action="delete" />
```

17. On the list of available policies on the right side of the Policy Editor, click the Find And Replace String In Body policy. Insert this policy below the two policies that you inserted in the previous step.

18. Modify the inserted policy by adding the values *from* and *to*. The policy should look like this:

```
<find-and-replace from="://conferenceapi.azurewebsites.net" to="://<your_APIM_
name>.azure-api.net/conference" />
```

19. Click the Save button at the bottom of the Policy Editor.

20. Repeat steps 6 to 8 to apply the transformation policies. You should notice that the *X-Powered-By* and *X-AspNet-Version* headers are missing. Also, the *href* properties are pointing to the correct URL using your APIM instance.

> **NEED MORE REVIEW?** **MORE ABOUT POLICIES**
>
> There are a lot of useful things you can do using policies—too many to cover in this section. If you want to learn more about APIM policies, see the following articles:
>
> - Error handling in API Management *https://docs.microsoft.com/en-us/azure/ api-management/api-management-error-handling-policies*
> - How to Set or Edit Azure API Management Policies *https://docs.microsoft.com/en-us/ azure/api-management/set-edit-policies*
> - Debug Your APIs Using Request Tracing *https://docs.microsoft.com/es-es/azure/ api-management/api-management-howto-api-inspector*

Skill 6.4: Develop event-based solutions

One of the main principles of code development is to reuse as much as possible. To make it possible to reuse the code, you need to ensure that the code is as loosely coupled as possible, which reduces the dependencies with other parts of the code or other systems to a minimum.

With this principle in mind, to make loosely coupled systems communicate, you need to use a kind of communication. Event-driven architectures allow communication between separate systems by sharing information through events.

In general, an event is a significant change of the system state that happens in the context of the system. An example of an event could be when a user adds an item to the shopping cart in an e-Commerce application or when an IoT device collects the information from its sensors.

Azure provides different services, like Event Grid, notification hubs, or event hubs, to cover the different needs when implementing event-driven architectures.

> **This skill covers how to:**
> - Implement solutions that use Azure Event Grid
> - Implement solutions that use Azure Notification Hubs
> - Implement solutions that use Azure Event Hub

Implement solutions that use Azure Event Grid

Azure Event Grid allows you to create an application using serverless architecture by providing a confident platform for managing events. You can use Azure Event Grid for connecting to several types of data sources, such as Azure Blob Storage, Azure Subscription, Event Hubs, IoT

Hubs, and others; Azure Even Grid also allows you to use different event handlers to manage these events. You can also create your custom events to integrate your application with the Azure Event Grid. Before you can start using the Azure Event Grid in your solution, there are some basic concepts that we should review:

- **Event** This is a change of state in the source (for example, in an Azure Blob Storage or when an event happens when a new blob is added to the Azure Blob Storage).
- **Event source** This is the service or application in which an event occurs; there is an event source for every event type.
- **Event handler** This is the app or service that reacts to the event.
- **Topics** These are the endpoints where the event source can send the events. You can use topics for grouping several related events.
- **Event subscriptions** When a new event is added to a topic, that event can be processed by one or more event handlers. The event subscription is an endpoint or built-in mechanism to distribute the events between the different event handlers. Also, you can use subscriptions to filter incoming events.

An important consideration that you need to bear in mind is that an event does not contain the full information about the event itself. The event only contains information relevant to the event itself, such as the source of the event, a time when the event took place, and a unique identifier. For example, when a new blob is added to an Azure Blob storage account, the new blob event doesn't contain the blob. Instead, the event contains a reference to the blob in the Azure Blob storage account.

When you need to work with events, you configure an event source to send events to a topic. Any system or event handler that needs to process those events subscribes to that topic. When new events raise, the event source pushes the event into the topic configured in the Azure Event Grids service. Any event handler subscribed to that topic reads the event and processes it according to its internal programming. There is no need for the event source to have event handlers subscribed to the topic; the event source pushes the event to the topic and forgets it. The following steps show how to create a custom topic. Then we will create console applications using C# to send events to the topic and process these events:

1. Open the Azure Portal (*https://portal.azure.com*).
2. Click All Services in the navigation menu on the left side of the Azure Portal.
3. On the Search Everything text box, type **event**.
4. Click Event Grid Topic in the results list.
5. On the Event Grid Topics blade, click the Create button in the top-left corner of the blade.
6. On the Create Topic panel, type a Name for the Event Grid Topic.
7. Select a subscription in the Subscription drop-down menu.

8. Select a resource group in the Resource Group drop-down menu. Alternatively, you can create a new resource group by clicking the Create New link below the drop-down menu.

9. Select a location in the Location drop-down menu.

10. Leave the Event Schema property as is.

11. Click the Create button at the bottom of the panel.

When the Azure Resource Manager finishes creating your new Event Grid Topic, you can subscribe to the topic to process the events. Also, you can send your custom events to this topic. Use the following steps to publish custom events to your newly created Event Grid Topic:

1. Open Visual Studio 2019.

2. On the welcome screen, click Create A New Project.

3. On the Create A New Project window, select the template Console App (.NET Core).

4. Click the Next button at the bottom-right corner of the window.

5. Type a Project Name.

6. Select a location for your solution.

7. Click the Create button.

8. Click Tools > NuGet Package Manager > Manage NuGet Packages For Solution.

9. On the NuGet – Solution tab, click Browse.

10. In the Search text box, type **Microsoft.Azure.EventGrid**.

11. Click *Microsoft.Azure.EventGrid* in the results list.

12. On the right side of the NuGet – Solution tab, click the name of your project.

13. Click the Install button.

14. On the Preview Changes window, click the OK button.

15. In the License Acceptance window, click the I Accept button.

16. Repeat steps 10 to 15 and install the *Microsoft.Extensions.Configuration.Json* NuGet Package.

17. In the Solution Explorer window, right click your project's name.

18. On the contextual menu, click Add > New Item.

19. On the Add New Item, type **json** in the Search text box.

20. Click the JSON File template.

21. Type **appsettings.json** in the Name text box.

22. Click the Add button at the bottom-right corner of the window.

23. On the Solution Explorer window, click the *appsettings.json* file.

24. On the properties window, set the Copy To Output Directory setting to Copy Always.

25. Open the *appsettings.json* file and replace the content of the file with the content of Listing 6-9. You can get the access key from the Access Key blade in your Event Grid Topic.

LISTING 6-9 *appsettings.json* file

```
{
    "EventGridAccessKey": "<Your_EventGridTopic_Access_Key>",
    "EventGridTopicEndpoint": "https://<Your_EventGrid_Topic>.<region_name>-1.eventgrid.
    azure.net/api/events"
}
```

26. Create a new empty C# class called *NewItemCreatedEvent*.

27. Replace the content of the *NewItemCreatedEvent.cs* file with the content of Listing 6-10.

LISTING 6-10 *NewItemCreatedEvent.cs*

```
// C# .NET
using Newtonsoft.Json;

namespace <your_project_name>
{
    class NewItemCreatedEvent
    {
        [JsonProperty(PropertyName = "name")]
        public string itemName;
    }
}
```

28. Open the *Program.cs* file.

29. Add the following using statements:

- *using Microsoft.Azure.EventGrid;*

- *using Microsoft.Azure.EventGrid.Models;*

- *using Microsoft.Extensions.Configuration;*

- *using System.Collections.Generic;*

30. Replace the content of the *Main* method with the content in Listing 6-11.

LISTING 6-11 *Program.cs* Main method

```
// C# .NET
IConfigurationBuilder builder = new ConfigurationBuilder().AddJsonFile("appsettings.
json");
IConfigurationRoot configuration = builder.Build();

string topicEndpoint = configuration["EventGridTopicEndpoint"];
string apiKey = configuration["EventGridAccessKey"];

string topicHostname = new Uri(topicEndpoint).Host;
TopicCredentials topicCredentials = new TopicCredentials(apiKey);
EventGridClient client = new EventGridClient(topicCredentials);

List<EventGridEvent> events = new List<EventGridEvent>();
events.Add(new EventGridEvent()
{
    Id = Guid.NewGuid().ToString(),
    EventType = "MyCompany.Items.NewItemCreated",
```

```
    Data = new NewItemCreatedEvent()
    {
        itemName = "Item 1"
    },
    EventTime = DateTime.Now,
    Subject = "Store A",
    DataVersion = "3.7"
});

client.PublishEventsAsync(topicHostname, events).GetAwaiter().GetResult();
Console.WriteLine("Events published to the Event Grid Topic");
Console.ReadLine();
```

At this point, your console application publishes events to the Event Grid topic that you previously created. Press F5 to run your console application to ensure that everything compiles and works correctly; you will not be able to see the published message. Use the following steps to create a subscriber Azure Function that connects to the Event Grid Topic and processes these events:

1. Open Visual Studio 2019.
2. On the Welcome screen, click Create A New Project.
3. On the Create A New Project window, click the template Azure Functions.
4. Click Next.
5. Type a Project Name.
6. Select a location for your project.
7. Click Create.
8. On the Create A New Azure Functions Application window, click the HTTP Trigger.
9. Click Create.
10. Install the *Microsoft.Azure.EventGrid* NuGet package.
11. Create a new empty C# class called *NewItemCreatedEvent*.
12. Replace the content of the *NewItemCreatedEvent.cs* file with the content of Listing 6-12.

LISTING 6-12 *NewItemCreatedEvent.cs*

```
// C# .NET

using Newtonsoft.Json;

namespace <your_project_name>
{
    class NewItemCreatedEvent
    {
        [JsonProperty(PropertyName = "name")]
        public string itemName;
    }
}
```

13. Replace the content of *Function1.cs* with the content in Listing 6-13.

LISTING 6-13 *Function1.cs*

```
// C# .NET

using System.Net;
using System.Net.Http;
using System.Threading.Tasks;
using Microsoft.Azure.WebJobs;
using Microsoft.Azure.WebJobs.Extensions.Http;
using Microsoft.Extensions.Logging;
using Microsoft.Azure.EventGrid;
using Microsoft.Azure.EventGrid.Models;

namespace <your_project_name>
{
    public static class Function1
    {
        [FunctionName("Function1")]
        public static async Task<HttpResponseMessage> Run(
            [HttpTrigger(AuthorizationLevel.Anonymous, "get", "post", Route = null)]
            HttpRequestMessage req,
            ILogger log)
        {

            log.LogInformation("C# HTTP trigger handling EventGrid Events.");

            string response = string.Empty;
            const string CustomTopicEvent = "Contoso.Items.ItemReceived";

            string requestContent = await req.Content.ReadAsStringAsync();
            log.LogInformation($"Received events: {requestContent}");

            EventGridSubscriber eventGridSubscriber = new EventGridSubscriber();
            eventGridSubscriber.AddOrUpdateCustomEventMapping(CustomTopicEvent,
            typeof(NewItemCreatedEvent));
            EventGridEvent[] eventGridEvents = eventGridSubscriber.DeserializeEventGridE
            vents(requestContent);

            foreach (EventGridEvent eventGridEvent in eventGridEvents)
            {
                if (eventGridEvent.Data is SubscriptionValidationEventData)
                {
                    var eventData = (SubscriptionValidationEventData)eventGridEvent.
                    Data;
                    log.LogInformation($"Got SubscriptionValidation event data,
                    validationCode: {eventData.ValidationCode},  validationUrl:
                    {eventData.ValidationUrl}, topic: {eventGridEvent.Topic}");
                    // Do any additional validation (as required) such as validating
                    // that the Azure resource ID of the topic matches
                    // the expected topic and then return back the below response
                    var responseData = new SubscriptionValidationResponse()
                    {
                        ValidationResponse = eventData.ValidationCode
                    };

                    return req.CreateResponse(HttpStatusCode.OK, responseData);
                }
                else if (eventGridEvent.Data is StorageBlobCreatedEventData)
```

```
        {
            var eventData = (StorageBlobCreatedEventData)eventGridEvent.Data;
            log.LogInformation($"Got BlobCreated event data, blob URI
            {eventData.Url}");
        }
        else if (eventGridEvent.Data is NewItemCreatedEvent)
        {
            var eventData = (NewItemCreatedEvent)eventGridEvent.Data;
            log.LogInformation($"Got NewItemCreated event data, item SKU
            {eventData.itemName}");
        }
    }

        return req.CreateResponse(HttpStatusCode.OK, response);
    }
  }
}
```

14. Publish the Azure Function to your Azure Subscription. Use the following procedure to publish an Azure Function to Azure: *https://docs.microsoft.com/en-us/azure/
azure-functions/functions-develop-vs#publish-to-azure*

15. Open your Event Grid Topic in the Azure Portal.

16. On your Event Grid Topic Overview blade, click the Event Subscription button.

17. On the Create Event Subscription blade, shown in Figure 6-20, type a Name for the
subscription.

18. In the Endpoint Type drop-down menu, select WebHook.

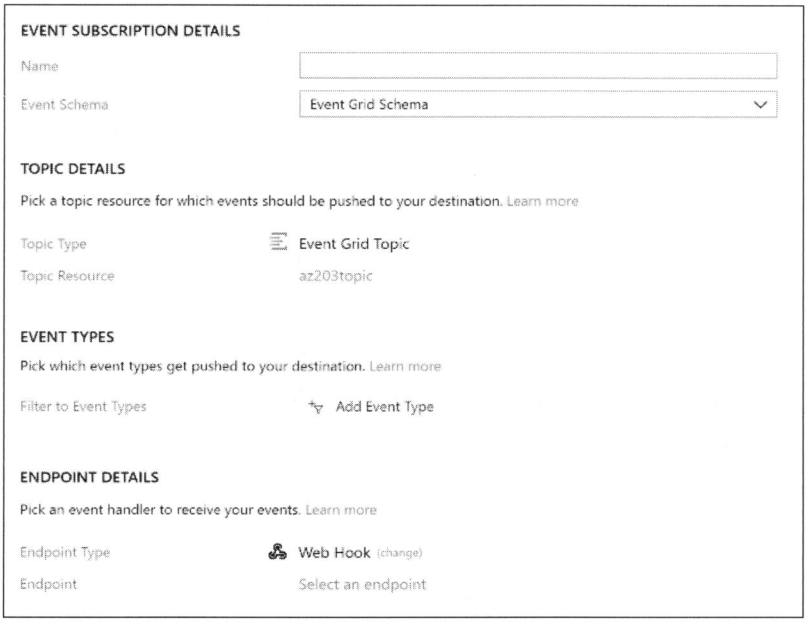

FIGURE 6-20 Creating a subscription using a WebHook endpoint

19. Click the Select An Endpoint link below the webhook endpoint type.
20. On the Select WebHook panel, type the following URL:

```
https://<your_azure_function_plan>.azurewebsites.net/
api/<your_azure_function_name>
```

21. Click Confirm Selection.
22. Click Create.

At this point, you should be able to publish and process events using the Event Grid Topic that you created previously. Use the following steps to ensure that everything works correctly:

1. Open the publisher console application in Visual Studio 2019.
2. Run the console application to publish an event to the topic.
3. Open the Azure Portal and navigate to your Azure Function.
4. In the Azure Functions blade, click Monitor in the tree control.
5. You should be able to see a list of invocations when the function has been called because a new event arrived at the Event Grid Topic.
6. Click one of the successful invocations; you will get a result similar to Figure 6-21.

> ***NOTE*** **AZURE FUNCTION MONITORING**
>
> **You need to have Application Insight integration enabled to be able to see the log messages generated from the Azure Function. Review the article about how to monitor Azure Functions using Application Insights at *https://docs.microsoft.com/en-us/azure/azure-functions/functions-monitoring*.**

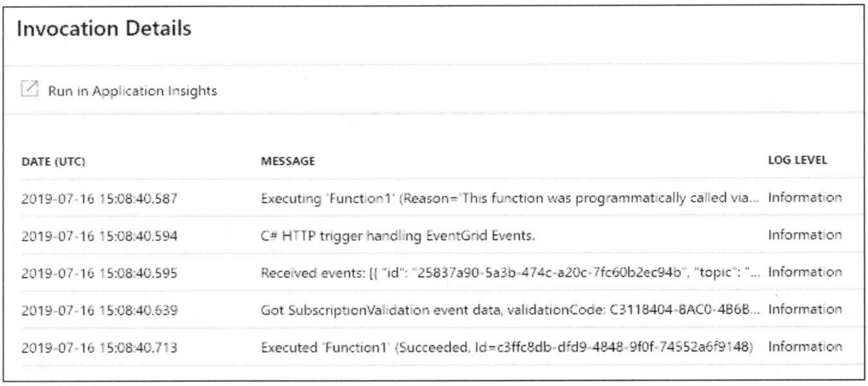

Invocation Details

Run in Application Insights

DATE (UTC)	MESSAGE	LOG LEVEL
2019-07-16 15:08:40.587	Executing 'Function1' (Reason='This function was programmatically called via...	Information
2019-07-16 15:08:40.594	C# HTTP trigger handling EventGrid Events.	Information
2019-07-16 15:08:40.595	Received events: [{ "id": "25837a90-5a3b-474c-a20c-7fc60b2ec94b", "topic": "...	Information
2019-07-16 15:08:40.639	Got SubscriptionValidation event data, validationCode: C3118404-8AC0-4B6B...	Information
2019-07-16 15:08:40.713	Executed 'Function1' (Succeeded, Id=c3ffc8db-dfd9-4848-9f0f-74552a6f9148)	Information

Figure 6-21 Log messages from a successful event processing

Implement solutions that use Azure Notification Hubs

Developing applications that can be accessed using mobile devices can be challenging because you usually need to allow access to your application from different mobile platforms. The challenge becomes even bigger because the different mobile platforms use different notification systems to send events. You need to deal with the Apple Push Notification Service (APNS), the Google Firebase Cloud Messaging (FCM), or the Windows Notification Service(WNS)—and these are just the main mobile platforms on the market.

The Azure Notification Hubs provide an abstraction layer that you can use for connecting to different push notification mobile platforms. Thanks to this abstraction, you can send the notification message to the Notification Hub, which manages the message and delivers it to the appropriate platform. You can also define and use cross-platform templates. Using these templates, you ensure that your solution sends consistent messages independently of the mobile platform that you are using.

In Skill 2.2 (see "Add push notifications for mobile apps" in Chapter 2) we discussed how to create an Azure Mobile App that integrates with the Azure Notification Hub service. Based on the example that we reviewed in that section, we can extend the architecture of an enterprise solution.

When you need to add push notification support to your solution, you should think of the notification hub as a part of a bigger architecture. An example of this could be a solution that needs to connect your line-of-business applications with a mobile application. In such a scenario, a possible architecture could be to use Event Grid topics. The line-of-business applications would be the publishers of events to the appropriate topic, and then you could deploy one or more Azure Mobile Apps that are subscribed to these topics. When one of the line-of-business applications publishes an event in the Event Grid topic, your Azure Mobile App, which is acting as an event handler, can process the event and send a notification to your mobile users by using the Azure Notification Hub. Figure 6-22 shows a schema of this architecture. As you can see in that figure, the key component of the architecture is the Event Grid service and the implementation of an event-driven architecture.

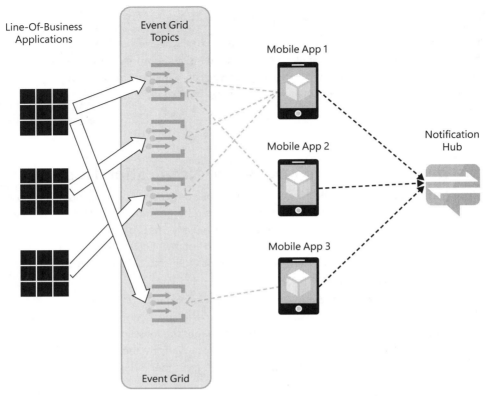

Line-Of-Business
Applications

Event Grid
Topics

Mobile App 1

Mobile App 2

Mobile App 3

Notification
Hub

Event Grid

FIGURE 6-22 Diagram of an event-driven architecture, including notification hubs

> ***NEED MORE REVIEW?*** **SAMPLE ARCHITECTURE IMPLEMENTATION**
>
> You can review a sample architecture implementation using Service Bus messages instead of Event Grid at *https://docs.microsoft.com/en-us/azure/notification-hubs/ notification-hubs-enterprise-push-notification-architecture.*

Implement solutions that use Azure Event Hub

Azure Event Grid is a great service for implementing event-driven solutions, but it is only one piece of a more complex pipeline. Although Event Grid is appropriate for working with event-driven, reactive programming, it is not the best solution when you need to ingest millions of events per second with low latency.

Azure Event Hub is a more suitable solution when you require a service that can receive and process millions of events per second and provide low-latency event processing. Azure Event Hub is the front door of a big data pipeline that processes millions of events. Once the Azure

Event Hub receives the data, it can deliver the event to Azure Event Grid, store the information in an Azure Blob Storage account, or store the data in Azure Data Lake Storage.

When you work with event hubs, you send events to the hub. The entity that sends events to the event hub is known as an Event Publisher. An Event Publisher can send events to the event hub by using either of these protocols: AMQP 1.0, Kafka 1.0 (or later), or HTTPS.

You can publish events to the Event Hub by sending a single event or grouping several events in a batch operation. If you publish a single event or a batch of them, you are limited to a maximum size of 1 MB of data per publication. When Azure Event Hub stores an event, it distributes the different events in different partitions based on the partition key provided as one of the data of the event. Using this pattern, Azure Event Hub ensures that all events sharing the same partition key are delivered in order and to the same partition.

A partition stores events as they arrive at the partition, which means newer events are added to the end of the partition. You cannot delete events from a partition. Instead, you need to wait for the event to expire and thus, removed from the partition. Because each partition is independent of other partitions in the Event Hub, the growth rates are different from partition to partition. You can define the number of partitions that your Event Hub contains during the creation of the Event Hub. You can create between 2 and 32 partitions, although you can extend the limit of 32 by contacting the Azure Event Hub team. Bear in mind that once you create the Event Hub and set the number of partitions, you cannot change this number later. When planning the number of partitions to assign to the Event Hub, consider the maximum number of parallels downstream that need to connect to the Event Hub.

You can connect event receiver applications to an Event Hub by using consumer groups. A consumer group is equivalent to a downstream in a stream-processing architecture. Using consumer groups, you can have different event receivers or consumers accessing different views (state, position, or offset) of the partitions in the Event Hub. Event consumers connect to the Event Hub by using the AMQP protocol that sends the event to the client as soon as new data is available.

The following procedure shows how to create an Azure Event Hub:

1. Open the Azure Portal (*https://portal.azure.com*).
2. Click All Services on the navigation menu on the left side of the Azure Portal.
3. In the Search Everything text box, type **Event**.
4. Click Event Hubs in the results list.
5. On the Event Hubs blade, click the Create button on the top-left corner of the blade.
6. On the Create Namespace panel, type a Name for the Event Hub namespace.
7. Select the Standard tier from the Pricing Tier drop-down menu.
8. Select a subscription from the Subscription drop-down menu.
9. Select a resource group from the Resource Group drop-down menu. Alternatively, you can create a new resource group by clicking the Create New link below the drop-down menu.
10. Select a location from the Location drop-down menu.

11. Click the Create button at the bottom of the panel.

12. On the Overview blade in the Event Hub Namespace, click the Event Hub button.

13. On the Create Event Hub panel, type a Name for the Event Hub.

14. For this example, leave the Partition Count as 2. (Remember that you cannot change this value once the event hub is created.)

15. Click the Create button.

16. Click Shared Access Policies in the navigation menu on the left side of the Event Hub namespace.

17. Click the *RootManageSharedAccessKey*.

18. Copy the *Connection String-Primary Key* value. You need this value step 9 in the next procedure.

Once you have created your Event Hubs namespace and your hub, you can start sending and consuming events from the hub. Use the following procedure to create two console applications—one for sending events and another for receiving events:

1. Open Visual Studio 2019.

2. On the Welcome screen, click Create A New Project.

3. Select the Console App (.NET Core) template.

4. Click Next.

5. Type a Project Name.

6. Select a location for the project.

7. Click Create.

8. Install the *Microsoft.Azure.EventHubs* NuGet package.

9. Replace the content of the *Program.cs* file with the content of Listing 6-14. You received the Event Hub Namespace connection string in the last step of the previous procedure.

LISTING 6-14 *Function1.cs*

```
// C# .NET
using System;
using System.Text;
using System.Threading.Tasks;
using Microsoft.Azure.EventHubs;

namespace <your_project_name>
{
    class Program
    {
        private static EventHubClient eventHubClient;
        private const string EventHubConnectionString =
        "<Your_event_hub_namespace_connection_string>";
        private const string EventHubName = "<your_event_hub_name>";
        private const int numMessagesToSend = 100;
```

```
static void Main(string[] args)
{
    var connectionStringBuilder = new EventHubsConnectionStringBuilder
    (EventHubConnectionString)
    {
        EntityPath = EventHubName
    };

    eventHubClient = EventHubClient.CreateFromConnectionString
    (connectionStringBuilder.ToString());

    for (var i = 0; i < numMessagesToSend; i++)
    {
        try
        {
            var message = $"Message {i}";
            Console.WriteLine($"Sending message: {message}");
            eventHubClient.SendAsync(new EventData(Encoding.UTF8.
            GetBytes(message)));
        }
        catch (Exception exception)
        {
            Console.WriteLine($"{DateTime.Now} > Exception: {exception.
            Message}");
        }

        Task.Delay(10);
    }

    Console.WriteLine($"{numMessagesToSend} messages sent.");

    eventHubClient.CloseAsync();

    Console.WriteLine("Press ENTER to exit.");
    Console.ReadLine();
    }
  }
}
```

At this point, you can press F5 to run the console application. This application console sends 100 messages to the Event Hub that you configured in the *EventHubName* constant. In the next procedure, you will create another application console for implementing an Event Processor Host. The Event Processor Host is an agent that helps you receive events from the Event Hub. The Event Processor automatically manages the persistent checkpoints and parallel event reception. The Event Processor Host requires an Azure Storage Account to process the persistent checkpoints.

Follow these steps to create the console application that implements the Event Processor Host:

1. Open Visual Studio 2019.

2. On the Welcome screen, click Create A New Project.

3. Select the Console App (.NET Core) template.

4. Click Next.

5. Type a Project Name.

6. Select a location for the project.

7. Click Create.

8. Install the following NuGet packages:

   - *Microsoft.Azure.EventHubs*

   - *Microsoft.Azure.EventHubs.Processor*

9. Create a new empty *C#* class and name it *SimpleEventProcessor*. In later steps, this class will implement the *IEventProcessor* interface that contains the signature of the methods needed for the Event Processor.

10. Replace the content of the *SimpleEventProcessor.cs* file with the content of Listing 6-15.

LISTING 6-15 *SimpleEventProcessor.cs*

```
// C# .NET
using Microsoft.Azure.EventHubs;
using Microsoft.Azure.EventHubs.Processor;
using System;
using System.Collections.Generic;
using System.Text;
using System.Threading.Tasks;

namespace <your_project_name>
{
    public class SimpleEventProcessor : IEventProcessor
    {
        public Task CloseAsync(PartitionContext context, CloseReason reason)
        {
            Console.WriteLine($"Processor Shutting Down. Partition '{context.
            PartitionId}', Reason: '{reason}'.");
```

```
            return Task.CompletedTask;
        }

        public Task OpenAsync(PartitionContext context)
        {
            Console.WriteLine($"SimpleEventProcessor initialized. Partition: '{context.
            PartitionId}'");
            return Task.CompletedTask;
        }

        public Task ProcessErrorAsync(PartitionContext context, Exception error)
        {
            Console.WriteLine($"Error on Partition: {context.PartitionId}, Error:
            {error.Message}");
            return Task.CompletedTask;
        }

        public Task ProcessEventsAsync(PartitionContext context, IEnumerable<EventData>
        messages)
        {
            foreach (var eventData in messages)
            {
                var data = Encoding.UTF8.GetString(eventData.Body.Array, eventData.Body.
                Offset, eventData.Body.Count);
                Console.WriteLine($"Message received. Partition: '{context.
                PartitionId}', Data: '{data}'");
            }

            return context.CheckpointAsync();
        }
    }
}
```

11. Replace the content of the *Program.cs* with the content of Listing 6-16.

LISTING 6-16 *Program.cs*

```
// C# .NET
using Microsoft.Azure.EventHubs;
using Microsoft.Azure.EventHubs.Processor;
using System;

namespace <your_project_name>
{
    class Program
    {
        private const string EventHubConnectionString =
        "<your_event_hub_namespace_connection_string>";
        private const string EventHubName = "<your_event_hub_name>";
        private const string StorageContainerName = "<your_container_name>";
        private const string StorageAccountName = "<your_storage_account_name>";
        private const string StorageAccountKey = "<your_storage_account_access_key>";
        private static readonly string StorageConnectionString = string.Format($"DefaultE
        ndpointsProtocol=https;AccountName={StorageAccountName};AccountKey={StorageAccount
        Key}");
```

```
static void Main(string[] args)
{
    Console.WriteLine("Registering EventProcessor...");

    var eventProcessorHost = new EventProcessorHost(
        EventHubName,
        PartitionReceiver.DefaultConsumerGroupName,
        EventHubConnectionString,
        StorageConnectionString,
        StorageContainerName);

    // Registers the Event Processor Host and starts receiving messages
    eventProcessorHost.RegisterEventProcessorAsync<SimpleEventProcessor>();

    Console.WriteLine("Receiving. Press ENTER to stop worker.");
    Console.ReadLine();

    // Disposes of the Event Processor Host
    eventProcessorHost.UnregisterEventProcessorAsync();
    }
  }
}
```

Now, you can press F5 and run your console application. The console application registers itself as an Event Processor and starts waiting for events not processed in the Event Hub. Because the default expiration time for the events in the Event Hub is one day, you will receive all the messages sent by your publishing console application in the previous example. If you run your Event Publisher console application without stopping the Event Processor console application, you will be able to see the messages in the Event Processor console almost in real time as they are sent to the Event Hub by the Event Publishing console. This simple example also shows how the Event Hub distributes the events across the different partitions.

EXAM TIP

The Azure Event Hub is a service appropriate for processing huge amounts of events with low latency. You should consider the Event Hub as the starting point in an event processing pipeline. You can use the Event Hub as the event source of the Event Grid service.

NEED MORE REVIEW?   **EVENT HUBS CONCEPTS**

The Azure Event Hub service is designed to work with big data pipelines where you need to process millions of events per second. In those scenarios, making a bad decision when planning the deployment of an Event Hub can have a big effect on the performance. You can learn more about the Event Hub service by reading the article at *https://docs.microsoft.com/en-in/azure/event-hubs/event-hubs-features*.

Skill 6.5: Develop message-based solutions

In the previous Skill, we reviewed how to use event-driven services in which a publisher pushes a lightweight notification, or event, to the events management system and forgets about how the event is handled or if it is even processed.

In this section, we are going to review how to develop message-based solutions using Azure services. In general terms, a message is raw data produced by a service with the goal of being stored or processed elsewhere. This means that the publisher of the messages has an expectation of some other system or subscriber process the message. Because of this expectation, the subscriber needs to notify the publisher about the status of the message.

> **This skill covers how to:**
> - Implement solutions that use Azure Service Bus
> - Implement solutions that use Azure Queue Storage queues

Implement solutions that use Azure Service Bus

Azure Service Bus is an enterprise-level integration message broker that allows different applications to communicate with each other in a reliable way. A message is raw data that an application sends asynchronously to the broker to be processed by another application connected to the broker. The message can contain JSON, XML, or text information.

There are some concepts that we need to review before starting to work with the Azure Service Bus:

- **Namespace**   This is a container for all messaging components. A single namespace can contain multiple queues and topics. You can use namespaces as application containers that associate a single solution to a single namespace. The different components of your solution connect to the topics and queues in the namespace.

- **Queue**   A queue is the container of messages. The queue stores the message until the receiving application retrieves and processes it. The message queue works as a FIFO (First-In, First-Out) stack. When a new message arrives at the queue, the Service Bus service assigns a timestamp to the message. Once the message is processed, the message is held in redundant storage. Queues are appropriate for point-to-point communication scenarios in which a single application needs to communicate with another single application.

- **Topic**   You use topics for sending and receiving messages. The difference between queues and topics is that topics can have several applications receiving messages used in publish/subscribe scenarios. A topic can have multiple subscriptions in which each subscription to a topic receives a copy of the message sent to the topic.

Use the following procedure to create an Azure Service Bus namespace; then you can create a topic in the namespace. We are going to use that topic to create two console applications to send and receive the messages from the topic:

1. Open the Azure Portal (*https://portal.azure.com*).
2. Click Create A Resource in the navigation menu on the left side of the Portal.
3. Click Integration in the Azure Marketplace column.
4. Click Service Bus in the Featured column.
5. On the Create Namespace panel, type a Name for the Service Bus namespace.
6. Select the Standard tier in the Pricing Tier drop-down menu. You cannot create topics in the Basic pricing tier; you need to use at least the Standard tier.
7. Select a subscription in the Subscription drop-down menu.
8. Select a resource group in the Resource Group drop-down menu.
9. Select a location in the Location drop-down menu.
10. Click the Create button at the bottom of the panel.
11. Go to the resource once the Azure Resource Manager finishes the deployment of your new Service Bus Namespace.
12. On the Overview blade in the Service Bus Namespace, click the Topic button.
13. Type a name for the Topic on the Create Topic panel, shown in Figure 6-23.

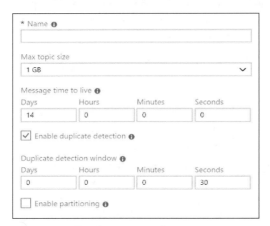

FIGURE 6-23 Creating a new topic

14. Leave the Max Topic Size and Message Time To Live parameter as is.
15. Check Enable Duplicate Detection. This option ensures that the topic doesn't store duplicated messages during the configured detection window.
16. Click the Create button.
17. Click Shared Access Policies in the navigation menu on the left side of the Service Bus Namespace.

18. Click the *RootManageSharedAccessKey* policy.

19. Copy the Primary Connection String. You are going to use the connection string later in this section.

20. Click Topics in the navigation menu on the left side of the Service Bus Namespace.

21. Click your topic.

22. On the Overview blade on the Service Bus Topic, click the Subscription button.

23. On the Create Subscription panel, shown in Figure 6-24, type a Name for the subscription.

FIGURE 6-24 Creating a new subscription

24. Leave the other properties as is.

25. Click the Create button at the bottom of the panel.

Now you are going to create two console applications. One console application will publish messages to the Service Bus Topic; the other console application will subscribe to the Service Bus Topic, process the message, and update the processed message. Use the following procedure to create the console application that publishes messages to the Service Bus Topic:

1. Open Visual Studio 2019.

2. On the Welcome screen, click Create A New Project.

3. Select the Console App (.NET Core) template.

4. Click Next.

5. Type a Project Name.

6. Select a location for the project.

7. Click Create.

8. Install the *Microsoft.Azure.ServiceBus* NuGet package.

9. Replace the content of the *Program.cs* file with the content of Listing 6-17.

LISTING 6-17 *Program.cs*

```csharp
// C# .NET
using Microsoft.Azure.ServiceBus;
using System;
using System.Text;

namespace <your_project_name>
{
    class Program
    {
        const string ServiceBusConnectionString =
        "<your_service_bus_connection_string>";
        const string TopicName = "<your_topic_name>";
        const int numberOfMessagesToSend = 100;

        static ITopicClient topicClient;

        static void Main(string[] args)
        {
            topicClient = new TopicClient(ServiceBusConnectionString, TopicName);

            Console.WriteLine("Press ENTER key to exit after sending all the
            messages.");
            Console.WriteLine();

            // Send messages.
            try
            {
                for (var i = 0; i < numberOfMessagesToSend; i++)
                {
                    // Create a new message to send to the topic.
                    string messageBody = $"Message {i} {DateTime.Now}";
                    var message = new Message(Encoding.UTF8.GetBytes(messageBody));

                    // Write the body of the message to the console.
                    Console.WriteLine($"Sending message: {messageBody}");

                    // Send the message to the topic.
                    topicClient.SendAsync(message);
                }
            }
            catch (Exception exception)
            {
                Console.WriteLine($"{DateTime.Now} :: Exception: {exception.Message}");
            }

            Console.ReadKey();
```

```
            topicClient.CloseAsync();
        }
    }
}
```

You can now press F5 and publish messages to the topic. Once you publish the messages, you should be able to see an increase in the Message Count column in the Overview blade of your Service Bus Topic. The next steps show how to create the second console application that subscribes to the topic and processes the messages in the topic:

1. Open Visual Studio 2019.

2. On the Welcome screen, click Create A New Project.

3. Select the Console App (.NET Core) template.

4. Click Next.

5. Type a Project Name.

6. Select a location for the project.

7. Click Create.

8. Install the *Microsoft.Azure.ServiceBus* NuGet package.

9. Replace the content of the *Program.cs* file with the content of Listing 6-18.

LISTING 6-18 *Program.cs*

```
// C# .NET
using Microsoft.Azure.ServiceBus;
using System;
using System.Text;
using System.Threading;
using System.Threading.Tasks;

namespace <your_project_name>
{
    class Program
    {
        const string ServiceBusConnectionString =
        "<your_service_bus_connection_string>";
        const string TopicName = "<your_topic_name>";
        const string SubscriptionName = "<your_subscription_name>";
        static ISubscriptionClient subscriptionClient;

        static void Main(string[] args)
        {
            subscriptionClient = new SubscriptionClient(ServiceBusConnectionString,
            TopicName, SubscriptionName);

            Console.WriteLine("Press ENTER key to exit after receiving all the
            messages.");

            // Configure the message handler options in terms of exception handling,
            number of concurrent messages to deliver, etc.
            var messageHandlerOptions = new MessageHandlerOptions
            (ExceptionReceivedHandler)
```

Skill 6.5: Develop message-based solutions **CHAPTER 6** **353**

```
        {
            // Maximum number of concurrent calls to the callback
            ProcessMessagesAsync(), set to 1 for simplicity.
            // Set it according to how many messages the application wants to
            process in parallel.
            MaxConcurrentCalls = 1,

            // Indicates whether the message pump should automatically complete the
            messages after returning from user callback.
            // False below indicates the complete operation is handled by the user
            callback as in ProcessMessagesAsync().
            AutoComplete = false
        };

        // Register the function that processes messages.
        subscriptionClient.RegisterMessageHandler(ProcessMessagesAsync,
        messageHandlerOptions);

        Console.ReadKey();

        subscriptionClient.CloseAsync();
    }

    static async Task ProcessMessagesAsync(Message message, CancellationToken token)
    {
        // Process the message.
        Console.WriteLine($"Received message: SequenceNumber:{message.SystemProperties.
        SequenceNumber} Body:{Encoding.UTF8.GetString(message.Body)}");

        // Complete the message so that it is not received again.
        // This can be done only if the subscriptionClient is created in
        // ReceiveMode.PeekLock mode (which is the default).
        await subscriptionClient.CompleteAsync(message.SystemProperties.LockToken);

        // Note: Use the cancellationToken passed as necessary to determine if the
        // subscriptionClient has already been closed.
        // If subscriptionClient has already been closed, you can choose to not call
        // CompleteAsync() or AbandonAsync() etc.
        // to avoid unnecessary exceptions.
    }

    // Use this handler to examine the exceptions received on the message pump.
    static Task ExceptionReceivedHandler(ExceptionReceivedEventArgs
    exceptionReceivedEventArgs)
    {
        Console.WriteLine($"Message handler encountered an exception
        {exceptionReceivedEventArgs.Exception}.");
        var context = exceptionReceivedEventArgs.ExceptionReceivedContext;
        Console.WriteLine("Exception context for troubleshooting:");
        Console.WriteLine($"- Endpoint: {context.Endpoint}");
        Console.WriteLine($"- Entity Path: {context.EntityPath}");
        Console.WriteLine($"- Executing Action: {context.Action}");
        return Task.CompletedTask;
    }
    }
}
```

You can now press F5 and run the console application. As the console application processes the messages in the topic, you can see that the count of the messages in the subscription is decreasing.

> **NEED MORE REVIEW?   SERVICE BUS ADVANCED FEATURES**
>
> You can learn more about Service Bus in the following articles:
>
> - **Queues, Topics, and Subscriptions**   *https://docs.microsoft.com/en-us/azure/service-bus-messaging/service-bus-queues-topics-subscriptions*
> - **Service Bus Performance Improvements**   *https://docs.microsoft.com/en-us/azure/service-bus-messaging/service-bus-performance-improvements*
> - **Topic Filters and Actions**   *https://docs.microsoft.com/en-us/azure/service-bus-messaging/topic-filters*

Implement solutions that use Azure Queue Storage queues

Azure Queue Storage is the first service that Microsoft released for managing message queues. Although Azure Service Bus and Azure Queue Storage share some features, such as providing message queue services, Azure Queue Storage is more appropriate when your application needs to store more than 80GB of messages in a queue. Also, although the queues in the service work as a FIFO (First-In, First-Out) stack, the order of the message is not guaranteed.

> **NOTE   AZURE QUEUE STORAGE VS. AZURE SERVICE BUS**
>
> You can review a complete list of differences between these two queuing services at *https://docs.microsoft.com/en-us/azure/service-bus-messaging/service-bus-azure-and-service-bus-queues-compared-contrasted*.

The maximum size of a single message that you can send to an Azure Queue is 64KB, although the total size of the queue can grow larger than 80GB. You can only access an Azure Queue using the REST API or using the .NET Azure Storage SDK. Here are the steps to create an Azure Queue Storage account and a queue for sending and receiving messages:

1. Open the Azure Portal (*https://portal.azure.com*).
2. Click Create A Resource in the navigation menu on the left side of the Portal.
3. Click Storage in the Azure Marketplace column.
4. Click Storage Account in the Featured column.
5. On the Create Storage Account blade, select a subscription in the Subscription drop-down menu.
6. Select a resource group in the Resource Group drop-down menu.
7. Type a Storage Account Name.

8. Select a location in the Location drop-down menu.

9. Select Locally-Redundant Storage in the Replication drop-down menu.

10. Leave the other properties as is.

11. Click the Review + Create button.

12. Click the Create button.

13. Click the Go To Resource button once the deployment finishes.

14. Click Access Keys on the navigation menu in the Azure Storage account blade.

15. Copy the Connection String from the *key1* section. You need this value later in this section.

At this point, you can create queues in your Azure Storage account by using the Azure Portal. You can also add messages to the queue using the Azure Portal. This approach is useful for development or testing purposes, but it is not suitable for applications. Use the following steps to create a console application that creates a new queue in your Azure Storage account. The application also sends and reads messages from the queue:

1. On the Welcome screen, click Create A New Project.

2. Select the Console App (.NET Core) template.

3. Click Next.

4. Type a Project Name.

5. Select a location for the project.

6. Click Create.

7. Install the following NuGet packages:

   - *Microsoft.Azure.Storage.Common*
   - *Microsoft.Azure.Storage.Queue*

8. Replace the content of the *Program.cs* file with the content of Listing 6-19.

LISTING 6-19 *Program.cs*

```
// C# .NET
using Microsoft.Azure.Storage;
using Microsoft.Azure.Storage.Queue;
using System;
using System.Collections.Generic;
using System.Linq;

namespace <your_project_name>
{
    class Program
    {
        private const string connectionString =
        "<your_storage_account_connection_string>";
        private const string queueName = "az203queue";
        private const int maxNumOfMessages = 10;
        static void Main(string[] args)
        {
```

```
CloudStorageAccount storageAccount = CloudStorageAccount.
Parse(connectionString);
CloudQueueClient queueClient = storageAccount.CreateCloudQueueClient();

//Get a reference to the queue.
CloudQueue queue = queueClient.GetQueueReference(queueName);

//Create the queue if it doesn't exist already
queue.CreateIfNotExists();

//Sending messages to the queue.
for (int i = 0; i < maxNumOfMessages; i++)
{
    CloudQueueMessage message = new CloudQueueMessage($"Message {i}
    {DateTime.Now}");
    queue.AddMessage(message);
}

//Getting the length of the queue
queue.FetchAttributes();
int? cachedMessageCount = queue.ApproximateMessageCount;

//Reading messages from the queue without removing the message
Console.WriteLine("Reading message from the queue without removing them from
the queue");
List<CloudQueueMessage> peekedMessages = (queue.PeekMessages((int)
cachedMessageCount)).ToList();
foreach (CloudQueueMessage peekedMessage in peekedMessages)
{
    Console.WriteLine($"Message read from the queue: {peekedMessage.
    AsString}");

    //Getting the length of the queue
    queue.FetchAttributes();
    int? queueLenght = queue.ApproximateMessageCount;
    Console.WriteLine($"Current lenght of the queue {queueLenght}");
}

//Reading messages removing it from the queue
Console.WriteLine("Reading message from the queue removing");
List<CloudQueueMessage> messages = (queue.GetMessages((int)
cachedMessageCount)).ToList();
foreach (CloudQueueMessage message in messages)
{
    Console.WriteLine($"Message read from the queue: {message.AsString}");
    //You need to process the message in less than 30 seconds.
    queue.DeleteMessage(message);

    //Getting the length of the queue
    queue.FetchAttributes();
    int? queueLenght = queue.ApproximateMessageCount;
    Console.WriteLine($"Current lenght of the queue {queueLenght}");
}
        }
    }
}
```

Press F5 to execute the console application that sends and reads messages from the queue. You can see how the messages are added to the queue by using the Azure Portal and navigating to your Azure Storage account and choosing Queues > az203queue. You will see a queue similar to the one shown in Figure 6-25.

FIGURE 6-25 Creating a new subscription

NEED MORE REVIEW? **PUBLISH/SUBSCRIBE PATTERN**

Although the Azure Queue Storage service doesn't provide the ability to create subscriptions to the queues, you can easily implement the publish-subscribe pattern for communicating applications using the Azure Queue Storage. You can learn how to implement this pattern by reviewing the article at *https://docs.microsoft.com/en-us/learn/modules/ communicate-between-apps-with-azure-queue-storage/.*

Chapter summary

- Azure App Service Logic Apps allows you to interconnect different services without needing to create specific code for the interconnection.
- Logic App Workflows define the steps needed to exchange information between applications.

- Microsoft provides connectors for sending and receiving information to and from different services.

- Triggers are events fired on the source systems.

- Actions are each of the steps performed in a workflow.

- Azure Logic Apps provides a graphical editor that eases the process of creating workflows.

- You can create custom connectors to connect your application with Azure Logic Apps.

- A Custom Connector is a wrapper for a REST or SOAP API.

- You can create custom connectors for Azure Logic Apps, Microsoft Flow, and Microsoft PowerApps.

- You cannot reuse custom connectors created for Microsoft Flow or Microsoft PowerApps with Azure Logic Apps.

- You can export your Logic Apps as Azure Resource Manager templates.

- You can edit and modify the Logic Apps templates in Visual Studio.

- Azure Search service is built on top of the Apache Lucene search engine.

- An Azure Search index contains the information you need to add to the search engine.

- Azure Search indexes are composed of documents.

- Azure Search indexes and documents are conceptually equivalent to tables and rows in a database.

- When defining an Azure Search index, you should use the Azure Portal for the initial definition.

- You cannot edit or change the definition of an Azure Search index by using the Azure Portal.

- You cannot upload data to a search index by using the Azure Portal.

- You should use code to edit or modify a search index.

- You need to use code to upload data to a search index.

- There are two methods to import data to a search index—push and pull.

  - The push method uploads the actual data, in JSON format, to the search index.

  - The pull method connects the search index to a supported data source and automatically imports the data.

  - The push method is less restrictive than the pull method.

  - The push method has lower latency when performing search operations.

- The attributes configured in the field definition affect the physical storage of the index.

- The attributes configured in the field definition affect the search queries that you can perform on your search index.

- The API Management service allows you to publish your back-end REST or SOAP APIs using a common and secure front end.

- You need to create subscriptions in the APIM service to authenticate access to the API.
- You need to create a Product to publish a back-end API.
- You can publish only some operations of your back-end APIs.
- APIM Policies allow you to modify the behavior of the APIM gateway.
- An event is a change in the state of an entity.
- In an event-driven architecture, the publisher doesn't have the expectation that the event is processed or stored by a subscriber.
- Azure Event Grid is a service for implementing event-driven architectures.
- An Event Grid Topic is an endpoint to which a publisher service can send events.
- Subscribers are services that read events from an Event Grid Topic.
- You can configure several types of services as event sources or event subscribers in Azure Event Grid.
- You can create custom events to send them to the Event Grid.
- You can subscribe to your custom application with an Event Grid Topic by using webhooks.
- The Azure Notification Hub is a service that unifies the push notifications on mobile platforms.
- You can connect the push notifications services from the different manufacturers to the Azure Notification Hub.
- The Azure Event Hub is the entry point for big data event pipelines.
- Azure Event Hub is specialized to ingest millions of events per second with low latency.
- You can use Azure Event Hub as an event source for the Event Grid service.
- You can use AMQP, Kafka, and HTTPS for connecting to Azure Event Hub.
- In a message-driven architecture, the publisher application has the expectation that the message is processed or stored by the subscriber.
- The subscriber needs to change the state once the message is processed.
- A message is raw data sent by a publisher that needs to be processed by a subscriber.
- Azure Service Bus and Azure Queue are message broker services.

Thought experiment

In this thought experiment, you will demonstrate your skills and knowledge of the topics covered in this chapter. You can find answers to this thought experiment in the next section.

Your organization has several Line-Of-Business (LOB) applications deployed on Azure and on-premises environments. The information managed by some of these LOB applications overlaps more than one application. All your LOB applications allow you to use SOAP or REST API for connecting to the application.

Your organization needs to implement business processes that require sharing information between the LOB applications. Answer the following questions about connecting Azure services and third-party applications:

1. You need to implement a business process that requires that an application be deployed in Azure to share information with an application deployed in your company's on-premises datacenter. How can you implement this business process?

2. Your company needs to share information managed by one of the LOB applications with a partner. The LOB application uses a SOAP API for accessing the data. You need to ensure that the partner is authenticated before accessing the information. Your partner requires information to be gathered from your application in JSON format, so you also need to ensure that the information provided by your application is published using a REST API. Which service should you use?

3. You need to improve the search features of the LOB applications. You decide to use Azure Search for that purpose. The information that you need to include in the Azure Search service is stored in different types of data sources. Which import data method should you use?

Thought experiment answers

This section contains the solutions to the thought experiment. Each answer explains why the answer choice is correct.

1. You should use Azure Logic Apps for implementing the business process. Azure Logic Apps allows you to create workflows that can be used to implement your business process. You can connect Azure Logic Apps with your on-premises LOB applications by using the on-premises data gateway. You also need to create custom connectors so that your Azure Logic Apps can work with your LOB applications.

2. You should use the API Management service. This service allows you to securely share your back-end APIs with partners and external developers. Using the APIM policies, you can also convert the XML messages provided by the SOAP API to JSON documents needed for REST APIs. You can use Azure AD, mutual certificate authentication, or API keys for authenticating the access to the API.

3. You should use the push method to import data to the Azure Search index. The push method is your only choice because the information that must be included in the Azure Search index is stored in different types of data sources, and the push method is the only method that is independent of the data source type. You need to convert the information stored in the data source to JSON documents and then upload to the Azure Search index. The pull method, using indexers, is appropriate only when the data source is stored in one of the following Azure services: Azure Blob storage, Azure Table storage, Azure Cosmos DB, Azure SQL database, and SQL Server deployed on Azure VMs.

Index

A

BeginForm() method, 180
bindings
    function, 78–83
    WebJobs, 54
blob storage. *See* Azure Blob Storage
Bounded Staleness consistency level, 146
Breaking state (blog leases), 168
Broken state (blog leases), 168
Build() method, 56

C

Cache-Aside pattern (Azure Cache for Redis), 259
Cache-Control HTTP Header, 268
caching. *See* Azure Cache for Redis
Caching Rules panel, 269–270
CaludateAntiForgeryToken, 186
Cassandra API, 130, 142, 147
CBAC (Claims-Based Access Control) authorization, 221-225
CDN Library for .NET, 267
CDN Library for Node.js, 267
CDNs (Content Delivery Networks)
    DSA (Dynamic Site Acceleration) versus, 268
    implementation of, 265–268
    invalid cache content, 268–271
    when to use, 268
CertificatePolicy object, 244
certificates
    self-signed, 243–244
    SSL (Secure Sockets Layer), 190–191
Certificates & Secrets panel, 228
child elements, 14
Choose An Action panel, 292, 298
Circuit pattern, 258
ClaimPrincipal, 92
Claims-Based Access Control. *See* CBAC (Claims-Based Access Control) authorization
cleanup, batch jobs, 31
Clients.cs file, 204–205
Cloud Explorer dialog box, 301
Cloud Services, 252
Cloud Shell, disk encryption with, 16–17
cloud synchronization, Azure App Service, 50
CloudBlobClient objects, 26–27, 165
CloudJob objects, 29
CloudStorageAccount class, 116
CloudTable class, 117
CloudTableClient class, 116

CloudTask objects, 30–31
clusters (AKS), creating, 32–36
cmdlets, New-Guid, 227
Cognitive Services. *See* Azure Cognitive Services API
collections, Cosmos DB storage, 142–143
Common.cs file, 118–120, 161, 163
compound key pattern, 129
compression, CDNs (Content Delivery Networks), 267
compute nodes
    defined, 18
    pools, 19, 22, 28–29, 31
conditional access, Azure AD, 196
Configure A Project For Google Sign-In dialog box, 189
Configure Policies panel, 152
Configure Your OAuth Client dialog box, 189
ConfigureAuth() method, 189, 199
Configured Actions panel, 284
ConfigureService() method, 230
ConfigureWebJobs method, 56
Connection String panel, 140, 141
connection strings, creating, 57
Connection Strings setting (Azure App Service), 51
ConnectionMultiplexer class, 261
connectors, Logic Apps
    custom, 295–300
    managed, 290
Consistent Prefix consistency level, 146
constructors, controller, 277
Container Instance, 40–41
Container Register, 38–41
Container-level SAS (Shared Access Signature), 232
containers
    ACR (Azure Container Registry), 38–39
    AKS (Azure Kubernetes Service) clusters, creating, 32–36
    blob storage items, moving, 161–165
    Cognitive Services. *See* Azure Cognitive Services API
    container images, 36–39
    Container Instance, 40–41
    Container Register, 38–41
    defined, 31
    overview of, 31–32
    running, 40–41
    runtime, 33
Content Caching pattern (Azure Cache for Redis), 259
Content Delivery Networks. *See* CDNs (Content Delivery Networks)
contentVersion template section, 7
continuous background tasks, 52

H

I

M

timers, 84, 87–88
TimeSpan expressions, 88–89
Timestamp property, 126
timestamps, 109
TimeToLive (TTL) value, 268, 270
TinkerPop, 131
TLS (Transport Layer Security), 234–235
TLS/SSL Settings panel, 235
token-based authentication, 187–191
TokenEndpointPath, 201
tokens, SAS, 110, 114–115
topics, Azure Service Bus
    creating, 350–351
    defined, 349
    online resources, 355
    publishing messages to, 351–353
    subscribing to, 353–355
topics, Event Grid
    defined, 334
    publishing events to, 335–337
Trace class, 279
TraceException() method, 279
TrackAvailability() method, 283
TrackEvent() method, 277
TrackValue() method, 278
transient faults, handling, 254–258
Transport Layer Security (TLS), 234
triggers
    activity, 95
    App Service Logic Apps, 290–292
    creating, 56
    function, 84–93
        CosmosDB trigger configuration, 84–86
        CRON expressions, 86–87
        HTTP, 89–93
        timers, 87–88
        types of, 84
    orchestration, 95
    triggered background tasks, 52
    WebJobs, 54
TTL (TimeToLive) value, 268, 270

U

uniform resource locators. *See* URLs (uniform resource locators)
updateAt field, 67

UpdateCertificatePolicyAsync() method, 244
upload action, Azure Search, 310
Upload Items panel, 318
UploadFromFileAsync() method, 27
URI parameters
    Account SAS (Shared Access Signatures), 110–111
    Service SAS (Shared Access Signatures), 112–114
UriFactory class, 137–138
URLs (uniform resource locators), 283–285, 296
UseCookieAuthentication, 184
UseOAuthAuthorization Server() method, 201
user authentication. *See* authentication
user counts, monitoring, 273
user session caching pattern (Azure Cache for Redis), 259
user-assigned managed identities, 217
user-defined metadata, 165–167
UserManager class, 181, 183–184
Users And Groups panel, 229
UserStore class, 181
uuidgen command, 227

V

variables section, templates, 7
vCore-based SQL Databases, 149
Verbose error logging, 60
vertical scaling, 250
Vertices API, 131
views
    ForgotPassword.cshtml, 178
    Login.cshtml, 178–180
    Register.cshtml, 178
Virtual Applications and Directories setting (Azure App Service), 51
virtual machines. *See* VMs (virtual machines)
virtual networks, 3
Virtual Private Networks (VPNs), 235
Visual Studio, 102–104, 283, 285
VMs (virtual machines)
    autoscaling with, 251
    Azure Disk Encryption configuration for, 14–17
    creating, 4–5
    deployment template, 7–11
    overview of, 1
    provisioning, 2–6
    supported operating systems, 2
    templates, creating, 6–14